D1244600

The Religion of Falun Gong

The Religion
of Falun Gong

BENJAMIN PENNY

The University of Chicago Press   Chicago and London

BENJAMIN PENNY is deputy director of the Australian Centre on China in the World in the College of Asia and the Pacific at the Australian National University.

The University of Chicago Press, Chicago 60637
The University of Chicago Press, Ltd., London
© 2012 by The University of Chicago
All rights reserved. Published 2012.
Printed in the United States of America

21 20 19 18 17 16 15 14 13 12   1 2 3 4 5

ISBN-13: 978-0-226-65501-7 (cloth)
ISBN-10: 0-226-65501-6 (cloth)

Library of Congress Cataloging-in-Publication Data
Penny, Benjamin.
  The religion of Falun Gong / Benjamin Penny.
    p. cm.
  Includes bibliographical references and index.
  ISBN-13: 978-0-226-65501-7 (hardcover : alkaline paper)
  ISBN-10: 0-226-65501-6 (hardcover : alkaline paper)
  1. Falun Gong (Organization). 2. China—Religious life and
  customs—20th century.   I. Title.
  BP605.F36P46 2012
  299.5'1—dc23   2011032780

♾ This paper meets the requirements of ANSI/NISO Z39.48-1992
(Permanence of Paper).

For Gillian and Tom

Contents

Acknowledgments

The research that led to this book began when I was awarded a Harold White Fellowship at the National Library of Australia, which enabled me to explore the superb collection of books and journals on Falun Gong and *qigong* in its Chinese collection and to begin to understand Li Hongzhi's teachings. It was when I gave a lecture at the NLA as part of my fellowship that I realized the degree of interest in Falun Gong beyond the academy, which led me to think of that early research on Falun Gong as the beginnings of a monograph. My first thanks therefore are due to Jan Fullerton, the then Director General of the NLA, and her staff, in particular Andrew Gosling and Ouyang Dipin. The other library I have relied on while working on this project has been that of my own institution, The Australian National University, and I would like to acknowledge the assistance there of both Darrell Dorrington and Renata Osborne.

The final revisions of this book were made while I was the fortunate recipient of another fellowship, at the Institute for Research in Humanities at the University of Kyoto. I was made most welcome at that superb and venerable institution, and my grateful thanks are due to its then director, Mizuno Naoki, and in particular to Tanaka Masakazu, who was kind enough to invite me and make my stay so enjoyable and stimulating.

Between this book's inception and its conclusion, many others have knowingly or unknowingly been of great assistance. There are too many to single out, but I would like to mention the following: Remco E. Breuker, Duncan Campbell, Benjamin Dorman, Thomas David DuBois,

Fan Shengyu, Herbert Freilich, Valmae Freilich, Vincent Goossaert, Inoue Nobutaka, John Jorgensen, Susan V. Lawrence, Liu Songfa, Dorothy McIntosh, Lewis Mayo, James Miles, John Minford, John Moffett, Brian Moloughney, Nakamaki Hirochika, David Ownby, Scott Pacey, David A. Palmer, Richard Rigby, Lindy Shultz, Wendy Smith, Francesca Tarocco, Barend ter Haar, Patricia M. Thornton, Stefania Travagnin, Utiraruto Otehode, Holly Wei, Kyle Wilson, Nathan Woolley, Anthony C. Yu, and Mayfair Mei-Hui Yang, and Zhu Yayun.

I especially wish to acknowledge the support of three outstanding scholars of Chinese history: Geremie R. Barmé, stimulating, rigorous, and encouraging in equal parts; T. H. Barrett, who in many ways inspired me to pursue the kind of research I do; and W. J. F. Jenner, a fine teacher, a superb critic, and an always generous friend.

I am also grateful to Alan G. Thomas for supporting and shepherding this project at the University of Chicago Press, and to Randy Petilos, Sandy Hazel, Andrea Guinn, Joe Claude, and Laura Avey for their assistance in the production process.

I would also like to thank my mother, Glen Rose, who once again has proofread my work with patience, indefatigability, and a keen eye.

Finally, and most important, I could not have written this book without the unfailing love and support of my partner, Gillian Russell, and our son, Tom Russell-Penny. They have endured my frustrations and my obsessions, and over the years I have imposed on them greatly to work on this project. Gillian has always been my sounding board, the person to whom I have gone with my puzzlements and intellectual confusions, and the best reader I could wish to have. I dedicate this book to her, and to Tom, with gratitude and love.

References and Translations

Falun Gong has always been aware of the need to disseminate its message as broadly as possible. It has, for example, translated Li Hongzhi's works, especially the major scriptures such as *Zhuan Falun*, into multiple languages, and has provided Chinese-language versions in both simplified and traditional characters. Appreciating the utility of electronic communications early on, it produced websites in China that allowed practitioners to read the most recent teachings and statements from Li Hongzhi, and had other functions related to publicity. Since the Chinese government's suppression of Falun Gong in 1999, the importance of these websites has grown as the expatriated Falun Gong community of practitioners spread across many countries. As a result, although Li's major works have been published over the years in multiple print editions, the web versions of his works have become the authoritative versions for his followers.

The online versions of Li Hongzhi's works cited in this book are listed in the bibliography (along with the earliest versions of *Zhuan Falun* and *Falun Gong*, which were only available in print), with page numbers referring to the PDF versions available on the relevant websites. The page number in the English translation is given first, followed by the original Chinese. Since the English and Chinese titles of *Zhuan Falun* and *Falun Gong* are the same, the page references simply appear one after the other. In addition, for *Zhuan Falun* and *Falun Gong*, I have adopted the traditional Chinese practice of providing chapters and subsections. *Zhuan Falun* is divided into nine "talks" or "lectures" that are, in turn, subdivided into between five and ten sections. Each section is typically only a few pages long. Thus, a reference that reads "*Zhuan Falun* 7/5" means the fifth section of lecture 7. *Falun Gong* has five chapters that are also divided into parts, so "*Falun Gong* 2/3" means the third section of chapter 2. For works that are found in compilations of lectures or short essays, I have referenced the individual text, adding the name of the collective work in the footnote. It should be noted that in a few cases the original Chinese version of a lecture is found as part of a compilation, while the English translation of the same lecture stands as an individual work.

Falun Gong is assiduous in translating Li's works, as noted above. Almost all of them are available in English, sometimes in several different versions. Falun Gong thus provides "approved" translations of its works, but using these translations unchanged would present several problems for readers. The most obvious is that translations of different texts—particularly the three different translations of *Zhuan Falun*—often render the same Chinese word or phrase differently. For example, the three-part moral teaching of *zhen*, *shan*, and *ren* is usually translated as "truth, compassion, and forbearance," but in some texts it becomes "truth, goodness, and endurance"; and the final goal of Falun Gong cultivation, *yuanman*, while usually translated as "Consummation," is sometimes rendered as "Spiritual Perfection." Similarly, the term *tianmu* is typically translated directly as "Celestial Eye," but occasionally appears as "Third Eye," while "cosmos" and "universe" are both used to translate the single term *yuzhou*. These are just some of the more important examples of inconsistencies found throughout the Falun Gong corpus of texts. To avoid confusion, I have amended cited passages from the authorized translations for reasons of consistency, and have chosen the most common rendition of any particular term. In these cases, as in all others where I have altered the "approved" translation, this is noted in the footnote with the word *amended*. In addition to changing translations for consistency, I have also lightly amended a few passages in which the English renderings are unnecessarily ungainly and distracting, a slight alteration would better represent the nuance or tone of the original, or a minor change would clarify the meaning.

A particular issue arises with *Zhuan Falun*, Li Hongzhi's major scripture, as three different translations (from 1998, 2000, and 2003) are provided on the relevant website. Of these three, the 1998 version is clearly the least polished. In general, I have cited the most recent one from 2003, since it clearly represents the latest interpretation of Li Hongzhi's words. This is not to suggest, however, that the 2000 translation is deficient: the major difference between it and the 2003 version is that while the earlier one renders Li's text in a straightforward and unadorned way, the latter, attempting to replicate his informal style, occasionally errs on the side of verbosity. When this interferes with the sense of the original Chinese, I have made small changes to the translation, usually on the basis of the 2000 version.

For *Falun Gong* citations, I have chosen the "5th Translation Edition" that was "updated" in July 2006. This is the most recent translation of *Falun Gong* before chapters 4 and 5 were replaced with *The Great Consummation Way of Falun Dafa*. Other texts are cited from the single translation provided. In addition, throughout this book, I refer to Falun Gong texts by the name Falun Gong itself gives them in translation, even when this is inconsistent; thus, I refer to *Zhuan Falun* and *Zhuan Falun Fajie*, but *Explaining the Content of Falun Dafa*.

The Great Consummation Way of Falun Dafa raises a specific issue: this title is the one by which the text has become known and under which it is listed on the website where readers can download a copy. At the time of writing, however, while the html version ("3rd translation edition, July 2006") also gives *The Great Consummation Way of Falun Dafa* as the title, the PDF version on the same site changes it to *The Great Way of Spiritual Perfection* while providing precisely the same details of the translation. To maintain consistency, I have used the former title throughout.

A final translation issue concerns certain key terms in Li Hongzhi's teachings. As will become clear, Li often uses the standard Chinese versions of Buddhist terms and concepts while giving them different meanings. The term *falun* itself is an example of this, as is the ubiquitous term that translates as "Law Body." *Fashen*, the original Chinese word for the latter term, is the way Chinese Buddhist translators have rendered the Sanskrit *dharmakāya* for centuries (as I explain in chapter 3). However, what Li means by *fashen*, and what a reader would understand by it when used in a Buddhist context, is completely different. Falun Gong translators who use "Law Body" throughout the translated corpus clearly feel that this term best renders what Li means by it in Chinese. To "correct" the Falun Gong translation and use *dharmakāya* instead would therefore be a mistake. Thus, in this case, and with several other key terms in the teachings, I use the authorized Falun Gong translations. Where I have departed from using the authorized translation—for example, with *yuanshen* and related terms—I have explained my reasons for doing so.

ONE

What Is Falun Gong?

Falun Gong first came to the attention of the world's media, and indeed some of the most senior figures in the Chinese government, on the morning of April 25, 1999. On that Sunday more than ten thousand of its practitioners congregated outside Zhongnanhai, the compound in the center of Beijing that houses the highest officials of the Chinese state and the Communist Party. The first protesters arrived late on the evening of the twenty-fourth, and by the early morning hours groups started gathering at the compound's northern gate on Wenjin Street and at its western gate on Fuyou Street. By eight o'clock the protesters had formed a line stretching more than two kilometers around the north and west walls of Zhongnanhai, in some places eight deep. Some had also gathered at the southern entrance on Chang'an Boulevard, one of Beijing's major east–west thoroughfares. The entrances to Zhongnanhai were guarded by groups of policemen, and police vehicles patrolled constantly. The protesters were corralled onto the western footpath on the other side of the road from the compound entrances and were guarded by police—"one policeman for every meter," according to a Hong Kong journalist, who also reported that "pedestrians were barred from approaching or joining the protest."[1]

---

1. "Sect Members Deliver Their Demands to Beijing in Huge Petition," *Ming Pao*, Hong Kong, April 26, 1999, as reported in BBC Summary of World Broadcasts, April 27, 1999. An important source on the demonstration and its aftermath is Zong Hairen's *Zhu Rongji zai 1999* (Carle Place, NY: Mingjing chubanshe [Mirror Books], 2001), translated in full as *Zhu Rongji in 1999* in *Chinese Law and Government* 35, no. 1 (January/February 2002). The fourth chapter of the book is entitled

This demonstration was easily the largest that the Chinese capital had seen since the 1989 Tiananmen Square protests—and it took place just weeks short of the tenth anniversary of their violent suppression. Unlike in 1989, however, the demonstrators at Zhongnanhai were neither young nor overtly political. Journalists reported that they were largely middle-aged or elderly, and they did not shout slogans, hold banners, or hand out leaflets. Instead, they stood or sat quietly, many in the lotus position; most of them, apparently, were reluctant to discuss the purpose of their demonstration with curious members of the press. While most of these Falun Gong adherents were from Beijing, many others had come from the city of Tianjin just over one hundred kilometers away or from the province of Hebei that surrounds both cities, with a small representation from more distant provinces to the north and south.[2] By nine o'clock that night, the locals had quietly made their way home, and those from outside Beijing had been taken by bus to the railway station and given tickets to their hometowns. By all accounts the police were polite and low-key, even if they were represented in force. Moreover, the protesters apparently collected their litter before they left.

The first member of the leadership to hear the news of the protest was Luo Gan, a protégé of Li Peng, the premier widely held responsible for the Beijing massacre of 1989. In 1999, Luo was a member of the Politburo and secretary of the Communist Party Central Committee's Politics and Law Commission. In the latter post he was effectively in charge of China's security services.[3] On the morning of the demonstration, Luo allegedly rang Jiang Zemin, general secretary of the Party and president of the People's Republic, who had just finished breakfast. When told of "the unexpected tidings that Falun Gong believers were besieging Zhongnanhai," Jiang reportedly replied, "What is Falun Gong?"[4] Luo, given permission to deal with the protest, called in officials from the Ministries of Public Security and State Security, the People's Armed Police, the Beijing Municipality, and senior members of the bureaucracy. This group, in turn, invited five

"Handling the Falungong Case." Zong Hairen is the pseudonym of an anonymous author—or authors—who appear to come from then Premier Zhu Rongji's inner circle. Another book and several articles under the name "Zong Hairen" have appeared outside China, but whether they all refer to the same person or people is unknown. In *Zhu Rongji in 1999*, Zong purports to demonstrate how the competent Zhu was consistently sidelined by the less competent but politically conniving Jiang Zemin. To do so, he quotes extensively from internal Party and government documents, the veracity of which cannot be proved.

2. "Falun Gong 'Paratroops' Reportedly Still in Beijing," *Sing Tao Jih Pao*, April 28, 1999, reported on BBC Monitoring Service, April 30, 1999.

3. John Ruwitch, "Luo Gan Knows Where China's Skeletons Lie," Reuters, May 11, 2002.

4. This citation and the discussion in the next few paragraphs are based on Zong, *Zhu Rongji in 1999*, pp. 53–58.

Falun Gong representatives into Zhongnanhai for discussions. These five were, no doubt to the surprise of the leadership, attached to organizations at the very heart of Chinese society: the Ministry of Public Security; the Second Department of the General Staff Headquarters, the unit of the People's Liberation Army that collects military intelligence; the Ministry of Supervision, which is charged with maintaining efficiency, discipline, and honesty in the Chinese bureaucracy; the Ministry of Railways; and Peking University, China's top-ranked tertiary education institution.

The Falun Gong representatives demanded that the authorities recognize the movement as a legitimate organization; that forty-five practitioners arrested the previous week in Tianjin be released; that the Zhongnanhai demonstration itself not be declared an antigovernment activity; and that no one be prosecuted for taking part in it.[5] They also asked to meet with the premier, Zhu Rongji. At about nine in the morning, Zhu, still jetlagged from a trip to the United States, saw them after having conferred with Jiang Zemin. While none of the Falun Gong demands were met, the representatives were clearly happy enough with the leadership's responses to suggest that the protesters disperse.

Less than three months later, the Chinese government banned Falun Gong, and since then the movement has been subjected to a harsh suppression.[6] Millions of those who had publicly professed Falun Gong no longer belong to the movement. Thousands of practitioners have been sent to "Re-education through Labor" camps under the administrative detention regulations. Some hundreds have been convicted of criminal offenses and have spent time in jail—the longest sentence was eighteen years. And, according to Falun Gong itself, as of September 2009, 3,369 practitioners have been killed in the suppression.[7]

---

5. Ibid., p. 55.

6. On the suppression of Falun Gong, see the Amnesty International reports "The Crackdown on Falun Gong and Other So-Called Heretical Organizations" (March 23, 2000), online at www .amnesty.org/en/library/info/ASA17/011/2000/en, and "Falun Gong Practitioners: List of Sentences, Administrative Sentences and Those Detained" (March 28, 2000), www.amnesty.org/en/library/ info/ASA17/012/2000/en, as well as subsequent updates, and Human Rights Watch's report written by Mickey Spiegel, "Dangerous Meditation: China's Campaign against Falun Gong" (January 2002), www.hrw.org/legacy/reports/2002/china. Falun Gong itself provides a great deal of information about the suppression on its websites, especially on its "Falun Dafa Information Centre," www .faluninfo.net, but its data, of course, are not independently verified. Another Falun Gong source is Jennifer Zeng's memoir *Witnessing History: One Woman's Fight for Freedom and Falun Gong* (Crows Nest, NSW: Allen and Unwin, 2005). One of the best journalists who reported the suppression is Ian Johnson of the *Wall Street Journal*, whose *Wild Grass: China's Revolution from Below* (London: Penguin, 2005) contains a long section on this topic (chap. 3, "Turning the Wheel").

7. See "Key Statistics Related to Falun Gong—2010 Annual Report" (September 27, 2009); online at www.faluninfo.net/article/909/?cid=162.

Over the past decade, the continuing suppression of Falun Gong has become an important issue in discussions of human rights in China, alongside older concerns such as the situation in Tibet. Inside the country the suppression has become part of the political and security landscape. However, it is clear that while Falun Gong may have been forced underground, and in all likelihood the numbers of people actively engaged in it have decreased dramatically, it has not been wiped out.[8] The movement has been analyzed from various perspectives, including those of political science, sociology, and law; but questions raised by Jiang Zemin's demand, "What is Falun Gong?" continue to resonate. This book responds by examining what it is that practitioners of Falun Gong believe and do; how Falun Gong teachings might relate to earlier Chinese religious ideas as well as to contemporary society and culture; and where its adherents understand that practicing Falun Gong will lead.

The Nature of Falun Gong

Falun Gong is a contemporary spiritual movement founded and led by Li Hongzhi, who comes from Changchun, a city of over seven million people that is a center of China's automobile industry and the capital of Jilin Province in the northeastern part of the country. Li's followers refer to him as Master Li or simply Master.

Adherents usually characterize Falun Gong as a cultivation or self-cultivation system, meaning that it is a practice involving physical movements, mental disciplines, and moral tenets that together can effect a positive change in the nature of ordinary human bodies. It emerged from a boom in gymnastic, breathing, and meditational activities in the 1980s and early 1990s, known by the general term *qigong*, which were thought to benefit a person's health and fitness. Specifically, *qigong* refers to "biospiritual" practices in which the manipulation of *qi* (or sometimes *chi* or *ch'i*, or in Japanese *ki*) is primary. Etymologically, the word *qi* is related to aspiration and vaporization and is thought of in material terms. The common English translation of it as "energy" does not, therefore, quite capture the meaning of the Chinese term.[9]

8. Falun Gong sources regularly report the activities of practitioners within China, and there are periodic mentions of Falun Gong activities in the Chinese and Western press.

9. An excellent discussion of the meaning of *qi* can be found in Stephen R. Bokenkamp, *Early Daoist Scriptures* (Berkeley: University of California Press, 1997), pp. 15–20. As far as I am aware, the term *biospiritual* was first used in studies of Chinese religion and philosophy by Russell Kirkland. See

The *gong* in Falun Gong and *qigong* is the same word, and in standard Chinese usage carries the connotations of "achievement," "merit," "efficacy," "skill," "power," or "work." In this context, *gong* is perhaps best understood to refer to "exercises" or "practice"; thus *qigong* might be literally translated as "practices involving *qi*." *Falun* is originally a Buddhist term and means the wheel of the Buddhist Law, or dharma. *Falun Gong* therefore means "the Practice of the Wheel of the Law." However, practitioners of Falun Gong generally refer to it by another name, Falun Dafa, which means "the Great Method of the Wheel of the Law." The distinction between the two names draws attention to the followers' view that what they do extends far beyond the physical exercises that they perform each day as Falun Gong devotees. Their practice, they would maintain, is a supreme method that elevates them above the condition of ordinary humanity. In this book, however, the more common term *Falun Gong* is used.

The *falun* in the name Falun Gong has a different meaning from that in Buddhism. Originally it was a symbol of the Buddha's teaching, the *dharmacakra* in Sanskrit, where its circular shape represented the completeness of the doctrine.[10] To "turn the Wheel of the Law" is to preach the Buddha's word as he himself did first in the Deer Park at Sarnath in northern India. In Falun Gong, however, the *falun* is an object that Li Hongzhi inserts into the abdomens of practitioners. Li insists that this *falun* is real, but he explains that its physical existence is in a parallel body in another dimension. It is fundamental in the cultivation process of practitioners—first spinning one way, collecting energy from the universe, then the other, sending it out to different parts of the body.

The word *falun*, then, is of Buddhist origin but has a distinct meaning in Falun Gong. Several other originally Buddhist terms also appear in Li's writings. Core terms in Falun Gong teachings such as *karma*, *gong*, and *Law Body* are, like *falun*, given new meanings. In fact, Li explicitly states that Falun Gong is not Buddhism and often criticizes that religion in his books and speeches—indeed, Li is explicit in his denial that Falun Gong is a religion at all. Rather, he says that it is a discipline associated with "Buddha Law" or the "Buddha School." He writes, "Our Falun Dafa is . . . one of the 84,000 teachings [*famen*], but it's never been related to Buddhism,

---

Kirkland, "Varieties of Taoism in Ancient China: A Preliminary Comparison of Themes in the *Nei Yeh* and Other Taoist Classics," *Taoist Resources* 7, no. 2 (1997): 73–86.

10. On the relationship between Falun Gong and Buddhism, see Benjamin Penny, "The Falun Gong, Buddhism and 'Buddhist *Qigong*,'" *Asian Studies Review* 29, no. 1 (March 2005): 35–46.

from the original Buddhism right on up to the one in the Age of the Law's End. And it doesn't have anything to do with today's religions."[11]

Soon after the Chinese authorities suppressed Falun Gong in July 1999, they characterized it as an "evil cult." "Evil cult" translates the Chinese term *xiejiao* that has been used for centuries by Chinese governments to categorize religious movements which they want to eradicate. A more literal translation of it would be "heterodox teaching." In imperial China, another term, *zhengjiao*, or "orthodox teaching," was used to refer to government-authorized religions. There were many reasons why the state may not have authorized a set of teachings and the activities associated with it. However, it was not necessarily because these religions were deemed "false" in the sense that they were nonsense, or their activities ineffective in gaining results. Often, indeed, they were designated in this way because they effectively threatened the fate or legitimacy of the state itself. Thus, in Chinese the term *xiejiao* specifically preserves the connotation of a teaching disapproved of by the authorities. The official government rendering of "evil cult," on the other hand, brings to mind recent violent and sometimes apocalyptic religious groups in the West and Japan, such as Aum Shinrikyō, Heaven's Gate, the Solar Temple, David Koresh's Branch Davidians, and Jim Jones's People's Temple. Historically and into the present day, groups defined as *xiejiao* are illegal and have been systematically suppressed and their leadership punished.[12]

The title of this book asserts that Falun Gong can indeed be considered a religion. As will be shown throughout, it has many of the features associated with religions in the present and in the past, and across the world. It has a charismatic founder who is believed by his followers to be more than human, whose message will save humanity from the disastrous position in which it finds itself. He has a scripture, which is considered true for all times, places, and cultures, and which he instructs should be read repeatedly, and even memorized. He has enunciated a moral code that he demands Falun Gong adherents follow, or else their cultivation will

11. Li Hongzhi, *Zhuan Falun* 3/2, p. 47; p. 83. Falun Gong translations render *famen* (literally "dharma gates") as "disciplines" (2003), "cultivation ways" (2000), and "schools" (1998), but I have chosen the more standard "teachings." In Buddhism, 84,000 is a meaningful number. William Edward Soothill and Lewis Hodous cite the 84,000 atoms in a human body, the 84,000 stupas of Asoka to house the 84,000 relics of the Buddha, and the 84,000 types of light shed by Amitabha, among other examples, in their *Dictionary of Chinese Buddhist Terms* (London: Kegan Paul, Trench, Trubner, 1937), p. 39.

12. On the history of *xiejiao* and suppressed religious groups in general in China, see Vincent Goossaert and David A. Palmer, *The Religious Question in Modern China* (Chicago: University of Chicago Press, 2011), pp. 336–42; B. J. ter Haar, *The White Lotus Teachings in Chinese Religious History* (Honolulu: University of Hawai'i Press, 1999); and Hubert Seiwert, in collaboration with Ma Xisha, *Popular Religious Movements and Heterodox Sects in Chinese History* (Leiden: Brill, 2003).

not work. He states that the end point of his cultivation method will lead to what he calls "Consummation," which he equates with the point of ultimate attainment in other religions, specifically mentioning the Buddhist nirvana as an example. The universe he describes has a past and a future on a cosmic time scale, and a geography that includes multiple dimensions populated by divine beings. Finally, he teaches that his followers should regularly perform a series of spiritual exercises, and that they should meet together to read his scripture and share their experiences in the faith.

However, a particular feature of Falun Gong that distinguishes it from many other religions is that it has no formal ritual of initiation into its community of believers. There is no point at which someone "officially" becomes a follower of Li Hongzhi. Anyone can become a "practitioner" of Falun Gong simply by practicing—no one needs to contract to any organization, no one receives a membership card, and no one has a bureaucratic designation. I have therefore avoided using the term *members* in this book and instead use *followers*, *devotees*, *adherents*, or, in other contexts, *practitioners* or *cultivators*.

The absence of formal membership requirements has several consequences, notably the difficulty of estimating the number of former and current Falun Gong followers. Various estimates were given after the suppression. Chinese government sources, as noted by James Tong, began at a low point of 2 million, with a general consensus of around 2.1 million to 2.3 million. One newspaper, however, suggested there were 40 million adherents in March 1999. Falun Gong estimates, on the other hand, have been higher, claiming 70–80 million adherents in China, with another 20 million or so overseas.[13] One well-informed news report from November 1998 says that Falun Gong itself claimed 20 million devotees at that time.[14]

The large discrepancies in these figures may be partly explained by the fact that they are necessarily approximations, and partly by what is being counted. During the 1990s, when Falun Gong practice sites were scattered across most of urban China and when other *qigong* groups also met and did their exercises nearby, it is easy to imagine that interested members of the public might have drifted from one group to another, trying out what was offered. Some people may have chosen to take part in Falun Gong group routines regularly. Of these, a proportion may also

13. James Tong, "An Organizational Analysis of the Falun Gong: Structure, Communications, Financing," *China Quarterly* 171 (September 2002): 636–60; statistic is from p. 636, note 1.

14. James Miles, *BBC Breakfast News*, November 6, 1998.

have become interested enough to buy a copy of Li Hongzhi's scripture. A still smaller group may have taken his words to heart and chosen to live their lives according to his teachings. In other words, much like any activity in human society, there were those more enthusiastic and committed to Falun Gong, and there were others whose connection to it was weak. It may have been the case that there were indeed between two million and three million highly committed adherents in the late 1990s, as the government claims, as well as several tens of millions more who attended the practice sites on a more or less regular basis, as Falun Gong maintains, but we have no way of knowing exact figures. We can, however, be reasonably certain that after the suppression the government would have tended to underestimate numbers of adherents, and Falun Gong would have overestimated them. It was certainly in Falun Gong's interests for its figure to be greater than sixty-three million, as that was the generally accepted membership of the Communist Party at the time of the suppression. David Palmer has looked critically at Falun Gong's claims about the numbers of practitioners and concludes that "a midrange estimate of 10 million would appear . . . more reasonable."[15]

Falun Gong in the *Qigong* Boom

Falun Gong's relationship with the Chinese authorities has not always been as oppositional as it is now; in fact, in the early years of the movement there was close cooperation, a circumstance downplayed by both parties since the suppression was launched. Falun Gong first appeared on the Chinese scene in May 1992 when Li Hongzhi launched it in Changchun, and it cannot be properly understood without considering it as part of the decade-long enthusiasm for *qigong*. In the 1980s and 1990s, hundreds of different *qigong* groups emerged across China, some gaining a national profile. In fact the growth in *qigong* activities reached such a scale that it was known in China as the "*qigong* fever."[16] The founders and

15. David A. Palmer, *Qigong Fever: Body, Science and Utopia in China* (London: Hurst, 2007), p. 261.
16. On the *qigong* boom, see Nancy N. Chen, *Breathing Spaces: Qigong, Psychiatry, and Healing in China* (New York: Columbia University Press, 2003); Kunio Miura, "The Revival of *Qi*: Qigong in Contemporary China," in *Taoist Meditation and Longevity Techniques*, ed. Livia Kohn, in cooperation with Yoshinobu Sakade (Ann Arbor: Center for Chinese Studies, University of Michigan, 1989); Utiraruto Otehode, "The Creation and Reemergence of *Qigong* in China," in *Making Religion, Making the State*, ed. Yoshiko Ashiwa and David L. Wank (Stanford, CA: Stanford University Press, 2009), pp. 241–65; Palmer, *Qigong Fever*; Jian Xu, "Body, Discourse, and the Cultural Politics of Contemporary Chinese *Qigong*," *Journal of Asian Studies* 58, no. 3 (1999): 961–91; and "The Qigong Boom," ed. Zhu

leaders of the groups—conventionally referred to as *qigong* masters—were often charismatic figures attracting thousands of people to their lectures and demonstrations. Some masters were credited with marvelous powers and claimed that their version of *qigong* not only would impart health benefits, including healing their followers of otherwise incurable diseases, but also would lead to practitioners acquiring superhuman strength, clairvoyance, and various other "supernormal abilities," as they came to be known.[17]

The Chinese government officially endorsed the teaching of *qigong* throughout this period, and most groups and masters were registered with the national *qigong* association. Many of the most powerful masters were directly supported by the authorities through employment in clinics and research establishments, and their powers were tested in government laboratories. It was into this environment that Falun Gong was launched in 1992, and at the time it was only one of many new *qigong* groups to appear. Duly registered with the authorities, it enjoyed all the rights and protections that any officially recognized *qigong* group could claim, but equally it had to abide by the restrictions that the association imposed. In May 1992, Li Hongzhi was no more notable on the national *qigong* scene than any other new self-proclaimed master.

This was not, however, how his followers saw him. In the first version of his biography that was later withdrawn by Falun Gong itself, Li Hongzhi's appearance was described in this way:

In 1992, while China's reforms advanced ever forward and it increasingly opened to the outside world, the great importance the Party and the Country placed on research into "somatic science" reached new levels. At this time an extraordinary man appeared in the north of China with a cultivation method so marvellous that people looked with new eyes. The man was Li Hongzhi, and the cultivation method—his Falun Gong—had qualified as an affiliated cultivation school with the Chinese Association for Research into Qigong Science.[18]

Xiaoyang and Benjamin Penny, special issue, *Chinese Sociology and Anthropology* 27, no. 1 (Fall 1994). On the new forms of religiosity that emerged in China in this period, see Goossaert and Palmer, *The Religious Question in Modern China*, chap. 11.

17. See Geremie R. Barmé and Linda Jaivin, eds., *New Ghosts, Old Dreams: Chinese Rebel Voices* (New York: Times Books, 1992), pp. 377–80, for a translated excerpt from Ke Yunlu's lightly fictionalized memoir of the period, *Da Qigongshi* (*The Great Qigong Masters*), describing a "*qi*-empowered lecture"; and Palmer, *Qigong Fever*, chap. 3, "The Grandmasters."

18. Li Hongzhi, *Zhongguo falungong* (Beijing: Junshi yiwen chubanshe, 1993), pp. 150–82; quotation is from p.150. This original biography clearly serves as the major source for that included in the first edition of *Zhuan Falun*, discussed in chapter 3 of the present text.

The Chinese Association for Research into Qigong Science was the national body with whom all *qigong* groups were registered. "Somatic science," or literally "science of the human body," was the name given to the academic field that investigated *qigong*, psychokinesis, ESP, and other anomalous interactions between the human body and the physical environment. The introduction to Li's biography also notes that

1992 represented a most important page in China's development. Comrade Deng Xiaoping's speeches on his "imperial tour of the south" led to reform being deepened and the economy growing more vibrant each day. With this great surge of reform, when even more people rushed to "dive into the sea of business," Li Hongzhi unexpectedly appeared in the world of *qigong*.[19]

In 1992, Deng Xiaoping was still regarded as China's "paramount leader," although he had retired from all party and government positions. After the massacre in Beijing in 1989, Deng's influence had waned, but his "imperial tour of the south" to Guangzhou, Shanghai, and the boom areas of Shenzhen and Zhuhai, on the borders with Hong Kong and Macau respectively, was his attempt to reignite the economic reforms he had initiated in the 1980s.[20] The speeches he gave on this tour were credited with stimulating new and rapid growth in private business activities in the years that followed. For the followers of Falun Gong, Li Hongzhi was clearly seen as parallel to Deng Xiaoping as a hero of the age, bringing reform to the world of *qigong* as Deng had in the national economy. *Qigong* itself (and more broadly somatic science) was also seen as central to the reform agenda, if not by Chinese society as a whole, then certainly by Li's supporters, by *qigong* circles, and, indeed, in some influential parts of the government.

In early publicity and even in Li Hongzhi's writings, Falun Gong is presented as a form of *qigong*, if a rather special one. For the first few years of its public existence, this categorization had profound consequences for the way Falun Gong was administered, the way it related to the Chinese state, and the discourse in which it expressed its teachings. Before I address these consequences, however, it is necessary to outline some basic ideas that underpin *qigong*.

Qi, the substance manipulated in *qigong*, has a venerable place in Chinese thought and is central to traditional understandings of cosmology,

19. Li, *Zhongguo falungong* (1993), p. 151.
20. On Deng's "imperial tour," see Suisheng Zhao, "Deng Xiaoping's Southern Tour: Elite Politics in Post-Tiananmen China," *Asian Survey* 33, no. 8 (August 1993): 739–56.

medicine, and the nature of all existence. *Qi* pervades all things: different varieties of *qi* constitute the various forms of living and nonliving entities. In medicine, *qi* is understood to pass along a set of channels, typically called meridians, which do not necessarily follow the routes marked out by blood vessels, nerves, muscles, or any other visible structures in the body. In *qigong* theory, *qi* is also understood to move through the body along the meridians used in medical procedures. However, *qigong* practitioners also believe it moves along other channels less well known to doctors called the "strange" or "marvelous" meridians, and can be induced to circulate in particular ways through either physical or mental exercises. Thus, many forms of *qigong* involve sets of physical movements performed in standing and seated positions, but in other forms, movements are not required at all. In these latter *qigong* forms, concentration and visualization are used—in particular, visualization of the movement of *qi* along the strange meridians.[21]

The origins of the term *qigong* are disputed. Certainly, this conjunction of the two characters is known in texts as far back as the Tang dynasty, but whether they had the same meaning at that time as *qigong* does today is doubtful.[22] In the way it is used currently, *qigong* is a twentieth-century coinage; however, it only really gained popularity at the end of the 1940s and 1950s. Whether or not the word itself is ancient or modern, it is clear from both textual and archeological evidence that exercises we would undoubtedly refer to as *qigong* today have been known in China for at least two thousand years and probably much longer. Known by various names, these practices were part of a broad interest in self-cultivation that had moral and ethical as well as spiritual and religious manifestations. These kinds of biospiritual cultivation methods were transmitted from master to student in a manner similar to most other forms of knowledge in premodern China. Thus, in this field as in many others, the idea of lineage was fundamental, and with lineage came a veneration of one's master as the embodiment of the line of transmission. Eventually, different schools of self-cultivation became more or less strongly associated with religious traditions and institutions and their doctrines. Specifically Buddhist and, in particular, Daoist forms of self-cultivation arose with correspondingly Buddhist or Daoist names. *Qigong* schools today often refer to the religious tradition from which they derived or with which

21. On these aspects of *qigong*, see Miura, "The Revival of *Qi*."

22. See Catherine Despeux, "Le *qigong*, une expression de la modernité chinoise," in *En Suivant la Voie Royale: Mélanges en hommage à Léon Vandermeersch*, ed. Jacques Gernet and Marc Kalinowski (Paris: Ecole français d'Extrême-Orient, 1997), pp. 267–81; and Palmer, *Qigong Fever*, pp. 18–19.

they were, or continue to be, associated. Yet it should be noted that some of them including, arguably, Falun Gong, claim false, or at best misleading, ancestries and affiliations, as will be shown in chapters 3 and 4.

In the 1950s, the new Chinese government sought to regularize and codify the practice of *qigong*, along with other traditional forms of knowledge and practice that were not thought necessary to wipe out completely, such as traditional Chinese medicine.[23] One important feature of this reformulation was to reclassify *qigong* from being part of religion to being a form of medical practice. In consequence, the vocabulary of science replaced that of transcendence in discussions of *qigong*, and the goal of its practitioners became, for the proponents of this reclassification at least, physical health rather than spiritual cultivation. Thus, *qigong* also became the subject of "scientific" research and the object of regulation. However, as in most areas of activity that could be thought of as traditional, progress in *qigong* matters was forestalled for most of the 1960s and 1970s during the Cultural Revolution. With the death of Mao in 1976 and the institution of the so-called reform period that began in 1978, limits on many of these activities were relaxed. Gradually a population exhausted by political campaigns sought out activities that were designated as apolitical but which allowed for the possibility of fulfillment at the level of the individual rather than of society as a whole.

It would be wrong, however, to see the extraordinary enthusiasm for *qigong* in the 1980s and 1990s as primarily a yearning for individual spiritual realization, filling a "vacuum" caused by the collapse of the ideology of the 1960s and 1970s.[24] Rather, it is clear from the vast archive of *qigong* books, journals, and electronic media from this period, as well as from the small amount of fieldwork that was undertaken in China at the time, that many of its enthusiasts were attracted to *qigong* in general (or to a specific *qigong* form) because of claims related to health and fitness. Nancy Chen has described how changes in the health-care system during the 1990s, particularly the move away from a socialist toward a fee-for-service model in which individuals incurred much greater expense, facilitated the growth in *qigong* as an alternative route to health. She writes,

23. On the modern history of "traditional Chinese medicine," see Kim Taylor, *Chinese Medicine in Early Communist China, 1945–63: A Medicine of Revolution* (London: RoutledgeCurzon, 2005).

24. This is not to dispute the apparently widespread crises in faith, trust, and confidence (*san xin weiji*) experienced particularly by young Chinese people at the beginning of the 1980s, as epitomized in the famous letter from "Pan Xiao" (a pseudonym made up of characters from the names of the two authors of the letter) to *China Youth* entitled "Why Is Life's Road Getting Narrower and Narrower?," and the ensuing discussions that went on across the country for almost a year. See Luo Xu, *Searching for Life's Meaning: Changes and Tensions in the Worldviews of Chinese Youth in the 1980s* (Ann Arbor: University of Michigan Press, 2002), pp. 51–71.

Deep concern about the disintegration of the existing medical system accompanied the increased popularity of *qigong* as an alternative form of healing. Biomedical clinics and hospitals in China during the post-Mao era were usually crowded, considered a last resort. Instead, many people relied on herbal remedies, special foods, or tonics, often prepared by family members, before seeking medical advice. . . . *Qigong* fit easily within this tradition of self-medication and self-sufficiency in healing. Moreover, most practitioners believed that *qigong* could cure *any* illness or ailment.[25]

Chen goes on to describe the scenes, common in Chinese cities throughout this period, of people gathering in parks in the early morning to practice *qigong* either individually or more often with a like-minded group. And in common with other observers of this phenomenon, she reports that most of those engaged in *qigong* practice were older people, more likely women than men, who often began their practice as an attempt to cure chronic or life-threatening illness.

These health-related concerns must be borne in mind when analyzing the various schools of *qigong*. Practitioners' engagement in what to Western eyes might seem to be "fringe" or alternative medicine was driven by practical, rational considerations. What they were doing was, to a large extent, responding to pressing social realities. These people were not "spiritual seekers"; they did not see their practice as a route to personal enlightenment. Yet among the many forms of *qigong* that arose during the boom years, several, including Falun Gong, developed theories and doctrines that were undeniably spiritual—even religious, as I have noted. Nonetheless, even with these groups we should bear in mind that many of those who adopted their forms of *qigong* as a daily practice did so because of their proponents' claims to heal disease. In the texts of these groups, including Li Hongzhi's lectures, discussions of health-related matters are at the core.

Along with the various social and economic activities that flourished in China during the 1980s and 1990s, including *qigong*, the publishing industry also experienced remarkable growth.[26] Many of the controls over what publishers could print and the restrictions on how books and magazines could be sold were lifted along with the removal of financial protections. In this new world of mass publication, where the number of books sold

25. N. Chen, *Breathing Spaces*, p. 46.

26. See Gayle Feldman, "The Organization of Publishing in China," *China Quarterly* 107 (September 1986): 519–29, and Yi Chen, "Publishing in China in the Post-Mao Era: The Case of *Lady Chatterley's Lover*," *Asian Survey* 32, no. 6 (June 1992): 568–82. On the Chinese publishing industry, concentrating on a later period, see Robert E. Baensch, ed., *The Publishing Industry in China* (New Brunswick, NJ: Transaction Publishers, 2004).

actually mattered to the publishers, the nationwide enthusiasm for *qigong* represented an as yet untapped market opportunity. Books and magazines about *qigong* began to appear in both state-owned and privately run bookshops as well as on the trestle tables of the countless bookstalls that filled markets, railway station forecourts, and other open areas. *Qigong*, in other words, was good business. As new forms of media (and the machines to run them) became more prevalent in China, *qigong*-related audio- and videocassettes, VCDs, and later DVDs also appeared. *Qigong* groups and masters including Falun Gong and Li Hongzhi undoubtedly made use of this phenomenon, and if the accusations of the Chinese authorities are to be believed, made a great deal of money from their products.

The *qigong* boom also saw the more or less formal establishment of a number of *qigong* organizations.[27] This is not surprising; in China the management and regulation of social activities is achieved through large-scale single-interest organizations linked to the state. Thus, there exist national organizations for labor, women, farmers, and other concerns as well as for religions, as we will see below.[28] The growth in interest in *qigong* in the first half of the 1980s necessitated the formation of its own official umbrella organizations. Some were local: the first was the Beijing Qigong Research Association formed in December 1979, followed by other city- or province-based *qigong* organizations. Some were formed around particular interest groups, such as the Medical Qigong Science Research Association established by the Chinese National Traditional Medicine Association,[29] and the National Sports Qigong Science Research Association. By 1985, *qigong* had become so popular and so many organizations had proliferated that the authorities deemed it necessary to institute a national umbrella organization that would gather these different groups, to promote *qigong* on the one hand and regulate its activities on the other. Thus, the Chinese Association for Research into Qigong Science (Zhongguo qigong kexue yanjiu hui) was established in December 1985 and had its first official meeting in Beijing on April 30, 1986.[30]

27. See Palmer, *Qigong Fever*, chap. 2, "Political Networks and the Formation of the Qigong Sector."

28. On social organizations, including NGOs, in China, see Jonathan Unger, ed., *Associations and the Chinese State: Contested Spaces* (Armonk, NY: M. E. Sharpe, 2008), and Qiusha Ma, *Non-Governmental Organizations in Contemporary China: Paving the Way to Civil Society?* (Abingdon, UK: Routledge, 2006).

29. It was originally named the National Qigong Science Research Organization; see Palmer, *Qigong Fever*, p. 59.

30. See ibid., pp.75–76, and Zhang Zhenhuan, "Address Given by Zhang Zhenhuan at a Meeting Held to Celebrate the Formation of the Chinese *Qigong* Scientific Research Association," in Zhu and Penny, "The Qigong Boom," 13–20.

The high-level nature of the organization was reflected in the eminence of its leadership. Its honorary president was Peng Chong (1915–2010), a former member of the Politburo, secretary of the Central Committee, and at that time vice chairman of the Standing Committee of the National People's Congress—he was later to become its secretary general. There were six honorary deputy presidents:

Qian Xinzhong (1911–2009), a member of the Central Committee Advisory Commission, a former Minister of Public Health, and later head of the State Family Planning Commission;

Zhao Puchu (1907–2000), longtime Chairman of the Religion Committee of the Chinese People's Political Consultative Conference, a Leading Member of the Religious Affairs Bureau, and President of the Chinese Buddhist Association;

Liu Jianzhang (1910–2008), a member of the Central Committee Advisory Commission, a former Minister of Railways, and an advisor to the Aging Committee;

Cui Yueli (1920–1998), like Qian Xinzhong, a former Minister of Public Health, a member of the Central Committee, and longtime President of the Traditional Chinese Medicine Association;

Li Menghua (1922–2010), a member of the Central Committee, Minister of the State Physical Culture and Sports Commission, President of the All-China Sports Federation, and Chairman of the China Olympic Committee; and

He Dongchang (1923–), a member of the Central Committee, former Minister of Education, and a member of the Leading Group on Science and Technology Education.[31]

That interest in *qigong* had grown in many fields by 1985 is evident in the affiliations of these men (senior Chinese leaders often hold many offices simultaneously): public health, traditional Chinese medicine, aging, religion, sport, science, and technology. Indeed, in an important speech given at the 1986 meeting by Zhang Zhenhuan (1915–1994), the first substantive as opposed to honorary president of the Chinese Association for Research into Qigong Science, many of these areas were noted as falling into its ambit. Significantly, Zhang saw *qigong* specifically assisting China's drive for modernization.

On the subject of *qigong*, we have always believed that it can be used to treat disease, to improve health, and to extend life, but as to why this should be the case, we have not conducted sufficient scientific research. . . . We want to be of service to the

---

31. Anon., "Zhongguo qigong kexue yanjiuhui lishihui mingdan," *Qigong yu kexue* 7 (1986): 2.

modernization of agriculture, industry, national defence, science and technology, of service in the building of a new socialist material and spiritual civilisation.[32]

And later:

Practicing *qigong* helps to maintain good health in elderly people; this is one benefit that is well known. In sport, while it is gratifying to obtain a gold medal, what we really want to achieve is good results and the maintenance of a good physique. *Qigong* can be used to good effect in this area. In military matters, how can *qigong* be used? The highest technological achievement is to travel in space, but travelling in space can cause space travel sickness. Chinese should be better off than people of other countries in this matter. Experiments have been conducted with people who do not practice *qigong*, sitting them on a chair and spinning it around. After only five turns these people feel quite sick, whereas people who practice *qigong* can be spun continually for 108 times and still feel no ill effects.[33]

These passages reveal the new association's profound interest in the nexus between *qigong* and experimental science. Throughout the 1980s and 1990s, *qigong* journals often published articles reporting experiments that purported to prove both the existence of *qi* and the measurable effects of *qi* directed onto specific living organisms. The language of science became the predominant mode of discourse in discussions of *qigong* in the official press and in the *qigong* bureaucracy. It is not surprising, then, that in the writings of *qigong* groups, including Falun Gong, discussions that used scientific language were at the forefront, even when those discussions did not appear to be about scientific topics or even to be scientifically plausible.[34]

One application of *qigong* mentioned by Zhang Zhenhuan that was not represented by the honorary president or his deputies was military research. Zhang's reference to this is intriguing, since before his appointment to the Chinese Association for Research into Qigong Science he had made a career in military science and technology. His professional life culminated with appointments as chairman of the Science and Technology Committee of the State Defense Science, Technology and Industry Commission (holding the rank of general), and vice president of the Chinese Nuclear Science Society. The possibility that part of the authori-

---

32. Zhang, "Address Given . . .," pp. 14–15.
33. Ibid., p. 19.
34. See Benjamin Penny, "*Qigong*, Daoism and Science: Some Contexts for the *Qigong* Boom," in *Modernization of the Chinese Past*, ed. Mabel Lee and A. D. Syrokomla-Stefanowska (Sydney: Wild Peony, 1993), 166–79; and Palmer, *Qigong Fever*, chap. 4, "*Qigong* Scientism."

ties' motivation for encouraging *qigong* was its potential for spinoffs in the field of weapons research or other military applications cannot be discounted—especially because by this time, both the Soviet Union and the United States reportedly had invested in military-linked research programs focusing on the paranormal.[35] Indeed, in China from the early 1980s onward, it was popularly thought that while *qigong* masters were publicly feted for their achievements in healing, their real role was military. Nonetheless, whether or not the idea of military applications was taken seriously, a scientific approach to *qigong* and *qigong* research became the ruling model.

Especially in the latter half of the 1980s, "scientific *qigong*" became the watchword in *qigong* practice and in the *qigong* press. However, the *qigong* world, like the rest of Chinese society, felt the effects of the 1989 democracy movement and subsequent massacre, or, to be more precise, the change in political mood that followed. During the early years of the 1990s, social and cultural activities that were imported from the West and therefore tainted with "bourgeois liberalization" were discouraged.[36] At the same time, activities that were clearly Chinese were supported and perhaps allowed more freedom than previously. *Qigong* was one such activity, and this encouragement allowed a broadening of its concerns. Increasingly during these years, the dryly rational approach to *qigong* gradually relaxed as new forms included religious elements in the explanations of how their systems worked. As indicated by their names, these new varieties of *qigong* typically appealed to established Chinese religious ideas from Buddhism or Daoism, but sometimes they developed their own cosmologies, ethical systems, and doctrines. Of course, the prevalent notion that a particular form of *qigong* was embodied in a *qigong* master encouraged the thought that the master possessed great wisdom and superior knowledge—in some cases, enlightenment. These ideas were in no way dispelled by *qigong* magazine covers, which increasingly depicted the masters dressed in saffron robes rather than in sober business suits. In other words, in the early 1990s some *qigong* groups appeared more and more spiritual and less and less scientific. In addition, some masters started propounding teachings that went far beyond instructions for their regime of exercises. In fact, the writings that accumulated around some of these masters grew both in volume and in status as their words

35. On these programs, see Jonathan D. Moreno, *Mind Wars: Brain Research and National Defense* (New York: Dana Press, 2006), especially pp. 76–78, 83–87. See Palmer, *Qigong Fever*, pp. 73–85, for the links between the promoters of *qigong* and Chinese political and military institutions.

36. See Richard Baum, *Burying Mao: Chinese Politics in the Age of Deng Xiaoping* (Princeton, NJ: Princeton University Press, 1996).

started to be treated as scripture. Falun Gong was in many ways typical of this trend, but Li Hongzhi was, and remains, insistent that it is not a religion. While Li's position will be challenged in this book, it is important to understand why, in the China of the 1990s, Falun Gong would disavow its being categorized in any way as "religion."

Religion and the State in Contemporary China

It is no coincidence that the years of the *qigong* boom also saw a flourishing of religious activities in China, with the renovation and rebuilding of temples, churches, and mosques, the rediscovery of religious culture, and the reinvigoration of religious networks. The authorities had closely regulated religion ever since the Communist victory in 1949, so it is relatively easy to pinpoint the moment this revival was allowed to begin: the Third Plenum of the Eleventh Party Congress in December 1978. This plenum was, in general, the political turning point between Maoism and the era of "reform." However, with the decision to accord religion a degree of autonomy from the state came the imperative to prevent its becoming a catalyst for action against the regime. To this day, the fear of religiously inspired uprisings remains deeply ingrained in Chinese political culture. As Pitman Potter argued in 2003,

The tension between autonomy and loyalty is particularly evident in the area of religion. . . . Religion represents a fault line of sorts in the regime's efforts to build legitimacy through social policy. As a rich array of religious belief systems re-emerges, the regime faces continued challenges of maintaining sufficient authority to ensure political control while still presenting a broad image of tolerance.[37]

Thus, as is the case with *qigong*, religious activities were at once granted an autonomous space to exist but were at the same time placed under systems of monitoring and regulation that subjected this autonomy to state intervention. Parallel to Potter's "tension between autonomy and loyalty," another tension came into being during the 1980s and 1990s: that between legal and administrative instruments of protection and of coercion.

The Party's general policy toward religious activities since 1979 was enunciated in a document entitled "The Basic Viewpoint and Policy on

37. Pitman B. Potter, "Belief in Control: Regulation of Religion in China," *China Quarterly* 174 (June 2003): 317–37; quotation is from p. 318.

the Religious Question during Our Country's Socialist Period."[38] Distributed widely to Party committees at all levels in early 1982, it represented a definitive statement of religious policy. "The Basic Viewpoint"—which has become known as "Document 19"—proposes that religion is a historical phenomenon dependent on particular class relations. Since in Socialist society there were no oppressive class relations anymore, "the class root of the existence of religion was virtually lost . . . [but] because the people's consciousness lags behind social realities, old thinking and habits cannot be thoroughly wiped out in a short period."[39] Thus, officially, the "question of religion" shifted from focusing on its elimination (as had been the goal during the Cultural Revolution and the years that followed) to understanding how it was to be managed. In other words, the Party accepted that among the Chinese population there were going to be practitioners of one religion or another for the foreseeable future.[40] Party members themselves, however, were expected not to hold religious beliefs.

In documents that have been issued on the management of religions since the establishment of the People's Republic, a common feature has always been the claim that the state protects the freedom of religious belief. Clearly, in some periods the state has not done so, but the claim is echoed in Document 19: "The basic policy the Party has adopted towards the religious question is that of respect for and protection of the freedom of religious belief. This is a long-term policy, one which must be continually carried out until that future time when religion itself will disappear."[41] At the same time, however, this document also states clearly the limits to religious freedom. There must be no religious involvement in "the administrative or juridical affairs of the state," or in education. No one, "particularly people under eighteen years of age," can be forced "to become a member of a church, to become a Buddhist monk or nun, or to go to temples or monasteries to study Buddhist scripture." And most important, "nor will religion be permitted to make use in any way of religious pretexts to oppose the Party's leadership or the Socialist system, or to destroy national or ethnic unity."[42] The same tension between

38. Document 19 can be found in translation in Donald E. MacInnes, *Religion in China Today: Policy and Practice* (Maryknoll, NY: Orbis Books, 1989), pp. 8–26.

39. Ibid., p. 8.

40. The idea that religion was not on the verge of disappearance was, in a sense, a reversion to a general theoretical position developed in the 1950s: it is "complex, mass-based, long-lasting, and has implications for relations with both ethnic minorities and the nations of the world" (ibid., p. 2).

41. Ibid., p. 14.

42. Ibid., p. 15.

autonomy and loyalty can be observed in Article 36 of the 1982 Constitution. It reads:

Citizens of the People's Republic of China enjoy freedom of religious belief. No state organ, public organization, or individual may compel citizens to believe in, or not to believe in, any religion; nor may they discriminate against citizens who believe in, or do not believe in, any religion. The state protects normal religious activities. No one may make use of religion to engage in activities that disrupt public order, impair the health of citizens or interfere with the educational system of the state. Religious bodies and religious affairs are not subject to any foreign domination.[43]

The category "normal religious activities" adumbrated in this article has been especially effective in restricting activities across all religions practiced in China: it is not, after all, religious practitioners themselves who define what "normal religious activities" are. Decisions about religious activities on the ground are made by the state Religious Affairs Bureaus that exist at all levels of government, and their dictates are enforceable. In addition, policy decisions concerning religious activities are transmitted down to the local level through each of the government-authorized religious associations. As Human Rights Watch's 1997 report *China: State Control of Religion* indicates, "As early as the 1950s, the Chinese government began to set up an elaborate bureaucratic supervisory structure so that religion might better serve the political ends of the state. With some shifts in emphasis, that structure remains."[44]

The theoretical positions, state policies, and bureaucratic structures outlined here—whether they allow the expression of religious aspirations or whether they limit them—apply only to those social activities defined as "religions." This statement would be banal if it were not for the definition of what constitutes the category of religions in the People's Republic of China. In legal and administrative terms, there are only five religions in China: Buddhism (including Tibetan Buddhism), Daoism, Islam, Protestant Christianity, and Catholic Christianity. Each of these has its own religious association and its own points of contention with the authorities that monitor religious activities. Limiting religious activity in China to these five nominated religions does not, of course, reflect the actual religious situation across the country, but the effect of so doing is to create a demarcation between what is "religious" and therefore protected

43. Article 36, Constitution of The People's Republic of China, online at english.peopledaily.com.cn/constitution/constitution.html.
44. Mickey Spiegel, *China: State Control of Religion* (New York: Human Rights Watch, 1997), p. 13.

(as long its activities remain "normal") and what is "nonreligious." This demarcation allows the authorities to suppress religious groups that do not fall under one of the five nominated religions. This includes those groups that, by all objective accounts, could be defined as belonging to one of the five religions but which refuse to accept the leadership of the relevant association; for example, Catholic groups that maintain links with the Vatican. The definition of the five as the only "religions" also excludes sectarian groups that are in some way related to them, such as the various Buddhist sectarian organizations that trace their lineages back several centuries, or more recent Protestant groups such as the "Shouters." But the demarcation between protected "religions" and suppressed (or potentially suppressed) "nonreligions" has a more profound effect on the religious life of Chinese people than even these cases.

Historically in China, religion has rarely been exclusive, in contrast to the situation in the West, in which affiliation to a particular religion (whether by inheritance or by conversion) meant the exclusion of others. Thus, a Christian cannot simultaneously be a Muslim, and vice versa. However, in China, it was quite possible, indeed typical, for a person to honor Buddhist, Daoist, or local deities and traditions across the religious calendar, varying from place to place. These observances were often made to gods who did not belong to any of the five named religions but were, rather, part of a popular pantheon.[45] In addition, whether a particular deity or spirit or immortal was honored, whether its cult flourished or died out, ultimately depended on the deity's reliability in granting requests made to it. Traditional popular Chinese religious practice was, in this sense, very practical, and the history of the rise and fall of gods speaks to the observed changes in spiritual power that they could exercise. Thinking about religious activity in China in this way, it becomes clear that the government's fivefold division of religions excludes a major proportion of China's religious activity—and therefore that the people who practice it have no protection for their observances in law or regulation.

In addition to activities that are clearly religious (but that are excluded from being designated as such by the definition of the state), there is also a range of activities that have been widespread and often the province of religious professionals, sometimes taking place in temples. Among these are various forms of divination, geomancy (*fengshui*), spirit healing, and certain rituals associated with rites of passage. Unlike the popular

---

45. On the nature of Chinese popular religion, see Stephen F. Teiser, "Popular Religion," *Journal of Asian Studies* 54, no. 2 (May 1995): 378–95. See also Adam Yuet Chau, *Miraculous Response: Doing Popular Religion in Contemporary China* (Stanford, CA: Stanford University Press, 2006).

religious practices outlined above, whether these should be regarded as "religious" or not depends on how *religion* is defined. Nonetheless, it is clear that by any reasonable definition of what constitutes "religion" or "religious activities," the definition of *religion* promulgated by the Chinese authorities is too narrow. Yet while this definition is restrictive and exclusionary, we should recognize that it performs important political and cultural work in Chinese society. First, in a positive sense, it valorizes certain religious forms: the five approved religions are organized, hierarchical, and text-based, and present a coherent view of the cosmos, its origins, and the place of humanity in it. Second, and in contrast, it downgrades religious activities that are randomly distributed, nonhierarchical, and practice-based, and have no coherent or systematized theology. On the one hand this allows the state to control what it allows to be religions, as each group has a leadership and an administrative structure through which government orders can be promulgated. At the same time, it disallows the potentially subversive position that coherent ideologies may not be necessary or sufficient to explain the complexities of human existence.

Earlier in this chapter, the term *xiejiao*—"heterodox teaching" or "evil cult"—was discussed. Another term that appears in the government's attacks on Falun Gong, as well as in Chinese discussions of religion in general, is *mixin*. "Superstition" is the translation typically given for this word, which means literally "disordered or confused beliefs." While the idea of *xie*, "heterodox," has a long-standing position in Chinese discourse about religions, *mixin* is relatively new in two senses: first, *mixin* entered Chinese, along with many other new words, from Japanese, where it is first found in 1889 as a neologism used to translate the Western idea (indeed, *xin*, "belief," was not a term that described religious activity, let alone defined the nature of religion, in premodern China).[46] Second, the idea that beliefs could be disordered or confused (as opposed to unauthorized) also derives from the West. Thus, in government documents that rail against superstition, the corrective that is diagnosed is consistently education and a scientific outlook. For *qigong* groups to evoke "science" in some way, or for their writings to use scientific language to explain their particular practice and its virtues, was therefore to erect a defense against the accusation of "superstition," an accusation that would render them susceptible to negative actions by the authorities. The word that translates as "feudal" is often linked to "superstition" in modern China,

---

46. See Rebecca Nedostup, *Superstitious Regimes: Religion and the Politics of Chinese Modernity* (Cambridge, MA: Harvard University Asia Center, 2009).

where it means, loosely, "of the old society" and therefore conforming to certain sets of class relations now no longer extant.

Superstition and especially feudal superstition have been consistent targets of the Chinese authorities for more than fifty years. One of the most visible manifestations of this has been the destruction of religious buildings, including "unauthorized" temples, churches, and tombs.[47] Generally speaking, however, the attitude toward ordinary believers in "feudal superstition" has been that punishment is an inappropriate response. Instead, these believers are regarded as being misguided and therefore in need of education; consequently, campaigns against superstition have been a regular feature of Chinese life since the 1949 revolution and indeed before.[48] On the other hand, those that profit financially from purveying feudal superstition are punishable by law. As Stephan Feuchtwang has written,

The category "superstitious activities" concentrated on the peddling of goods and services. The services most often listed are those of horoscopy, geomancy, spirit-mediumship, and all forms of telling fate and calculating taboos. . . . They are . . . denounced as fraud, as being used to exploit people gulled into believing them, an economic offence.[49]

In addition to economic crime, the other legal arena in which superstition is regarded as an offense is when it is used to endanger social stability. Thus, "using superstitious beliefs to damage the implementation of state law and administrative regulation" attracts a seven-year prison sentence.[50]

Religion in contemporary China is, in short, highly regulated, even—perhaps especially—when it conforms to the models approved by the authorities. Over the years, various religious figures have complained about the restrictions under which they work, and on occasion overzealous local Religious Affairs Bureau officials have been upbraided for their maladministration. Nonetheless, the injunction to keep religious activities within the bounds set by the authorities has proved onerous for many believers and religious professionals. No such restrictions faced *qigong*

---

47. Spiegel, *China*, pp. 37–38.

48. See Prasenjit Duara, *Rescuing History from the Nation: Questioning Narratives of Modern China* (Chicago: University of Chicago Press, 1995), chap. 3, "The Campaigns against Religion and the Return of the Repressed"; and Nedostup, *Superstitious Regimes*.

49. Stephan Feuchtwang, "The Problem of Superstition in the People's Republic of China," in *Religion and Political Power*, ed. Gustavo Benavides and M. W. Daly (Albany: State University of New York Press, 1989), p. 56.

50. Spiegel, *China*, p. 36.

organizations: one Buddhist official complained in the mid-1990s that Falun Gong had, in fact, enjoyed a much freer rein than did Buddhism in bringing its message to the public. He pointed out that Party members who were precluded from practicing Buddhism by the official policy of atheism were initially attracted to Falun Gong as an apparently nonreligious form of spirituality.[51]

Falun Gong's disavowal of the category of religion to describe itself is therefore quite understandable under these circumstances. It is clearly not one of the five religions authorized by the state, and to claim to be a religion and not be one of the five would invite suppression. None of this, of course, affects whether outside observers of Falun Gong should, or should not, describe it as a religion. Indeed, this book will draw attention to many features of Falun Gong's doctrines, its practices, and the activities of its practitioners that point in that precise direction.

Religion and the Study of Falun Gong

When Falun Gong, the Chinese government, or a disinterested outsider asserts that Falun Gong is or is not a religion, it is worth remembering that the Chinese word for "religion"—*zongjiao*—is, like *mixin*, a relatively new arrival in the lexicon.[52] Although this combination of characters is found in texts dating to the sixth century, its modern usage appears to date from the middle of the nineteenth when it was imported from Japan after the neologism was formed in the late 1860s.[53] In earlier texts, it appears only in specifically Buddhist contexts and means the principles

51. See the comments of Chen Xingqiao as reported by Craig S. Smith, "Confounded China Considers Response to Challenge from Spiritual Group," *Wall Street Journal*, April 27, 1999.

52. In this context, it should be noted that in English and other European languages, the definition of the word *religion* has been the subject of considerable debate in academic writing. See Winston L. King, "Religion," and Gregory D. Alles, "Religion [Further Considerations]," in *Encyclopedia of Religion*, ed. Lindsay Jones, 2nd ed. (Farmington Hills, MI: Macmillan Reference USA, 2005), pp. 7692–701 and 7701–706 respectively; and Jonathan Z. Smith, "Religion, Religions, Religious," in *Critical Terms for Religious Studies*, ed. Mark C. Taylor (Chicago: University of Chicago Press, 1998), pp. 269–84, for relevant discussions of the issues involved. In this book, quoting Benson Saler, "religions" are understood not to possess any particular "feature in common, nor do they all necessarily resemble one another with respect to some trait or quality" but rather to share in "family resemblances." To use the formulation of Saler, "they collectively reveal a multiplicity of 'similarities overlapping and criss-crossing'" (*Conceptualizing Religion: Immanent Anthropologists, Transcendent Natives, and Unbound Categories*, paperback ed. [New York: Berghahn Books, 2000]), p. 160.

53. On the question of the origins of *zongjiao*, see Goossaert and Palmer, *The Religious Question in Modern China*; Nedostup, *Superstitious Regimes*; Mayfair Mei-Hui Yang, introduction to *Chinese Religiosities: Afflictions of Modernity and State Formation*, ed. Yang (Berkeley: University of California Press, 2008), 1–40; and Anthony C. Yu, *State and Religion in China: Historical and Textual Perspectives* (Chicago: Open Court, 2005).

and teachings of different strands of Buddhist thought or "the revered teaching/religion."[54] Whenever the term entered the Chinese language, however, it gained real currency as the translation for "religion" only in the works of the Chinese "public intellectual and Buddhist sympathiser" Liang Qichao (1873–1929) in the early twentieth century.[55]

We should bear in mind, though, what idea of religion this term conjured up for Chinese people in modern times. Mayfair Yang observes that "throughout the twentieth century in China, ideas of religion implicitly took Christianity, and more specifically Protestantism, as the standard and quintessential model of religion," and that any "legitimate" religion should have "a church-like organisation, an organised clergy and ordination system, a textual history, theological doctrines and scriptures, and so forth." What this meant was that "other forms of popular religion"—Yang nominates geomancy, exorcism, divination, spirit possession and shamanistic travel, and the placating of ghosts and demons—were relegated to the category of superstition.[56] In the introduction to their monumental work *The Religious Question in Modern China*, Vincent Goossaert and David A. Palmer make a related point forcibly:

The category of religion is a contested one, and the history of China's religious question is to a great extent the story of how the category has been imposed, rejected, appropriated, expanded, contracted, and assigned a place within ideological systems by different actors over the past century.[57]

Irrespective of the way *religion* or *zongjiao* has been defined by Chinese governments in modern times, Chinese religions have been practiced throughout history and in different places across the country in immensely varied ways, which Adam Yuet Chau refers to as collectively "doing religion." He finds five modalities of doing religion in his research, the first two of which are of particular interest here. The first of these is the "discursive or scriptural" modality, which "requires a high level of literacy and a penchant for philosophical or 'theological' thinking." The second is the "personal or cultivational":

54. See T. H. Barrett and Francesca Tarocco, "Terminology and Religious Identity: Buddhism and the Genealogy of the Term *Zongjiao*," in *Dynamics in the History of Religions*, ed. Volkhard Krech (Leiden: Brill, 2011), and Yu, *State and Religion in China*, p. 12. Barrett and Tarocco's research has indicated, however, the possibility that something like the modern usage of *zongjiao* was actually appearing in Chinese Buddhist circles in the earlier nineteenth century.

55. The quotation is from Barrett and Tarocco, "Terminology and Religious Identity."

56. Yang, introduction, pp. 12, 17.

57. Goossaert and Palmer, *The Religious Question in Modern China*, p. 9.

Practices such as meditation, *qigong*, alchemy, personal sutra chanting, and keeping a merit/demit ledger belong to this modality. This modality presupposes a long-term interest in cultivating and transforming oneself (whether Buddhist, Daoist, or Confucian). Sometimes sectarian movements might precipitate out of these personal-cultivational pursuits (e.g. Falungong).[58]

Falun Gong, with its concerns with cultivation and its extensive scriptural corpus, is one of the newest of Chinese religions, and it claims no immediate predecessor in the sense of asserting its position in a lineage of religions. Nonetheless, as will be clear throughout this book, many of the terms Li Hongzhi uses and the ideas that underpin Falun Gong teachings are found in Chinese religions of the past. We know very little about Li's own religious background or that of his family, only what we can glean from his own writings about what he has read, as we will see in chapter 3; so any attempt to be precise about his specific religious influences would be speculative. Thus, in this book, when Li uses a term or alludes to a religious concept that comes from or echoes some other religion, I have simply noted its origin (as far as we can tell) and have tried to explain how his use of it differs from earlier usages.

The question of whether Falun Gong is a religion is relevant to how it has been seen in the West. Since the suppression of Falun Gong that began in July 1999, the nature of the movement has changed. What had been, explicitly at least, a nonpolitical movement interested in the transformation of practitioners through cultivation chose to take a stand against an aggressive state. Thus, what has become essentially an expatriate movement has attempted to transform itself into an activist organization, adopting the discourses of human rights familiar to its now largely Western audience. In some cases, claims made outside China for the human rights of Falun Gong practitioners have taken place specifically in relation to "freedom of religious belief." In 2001 Falun Gong itself accepted an International Religious Freedom Award from the Center for Religious Freedom of the US non-government organization Freedom House (along with the Cardinal Kung Foundation, Friends of the Christian Unregistered Churches, the International Campaign for Tibet, and the Uyghur American Association).[59] Also notable in this context are the annual reports on religious freedom published by the Department of State of the

58. Chau, *Miraculous Response*, p. 75. The remaining three modalities are "liturgical/ritual," "immediate/practical," and "relational."

59. See "Freedom House Honors Chinese Defenders of Religious Freedom: Annual Award Going to Five Chinese Religious Groups," online at web.archive.org/web/20010715213704/http://www.freedomhouse.org/religion/news/bn2001/bn-2001-03-12.htm.

United States, where Falun Gong features in the China section.[60] Reports such as these have been produced because of the way practitioners have been treated in China and not because of any particular characteristics of Falun Gong itself, save the sufferings of its adherents. In other words, the specific teachings of Falun Gong—what its practitioners believe and do—are strictly not relevant to the concerns of such organizations. Human Rights Watch makes its position explicit: "From a human rights perspective it is irrelevant whether Falun Gong is termed a 'cult,' a 'sect,' a 'heretic' organization, etc. What is critical is that individuals not be punished for the substance of their beliefs."[61]

This exclusion of the substance of what adherents believe they are doing when they practice Falun Gong also occurs in some recent academic discussions of the movement, where the actual content of its religious teachings has largely been absent, or dealt with only briefly.[62] It is this lacuna that the present book seeks to fill. One perspective evident in several studies sees Falun Gong in a tradition of popular protest movements in late imperial and modern China, representing a potential challenge to the state.[63] Specifically, some authors see the motivations for the government's violent response to Falun Gong as lying in its fear of religiously inspired uprisings. According to this view, when the Chinese authorities suppressed Falun Gong they saw parallels between that movement and earlier popular religious sects that threatened the regimes of their times. Jeffrey N. Wasserstrom calls this the "religious revolt specter."[64]

David Ownby, on the other hand, in his *Falun Gong and the Future of China*, invokes the tradition of Chinese "redemptive societies" of the Republican period, which themselves "stand in some kinship relation to what we have called the late Imperial White Lotus tradition," to

60. The currently available report—*International Religious Freedom Report, 2010*—is available from www.state.gov/g/drl/rls/irf/2010/148863.htm. Earlier annual reports are archived on the US State Department's website. See also Michael Dillon, *Religious Minorities and China* (London: Minority Rights Group International, 2001), which discusses Falun Gong with a focus on the rights of religious minorities.

61. Spiegel, "Dangerous Meditation," note 1, p.8.

62. Notable exceptions include David Ownby, *Falun Gong and the Future of China* (New York: Oxford University Press, 2008), pp. 89–123, and Palmer, *Qigong Fever*, pp. 225–40, as well as Benjamin Penny, "Falun Gong, Prophecy and Apocalypse," *East Asian History* 23 (June 2002): 149–68; "The Life and Times of Li Hongzhi: Falun Gong and Religious Biography," *China Quarterly* 175 (September 2003): 643–61; and "Animal Spirits, Karmic Retribution, Falungong, and the State," in Yang, *Chinese Religiosities*, 135–54.

63. See, for instance, the introduction to Elizabeth J. Perry, *Challenging the Mandate of Heaven: Social Protest and State Power in China* (Amonk, NY: M. E. Sharpe, 2002), especially pp. xv–xxiii. Another version of the introduction can be found in *Critical Asian Studies* 33, no. 2 (2001): 163–80.

64. Jeffrey N. Wasserstrom, "The Year of Living Anxiously: China's 1999," in his edited volume *Twentieth-Century China: New Approaches* (London: Routledge, 2003).

illuminate the history of Falun Gong. As he notes, the groups designated by the term *White Lotus* usually did not describe themselves in this way, but the designation itself was used during the Qing dynasty and into the Republican period as a generic term to justify suppressing them if they were considered threatening to the government.[65] The redemptive societies, for Ownby, act as a kind of bridge between a centuries-long sectarian movement and the *qigong* world of the 1980s and 1990s. These groups, he says, all "share the following basic characteristics":

At the most fundamental level, many of these groups appear to have been organised by and around charismatic masters, who generally claim independence from other recognised religions (or "cultivation systems") and from one another. These masters preach what they claim to be a unique message of salvation often experienced first and foremost through the body—almost always as renewed health, sometimes in the cultivation of paranormal powers—and grounded in traditional moral practices. Morality is a necessary but not sufficient condition for salvation; the master's message contains corporal techniques ranging from rituals to mantras to meditation to miracle cures, and the master's individual guidance, or presence, is often necessary to the success of the practitioner's efforts. The master's message is generally—but not always—consigned to scripture, and often sounds apocalyptic themes, driving home the need for repentance and moral rectitude. Although most of these groups have been peaceful, some have maintained problematic relations with authority, either because the state considers the teachings to be heterodox, or because the groups sometimes fall outside (or cut across) the orbit of such familiar authority structures as lineages or villages, or because some groups have been involved in millenarian movements or rebellions.[66]

It is certainly true that these characteristics were shared by "*qigong*, Falun Gong, and the traditions from late imperial and Republican China known as White Lotus, folk Buddhist, sectarian, syncretic and redemptive societies," as Ownby argues.[67] However, to draw links between any two movements across time—Falun Gong and one of the Republican-period redemptive societies, say—surely requires that they both possess certain particular or distinctive features. This list of "basic characteristics," on the other hand, can be observed in many religious groups from China's past and present (and many religious groups that experienced no influences at all from China). Thus, the fact that Falun Gong has a charismatic

65. Ownby, *Falun Gong and the Future of China*, p. 24. An earlier version can be found in his "A History for Falun Gong: Popular Religion and the Chinese State since the Ming Dynasty," *Nova Religio* 6, no. 2 (April 2003): 223–43.

66. Ownby, *Falun Gong and the Future of China*, pp. 25–26.

67. Ibid., p. 25.

master who preaches a message of salvation, who wrote scriptures that sometimes sound apocalyptic, and so on, does not necessarily point to the kind of continuity Ownby sees—Christianity, for instance, could also plausibly claim most of the characteristics listed above.

Arguably, this analysis also does not sufficiently take into account much of what makes Falun Gong different from any other group. As well as drawing on a wide range of Chinese religious traditions, Li Hongzhi refers extensively (though often silently) to ideas and books that first came into China in the 1980s, notably works of the Western New Age. Thus, Ownby's attempt to see Falun Gong as having a kinship relation to earlier redemptive societies and through them to groups labeled as belonging to the White Lotus tradition is provocative, but it does not, in my opinion, reveal the nature of Falun Gong as a religious movement in its own right.

Ownby is undoubtedly correct, however, to point to Falun Gong's links to earlier religious traditions in China in order to explain some of its success. To understand how the spiritual teachings of Master Li became interleaved with people's lives, to come to terms with this insertion of the doctrinal into the social, of religion into history, requires an approach perhaps more commonly seen in studies of religious and spiritual movements of the distant past than in those that focus on contemporary issues and topics. Such an approach takes the category of religion seriously and allows for the possibility that spiritual matters can be placed at the center of an analysis and not relegated to the margins. It argues that religious and spiritual claims should be approached with respect, and appropriate effort should be made to understand them on their own terms. It contends that the people who choose to mold their lives around these claims do not, thereby, leave the historical stage. Finally, it regards the texts produced by religious and spiritual movements as illuminating documents, not just for the groups that produced them, but for the society as a whole, adumbrating that society's imaginative possibilities, its plausible logics, its effective discourses.

Most of those who became Falun Gong practitioners throughout the 1990s were also, it should be remembered, people who lived ordinary day-to-day lives in China's vast cities, who experienced the effects and uncertainties of the economic reforms, who moved in their own social and familial networks. The people who became adherents had lived through the same history as their family members, friends, and neighbors who did not become adherents. Before the suppression, Falun Gong practitioners could be found in factories, military establishments, offices, classrooms, and every other kind of workplace across the country. In short, Falun Gong was not apart from contemporary China but rather a product of it. The nature of contemporary Chinese society therefore cannot be properly understood without taking its ability to produce Falun Gong into account.

The focus of this book is on Falun Gong's own extensive body of texts and the material that has circulated around them. This includes, of course, Li Hongzhi's own writings, writings by practitioners that appear on Falun Gong websites, articles by journalists in *qigong* journals, commentaries on Falun Gong in the Chinese religious press and in general circulation, and, finally, the copious quantities of material produced by the Chinese authorities since the crackdown. For Falun Gong practitioners, texts are of immense importance and occupy central doctrinal and organizational roles in the movement. As we will see, Li Hongzhi regards the reading (and rereading) of *Zhuan Falun* (*Turning the Wheel of the Law*), the primary scripture of Falun Gong, as a fundamental part of the cultivation practice he teaches, along with the performance of the five sets of exercises and the maintenance of his moral code. To this day, small groups of practitioners around the world meet regularly to recite *Zhuan Falun*, paragraph by paragraph. They also study Li Hongzhi's copious later writings, lectures, and collections of poetry.

All these works are freely available on Falun Gong websites, and the most important material has been translated into many languages. In addition, the websites are full of other textual material: testimonies from practitioners, discussions of the teachings, news from practitioner groups worldwide, updates on the suppression, remembrances of Li Hongzhi's lectures in China, and so on. Indeed, as Falun Gong has been transformed into an expatriate movement with many relatively small groups of practitioners scattered across the globe (rather than the fewer, larger concentrations that existed in China before 1999), the importance of web-based text has grown significantly. These texts now serve as a unifying agent; a practitioner in Canberra knows that he or she is reading the same scripture as a practitioner in Hong Kong or Paris or New York. Returning regularly to the websites to study the latest postings or delve into the Falun Gong archive maintains a community of belief and practice in spite of the great dispersal of the movement.

The texts on Falun Gong websites are clearly authorized at the highest level of the movement. The main website for practitioners is called Minghui.org, and its English-language equivalent is Clearwisdom.net. In July 2000, within a week of the first anniversary of the suppression, a notice appeared on the sites entitled "On Important Matters, Practitioners

Must Pay Attention to the Attitude of Minghui Net."[68] It explains that this website "has taken on the responsibilities of connecting Dafa [that is, Falun Dafa, or Falun Gong] disciples around the world, spreading Dafa information, and exchanging practitioners' thoughts and understandings." It also notes that all contributions to the website have undergone a process of "careful and detailed proofreading, editing, and approval." The position of authority granted to these websites comes directly from Li Hongzhi. As the website's editors state,

On June 15, 2000, Minghui Net was instructed to give an advanced notice of an upcoming new article. The notice clearly announced, for the first time, Master Li's words: "It is not that Minghui Net does not make mistakes, however, on important matters, practitioners watch the position of Minghui Net . . ."[69]

They conclude "On Important Matters" with the following:

Therefore, within the current complicated and difficult environment, it is imperative and of great urgency for all practitioners to know about the materials posted on Minghui Net thoroughly and to spread them widely.[70]

Thus, relying on the authorized textual corpus of Falun Gong guarantees that the doctrines, instructions, and observations being discussed form core teachings of the movement and are not simply the opinions of one informant or a group of local practitioners.

In addition, studying the texts of Falun Gong in this way places us in the position of a practitioner coming to grips with Li Hongzhi's teachings (but perhaps with different motivations). Many of Li Hongzhi's lectures—all of which are recorded, transcribed, and published— include question and answer sessions. These are particularly useful as a resource

68. "On Important Matters, Practitioners Must Pay Attention to the Attitude of Minghui Net" (July 14, 2000), online at www.clearwisdom.net/emh/articles/2000/7/16/7662.html; "Zhongda wenti kan minghuiwang de taidu," www.minghui.org/mh/articles/2000/7/15/2624.html.

69. This citation comes from an article entitled "A Second Authentic New Article of Master Li since July 22, 1999 Will Be Published in a Few Days" (June 15, 2000), online at www.clearwisdom .net/html/articles/2000/6/15/8785.html; "Jinrinei jiangyou qi yue ershier ri yilai dier pian zhen-zheng de xin jingwen fabiao," www.minghui.org/mh/articles/2000/6/15/1461.html.

70. According to a Falun Gong report, "As the Tenth Anniversary of the Minghui Website Draws Near, Editors Answer Readers' Questions" (April 19, 2009), some "12.2 million unique IP addresses outside of China went to the Minghui website in 2008," and "there have been at least 40 million practitioners in mainland China who have exchanged information on Minghui." See www.clearwisdom .net/html/articles/2009/4/22/106718.html; "Shi zhounian jianglin zhi ji, Minghui bianjibu da duzhe wen," www.minghui.org/mh/articles/2009/4/19/199284.html.

for research, as they not only indicate what issues practitioners find troubling but also put Li Hongzhi on the spot, forcing him to give an immediate answer to a specific question. They also allow Li to add nuance to teachings he has outlined in earlier texts, and to provide a commentary to his own writings as circumstances change. Since the suppression, Li has provided new interpretations of many of his core teachings to take account of the vastly different situation in which Falun Gong has found itself.

The realization that Falun Gong's teachings have not remained unchanged over its relatively short history emphasizes another reason for the importance of the study of texts. Although there have been important cases of Falun Gong books being rewritten and texts being withdrawn, in most cases the written material has not undergone revision or reediting. This is not surprising, as doctrinally, Li Hongzhi's words are true in a singular way, and changing them would be tantamount to altering scripture. This respect for the Master's words enables analysis of how Falun Gong teachings have changed. It provides an insight into the development of Li Hongzhi's ideas as he progressed from being just another new *qigong* master to being the leader of a movement of possibly tens of millions of adherents—and then, of course, to being persona non grata in his homeland. Tracking changes in the teachings is therefore important and can only really be done through textual study.

It has been argued that while there are followers of Li Hongzhi practicing Falun Gong in the West, textual study should be set aside in favor of fieldwork, or at most play a supplementary role to it. David Ownby, for example, has gone to great efforts to survey practitioners in North America. He argues, "Fieldwork allows us to go beyond Li Hongzhi's written message, beyond the representations of Falun Gong by the Chinese state, to understand how Falun Gong as a redemptive society, is understood and lived by practitioners." However, he continues, "no claim is made that Chinese practitioners in Canada and the United States are *identical* to Li Hongzhi's followers in China."[71] The importance of this observation cannot be overstated. In Ownby's own surveys, he found that "slightly more than three out of five" of the practitioners in North America he questioned between 1999 and 2002 had started practicing Falun Gong only after they had left China. Most practitioners "were relatively young," and were typically "well-educated and reasonably materially well off." Indeed, from his cohort, "roughly 77% of those responding

---

71. Ownby, *Falun Gong and the Future of China*, p. 126; emphasis in the original.

had completed at least a university-level degree," and a staggering 22.2% in one survey had a PhD. In terms of income, Ownby concludes that "significant numbers of Falun Gong practitioners [in Canada and the USA] are . . . doing considerably better than the average North American," and that they include "many engineers, scientists, computer programmers, accountants, and professors."[72] He observes,

> When I attended an anti-Falun Gong conference in Beijing in the fall of 2000, one Chinese researcher remarked that Falun Gong practitioners he had met were "weak elements" (or more colloquially, "losers"; *ruanzhe*), by which he meant the sick, the poor, the downtrodden, those without resources to make much of their lives (those who, one might add, might reasonably wish to make claims on a socialist state). This assertion may or may not paint an accurate picture of Falun Gong practitioners in China, but it is certainly not true of Falun Gong practitioners in North America. The average Chinese practitioner in North America is young, urban, dynamic, a successful recent immigrant largely living the American dream, at least from the material point of view.[73]

While fieldwork among expatriate practitioners is undoubtedly valuable, attempting to draw conclusions about the nature of Falun Gong inside China before 1999 based on interactions with these adherents overseas is fraught with difficulty. There are three clear problems. First, as Ownby himself shows, by almost any measure, practitioners in North America are very different from their counterparts in China before the suppression—and from my observations this situation is the same in Australia, New Zealand, and the United Kingdom. Second, most current practitioners, as he also notes, were not involved with the movement in its early days or in China at all; many, indeed, did not become adherents until the late 1990s or even after the suppression. Third, and perhaps most important, irrespective of when practitioners began cultivating, whether they first heard about Falun Gong in China or outside, or whether they are ethnically Chinese or not, they have all been subject to the reinterpretations of Falun Gong teachings that have occurred since 1999. Thus, to avoid a view of Falun Gong that is overwhelmingly and unavoidably defined by its current relationship with the Chinese government, and to go beyond the hurly-burly of the practitioners' present activism, the study of the textual corpus of Falun Gong is fundamental.

72. Ibid., pp. 136–37.
73. Ibid., p. 138; emphasis in the original.

In addition to these concerns, the study of Falun Gong has one particular characteristic that distinguishes it from the study of most other contemporary religious or spiritual movements: the fact of the suppression. In practical terms, it has been impossible to research Falun Gong in China since 1999. Those practitioners who have not recanted—but are not, or not yet, detained—are forced to operate in clandestine ways.[74] Even if they were to make themselves available as informants, the dangers in which they would therefore place themselves mean that it is simply not ethical to pursue such a project.

My goal in this book is to focus on Li's textual corpus, to investigate what it is that makes Falun Gong distinctive as a set of teachings. This approach forces us to take notice of those aspects of Li Hongzhi's writings that seem familiar as well as those that appear obscure; to take him seriously when he writes about subjects regarded in the West as the preserve of fringe groups; and to appreciate the deep debt he owes to premodern Chinese traditions of cultivation as well as to ideas that only appeared in China in the 1980s. Falun Gong is, after all, a movement that sets great store on the written word: Li himself states that reading the scriptures is more important in a practitioner's cultivation than performing the exercises, as we will see in chapter 5. Li's teachings make Falun Gong the movement it is; they hold it together, and give guidance to practitioners. They are therefore at the core of this study, the first to analyze comprehensively the religion of Falun Gong.

In methodological terms, this study exemplifies what has become known as the New Sinology. Geremie R. Barmé writes that New Sinology has a "robust engagement with contemporary China" that "emphasizes strong scholastic underpinnings in both the classical and modern Chinese language and studies."[75] John Minford sees it as transcending "the narrow concerns of the prevalent Social Sciences-based model. We recognise . . . the urgency of applying the past to the present, the pressing need to understand today's China, as the world's rising power. In doing so, we are deeply aware of the need to understand the historical roots of China's contemporary consciousness."[76] This book therefore approaches the study of Falun Gong cognizant of both its profound importance for

---

74. See, for instance, Mary-Anne Toy, "Screws Tighten on Persecuted Sect," *Sydney Morning Herald*, July 26, 2008.

75. Geremie R. Barmé, "On New Sinology," online at rspas.anu.edu.au/pah/chinaheritageproject/newsinology/.

76. John Minford, foreword to a new edition of Lionel Giles's translation of *Sunzi: The Art of War* (North Clarendon, UK: Tuttle, 2008), online at rspas.anu.edu.au/pah/chinaheritageproject/newsinology/.

understanding contemporary China and the necessity to see it as a product of the particularities and specificities of the Chinese people's long involvement in self-cultivation.

Practitioners' lives clearly changed in a fundamental manner when the suppression occurred and in the decade that followed, but even before July 1999 the nature of Falun Gong had altered. Many of the changes the movement experienced in those early years were, in fact, also determined by the relationship it had with the Chinese authorities, if not so crucially as the state's declaration of its illegality. We need to understand this history of the movement, beginning with its inception in May 1992, to appreciate fully the contexts in which these changes occurred. Thus, before approaching the detailed analysis of Li Hongzhi's teachings in the last four chapters of this book, it is necessary to outline the path of Falun Gong from its launch to its suppression. I approach this task as a historian, using the textual record for my evidence. It is obvious, however, that a clear distinction must be drawn between writings from before and after Falun Gong was banned. Those from the second half of 1999 and later must be assessed as weapons in a propaganda war, whatever else they may be. This is clear in the history I present in the next chapter, and even more so in the discussion of the figure of Li Hongzhi himself in chapter 3, where many assertions made by the Chinese authorities and Falun Gong itself are simply not commensurable. The best evidence we have for how Falun Gong began and grew, how its relationship with the government soured, and what led to the suppression must, therefore, be the writings produced at the time, writings that preserve the voices of participants in the events of the 1990s without the inevitable reinterpretations of the suppression period.

TWO

The History of Falun Gong, 1992–99

All established religions were once new. In their infancy, they must have appeared as strange aberrations on the religious landscape of the times, with their teachers seeming to be mavericks, oddities, or even madmen. Certainly, the purveyors of new religious approaches, past and present, have come into society with no followers or organization. Many have, presumably, died or given up their vocation in the same state, but history rarely records the lives of failed prophets and visionaries. Each of those newly founded religions that do attract enough followers to survive and therefore become, in some sense, established generally commemorates the early days of the faith in stories of the founder's life, the struggle to form a community of believers, and the spread of the message beyond its geographical origin. Notable events are also marked in the ritual calendar. In this, Falun Gong is no different from any other religion. It has an authorized (though now withdrawn) biography of Li Hongzhi, and an official chronicle of its history is available on its websites. Practitioners celebrate World Falun Dafa Day on May 13, which marks both Li's birthday (although this date is disputed by the government) and the beginning of his first series of lectures in 1992. They also commemorate the anniversary of the Zhongnanhai demonstration on April 25.

The early days of the formation of a newly established religion are also usually the time when its basic teachings are devised. Just as the founder's life is lived in specific places at particular times, so his or her teachings are directed toward a community embedded in a certain history and geography. Nonetheless, many religions—perhaps most—assert the universality of their message. This tension between the idea that a set of teachings is true for all times and places and, at the same time, that it derived from a specific historical and geographical context remains an important issue for religions across the world. Again, Falun Gong embodies this tension as much as any other faith. This is especially so now that most active practitioners live outside China, the origin of the religious traditions and practices that form the foundations of Falun Gong's teachings.

It is therefore important to place Li Hongzhi's religious teachings in their historical context. This chapter traces the history of Falun Gong from its official launch in 1992 in Changchun to the period after the Chinese government suppressed it in 1999—a history that is more detailed for some periods than others, partly due to the availability of source material and partly because the narrative is intended to serve the purpose of contextualizing Li's teachings. Thus, the early period in which the basic ideas of Falun Gong were first taught is discussed in greater detail than the decade following the suppression. However, where events from the later period have led to important changes or reinterpretations in the teachings, they are given more attention.

Master Li Comes Down from the Mountains

With the launch of Falun Gong, Li Hongzhi declared himself to be a *qigong* master. He had "come down from the mountains," a phrase often used in Chinese to describe the appearance of a new master who has refined his powers and is ready to pass them on to disciples. For Li this moment came on May 13, 1992, when he delivered the first of many sets of nine lectures across China in order to transmit his teachings. The original series was held in the auditorium of the No. 5 Middle School in Changchun and was sponsored by the Changchun Somatic Science Research Association.[1] Falun Gong sources indicate that about 180 people attended. Within three days of the conclusion of these lectures, Li gave a second set in the same place. This time 250 people went. Only three weeks later he took perhaps the most important step in his short career,

1. Anon., "A Chronicle of Major Events of Falun Dafa" (March 2, 2004), online at www.clearwisdom .net/emh/articles/2004/8/27/chronicle.html; "Falun dafa dashiji nianjian," www.zhengjian.org/zj/ articles/2004/3/2/26013.html.

moving to Beijing to deliver his lectures there. The Chinese Association for Research into Qigong Science sponsored the first series in the capital that again attracted between 200 and 300 people. By December 1992, only seven months after Falun Gong's launch, Li had given five series of these lectures in Beijing, four in Changchun, one in Taiyuan, the capital of Shanxi Province, and one in Guan County in the northeastern province of Shandong, to a total of about 5,000 people.

Until the end of 1994, Li Hongzhi gave no fewer than fifty-six series of lectures, with only a few days' pause between each one. They were held in many different places, but they were not spread evenly across the country. Almost all the lectures took place in large cities, mostly provincial capitals: thirteen series in Beijing, seven in Changchun, five each in Guangzhou and Wuhan. Only a handful was held in county towns. Even at the height of its popularity in the late 1990s, the reach of Falun Gong did not extend far beyond urban areas. In addition, by far the majority of Li's teaching took place in the north of China—in Beijing and Changchun, as already noted, but also in Tianjin, Taiyuan, Jinan, and other towns in Shandong, Dalian, Harbin, Qiqihar, and the ethnic Korean center of Yanji.

We are fortunate that considerable photographic evidence of these early lectures survives in Falun Gong online archives.[2] They took place in all sorts of halls: an old theater with dress circle and gallery in Wuhan, the auditorium of the Trades Union headquarters in Guangzhou, a basketball stadium in Jinan. In all the photographs Li Hongzhi sits alone at an ordinary desk in the centre of the stage, dressed in a sober business suit or a plain white shirt. In the early lectures the stage is completely unadorned, but by February 1994 the Falun Gong symbol of a large Buddhist swastika surrounded by four small swastikas and four small *taijitu* or *yinyang* symbols adorns the curtain behind him. Usually a banner hangs above the stage: "We Welcome Li Hongzhi, the Founder of Falun Gong, to Lecture at such-and-such a place" or "Opening Ceremony for the Commencement of the Falun Gong Transmission Class at such-and-such a place." In some of the later lectures, an array of video cameras is trained on him. In most of the photos, the audience is seated, listening to his lecture, but in two they are on their feet learning one of the Falun Gong exercises, following an instructor onstage who is standing on a table.

Falun Gong made an appearance in the Western press not long after it had been launched. Lincoln Kaye of the *Far Eastern Economic Review*

2. See Anon., "Zhengfa zhi lu" (no date), at photo.minghui.org/photo/images/exhibition/newest_1.htm.

attended one of Li's first Beijing lectures in July 1992. Characterizing the assembly as a "charismatic cult," Kaye describes an audience made up of all kinds of Beijingers: youths, old people, farmers, bureaucrats, and students. The crowd included two "svelte expatriate wives" who arrived in a limousine, a long-haired man wearing a hologram of the Buddha on a chain around his neck, and a "haggard middle-aged matron and her retarded daughter." Li preached a message opposing a "single-minded pursuit of prosperity" and advocating "patience" (usually rendered "forbearance" in Falun Gong's translations). Kaye paints a picture of a congregation in a state of frenzy.

An old man started grunting gutturally. A girl cried, her quiet whimper accelerating into wracking sobs. Someone else cackled hysterically. One of the expatriate wives rose to her feet, twitching and jerking violently (while her companion sat hunched in consternation). The young man with the amulet sank to the floor in a cross-legged trance. A frumpy matron in a pink polo shirt stood up and started caressing her shoulders, hair and breasts. Another woman batted herself in the head rapidly with her fists. Someone tap-danced loudly in the front of the hall. The haggard woman in the back row rocked in her chair, arms akimbo in the air and eyes shut behind thick spectacles. The retarded daughter, worried at her mother's distraction, laughed and crooned and finally tugged at her hands to pull her out of her trance.[3]

The first version of Li Hongzhi's biography also recalls an early lecture in Beijing. Although it does not describe the audience's reaction to Li's power as frenzied, the event appears numinous and full of miracles, especially in contrast with the plainness of the scene as depicted in photographs.

Many of the students could see a column of light on top of the teacher's head, a white light on his body and balls of light surrounding him. The balls of light were as big as basketballs, continuously moving. . . . Beijing student Wang Changsi said, "As I was listening to the lecture, I saw a gleaming gold Buddha with my own eyes, and I saw four gold Buddhas revolving together one after the other. During the night of the fifteenth day of the seventh lunar month of 1992, I saw a great Buddha in a nearby square filling the entire sky."[4]

---

3. Lincoln Kaye, "Traveller's Tales," *Far Eastern Economic Review*, July 23, 1992, p. 24. This description accords with what we know of many *qigong* lectures that took place in the 1980s and early 1990s. See the excerpt from Ke Yunlu's *The Great Qigong Masters* in Barmé and Jaivin, *New Ghosts, Old Dreams*, pp. 375–80.

4. Li, *Zhongguo falungong* (1993), pp. 180–81.

Since 2004, practitioners have published on Falun Gong websites additional recollections of some of these early lectures, including accounts of strange and wonderful happenings both within the lecture halls and in the nearby streets and squares. At a lecture in Guangzhou, for instance, "from the four sides of the stadium, no matter on which side practitioners sat, they all sat facing Master listening respectfully, and were bathed in his Buddha light. During the entire time Master lectured on the Fa and transmitted his *gong* energy, there were three big Buddha images in yellow *kaṣāyas* [Buddhist monks' robes] where he sat." Later, outside their hotel, practitioners saw "two white dragons coiling together in the sky above the hotel. We even clearly saw the dragons' moustaches."[5] On another occasion, also in Guangzhou, "big Faluns" could be seen in the sky "rotating nine times clockwise and nine times counter-clockwise. . . . There were some small Faluns rotating around the big Falun, rotating on their own axis. . . . The sky was half red and half green."[6] Such signs and wonders indicated that Li Hongzhi was no ordinary man. His powers and spiritual eminence seemed to induce a response from deities, from creatures of good omen, and from the cosmos itself.

As Li was traveling the country teaching Falun Gong to the thousands of people who attended his lectures, some of whom claimed to be privileged enough to see the manifestations of Falun Gong in the heavens, he was—on a much more mundane level—simultaneously establishing an institutional foothold for this new *qigong* form and gaining publicity for it in other ways. Not long after Falun Gong was launched, Li formed a peak organization, the Falun Dafa Research Association, which he led himself. According to James Tong, among his associates at this stage were Li Chang, Wang Zhiwen, and Yu Changxin.[7] All three received lengthy prison sentences after the suppression in 1999. In 1992, however, relations with the authorities were rather different. According to the Chinese government website Facts.org.cn, in September of that year Li Hongzhi "got connected with Zhang Zhenhuan," who as we saw in chapter 1 was the first president of the Chinese Association for Research into Qigong Science, and Falun Gong was recognized as a school under its authority.

5. Ming Xuan, "Recalling Master's Lectures in Guangzhou" (February 21, 2008), online at www .clearwisdom.net/emh/articles/2008/3/13/95309.html, amended; "Yi shizun Guangzhou chuangong jiangfa diandi," www.minghui.org/mh/articles/2008/2/22/172909.html.

6. A Falun Dafa Practitioner from Shandong Province, "My Experiences Attending Master's Fifth Lecture Series in Guangzhou" (January 1, 2008), online at www.clearwisdom.net/emh/ articles/2008/2/19/94593.html, "Huiyi shifu Guangzhou diwuqi jiangfa," www.minghui.org/mh/ articles/2008/1/1/169412.html.

7. Tong, "An Organizational Analysis of the Falun Gong," p. 640.

On July 30, 1993, "with the help of Li Chang and the others," Falun Gong was upgraded to become a branch of the national association; then on August 14 it was "formally registered" as one of the association's "special committees."[8] This recognition gave Falun Gong an official status, enabling it to organize, have public displays, and rent offices, as well as teach publicly. This status also meant that *qigong* magazines and newspapers, which by this time were well established and had formidable circulations, could run articles about Falun Gong without fear of criticism. In the early 1990s as today, having an official status was vital for any organization that wanted to exist without conflict with the Chinese government.

In December 1992 Li Hongzhi, accompanied by some of his close colleagues, attended the Oriental Health Expo in Beijing, a public exhibition of various *qigong* forms and presentations by *qigong* masters. A year later, according to Falun Gong sources, he served as a member of the organizing committee of the 1993 event, gave three speeches, and received the Award for Achievement in Borderline Science, a Special Gold Award, and the title a Popular Qigong Master, according to the authorized biography that is discussed in detail in chapter 3.[9] It was at these Expos, the sources claim, that the world of *qigong* first recognized Li Hongzhi as China's *qigong* master par excellence.[10] A 2005 article from the Falun Gong–linked newspaper the *Epoch Times* recalls the 1992 Expo in this way:

Li's name and Falun Gong spread like wildfire there, quickly creating a stir. The Executive Director of the health expo, a Mr. Li Rusong, and the chief consultant to the event, Professor Jiang Xuegui, spoke highly of Li Hongzhi's *qigong* powers and the contributions his Falun Gong were making. Professor Jiang said of this: Li Hongzhi can be considered a star at the 1992 Oriental Health Expo. I have seen Li create many miracles. I saw patients with canes, patients in wheelchairs, and those who had challenges moving about come to him for help. After receiving treatments from Li they could miraculously stand up and walk. As the chief consultant to the expo, I am here to responsibly recommend Falun Gong to you.[11]

8. Anon., "Investigation and Analysis of Establishment and Development of Falun Gong in Jilin Province" (January 11, 2008), online at www.facts.org.cn/Data/aboutfg/200801/t76201.htm.

9. Li Hongzhi, *Zhuan Falun* (1994), p. 344.

10. It should be noted, however, that several articles from nationally distributed *qigong* magazines at the time make no mention of his presence at the 1992 and 1993 Expos. See, in particular, Li Jianxin, "Qigong qunxing jinghua da juhui," *Zhonghua qigong* 2 (1993): 4–6, and Ji Zhe, "'93' dongfang jiankang bolanhui teyi gongneng yanshi '93,'" *Zhonghua qigong* 2 (1994): 42–44.

11. Anon., "Anything for Power: The Real Story of China's Jiang Zemin—Chapter 8" (June 7, 2005), online at en.epochtimes.com/news/5-7-24/30542.html; "Jiang Zemin qiren, 8: qiangtan Beijing xitong shushou," www.epochtimes.com/b5/5/6/7/n946915.htm.

From this report it is clear that in late 1992, Li's public face was that of a miracle worker, a *qigong* master whose personal powers were exceptionally strong and who had the ability to cure disease. This reputation, and the idea that Falun Gong was particularly effective in healing, continued throughout 1993. At an event at the end of August of that year for the Jianyi Yongwei Foundation, an organization under the Ministry of Public Security that encourages ordinary people to fight criminal activities, Li agreed to treat one hundred people. A letter of thanks from the foundation, addressed to Zhang Zhenhuan at the Chinese Association for Research into Qigong Science and preserved on Falun Gong websites, says the following:

Prior to the treatment, some people were suffering from ailments left over from knife and gunshot injuries. After the treatment, they were relieved of symptoms such as pain, numbness and chronic weakness. Those suffering from brain illnesses recovered and became sober minded after the treatment. They were relieved of symptoms such as headache and dizziness. Some people were relieved of tumors right on the spot. Some excreted gallstones within 24 hours of receiving the treatment. Some people suffered from stomach diseases, heart diseases or arthritis. After the treatment, all of them were relieved of symptoms right on the site. Among almost 100 people who received the treatment, only one person claimed no obvious effects. All others felt obvious improvements to various degrees.[12]

In his role as a healer, Li Hongzhi was following the standard path of a *qigong* master. In March 1993, he even appeared on the radio program *Happy Train* while lecturing in the city of Wuhan and conducted "hotline consultations" during a phone-in segment, performing remote healing.[13] *Qigong* was understood during the 1980s and early 1990s as primarily a technique for curing disease. For instance, Guo Lin, who in David A. Palmer's words "triggered the *qigong* wave of the 1980s," developed her "New Qigong Therapy" to treat her own uterine cancer, and this school spread rapidly with government support.[14] Yan Xin, one of the most celebrated *qigong* masters of the period, burst onto the scene in 1985 when his healing exploits were publicized in a local newspaper.[15] It was therefore

---

12. Anon., "A Brief History of Events Leading Up to Jiang Zemin's Irrational Persecution of Falun Gong in China" (November 20, 2004), online at www.clearharmony.net/articles/200411/23203p .html. A photographic reproduction of the letter is shown at photo.minghui.org/photo/images/ u_worldwide_recongnition/china/images/GonganBu_BiaoyangXin.jpg.

13. Zhu Huiguang, "'Rexian' xian shengong," *Qigong yu kexue* 9 (1993): 15.

14. Palmer, *Qigong Fever*, p. 46.

15. Ibid., p. 138.

to be expected that Li Hongzhi would first gain fame as a healer, and that his followers would be inspired by Falun Gong's reputation as a *qigong* form that was efficacious in curing disease. However, by the time Falun Gong's main scripture, *Zhuan Falun*, was published in early January 1995, Li was proclaiming that Falun Gong practitioners were specifically forbidden from treating the sick. Nonetheless, his fame at the Oriental Health Expos was primarily based on precisely these activities. He explains this apparent anomaly in *Zhuan Falun*, essentially by saying that curing diseases was good for publicity.

To support the country's large-scale *qigong* events, I took some disciples with me to participate in the Oriental Health Expos in Beijing. . . . At the second Expo, there was such a huge crowd there was nothing we could do. There weren't many people at other booths, but our booth area was packed. There were three waiting lines: there were so many people in the first line that by the end of the early morning all the slots for the first half of the day were gone; the people in the second line were waiting to register for the afternoon; and the people in the other line were waiting for my autograph. We don't do healing, so why did we do that? It was to support the country's large-scale *qigong* events, to contribute to that cause. That's why we participated.[16]

The middle months of 1993 saw Falun Gong's major publicity drive begin. In April, Li produced his first book, or at least the first book to appear under his name, *China Falun Gong*. Revised and reissued in December of that year, it has come to be known as *Falun Gong (Revised Edition)*; both versions are discussed at greater length in the next chapter. Introductory articles on Falun Gong appeared in various nationally distributed *qigong* magazines and newspapers in these months: *China Qigong* (*Zhonghua qigong*) and *Qigong and Science* (*Qigong yu kexue*) in March; *Qigong News* (*Qigong bao*) in April, May, and June; and *Eastern Qigong* (*Dongfang qigong*) and *Chinese Qigong* (*Zhongguo qigong*) in June. Some of these magazines also featured Li on the cover, dressed in yellow silk in the full lotus position. Others had images of him in suit and tie.

A representative article from this period argues for the superiority of Falun Gong over other *qigong* forms on the grounds that it is supremely powerful yet suited to modern lifestyles.[17] The *falun* that is inserted into practitioners' bodies by Li Hongzhi, this article claims (as do small notices from this period advertising Li's lectures), enables them to cultivate constantly, awake or asleep, as the *falun* itself cultivates its host. Indeed,

16. Li, *Zhuan Falun* 7/4, p. 146, amended; p. 252–53.
17. Zhu Huiguang, "Falun changzhuan, shengming changqing," *Zhonghua qigong* 3 (1993): 32–33.

Falun Gong cultivation is, in general, much faster than other forms. The article says that to attain the exalted state of "three flowers gathering at the head" takes one or more decades of bitter exertion in other practices, but Falun Gong practitioners can reach this point in only two years. In addition, the movements are simple and easy to learn, there are no special requirements or excessive prohibitions, and there is no danger of falling into "deviations" in its practice. Moreover, the article says, Li Hongzhi's "Law Bodies" (discussed in the next chapter) protect all practitioners and the "*qi* field" of each practice site. Thus, from the first, Falun Gong publicity claimed extraordinary results from the practice and miraculous powers for Li Hongzhi.

This deliberate use of the *qigong* press by Falun Gong during 1993 is striking, but the movement has always been assiduous in pursuing all possible means for disseminating its message and has adapted quickly to changes in technology. In September 1994, for instance, it issued its first videotape for teaching the five sets of exercises. According to a Falun Gong notice from June 1997, it started to use the Internet to spread the teachings as early as 1995.[18] This was just the start of its venture into cyberspace: various Falun Gong websites now constitute the most important means of maintaining links between practitioners and introducing the movement to new students. It also appears to have used the extraordinary uptake of mobile phones in China to organize its daily activities through the late 1990s, including the Falun Gong demonstration of April 1999 outside Zhongnanhai.

Li Hongzhi's lecturing activities during 1992 and 1993 laid the groundwork for what had become a large movement with a network of branches across China. This is clear from the speeches he gave and documents he issued in 1994 that dealt with the administration of Falun Gong practice centers. In the course of that year he traveled to Changchun, Beijing, and Guangzhou to talk to "Falun Dafa Assistants" and answer the questions of the relatively experienced practitioners in the audience. Transcripts of these events were not initially intended for ordinary practitioners, but in August 1995 they were collected and published under the title *Explaining the Content of Falun Dafa*, and so became generally available. Sections of these speeches are concerned with running Falun Gong's branches. In addition, in April 1994 Li issued a list of "requirements" for Assistance Centers and regulations for the transmission of the teachings. These vari-

18. The Foreign Liaison Group of Falun Dafa Research Society, "Falun Dafa's Transmission on Internet Notice" (June 15, 1997), online at web.archive.org/web/19990209113803/falundafa.ca/ FLDFBB/gongga0970615.htm.

ous documents give some indication of the growth of Falun Gong in the two years of its existence up to that time. The simple fact that Li felt it was important to publish guidelines shows that Falun Gong had grown into a movement large enough to have outlying centers with a degree of autonomy. Moreover, specific regulations indicate that among the people in positions of authority in the branches, there were some whose behavior needed to be corrected.

Several general themes emerge from these documents. First, Li is insistent that the purity of his teachings not be diluted or polluted with other messages, and that his authority as Master not be challenged. He demands that experienced practitioners who are instructing new students always use the words "Shifu [Master] Li Hongzhi has taught that . . ." or "Shifu [Master] Li Hongzhi says . . ." when referring to his teachings. He states, "You are strictly forbidden to use what you experience, see, or know, or to use things from other teachings, as if they were Li Hongzhi's Dafa."[19] On the one hand this refers to teachings from other *qigong* schools, but on the other it points to the possibility of practitioners thinking they have acquired new spiritual insights of their own. Li warns against this latter phenomenon in one of the regulations.

No disciple is allowed to promote what he sees, hears, or awakens to at his own low level as the content of Falun Dafa, and then "transmit the Law." That's not allowed even if he wants to teach people to do good, because that's not the Law, but merely exhorting everyday people to do good and it doesn't carry the power that the Law has to save people. Anyone using his or her own experience to teach the Way is considered to be severely disrupting the Law.[20]

Since it is not usually regarded as necessary to ban something that does not exist, we may presume that the transmission of personal revelation had in fact been taking place. Moreover, Li warns against practitioners passing on the teachings by making speeches in an auditorium, something that only he is allowed to do. Rather, they should introduce Falun Gong in "book-reading sessions, group discussions, or at practice sites," and he insists that when they teach, they must "make it clear" that it is only their personal understanding.[21]

This concern with the purity of the message and Li Hongzhi's authority to decide exactly what should constitute it has been maintained

19. Li Hongzhi, *The Great Consummation Way of Falun Dafa*, appendices, p. 3, amended; *Falun dafa da yuanman fa*, p. 64.

20. Ibid., appendices, p. 1; p. 63.

21. Ibid., appendices, p. 3; p. 64.

throughout Falun Gong's existence. A particularly good example comes from June 1997, when Li published a short essay called "Bear in Mind Forever." This demonstrates not only that unacceptable teachings were still being independently circulated three years after the regulations were issued, but that some of them were speeches Li had delivered himself. Unfortunately, from the point of view of an outsider studying the movement, none of the texts Li mentions have survived.

I suggest that every disciple immediately, on the spot, destroy everything that I have not publicly issued but that is in circulation without permission, such as: my speeches that came out of Chengde; the things about supernormal abilities that a practitioner from Beijing discussed; the speech of the assistance center coordinator in Dalian; the cave story from the coordinator of the Guizhou assistance center and other speeches; not to mention the speeches made by people in charge of different regions; what was said by students after seeing me; the speech given by people in charge of the Dafa Research Association, and so on, plus texts, recordings, videotapes, etc., that have been transcribed from my speeches without permission. All of these must be destroyed on the spot, and they cannot be kept regardless of the excuse. . . . From now on, nobody should tape record or videotape speeches given by any of the people in charge in different regions or by any disciples; even less can they be edited into texts or be spread around for people to read. . . . Bear in mind: Except for Dafa students' experience sharing conferences for studying the Fa and activities organized by major assistance centers with the endorsement of the Research Association, anything that does not belong to Dafa but is being circulated in Dafa undermines Dafa.[22]

The desire to maintain purity was of particular concern in relation to Falun Gong teachings on the Internet. In 1997 and 1998, notices were sent out on the then relatively new websites, insisting that only formally published works by Li Hongzhi be posted and that any other material first be submitted to the local Falun Gong center to be "proofread," to avoid "misspreading [sic] and misrepresentation."[23] In addition, these notices expressed concern over the proliferation of "personal web sites and pages" where unauthorized postings "have caused misunderstandings to people not familiar with Dafa, and have misled practitioners' cultivation."[24]

22. Li Hongzhi, "Bear in Mind Forever" (June 18, 1997), in *Essentials for Further Advancement*, p. 40; "Yongyuan jizhu," in *Falun dafa jingjin yaozhi*, p. 88.

23. Foreign Liaison Group of Falun Dafa Research Society, "Falun Dafa's Transmission on Internet Notice."

24. Falun Dafa Research Society, "Notice on Setting Up of 'Falun Dafa Bulletin Board'" (August 8, 1998), online at web.archive.org/web/19990429144533/falundafa.ca/FLDFBB/index.htm.

Another theme raised from the 1994 documents relates to financial administration. Li insists that all work related to Falun Gong is voluntary. "We don't charge any membership fee," he said in a speech to Assistance Center heads in December 1994, "nor do we collect people's money."[25] Neither is any Falun Gong center to engage in business activities. As a result of Falun Gong's voluntary status and consequent lack of funds, Li insists on branches being "managed in a loose manner." In practice, he says, this means they do not operate like work units (or *danwei*, as they are known in China): they provide no housing, have no telephones, and pay no electricity and water bills.[26] This loose management style does not mean that regional centers can operate without supervision, however. New branches should "report to the one in Beijing or to one of the several main Assistance Centres," and branches in major cities should oversee those "within their administrative areas," including entire provinces. The one in Wuhan apparently oversaw "several nearby provinces."[27] To become the head of an Assistance Center, a practitioner must have attended one of Li's series of transmission lectures in person, must not have held any position in an organization responsible for administering *qigong*, and must be approved by the central Falun Gong organization, the Falun Dafa Research Association. Actually, Li says, "most of them are appointed or designated by me personally."[28]

When Falun Gong was banned in July 1999, one of the Chinese government's attacks was on Li's assertions that the movement had no organization. The government claimed that the Falun Dafa Research Association headed by Li was in charge of thirty-nine instruction centers, which themselves administered more than 1,900 "exercise venues" and 28,000 "exercise points." Together these formed "a complete organizational structure." It then noted the existence of the documents discussed above and Li's regular publication of short essays, which it characterized as "orders" so as to prove its contention that Falun Gong "possessed a tightly organised administrative system and a complete set of functions."[29]

In some ways the contention between Falun Gong and the Chinese government over whether or not the movement possessed an "organization" is simply a matter of definition. It is undeniable that during the

25. Li Hongzhi, "Talk in Guangzhou to Some Assistance Center Heads from around the Country" (December 27, 1994), in *Explaining the Content of Falun Dafa*, p. 54; "Guangzhou dui quanguo bufen fudaozhan zhanzhang de jiangfa," in *Falun dafa yijie*, p. 108.

26. Ibid., p. 54; p. 108.

27. Ibid., p. 56; p. 112.

28. Ibid., p. 57; p. 114.

29. Research Office of the Ministry for Public Security, "Li Hongzhi: The Man and His Deeds," *Chinese Law and Government*, 32, no. 5 (September/October 1999): 56–64; quotation is from pp. 59–60.

1990s, the Falun Dafa Research Association was a peak body, to which a large network of regional branches reported. The branches, in turn, oversaw local practice groups. As founder and leader of Falun Gong, and with the beliefs about his status held by practitioners, Li Hongzhi's words would obviously have carried great weight, and would undoubtedly have been followed under most circumstances. Whether this amounts to "loose" management or "a tightly organised administrative system" is determined, in practice, by whether the opinion of Falun Gong or that of the Chinese authorities is being cited. What the network of instruction centers, exercise venues, and exercise points certainly points to, however, is the rapid growth that Falun Gong enjoyed in this period.

Finally, and of great importance, considering Falun Gong's later history, Li insisted that "all Principal Assistance Centers must take the lead to observe the laws and rules of the country, and they must not meddle in politics."[30] This straightforward injunction came at a time, of course, when the Chinese government regarded Falun Gong as completely acceptable, and even, it would appear, a standard-bearer for the *qigong* movement as a whole. After Falun Gong was suppressed, this position naturally changed. In 2001 (significantly on June 4, the anniversary of the Beijing massacre of 1989), Li published a short essay, "No Politics," in which he effectively redefined what "politics" meant for Falun Gong practitioners. The word *politics*, he says, only exists in "modern, warped society." The word, and what it represents, did not exist in "societies of genuine people" of the past, and only exists now to satisfy base desires for fame and profit. Politics, that is, "everyday people's politics," is "filthy" by its very nature. Falun Gong adherents, on the other hand, who take an apparently political stance against "evil regimes wrecking the country and ruining the people," are, in fact, upright; they "have grasped the truths in higher realms, and what they understand transcends the realm of everyday people."[31]

These moves toward sustaining and regulating Falun Gong during 1994 were clearly aimed at creating a structure that would maintain the movement's strength and unity as it grew. In addition, Falun Gong needed to be sufficiently organized to continue to thrive without Li giving his transmission lectures month after month. As we have seen, the last set of nine lectures that he gave in China was in December 1994 in

---

30. Li, *The Great Consummation Way*, appendices, p. 1, amended; *Falun dafa da yuanman fa*, p. 62.
31. Li Hongzhi, "No Politics" (June 4, 2001), in *Essentials for Further Advancement, II*, p. 37; "Bu zhengzhi," in *Falun dafa jingjin yaozhi er*, p. 54.

Guangzhou. In the same month, Li published his second book, *Zhuan Falun*, that was to become the primary scripture of the movement, and which is discussed more fully in the next chapter. A few months later, in March 1995, he gave his first set of lectures outside China, in Paris. On the same trip, in April, he gave lectures in Gothenburg, Stockholm, and Uddevalla in Sweden. The Gothenburg series of lectures was, according to Falun Gong, the last set of transmission classes that Li ever gave. This was, of course, only four months after *Zhuan Falun* was launched, and it is clear that one role the book was intended to play was as a substitute for the transmission lectures at which new adherents learned about Falun Gong, were cleansed, and had the *falun* inserted in their bodies.

The Beginnings of Contention

After the launch of Falun Gong in May 1992, it had enjoyed a mutu-ally supportive relationship with the Chinese *qigong* authorities. At the end of 1995 and the beginning of 1996, however, this situation came to an abrupt conclusion when Falun Gong left—or was expelled from—the Chinese Association for Research into Qigong Science. Although Falun Gong numbers were increasing at this time, David A. Palmer notes that 1995 had seen a critical campaign against *qigong* in the press, which had placed "the *qigong* sector as a whole . . . on the defensive." He notes, "We cannot exclude the hypothesis that Li Hongzhi's decision to leave the [Association] was motivated by the desire to jump ship."[32] "Reveal the Scheme of the Very Few People from Changchun," an important Falun Gong document that gives one version of this development, emerged soon after the Zhongnanhai demonstration in 1999. The editor's note that precedes it reads:

This article is provided by veteran disciples who have witnessed and attended all the important events of Falun Gong from its initial public introduction till now. With so many rumors targeting Falun Gong, and under the harsh situation of increasingly esca-lated political pressure, we are revealing the truth of several tribulations experienced by Falun Gong. It is intend [*sic*] to provide the truth for those who don't know Falun Gong or have misunderstanding towards it due to misleading information.[33]

32. Palmer, *Qigong Fever*, p. 247.
33. "Reveal the Scheme of the Very Few People from Changchun," July 21, 1999, online at web .archive.org/web/20040426043044/http://www.clearwisdom.net/emh/articles/1999/7/21/11163.html.

"Reveal the Scheme . . ." presents the decision to leave the Chinese Association for Research into Qigong Science as entirely straightforward and deriving from Li Hongzhi himself. It claims that in September 1995, Li informed the association that he intended to withdraw, as he had concluded his teaching in China. In March 1996, it says, he sent long-standing students—Ye Hao, now a senior figure in Falun Gong's US operations, and Wang Zhiwen, imprisoned for sixteen years following the Zhongnanhai demonstration—to report to the association and formally request withdrawal. The response from "people with authority"—the document names them as Zhang Jian, the association's general secretary, and Qiu Yucai—was to "repeatedly urge" Falun Gong not to go. After these entreaties were resisted, Falun Gong obtained formal approval, and duly withdrew.

This simple account presents the matter as purely bureaucratic and procedural, with the association keen to keep Falun Gong on board. Records from the association side, however, tell another story. A report entitled "The Situation concerning the Falun Gong (Li Hongzhi) Question" was written by its officers and submitted on September 12, 1996. Made public after the suppression, the report contained detailed criticisms of Falun Gong, including that Li engaged in "large-scale self-spiritualisation," "large-scale propagation of feudal superstition," and "large-scale fabrication of political rumours," backing up these charges with quotations from his books. Each of these accusations would be sufficient to have had Falun Gong censured; the three together make for a damning indictment of Li Hongzhi. The report was widely circulated within the Chinese Association for Research into Qigong Science and was also sent to related organizations and authorities.[34] It led, in due course, to the association leadership issuing a "Resolution concerning the Cancellation of Falun Gong as an Affiliated Practice" dated November 28, 1996. In it the association claims that Falun Gong was expelled as a result of Li's contravention of its rules, and his refusal to be counseled. The resolution reads:

Falun Gong, transmitted by Li Hongzhi, was formally admitted as an affiliated practice by this Association in August 1993. In the last three years the number of people

34. The full text of the report from 1996 can be found in Zhang Weiqing and Qiao Gong, *Falun Gong chuangshiren Li Hongzhi pingzhuan* (Taipei: Shangye zhoukan chuban gufen youxian gongsi, 1999), pp. 99–104. "Reveal the Scheme . . ." claims that this report and most of the other material critical of Falun Gong, including the attacks on it following the 1999 suppression, were based on information supplied by a small number of disgruntled early followers of Li Hongzhi. Three of these are named as Song Bingchen, Zhao Jiemin, and someone with the family name Liu.

who cultivate Falun Gong has gradually increased and they have attained unparalleled results in terms of fitness and disease prevention, and the cure of difficult illnesses. However, while Li Hongzhi has transmitted his practice he has propagated theology and superstition, and opposed and departed from the correct aims and objectives of *qigong* activities. This has given rise to much censure and criticism. Falun Gong's leader Li Hongzhi has also not attended meetings associated with our Association administering rectification.

In view of Li Hongzhi opposing and departing from the procedures of this Association in the transmission of his practice and refusing to receive education, we have decided that Falun Gong's affiliation be cancelled.[35]

Clearly, these two versions of how Falun Gong and the Chinese Association for Research into Qigong Science parted company cannot be easily reconciled. (We should bear in mind that discrepancies between historical accounts presented by Falun Gong and the Chinese authorities are not uncommon.) In one version Falun Gong initiates its withdrawal for pragmatic reasons; in the other the association expels it for Li Hongzhi's wrongdoings. Falun Gong has an explanation for this discrepancy. In "Reveal the Scheme . . . ," it claims that in 1996 the Chinese government planned to reform the management of *qigong*, placing it under the jurisdiction of the national organization that administers sports. If this had happened, claim the authors, the Chinese Association for Research into Qigong Science would have been disbanded. To ensure its own survival, the association's leadership decided to criticize Falun Gong "as a way to save itself."[36] This version of events, of course, renders Li Hongzhi blameless, representing him as a pawn in a larger bureaucratic game. Maneuvers within the Chinese bureaucracy are often complex and opaque, but even so, this explanation appears excessively convoluted.

A simpler explanation is possible. Falun Gong may well have withdrawn (or sought to withdraw) in March 1996, as it claims. In response, the Chinese Association for Research into Qigong Science could have refused the request, realizing that relations with Falun Gong were likely to get worse and understanding that the voluntary withdrawal of one of its largest and most prominent affiliates would have been a serious blow. Instead, it took the initiative by commissioning a report it knew would be negative and from which expulsion would necessarily follow—the report submitted in September. It is plausible, then, that as a direct response to Falun Gong's application to withdraw, the association set in motion

35. Zhang and Qiao, *Li Hongzhi pingzhuan*, pp. 96–97.
36. "Reveal the Scheme . . ."

procedures that would lead to its expulsion in order to maintain the association's own authority and reputation with the government.

During this period, however, contention between Falun Gong and the Chinese authorities was taking place beyond the limited world of *qigong*, with aggressive actions being launched by the government. In 1995, the city authorities of Hangzhou, south of Shanghai, banned the teaching of Falun Gong. Not long after, an occurrence with far more serious consequences took place in the media. On June 17, 1996, *Guangming Daily*, traditionally the newspaper aimed at the intelligentsia, published an article, "Opposing Pseudo-Science Requires a Great Cry of Alarm: A Discussion Prompted by *Zhuan Falun*." The article begins with the strident tone that characterizes the whole.

Around 1992, some books that propagated feudal superstition and pseudo-science came onto the market, disrupting the normal state of publishing and producing negative influences on the spiritual life of the masses.[37]

Later in the article, *Zhuan Falun*, which it says had recently appeared in street bookstalls, is directly accused of "spreading the pseudo-science of feudal superstition." This was the first of many attacks on Falun Gong in the media. The article continues by relating how various concerned citizens, representatives of the people, experts, scholars, and journalists were so worried by the appearance of *Zhuan Falun* that they were moved to appeal to the leadership of the government and the Communist Party. As a result, the Central Committee of the Party and the State Council took action, promulgating a document called "Some Views on Strengthening Work in Popularizing Science and Technology."

The tone of this first attack and the actions that flowed from it illustrate the nature of anti-*qigong* discourse in general, and attacks on Falun Gong in particular, in the middle 1990s. The way supporters of *qigong* had striven for respectability ever since the movement had reappeared on the scene fifteen or so years earlier was to appeal to its supposedly scientific nature. However, the forces aligned against *qigong* in this later period represented some of the most notable members of the Chinese scientific establishment, who launched their attacks under the banner of opposing "pseudo-science." This campaign in mid- to late 1995 saw a series of articles appear in newspapers across the country, organized by the Chinese Association for the Study of the Dialectics of Nature.[38]

37. Xin Ping, "Fandui weikexue yao jingzhong changming," *Guangming ribao*, June 17, 1996.
38. Palmer, *Qigong Fever*, p. 172.

The article specifically attacking Falun Gong should therefore be seen as part of a larger move against *qigong* organizations. However, as Palmer notes, it presaged some twenty more anti–Falun Gong articles in newspapers across China as well as television programs on national and regional networks. The Falun Gong response to the *Guangming Daily* article was striking. Practitioners were mobilized to write letters of complaint to the newspaper and to the national *qigong* association. In this they were supported by the *qigong* associations of the city of Changchun and Jilin Province.[39] Li Hongzhi explicitly condoned these activities in an essay from August 28, 1996, "Huge Exposure," in which he defined the activities of those who protested against the article as a kind of "genuine cultivation."

From the incident with the *Guangming Daily* until now, each Dafa disciple has played a role: some were determined to steadfastly cultivate; some wrote without reservation to the authorities for the sake of Dafa's reputation; some spoke out against the injustice done by the irresponsible report.[40]

In this way, Li not only supported the actions taken against *Guangming Daily* but also made protesting against criticism a required action for serious practitioners. Other practitioners, however, appear to have wilted under official criticism and "engaged in divisive activities," acted against Falun Gong to protect their reputations, or circulated rumors.

Across China, protests continued against any media outlets that attacked Falun Gong. In November 1999, the *People's Daily* reported, "Since August, 1996, when it held its first illegal demonstration outside a national newspaper the *Guangming Daily*, Falun Gong has organized a total of 78 illegal demonstrations with at least 300 followers participating on each occasion."[41] Referred to as "clarifying the truth" in Falun Gong sources, these demonstrations were consistently criticized by organs of the government as "illegal gatherings" that "disrupted social order." One of the most notable of these protests was in response to an interview given on Beijing television in May 1998 by He Zuoxiu, one of the leaders of the attacks on pseudo-science. In it, he related that a postgraduate student at his institute became a Falun Gong practitioner and was subsequently struck down by mental illness.[42]

39. Ibid., pp. 249–50.

40. Li Hongzhi, "Huge Exposure" (August 28, 19), in *Essentials for Further Advancement*, p. 31; "Da Baoguang," in *Falun dafa jingjin yaozhi*, p. 65.

41. "Cult Crimes Must Be Punished," *People's Daily Online*, November 16, 1999; english. peopledaily.com.cn/english/199911/06/eng199911060101.html.

42. Zhang Pengwen, "An Interview with He Zuoxiu: How He Exposes and Fights against Falun Gong," online at www.facts.org.cn/Views/200801/t75537.htm.

Since its suppression in 1999, Falun Gong has sought the good offices of Western governments and media organizations to present itself in the best possible light and to force the Chinese authorities to cease their aggressive activities. In November 1998, however, it did not seem to make such a distinction between local and foreign media, when practitioners took exception to a television and radio report by BBC correspondent James Miles. In this broadcast, Miles referred to Falun Gong as a "new religious movement" and a "faith," and noted that the Chinese government was "keeping a wary eye on the Falun Gong phenomenon." Practitioners apparently objected to any statements that Falun Gong was religious, and that the authorities were concerned about it, implying that this was "an attempt to incite differences between the government and the people."[43]

Protests against media and government in China were rare enough in the 1990s to make these Falun Gong actions remarkable in themselves. What makes them even more extraordinary was that they often generated retractions or apologies from the authorities responsible for the newspaper, journal, and television coverage. Regarding He Zuoxiu's interview on Beijing television and the subsequent Falun Gong demonstration, Palmer reports that "its director apologized, aired another report favourable to Falun Gong, and fired Li Bo, the journalist who had interviewed He Zuoxiu."[44] He adds, "The fact that Falun Gong successfully pressured a major television station to have a skeptical journalist fired, clearly demonstrates the social influence it was seen to possess, as well as its strong backing in the Propaganda Department—or, lacking such backing, the fear the department had of offending Li Hongzhi's followers."[45]

At the same time that negative stories about Falun Gong were appearing in the media and Li Hongzhi's followers were protesting against them, other newspapers were publishing positive reports. In Falun Gong's own version of its history, these feature prominently. It mentions, for instance, an article in a newspaper from Dalian, a port in the north of China, that describes how "an elderly man, Sheng Lijian, built a road that was over 1,100 meters long for his village on his own after he started to practice Falun Gong."[46] Also typical is a July 1998 report from the *China Economic Times* concerning "Xie Xiufen, a housewife from Handan City,

43. James Miles, *BBC Breakfast News*, November 6, 1998. Miles recalls receiving letters of complaint from Falun Gong practitioners in both China and North America (private communication, September 7, 2008).

44. Palmer, *Qigong Fever*, p. 252.

45. Ibid., p. 256.

46. Anon., "Positive Reports on Falun Gong by Mainland China Media before the Persecution of Falun Gong Began in 1999" (August 25, 2004), online at www.clearwisdom.net/emh/articles/

Hebei Province, who had been paralyzed for over 16 years, but was able to walk after she started practicing Falun Gong."[47] In fact, the theme of miracle cures is found in several of these reports, at least as late as 1998—Falun Gong's curative powers were clearly seen as one of its most newsworthy attributes.

In July 1996, a month after the *Guangming Daily* article appeared, a publication ban on Falun Gong books was instituted. Ostensibly, this meant that earlier works, such as *China Falun Gong* and *Zhuan Falun*, could not be reprinted and new works could not be released. In practice, however, the books were still produced in Hong Kong and Taiwan and by presses in China more distant from the capital. Anecdotal evidence indicates that some mainland presses of lower status, forced to pay their own way after decades of government support, made up the shortfall in their funds by selling ISBNs, or International Standard Book Numbers, that they had been issued by the central publishing authorities. Falun Gong, among many others, used these official numbers—and the names of the presses that had sold them—to publish books that would not have been approved by higher-status publishing houses based in the bigger cities. In this way, independently published books appeared in the many informal bookstalls across the country when officially they could be neither produced nor sold in government-owned bookshops.

Thus, from 1996 until the beginning of 1999, although Falun Gong was being lauded by some media outlets, it became the object of criticism by others but was often able to deflect the attacks with protests. This pattern of support from some sections of the official apparatus and scorn from others is also seen in the actions of government at that time. Falun Gong sources claim that from early 1997 until the end of 1998, various official organizations launched investigations into its activities. The first, by the Public Security Ministry, apparently sought evidence that it was an "evil cult," but found none. Eighteen months later, in July 1998, the same ministry launched a fresh investigation into the same question, this time using methods Falun Gong sources list as "tapping Falun Gong Assistants' phones, tailing Falun Gong Assistants, closing down Falun Gong practice sites, forcefully dispersing the practitioners during group exercise practice, ransacking practitioners' houses, confiscating their personal property, and other things."[48] Later that year, in response to letters of complaint about these actions, the leader of the National People's

---

2004/9/20/52631.html; "1999 nian quanmian pohaiqian dalu meiti dui falungong de zhengmian baodao 1999," www.minghui.org/mh/articles/2004/8/25/82595.html.

47. Ibid.

48. Anon., "A Chronicle of Major Events," amended.

Congress, Qiao Shi, led a further investigation into Falun Gong, concluding that "Falun Gong has hundreds of benefits for the Chinese people and China, and does not have one single bad effect."[49] Also opposing the Public Security Ministry's position were two sporting organizations, the national body in charge of athletics and the National Sports Bureau, which praised Falun Gong's health benefits in May and October 1998 respectively.

It is difficult to ascertain to what extent Li Hongzhi himself directed any of the protest actions or negotiations during this period. His direct day-to-day control of any organization would, however, have been hampered by the fact that he immigrated to the United States in October 1996. In that month he made his first speech in that country, in Houston, and a week later attended a Falun Gong conference in New York. These talks were, it should be stressed, single occasions rather than sets of nine lectures like those he gave in China to transmit the teachings in the early years of the movement. From the second half of August 1996 until early 1999, Li crisscrossed the globe, spreading the word in Sydney, Bangkok, San Francisco, Hong Kong, Taipei, Frankfurt, Toronto, Singapore, Geneva, and Los Angeles, as well as Houston and New York. During this time he also returned to China to attend the first international Falun Gong conference in Beijing in November 1996, and an Assistants' conference in Changchun in July 1998. His next—and last—visit to China occurred only three days before the Zhongnanhai demonstration in April 1999, and has become a matter of contention between the Chinese authorities and Falun Gong.

The Zhongnanhai Demonstration and the Suppression of Falun Gong

The famous demonstration of April 25, 1999, outside Zhongnanhai in central Beijing occurred as a reaction to how a Falun Gong protest in Tianjin had been handled by the Public Security authorities only a few days before. The Tianjin protest was similar to those against media organizations that had published articles or broadcast programs critical of Falun Gong. In this case the article was entitled "I Do Not Approve of Teenagers Practicing *Qigong*," and the magazine was *Youth Science and Technology Outlook*. Its author was He Zuoxiu, one of the leaders of the anti-pseudo-

49. Ibid.

science group; as noted above, he had already been subject to Falun Gong action after his Beijing television interview the previous year. Following the pattern of the many similar protests made since 1996, Falun Gong practitioners launched a sit-in on April 18 at Tianjin Normal University, where the magazine was published.[50] On the twenty-third and twenty-fourth, according to Falun Gong sources, riot police were dispatched to the university, where they beat some adherents and detained forty-five of them. The report continues: "When Falun Gong practitioners requested the release of the detained practitioners, they were told at Tianjin City Hall that the Public Security Bureau had become involved in this matter, so the arrested Falun Gong practitioners would not be released without authorization from Beijing. The Tianjin police suggested to Falun Gong practitioners, 'Go to Beijing. Only going to Beijing can resolve the problem.'"[51] The first practitioners arrived at the gates of Zhongnanhai that evening.

One of the ongoing points of disagreement about the Zhongnanhai demonstration concerns the role played by Li Hongzhi. Both the Chinese authorities and Falun Gong agree that he was not in Beijing on the day of the protest. In early May, he was in Sydney to attend the 1999 Australian Experience Sharing Conference, and on May 2 (a week after the protest) he also gave a press conference to both the Chinese-language and the Western media.[52] Asked whether he was concerned about the safety of his followers who had participated in the Zhongnanhai rally, Li replied,

I was not aware at all ahead of time when Falun Gong practitioners went to Zhongnanhai. At the time, I was on the way from the United States to Australia. As for their safety, since I did not know anything about it, they did it themselves. But I know students [of Falun Gong] will not do anything bad. They were very peaceful and calm and didn't use any slogans or signs. They went only to present the facts to the Government out of kindness. It was not a demonstration or a sit-in. Because all the practitioners wanted to go, there were a lot of people.

50. A translation of He's article can be found in *Chinese Law and Government* 32, no. 5 (September/October 1999): 95–98. He's article, "How 'Falun Gong' Harassed Me and My Family," can be found on the Internet archive at replay.waybackmachine.org/20030121122938/http://211.99.196.218/fanduixiejiao/eng/07/001.htm.

51. Gu Anru, "On the Fifth Anniversary of the 'April 25 Appeal'—Remembering April 25, 1999 (Part 2)" (April 24, 2004), online at www.clearharmony.net/articles/200405/19428.html; "Zhongnanhai shijian zhenxiang (er): heping shangfang yuanman jiejue da gongshi," www.yuanming.net/articles/200404/30754.html.

52. A Chinese transcript of this press conference can be found at thunderer.9.forumer.com/index.php?showtopic=583, with an English version at www.zhuichaguoji.org/en/upload/docs/ThirdPartyDoc/G_3.doc.

Asked how the practitioners knew to go to Zhongnanhai, he replied,

> You know there is the Internet, they learned it from the Internet. Also Falun Gong
> practitioners in many different areas are friends, and they would pass the message to
> other practitioners because they all practice Falun Gong, and they are all concerned
> about Falun Dafa.

Throughout the press conference, Li insisted that the Zhongnanhai gathering was simply intended to present the facts of the Tianjin incident to the government and not to apply pressure to it, since the participants were simply pointing out the errors of some Public Security Bureau officers in Tianjin. Thus, a week after the event, Li drew a sharp distinction between the Party and the government and its public security organs, on the one hand, and specific individuals who did wrong, on the other. Therefore, according to Falun Gong, the Zhongnanhai gathering was the spontaneous action of individual adherents of Falun Gong. Yet a few months later after Falun Gong had been suppressed, government news outlets began to reveal what they claimed was Li's pivotal role in organizing the Zhongnanhai protest. A typical example from a Xinhua Newsagency report of August 19 claims that the figure who had "directly plotted and controlled the incident behind the scenes was Li Hongzhi, the ringleader of Falun Gong cult."[53] Li, it maintains, had arrived in Beijing from New York on April 22, three days before the demonstration, and left for Hong Kong on April 24. It also describes how he had been informed of the progress of the Tianjin sit-in and coordinated the planning of the Zhongnanhai gathering. It claims that he deputized the logistics to several of his associates and left for Hong Kong at 1:30 in the afternoon the day before the event took place. Nonetheless, it claims that "evidence shows that there were over 20 calls placed between Li and the 'headquarters' on April 25, and that all the actions in Beijing were taken after being directed by Li Hongzhi." These calls allegedly included instructing the Falun Gong team that entered Zhongnanhai to negotiate with the government leaders.

Nine weeks later, Falun Gong was banned and the concerted government action against it was begun, action that continues to this day. Exactly what happened between April and July within the upper reaches of

53. Xinhua News Agency, "China Bans Falun Gong. Li Hongzhi's Role in Illegal Gathering at Zhongnanhai" (August 19, 1999), available at english.peopledaily.com.cn/english/199908/13/enc_19990813001031_TopNews.html.

government is not known with certainty, although *Zhu Rongji in 1999* presents a plausible narrative. By this account, as we saw in chapter 1, the Zhongnanhai demonstration caused panic in the upper reaches of the Party: a flurry of communications was sent on the day of the demonstration and a meeting of the Standing Committee of the Politburo was held the day after, on April 26. At this meeting President Jiang Zemin apparently produced a wad of printouts from the Internet about the demonstration. Reportedly angrier than he had been for a decade, he said,

The Ministry of Public Security has already been conducting surveillance over Falun Gong for three years, yet more than 20,000 people far and near came into Beijing individually and in small groups and, by previously organised dispositions, surrounded Zhongnanhai overnight. And in all this time, the public security departments were completely unaware that this was happening. Such dereliction of duty cannot be countenanced in future. Who says that no inkling was present of Falun Gong believers gathering at Zhongnanhai? Notifications for Falun Gong believers to assemble at Zhongnanhai have been found on the Internet. A huge matter like that, yet our public security and safety departments and the Beijing municipality have been so imperceptive! [Our] political power itself has been endangered, yet they did not sense anything at all. Comrades, how frightening this is! If we do not draw lessons from this, who can guarantee that there will not be a second or a third time?[54]

Luo Gan, a member of the Politburo, then described the way Falun Gong practitioners had used "modern communications equipment, such as cell phones, the Internet, and long-distance phones," to arrange the demonstration, and that "currently" Falun Gong ran more than eighty websites across the country. In addition, "among Falun Gong's trainees are Communist Party members, functionaries of state organs, military people, armed police, medical practitioners, teachers, and even diplomats."[55]

While *Zhu Rongji in 1999* claims that some Politburo members took a conciliatory stance toward Falun Gong, the hard-line position won the day. Reports that emerged in early May indicate that Jiang had placed Luo Gan and then vice president (and current president) Hu Jintao in charge of a special task force to deal with Falun Gong by "preparing a

54. Zong, *Zhu Rongji in 1999*, pp. 60–61.

55. Ibid., pp. 61–62. On the presence in Falun Gong of senior officials, see "Hong Kong Paper—Mainland Schools 'Invaded' by 'Cult' of Falun Gong," *Ming Pao*, April 27, 1999, reported on BBC Monitoring Service, April 28, 1999; and Craig S. Smith, "China's Retired Elite Aid Spiritual Group—Protest Draws Strength from Some Prominent Communist Party Members," *Asian Wall Street Journal*, April 30, 1999.

methodical campaign to discredit and rein in the martial arts sect [*sic*] they now see as a threat to Communist Party power."[56]

At the press conference in Sydney on May 2, Li seems not to have been prepared for any particularly strong reaction from the government. In a revealing exchange, one journalist asked him what he thought would happen if his followers, believing they were "doing good," did something that officials regarded as disrupting the social order. The journalist noted, perhaps with the 1989 demonstrations in mind, that officials "will kill people, they will imprison people, such as your disciples," to maintain social order. Li answered,

Li: First of all, practitioners will never go against the law. In terms of the scenario you described, I don't think it will happen. The Chinese government will not treat the masses like that . . .

Journalist: Does the government feel that your activities will threaten their long-term stability?

Li: You know, since the economic reform and opening up, the Chinese government has been quite tolerant in this respect. They are able to accept different opinions and they also allow the existence of religions and other mass organisations. This has been the case for the past few years. They allow *qigong* to exist and have never banned Falun Gong.

Journalist: If Chinese government banned Falun Gong and your disciples' activities, would you still think that Falun Gong is in conformity with Chinese law?

Li: I can only tell you that at present the Chinese government has not opposed Falun Gong. Although they went to Zhongnanhai to present the facts, the Chinese government did not oppose Falun Gong. As for what will happen in the future, I think that since the government allows it to exist now, it will also allow it to exist in the future. We do not get involved with politics and we obey the country's laws, in fact, it benefits the country and the people. Everyone knows this.[57]

Li Hongzhi's confidence that continuing to practice Falun Gong would not lead to punishment was apparently shared by practitioners around the country. Visitors to Li's hometown of Changchun, where Falun Gong was launched, said that "thousands" of people were still practicing regularly and publicly about two weeks after the protest.[58] Similarly, the *Far Eastern Economic Review* reported that "in a park in western Beijing, 100

56. Charles Hutzler, "Chinese Leaders Prepare Careful Crackdown Against Secretive Group," Associated Press, May 8, 1999.

57. See note 53 above, amended.

58. Mark O'Neill, "Thousands Gather for Falun Gong Despite Criticism, Ban," *South China Morning Post*, May 9, 1999.

or so Falun Gong practitioners exercised under a bold yellow banner proclaiming their affiliation." In the journalist's words, they were "far from running scared."[59]

Six days after his Sydney press conference, on May 8 Li Hongzhi released on one of Falun Gong's websites the first formal statement directed to his followers since the Zhongnanhai protest. It has subsequently appeared in print. Perhaps perversely, given that adherents could well have been seeking clear explanations and guidance about where the movement stood in relation to the government, he offered them a four-line poem:

TRUE NATURE REVEALED

Steadfastly cultivate Dafa, the will unflinching

The raising of levels is what's fundamental

In the face of tests one's true nature is revealed

Achieve Consummation, becoming a Buddha, Dao, or God[60]

Nothing in this poem is controversial or would look out of place in Li's teachings as a whole.[61] However, keen adherents might have seen a reference to contemporary events in the third line. In Falun Gong doctrine, "tests"—more usually rendered "trials" or "tribulations"—are to be expected by the practitioner in his or her cultivation practice. They are necessary obstacles to be overcome and are, in fact, an aid to further development. Throughout Li's writings, it is not unusual to find statements that echo the line "In the face of tests one's true nature is revealed." Yet given recent events and the undoubted possibility of some kind of negative government response, this line can be read as a warning that new "tests" will come, but should not be treated differently from other trials in cultivation. Indeed, any concerted action against Falun Gong or its adherents would, in this reading, only serve to confirm the practitioner's certainty that Master Li's teachings are real and true and efficacious. Thus, cultivation should remain the primary objective, and distractions should be ignored.

About four weeks later, Li released a much bolder and more politically engaged statement. On June 2, he bought space and issued a statement in several Hong Kong newspapers, including *Apple Daily*, as well as on one of the Falun Gong websites. This statement is called "Some Thoughts

59. Susan V. Lawrence, "Religion: Pilgrim's Protest," *Far Eastern Economic Review*, May 13, 1999.

60. Li Hongzhi, "True Nature Revealed" (May 8, 1999), in *Essentials for Further Advancement, II*, p. 1; "Jian zhenxing," in *Falun dafa jingjin yaozhi er*, p. 1.

61. Li's verse from 1976 until November 1998 is collected in *Hongyin*.

of Mine."[62] It opens with the claim that the Chinese government had sought Li's extradition from the United States in exchange for a reduction in the $500 million trade surplus. After restating his goals in the teaching of Falun Gong—to make people more compassionate, to eliminate their illnesses, to reach higher levels of mind—and denying his interest in politics and material reward, he insists that practitioners not be accused of engaging in "superstition." He continues,

How could something that helps people to get well and stay healthy, and that raises people's moral level, be labeled an "evil religion"? Every Falun Gong practitioner is a member of society, and each has his own job or career. It's only that they go to the park to do Falun Gong exercises for half an hour or an hour every morning, and then they go to work. We don't have various provisions that people have to follow, as religions do, nor do we have any temples, churches, or religious rituals. People can come to learn or leave as they please, and we have no membership rosters. How is it a religion? As to "evil," could teaching people to be good, not charging people money, and doing things to heal people and help them stay healthy be categorized as "evil"? Or, is something "evil" simply because it's outside the scope of the Communist Party's theories? Besides, I know that evil religion is evil religion, and it's not something a government determines. Should an evil religion be labeled "upright" if it's in keeping with the notions of certain people in the government? And should an upright one be labeled "evil" if it doesn't conform to their personal notions?[63]

In this essay, Li raises three points, namely his extradition, the accusation that Falun Gong practitioners engage in superstition, and the designation of the movement as an "evil religion," that is, a *xiejiao*, translated in government documents as "evil cult." The way that Li links the accusation of being an "evil religion" with "the Communist Party's theories" in this article is new, however. Although, as noted below, many of Falun Gong's attacks on the Chinese government after the suppression focused on specific individuals rather than the Party as a whole, or else on Communist ideology, this theme would return with the "Nine Commentaries on the Communist Party" that was published in 2004.

If Li's intention in publishing "Some Thoughts of Mine" was to rally his troops, it appears to have been a success. Falun Gong sources reported that on June 3, the day after Li's essay was published, seventy thousand practitioners from the northeastern provinces of Jilin and Liaoning had

---

62. Li Hongzhi, "Some Thoughts of Mine" (June 2, 1999), in *Essentials for Further Advancement, II*, p. 2; "Wode yidian ganxiang," in *Falun dafa jingjin yaozhi er*, p. 2.
63. Ibid., pp. 2–3; pp. 3–4.

arrived in Beijing. This time the security services were ready. In the words of the Hong Kong newspaper *Sing Tao Jih Pao*, they "stepped up surveillance, intercepted crowds of Falun Gong members in the streets and lanes, conducted strict checks on hotels and guest houses, and sent Falun Gong members to the Shijingshan stadium before transferring them in groups to a railway station where they were sent home by railway police and referred to local public security officers for surveillance."[64] On June 7, at a news conference in Hong Kong, a government official characterized reports of a mass expulsion of Falun Gong practitioners from Beijing and Li's accusation about his extradition as "sheer rumour," "absolutely not true," "absurd," and "fabricated."[65]

Despite these specific denials, Chinese authorities were attempting to exert control on Falun Gong activities, including closely monitoring leading figures in various cities and tapping the telephones of local Falun Gong instructors.[66] In response, a meeting was held between Falun Gong representatives and the "Person in Charge of Bureaus [*sic*] of Letters and Petitions of the General Secretariat of the Chinese Communist Party (CCP) Central Committee and of the General Secretariat of the State Council." That meeting resulted in a report on June 14 which stated that "rumors [which] included claims that the public security departments are preparing to crack down on Falun Gong practitioners, officials practicing Falun Gong will be expelled from their positions, and CPC and Chinese Communist Youth League members engaged in related activities will also be expelled" were "completely baseless and were made to confuse people. The purpose for spreading the rumors was to incite large gatherings, create chaos, and disrupt social stability."[67] It specifically reiterated that "governments at various levels have never banned any type of normal *qigong* practice or health building activity." Along with these reassurances, however, came the standard injunction to maintain social stability above all else.[68]

64. "Police Break Up Falun Gong Gathering of 70,000 in Beijing," *Sing Tao Jih Pao*, June 7, 1999, as reported on BBC Monitoring Service, June 8, 1999.

65. "Report on Extradition of Falun Gong Founder Li Hongzhi 'Sheer Rumours,'" Zhongguo Tongxun She News Agency, as reported by BBC Monitoring Service, June 7, 1999.

66. Vivien Pik-kwan Chan, "Phone Taps and Close Monitoring of Cult Members—Falun Gong Faithful Kept on Tight Leash," *South China Morning Post*, June 8, 1999.

67. Xinhua News Agency, "Official on Rumors concerning Falun Gong Practitioners," June 14, 1999.

68. A translation of the full text of the statement, Anon., "Main Points of a Talk Given by Person in Charge of Bureaus of Letters and Petitions of the Chinese Communist Party (CCP) Central Committee and of the General Secretariat of the State Council When Receiving a Number of Falun Gong Appellants," can be found in *Chinese Law and Government* 32, no. 5 (September/October 1999): 19–21.

Meanwhile, on June 13, Li Hongzhi issued two statements of his own, "Position" and "Stability." It is unclear whether these were made with knowledge of the meeting that took place between Falun Gong representatives and the person in charge of letters and petitions some time after June 7. The first, "Position", could have been written at almost any time, stressing as it does the need for practitioners to maintain their concentration on cultivation and overcome any trials encountered along the way.[69] "Stability," however, specifically addresses "the things that have transpired in recent times [that] have already done serious harm to many Falun Dafa students." In this essay, Li urges his followers to report cases of practice session disruptions "through the normal channels to different levels of the government or to the country's leaders."[70] This is an ambiguous instruction given practitioners' activities in general since 1996 and specifically since the Tianjin and Zhongnanhai demonstrations. Depending on how his readers chose to interpret the phrase "the normal channels," it could show that Li was either maintaining a possibly naïve degree of confidence in the existing political structures or else instructing his followers to continue with the strategy of drawing the leadership's attention to the transgressions of lower officials by gathering outside government offices in large numbers.

However, a clear change in his attitude occurred not long after. On June 16, the Japanese Kyodo Newsagency published an interview Li had granted it in New York in which his attitudes had appreciably hardened. It wrote,

Li Hongzhi . . . told Kyodo News . . . that Beijing would be foolish to escalate its persecution of the group that China's state security apparatus has targeted as a "cult." "They are attacking us, spreading rumors about us being a cult, about what kind of person I am. Well, I want to see where this will lead to," Li said. Li called it "crazy" for China's communist leaders to persecute his followers in China . . . because it would involve a friend, spouse, or family member of almost everyone in China. "It is as good as cracking down on everyone in China, so it seems crazy that they would do such a thing—inconceivable," Li said.

In the first direct statement of who was regarded as responsible for the attacks on Falun Gong, Kyodo reported that

---

69. Li Hongzhi, "Position" (June 13, 1999), in *Essentials for Further Advancement, II*, p. 5; "Weizhi," in *Falun dafa jingjin yaozhi er*, p. 7.

70. Li Hongzhi, "Stability" (June 13, 1999), in *Essentials for Further Advancement, II*, p. 6; "Anding," in *Falun dafa jingjin yaozhi er*, p. 8.

Specifically, Li blames Luo Gan, the head of China's state security apparatus and a Politburo member, for spreading false rumours that Falun Dafa practitioners threaten state security and initiating the Tianjin crackdown to further his own political career. "If this is a conspiracy, it is by Luo Gan," Li proclaimed.[71]

The timing of this interview is intriguing. According to the pseudonymous author of *Zhu Rongji in 1999*—who is solely concerned with affairs within the Party and pays no attention to any of Li's comments—it was on June 17—that is, the very next day—that Jiang Zemin declared in a Politburo meeting speech that Falun Gong was "the most serious political incident since the 'June 4' political disturbance in 1989." The meeting decided that a "Central Committee Leading Group for dealing with Falun Gong" be set up that would include Luo Gan.[72] The possibility must remain open that before this meeting, Li Hongzhi had received information that serious action against Falun Gong would be taken at it. Given what we know of the high-level Party membership of some Falun Gong practitioners, this is perhaps not as farfetched as it might initially appear.

From the end of June, both the government's harassment and Falun Gong's reactions to it continued to intensify. A total of 13,742 practitioners from Hebei signed an open letter addressed to President Jiang and Premier Zhu and delivered it to the offices of the provincial government in Shijiazhuang on June 18.[73] The letter claimed that four Falun Gong leaders had been detained in the city for twenty-four hours on June 4, and that a military plant there had threatened forty-two of its staff with dismissal if they did not cease practice of Falun Gong. On June 26, between five and eight in the morning, thirteen exercise sites outside major public buildings along Chang'an Boulevard were "cleaned up" by Beijing public security officers. *Tung Fang Jih Pao* reported that, in addition, "it has been learned that with Chang'an Avenue as a beginning, Beijing police will, as a next step, straighten out Falun Gong activities across the city in a big way."[74] On July 6 and 7, some one thousand Falun Gong

71. Kyodo News International, "Chinese Spiritual Leader Cautions Beijing on Crackdown," June 16, 1999.

72. This may be a mistake on the part of Zong Hairen. Falun Gong has long maintained that the group designed to run the suppression was called the "610 Office," which refers in standard Chinese manner to June 10, the date on which the office was set up, a week earlier than Zong's narrative would indicate.

73. Information on this open letter deriving from the Information Center for Human Rights and Democratic Movement in China was reported by Reuters (June 24, 1999), AP (June 25, 1999), *South China Morning Post* (June 25, 1999), and *The New York Times* (June 29, 1999).

74. "Beijing Restricting Falun Gong Sect Activities—Hong Kong Press," *Tung Fang Jih Pao*, June 28, 1999, as reported on BBC Monitoring Service, July 17, 1999.

practitioners staged a demonstration inside the Jiangxi provincial government headquarters in Nanchang, protesting against a critical article published in a local journal. The demonstrators dispersed only when government officials gave assurances that the article did not express the official view of the government or the magazine.[75]

On July 12, according to *Sing Tao Jih Pao*, 2,000 to 3,000 Falun Gong adherents from Hubei Province surrounded the entrance to the building of Chinese Central Television (CCTV) to protest the upcoming broadcast of a program produced by Hubei Television that attacked feudal superstition and mentioned Falun Gong. A CCTV official received a petition from the demonstrators but did not withdraw the program. The Hubei protesters were taken by bus to the railway station and sent home. The article that describes this protest also notes that

The CCP leadership expects the handling of protest in Beijing by "Falun Gong" followers to be a long-term issue. A relevant department of the State Council has issued a circular to provincial, provincial [sic], municipal and autonomous regional governments, demanding that to ensure Beijing's stability, all local governments should prevent "Falun Gong" followers from going to Beijing to stage protests. If "Falun Gong" members stir up trouble in Beijing, government officials from their localities, including leading ones, shall be held responsible.

Furthermore, all hotels and guesthouses were to report the arrival of Falun Gong adherents from outside the capital. If it was determined that they were in Beijing to protest, they would be required to leave.[76]

On July 14 and 15, some five thousand practitioners gathered on the square outside the government offices in Weifang in eastern Shangdong Province to protest against a local scientific magazine that had criticized Falun Gong and Li Hongzhi. The protest only ended after the mayor met with the participants and the city government promised that the magazine and other local media would not publish criticisms of Falun Gong in the future.[77]

According to *Zhu Rongji in 1999*, "by the middle of July, the national public security system had basically completed its investigations of

75. Information on this demonstration also derives from the Information Center for Human Rights and Democratic Movement in China, and was reported by AP (July 10, 1999), Central News Agency (Taiwan, July 10, 1999), and the *New York Times* (July 11, 1999).

76. "Falun Gong Sect Members Protest against TV Programme," *Sing Tao Jih Pao*, July 15, 1999, as reported on BBC Monitoring Service, July 17, 1999.

77. Information on this demonstration comes from the Information Center of Human Rights and Democratic Movement in China, and was reported by AP (July 18, 1999), Central News Agency (Taiwan, July 18, 1999), and Hong Kong Voice of Democracy (July 18, 1999).

Falun Gong's activities nationwide. Rigorous registrations and statistics revealed that there were 2.3 million Falun Gong believers in China, of whom 15.6% were Party members. . . . For this reason, a decision to ban Falun Gong was tabled before the highest level of the CCP."[78] Hu Jintao, the vice president at the time, announced the decision to ban to senior cadres. On July 19, by Jiang's direction, it was promulgated by the Politburo.

Concerted action was to have begun on July 21, but apparently the decision had been leaked, so early on July 20 police launched an attack on Falun Gong, arresting leaders in cities across China, including Dalian, Tianjin, Beijing, Shenyang, Benxi, Taiyuan, and Nanchang. Reports of how many were arrested varied, with seventy being the number given by the Information Center for Human Rights and Democratic Movement in China,[79] and fifty-five by the Japanese Kyodo News International.[80] According to the *Asian Wall Street Journal*, the arrests targeted Falun Gong's local leadership.[81] One prominent detainee was Li Chang, who was an organizer of the Zhongnanhai demonstration, one of the delegates who met with Zhu Rongji, and later the recipient of the longest prison sentence—eighteen years—handed down to a Falun Gong practitioner thus far. He was also the "chief contact person for the Foreign Liaison Group of the Falun Dafa Research Association in Beijing."[82] The same article also noted that the government had blocked Falun Gong's websites.

The government's increasingly harsh measures against Falun Gong produced a predictable reaction. Protests were reported throughout the country in more than thirty cities, including Harbin, Dalian, Weifang, Taiyuan, Guiyang, Shenzhen, Guanzhou, and Guangzhou. The Information Center for Human Rights and Democratic Movement in China estimated that more than thirty thousand people in all had protested. In Hong Kong and Tokyo, supporters held protests outside the Xinhua Newsagency offices and the Chinese Embassy respectively.[83]

---

78. Zong, *Zhu Rongji in 1999*, p. 67.

79. Reported by AP (July 20, 1999).

80. Kyodo News International, "H. K. Followers of Falun Gong Protest Arrests in China," July 20, 1999. Reports two days later in the *New York Times* said the number of arrests was "more than 100" (Mark Landler, "China Said to Prepare Ban on Sect; Protests Go On").

81. Leslie Chang, "China Arrests Sect's Leaders across Nation," *Asian Wall Street Journal*, July 21, 1999.

82. See Craig S. Smith, "China's Retired Elite Aid Spiritual Group."

83. See Pollock, "Beijing Police Clamp Down on Meditation Group" ; Michelle Chak, "Falun Gong Leaders Arrested," *South China Morning Post*, July 21, 1999; Dow Jones International News, "Falun Gong Protests Reported in More Chinese Cities," July 21, 1999; Landler, "China Said to Prepare Ban on Sect; Benjamin Kang Lim, "China Cracks Down on Sect, Thousands Protest," Reuters,

Reactions to the Suppression

On July 22, 1999, the Chinese Ministry of Civil Affairs declared "the Research Association of Falun Dafa and the Falun Gong organization under its control" to be illegal organizations. That same day, the Ministry of Public Security spelled out what this meant by issuing what have become known as the "six prohibitions":

1. Everyone is prohibited from displaying in any public place scrolls, pictures and other marks or symbols promoting Falun Dafa (Falun Gong);
2. Everyone is prohibited from distributing in any public place books, cassettes and other materials promoting Falun Dafa (Falun Gong);
3. Everyone is prohibited from gathering a crowd to perform "group exercises" and other activities promoting Falun Dafa (Falun Gong);
4. It is prohibited to use sit-ins, petitions and other means to hold assemblies, marches or demonstrations in defence and promotion of Falun Dafa (Falun Gong);
5. It is prohibited to fabricate or distort facts, to spread rumours on purpose or use other means to incite [people] and disturb social order;
6. Everyone is prohibited from organising or taking part in activities opposing the government's relevant decision, or from establishing contacts [with other people] for this purpose.[84]

In the period after the Zhongnanhai demonstration but before the suppression was launched, Falun Gong practitioners, as we have seen, continued to express their opinions publicly and collectively against media and government criticism. It is not surprising, then, that the promulgation of the suppression did not silence them. In the months following July 1999, groups of Falun Gong adherents continued to gather to practice in the parks where they had been meeting for several years. Now, however, the authorities did not hesitate to round them up and place them in detention. Falun Gong sources indicate that the first of such actions took place on August 8 in the city of Haikou, on the island of Hainan in the far south of China, when police apprehended 138 people after a group practice.[85]

At the same time, practitioners, individually or in groups, began to write letters of protest to the government or to appear in person at gov-

---

July 21, 1999; and Mark Landler, "Beijing Detains Leaders of Sect, Watchdog Says," *The New York Times*, July 21, 1999.

84. See Amnesty International, "The Crackdown on Falun Gong," p. 16.

85. Anon., "A Chronicle of Major Events."

ernment offices. Sometimes these protesters—following the same logic that took them to Zhongnanhai in the first place—made their way to Beijing to confront the government at its heart. January 2000 saw a concerted campaign of protest in Tiananmen Square, where Chinese and later overseas practitioners openly defied the authorities by unfurling banners (often simply saying "Falun Dafa Is Good") and performing their exercises. Foreigners seem to have taken over this action from Chinese nationals when it was realized that they would be deported rather than detained and allegedly beaten. Expatriate followers of Falun Gong and politicians and activists outside China were not, of course, constrained in the same way as practitioners at home. When news of the suppression broke and appeared on the front pages of newspapers around the world, petitions were compiled, official statements of protest were lodged with embassies, and sit-ins, demonstrations, and other forms of activism were held in different countries.

In these first few months of the suppression, practitioners were typically detained for periods of up to fifteen days. These detention orders did not require ratification by any court and could take place at a local level. For these reasons, we have no reliable figures for how many Falun Gong devotees were placed in detention, but the numbers are undoubtedly in the thousands and probably exceed ten thousand. It would appear that many practitioners' level of commitment was greater than the authorities had expected: upon release from their fifteen days, many took up the cause again and were detained once more. This apparently happened so often that, as Human Rights Watch puts it in its report *Dangerous Meditation*,

it became evident that dismantling Falungong could not be accomplished quickly, and as demonstrations became daily occurrences, officials apparently grew impatient with briefly detained practitioners who, as soon as they were released, rejoined public protests in Tiananmen Square. In October 2000, China's policy changed. Instead of the Public Security Bureau rounding up protestors and escorting them home or detaining them for a few days or weeks, "relevant Beijing departments . . . decided to practice a 'close style management' on stubborn Falungong members." In the hope of facilitating the permanent "transformation" of identified "recidivists," such individuals were to be immediately sentenced administratively to reeducation through labor, in some cases for as long as three years.[86]

These three-year sentences could be "imposed judicially or administratively," as the report notes. The reeducation camps to which Falun

86. Spiegel, *Dangerous Meditation*, quoting *Ming Pao*, October 12, 2000.

Gong adherents were sent are located all over China and are administered variously by national, provincial, city, and county governments. Under these circumstances it is impossible to tell exactly how many people were, or still are, detained. Anecdotal evidence suggests that when many practitioners were detained—sometimes far from home—they refused to provide their names or addresses or any other identifying detail (such as work unit) for fear of repercussions for their families or coworkers. As a result, a proportion of detainees have only been assigned identification numbers and have simply disappeared, as far as their families are concerned.[87] Even if this were not the case, it is not routine for detainees' families to be informed of their whereabouts.

The vast majority of Falun Gong adherents detained since 1999 have been dealt with under administrative measures, including detention. A relatively small number, however, have passed through the judicial system and been found guilty of criminal offenses. These people were generally more senior in Falun Gong than the mass of followers detained, and have typically received sentences greatly exceeding the standard three years of administrative detention. Notable among the people accused under this category was a group of "four former senior government officials," as the director general of the State Council Information Office put it. In the words of the Amnesty International report,

Li Chang, aged 59, is a former departmental deputy director at the Ministry for Public Security; Wang Zhiwen, aged 50, is a former official with a company under the Ministry of Railways; Ji Liewu, aged 36, was the manager of a Hong Kong subsidiary of a government metals company; and Yao Jie, 40, was the Communist Party secretary of a large real estate company in Beijing.[88]

They were charged with "organizing and using a heretical organization to undermine the implementation of the law," "causing deaths by organizing and using a heretical organization," and "illegally obtaining and leaking state secrets."[89] All four were sentenced to long jail terms: 18 years for Li, as noted above, 16 for Wang, 12 for Ji, and 7 for Yao. It is likely that the actual reason they were dealt with so harshly was that they were all closely involved with the organization of what government documents routinely call "the siege of Zhongnanhai." Like Li Chang, Wang Zhiwen

87. See David Matas and David Kilgour, "Report into Allegations of Organ Harvesting of Falun Gong Practitioners in China," section F6, online at pkg.dajiyuan.com/pkg/2006-07-07/Kilgour-Matas-organ-harvesting-rpt-July6-eng.pdf.

88. Amnesty International, "The Crackdown on Falun Gong," p. 24.

89. Ibid.

was also one of the group who met with senior leaders at that time to present Falun Gong's claims.

Li was among the earliest followers of Li Hongzhi, attending the first series of lectures he gave in Beijing in mid-1992. He was among those arrested in the first major roundup of Falun Gong figures, as noted above.[90] This high-ranking and long-standing practitioner, who also had a career in the Chinese internal security services, had been a Communist Party member for almost forty years when he was arrested. Interviewed in 2006 in prison by the government-run anti–Falun Gong website Facts.org.cn, Li was apparently reconciled to his imprisonment, acknowledging that "Falun Gong should not be engaged in political affairs." He "recalled that on April 25, in the early morning, he intentionally drove around Zhongnanhai for some time. When he found that more and more people gathered around Zhongnanhai, he couldn't help feeling afraid for he knew what was happening was totally beyond his control. Used to being an official in the Ministry of Public Security, he figured out that he would be punished by law."[91]

Interviews with two more of this group, in which they praise the actions of the authorities and regret their lives wasted in Falun Gong, have also appeared on Facts.org.cn. Wang Zhiwen had started practicing extraordinarily early—in 1990, two years before Falun Gong was even launched—having been given a personal introduction to Li Hongzhi. Wang was in charge of maintaining contact with Falun Gong groups around the country.[92] Ji Liewu was also a longtime practitioner and was based in Hong Kong as representative of two Chinese nonferrous metals trading groups. From this base he assisted Li Hongzhi with his international travel arrangements—including arranging Li's flights into and out of Beijing just before the Zhongnanhai protest—and hosted him in his apartment.[93] There is less information about Yao Jie, the fourth member of the group, who by now would have served her sentence. She was apparently a "core member" who is "now no longer a Falun Gong follower."[94]

90. Craig S. Smith, "China's Retired Elite Aid Spiritual Group."

91. Tan Deyin, "Li Chang: It's Tragic for Falun Gong to Go to Politics," online at www.facts.org .cn/krs/wfem/200801/t75987.htm.

92. Tan Deyin, "Wang Zhiwen: '4·25' Affair Was Plotted in This Way," online at www.facts.org .cn/krs/wfem/200801/t75991.htm.

93. Tan Deyin, "Ji Liewu: Falun Gong Made Me Lose My Mind," online at www.facts.org.cn/krs/ wfem/200801/t76811.htm.

94. Anon., "Former Falun Gong Follower Leads New Life," online at *People's Daily Online*, english .peopledaily.com.cn/200111/21/eng20011121_85012.shtml; "Recent Situation of Yao Jie: Well-known Member of Falungong Cult (1)," online at au.china-embassy.org/eng/zt/jpflg/t46159.htm.

Another category of people convicted under criminal law was charged with offences related to the dissemination of Falun Gong publicity materials. These people printed pamphlets, made banners, duplicated and distributed compact discs, and sold Falun Gong books and other materials. They were imprisoned for periods between six and thirteen years.[95]

Three months after the suppression of Falun Gong, government actions against religious and spiritual groups that raised the suspicions of the authorities were generalized and formalized in a resolution of the National People's Congress. The Legislative Resolution on Banning Heretic Cults passed on October 30, 1999, was brief but sweeping in its effects. "Heretic cult" is another translation of *xiejiao*, rendered more commonly in government documents as "evil cult," as we have seen. The resolution is little more than a page long and outlines four measures. So-called heretic cult organizations are to be banned, and "those who manipulate members of cult organizations to violate national laws and administrative regulations, organize mass gatherings to disrupt social order, and fool others, cause deaths, rape women, swindle people out of their money and property or commit other crimes with superstition and heresy" are to be dealt with severely. Second, since most followers of these "cults" had been deceived into joining them (according to this resolution), they should receive education. At the same time, the "organizers, leaders and core members who committed crimes" should be punished. Third, education campaigns should be carried out among the citizenry at large, instructing them especially in science and technology, literacy, and the law. Finally, "all corners of society shall be mobilized in preventing and fighting against cult activities, and a comprehensive management system should be put in place."[96]

Thus, in the initial phase of dealing with these "cults," a distinction is drawn between credulous followers and criminal leaders. There are two assumptions underlying this distinction. The first is that none of the beliefs of these groups has any merit or worth, and anyone deciding to adhere to them is foolish, irrational, and wrong. The second is that the leaders of such groups do not believe the teachings they promote and simply concoct them to trick people for profit. The consequences for these two classes of people are different in commensurate ways. Whereas the leaders are dealt with under criminal law, the followers are subject to "education." The latter takes the form of administrative detention,

---

95. Spiegel, "Dangerous Meditation," pp. 55–56.

96. Anon., "China Issued Anti-Cult Law" (November 2, 1999), online at www.chinaembassycanada .org/eng/xw/xwgb/t38871.htm.

as we have seen in the Falun Gong case; the detention centers are, formally, "Re-education through Labour" camps. The resolution also calls for mass mobilization against "cults," and mass education in areas considered vital to preventing their reappearance. One of the primary areas for education, harking back to the first anti–Falun Gong article in *Guangming Daily* in 1996, is science and technology. Fundamentally, Falun Gong and the other "heretic cults" attacked in this drive were considered antiscientific.

Several other groups that emerged from the *qigong* boom were caught up in the backwash of the Falun Gong suppression and closed down in the second half of 1999. Notable among these were Guogong, Cibei Gong, and especially Zhong Gong.[97] Zhang Hongbao, the leader of Zhong Gong, escaped arrest and had found his way to Guam by early 2000. Subsequently, he was granted political asylum in the United States and died in a car accident in Arizona in 2006. Yet it was not just *qigong* groups that suffered under this crackdown. Several quasi-Christian groups, including those commonly translated as the Spirit Church, the Disciples Organization, Eastern Lightning, and the Elijah Church, have had leaders arrested and activities disrupted.[98] It is likely that many smaller and less well-known groups have also been attacked in this campaign, but news of them has not reached Western human rights monitors or other interested parties.

The suppression has forced many changes on Falun Gong. Some of these are obvious: the number of active participants has fallen sharply, communication with practitioners who continue to practice secretly in China is extremely difficult, the community of adherents now comprises many relatively small groups in numerous centers worldwide, and practitioners have become active campaigners for the rights of their fellows rather than concentrating solely on their cultivation. Some other changes have been more subtle. As Falun Gong practitioners in China faced the real possibility of detention, and allegedly beatings and torture, as well as the innumerable constraints on their practice caused by its being declared illegal, Li Hongzhi has changed the emphasis in parts of his teachings to take account of the new realities.

The suppression has had a major effect on two sets of teachings that may be summarized under the categories of tribulations and forbearance, and the place of the Communist Party in the doctrine. As noted earlier,

---

97. Amnesty International, "The Crackdown on Falun Gong," section 2.3, "The Purging of *Qigong* Based Groups."

98. Ibid., section 2.2, "Other Groups—the Ongoing 'Anti-Superstition' Campaign."

Li maintains that the negative consequences of sin and transgression which humans have accumulated in this and previous lives can only be overcome and transformed into positive attributes by passing through what he calls tribulations. In the early teachings, notably in *Zhuan Falun*, tribulations are described as occurring in everyday life and are often discussed in terms of disease. The tribulations are positive for cultivation, as enduring them eliminates karma—though Li's understanding of karma is very different from the orthodox Buddhist position, as we will see in chapter 5. This suffering is called "forbearance" in the standard Falun Gong translation. After the suppression, opportunities for practicing forbearance greatly expanded, and a few lines from early in *Zhuan Falun* took on a new significance. Maintaining that practitioners should not engage in shouting or swearing at other people, Li explains that a portion of a substance called virtue, or *de*, that will counteract karma passes from the aggressor during any attack. Thus,

The worse that person insults him, the more virtue he gives him. And the same goes for hitting people and picking on them. When a person punches somebody, or gives him a good kick, however hard the hit, that's how much virtue lands on him.[99]

In the context in which Falun Gong practitioners in China who protested the suppression were almost certain to be detained and possibly beaten, this aspect of the doctrine would have been not just a comfort in their pain but possibly an encouragement to resist: every punch and every kick from a policeman or a guard would be transferring valuable *de* to them and depriving their attacker of it. Thus, the suppression itself became a vast new opportunity for practitioners to show forbearance and promote their cultivation.

The second major way the teachings have changed since the suppression involves Falun Gong's attitudes toward the Communist Party. Earlier in this chapter, I outlined the way Li Hongzhi reinterpreted "politics" to allow for followers to protest against the actions of the government. In the first few years after July 1999, Falun Gong largely focused its attention on specific members of the Chinese government whom they considered instrumental in banning Falun Gong and ordering action against practitioners. Notable among these were the president at the time of the suppression, Jiang Zemin, and Luo Gan, the Politburo member most closely associated with the policy of arrest and detention. Practitioners from around the world launched legal cases against these two men and some

99. Li, *Zhuan Falun* 1/6, pp. 16–17, amended; pp. 28–29.

other high-ranking officials. In addition to accusing these individuals of crimes against Falun Gong, the movement also routinely listed on its websites the names of low-level government employees who did the dirty work of the suppression—prison officers, policemen, local government officials—and described dreadful diseases, accidents, and other misfortunes that had befallen them as a result of their actions.[100] Thus, at this stage Falun Gong still maintained that *individuals* were responsible for the suppression, much in the same way that the protests against various media outlets were explicitly asking for redress against the actions of specific journalists, authors, or interviewers.

In 2004, this approach changed with the publication of the "Nine Commentaries on the Communist Party" in the Falun Gong–aligned newspaper the *Epoch Times* and widely on the Internet. Falun Gong's use of the name "Nine Commentaries" is a reference to the Chinese Communist Party's own "Nine Commentaries on the Open Letter of the Central Committee of the Communist Party of the Soviet Union," which it issued at the height of the Sino-Soviet split in 1963 and 1964.[101] Falun Gong's "Nine Commentaries" shifts the focus from individuals to the Party itself and to Communism as an ideology. Moreover, Communism becomes regarded as "anticosmos"; that is, Falun Gong's objections to it are based not on a criticism of how it runs a society, or whether it is fair and just, but on its very nature, understood in spiritual terms. The title of the fourth commentary makes their objection clear: "On How the Communist Party Is an Anti-Universe Force." Part of that essay reads:

In the last hundred years, the sudden invasion by the communist specter has created a force against nature and humanity, causing limitless agony and tragedy. It has also pushed civilization to the brink of destruction. Having committed all sorts of atrocities that violate the Tao and oppose heaven and the earth, it has become an extremely malevolent force against the universe.[102]

As the clash with the Communist Party became reinterpreted as a cosmic struggle, action against it has also taken on cosmic dimensions. As we will see in chapter 4, some Falun Gong practitioners have been vouchsafed visions of the battle currently under way in all dimensions of the

100. See Penny, "Animal Spirits, Karmic Retribution, Falungong, and the State."
101. I thank Geremie R. Barmé for this reference.
102. "Commentaries on the Communist Party—4" (November 25, 2004), online at en.epochtimes .com/news/4-12-14/24953.html; "Jiuping zhi si," www.epochtimes.com/gb/4/11/25/n727814.htm. The use here of "communist specter" is a reference to the opening lines of *The Communist Manifesto*: "A spectre is haunting Europe—the spectre of communism."

universe in which the true, cosmically evil nature of the Communist Party is revealed.

It is clear that when Falun Gong was launched in 1992 and in the first period of its existence, Li Hongzhi was essentially uninterested in challenging the authorities politically. Indeed, he was quite successful in finding a place for it within state-endorsed structures. The movement only launched demonstrations in response to broadsides from newspapers, journals, and television stations, and it only became a truly oppositional force when it was explicitly attacked by the Chinese government and the Communist Party. Throughout this history, from the early days to the present, one feature has remained constant: Li Hongzhi himself. More than a participant in events, he has led the movement since it began. To the government he is the ringleader of a subversive movement that must be eradicated, but to practitioners he is their highly cultivated spiritual guide.

———

In the next chapter, the focus turns to Li Hongzhi himself: how he is represented in Falun Gong texts, how practitioners view him, the scriptures he has written, and, insofar as we can determine them, the books he has read.

THREE

The Lives of Master Li

Li Hongzhi has always been, and continues to be, at the center of Falun Gong. He developed its teachings, launched it to the public, and has led Falun Gong since it began. All through its years of astonishing growth and its initial confrontation with the Chinese government, and since its suppression, Li Hongzhi has been guide and master for practitioners. More than this, however, Li is central to Falun Gong doctrine itself. According to the teachings, he has revealed truths about the nature of the cosmos and the human condition no one else has ever communicated. He has shown people how to live their lives and escape the dire predicament in which they find themselves. To spread the word, he has produced a scripture, *Zhuan Falun*, from which all people can learn these truths. On its first page he states that his system of cultivation achieves nothing less than "saving people."[1] Falun Gong could not exist without Li Hongzhi, and he remains at its heart.

Claims made about Li may seem extravagant to outsiders. The biography that will be discussed in the first section of this chapter states, for example, that after many years of assiduous cultivation he "saw the truth of the cosmos . . . as well as the origin, development and future of mankind."[2]

1. Li, *Zhuan Falun* 1/1, p. 1; p. 2.
2. This biography can be found in Li, *Zhuan Falun* (1994), pp. 333–45, and online at en.wikipedia.org/wiki/User:Colipon/Biography_of_Li_Hongzhi. One translation credited to the "Translation Group of Falun Xiulian Dafa" is available at web.archive.org/web/20010109225900/http://www.compapp.dcu.ie/~dongxue/biography.html. Another translation is available in *Chinese Law and Government* 32, no. 6 (November/December 1999): 14–23. I have used the "Translation Group" translation as the basic text, but have amended it for accuracy.

According to his own teachings, he routinely intervenes in the bodies of practitioners at the beginning of their cultivation process, and consistently throughout it. This enables them to move forward, step by step, on the path to Consummation, the final goal of a Falun Gong adherent. For practitioners, he is like no other person alive: he is wisdom, compassion, and spiritual power personified. His exalted status appears to have led some of his followers to question whether he is, in fact, the same sort of being as they are. A practitioner interviewed, in English, by the BBC said that "he is even higher than Jesus."[3] In the first version of the biography, from 1993, the author says, "There are some people who ask, 'Is Li Hongzhi actually a man? Or is he a Buddha?' "[4]

At the same time, though, Li presents himself as an ordinary person. When he appears in public, as he still does at some meetings of followers, he wears a sober business suit. Practitioners recollecting his early lectures in China speak of him moving easily among people, chatting to them while he cured their illnesses. One remembered him as being "very amiable and approachable. He did not show any arrogance."[5] Indeed, the author of the 1993 biography answers the question of whether he is a Buddha like this:

When you see him wearing a knitted jumper with holes in it or patched underwear, when you see the simple way that he lives, when you hear his unaffected language, he really is a genuinely common man. Although he has spiritual powers that surpass those of ordinary people, you don't sense that he is special because he is so down-to-earth.[6]

In 1999, an Australian practitioner, interviewed in response to the announcement of the suppression of Falun Gong, said of Li: "He's not a guru, I don't worship him; I respect him in every way, just like I respect you and the people around me."[7]

This chapter focuses on the figure of Li Hongzhi himself and his textual corpus. As we saw in chapter 2, Li has been central to Falun Gong

3. Interviewed by James Miles, *BBC Breakfast News*, November 6, 1998.

4. Li, *Zhongguo falungong* (1993), pp. 179–80.

5. Anon., "Memories of Attending Master's Fourth Lecture Series in Guangzhou" (May 14, 2008), online at www.clearwisdom.net/emh/articles/2008/6/5/97893.html, amended; "Canjia shizun Guangzhou disi chuangdong jiangfaban de rizi," www.minghui.org/mh/articles/2008/5/16/178490.html.

6. Li, *Zhongguo falungong* (1993), p. 180.

7. This statement comes from Caroline Lam, an Australian spokesperson for Falun Gong, interviewed on *The Religion Report*, ABC Radio National, July 28, 1999; transcript at www.abc.net .au/rn/religionreport/stories/1999/39480.htm.

at all stages in its development. His own life story therefore occupies a fundamental position in the construction of its teachings, but this story has also been a matter of contention. The aim here is not to present a factually reliable version of Li's biography (even if that were possible) but rather to understand the meanings of his life as presented by the movement. Thus, this chapter begins with a consideration of the official Falun Gong biography of Li Hongzhi that narrates his life from his birth until 1993, before examining how some details in that narrative were disputed by the Chinese authorities. I will argue that just as significant features of Falun Gong's teachings can only be understood with reference to Chinese religious traditions, Li's biography is best seen as a contemporary example of a traditional Chinese religious life of the sort that has been written and read by Buddhists and Daoists since the early centuries CE. The second section of the chapter discusses what we know of the particular context from which Li emerged in the late 1980s and early 1990s, focusing specifically on the books he might have read. Following this is a discussion of Li's major writings, focusing on three works: the first Falun Gong book, *China Falun Gong*; the movement's primary scripture, *Zhuan Falun*; and the first collection of shorter talks and writings, *Zhuan Falun, Volume II*. The final section of the chapter investigates the great powers Master Li is said to possess and how he is viewed by practitioners.

The Early Life of Li Hongzhi

The original version of Li Hongzhi's official biography was published as an appendix to the first edition of *China Falun Gong* in April 1993. Written by a *qigong* journalist called Zhu Huiguang, it traced Li's life from his birth to the launch of Falun Gong in 1992, and included testimonies from practitioners whose diseases had been healed. Entitled "The New Cosmos Revolves around the Wheel of the Law—on Li Hongzhi and the Falun Gong He Founded," it is provided, it says, "to let readers understand the author's situation and the background to why the book was written." This version of the biography was replaced when *Zhuan Falun* was published in early 1995. The new biography, by contrast, appears over the signature of the Falun Dafa Research Association and has a much more neutral title: "A Short Biography of Mr Li Hongzhi, Founder of Falun Gong, President of the Falun Dafa Research Association." The main difference between the two versions is that the latter concentrates solely on Li's life and includes no testimonies (although there are significant changes in the text throughout).[8] Probably completed late in 1993 or in 1994, this biography appears to have circulated freely for some five or six years both as part of *Zhuan Falun* and as an independent text on the Internet, but it is no longer available in either form. Li ordered its withdrawal in a lecture he gave in Toronto in May 1999, explaining that he wanted practitioners to concentrate on their cultivation practice and not be distracted by his life story.[9] Another reason for the withdrawal may have been that some parts of it present Li as possessing superhuman powers, and thus had the potential to embarrass the movement at precisely the time Falun Gong was trying to appear as the noncontroversial victim of Chinese government oppression. The official English translation was last available in March 2001 on a practitioner's private site (rather than on an official site of the movement) but had disappeared by May 1 of that year.

It is important to examine Li's biography for several reasons. Leaving aside the question of whether the events narrated in it actually took place in the way that is indicated, Li's life story can be seen as the embodiment of Falun Gong teachings, demonstrating for practitioners not only that their teacher is a supreme spiritual master but also the heights of achievement they may attain by emulating him. In general, the biographies of founders of religions the world over serve these purposes; in this sense, Falun Gong is not unusual. Master Li's biography is, however, of particular interest, as it belongs to a long tradition of Chinese biographies of religious figures. There are both Daoist and Buddhist subtraditions within the greater stream of religious biography, but they share a great deal, especially from the structural point of view.[10]

One feature of these biographies is that their narrative generally climaxes in the transcendence of the central figure. The form that transcendence takes may vary, encompassing immortality, nirvana, or resurrection,

8. On the original biography from the first edition of *Zhongguo falungong*, see chapter 1, note 18 of the present text; on the revised, *Zhuan Falun* biography, see note 2, above.

9. Li Hongzhi, "Teaching the *Fa* at the Conference in Canada" (May 23, 1999), online at www .falundafa.org/book/eng/pdf/canada1999.pdf, p. 35; "Falun dafa Jianada fahui jiangfa," pp. 80–81.

10. On the Daoist biographical tradition, see, for an overview, Benjamin Penny, "Immortality and Transcendence," in *Daoism Handbook*, ed. Livia Kohn (Leiden: Brill, 2000), pp. 109–33. For studies on particular collections, see Stephan Peter Bumbacher, *The Fragments of "Daoxue zhuan": Critical Edition, Translation and Analysis of a Medieval Collection of Daoist Biographies* (Frankfurt am Main: Peter Lang, 2000); Robert Ford Campany, *To Live as Long as Heaven and Earth: A Translation and Study of Ge Hong's "Traditions of Divine Transcendents"* (Berkeley: University of California Press, 2002); and Maxime Kaltenmark, *Le Lie-sien tchouan* (Beijing: Université de Paris Publications, 1953). On Chinese Buddhist biographies, see Arthur F. Wright, "Biography and Hagiography: Hui-Chiao's Lives of Eminent Monks," in Wright, *Studies in Chinese Buddhism*, ed. Robert M. Somers (New Haven, CT: Yale University Press, 1990), and John Kieschnick, *The Eminent Monk: Buddhist Ideals in Medieval Chinese Hagiography* (Honolulu: University of Hawai'i Press, 1997).

but the narrative force of the genre is found in the inexorable movement toward the passage from a mundane human existence to something higher. As we will see, Li Hongzhi's biography follows exactly this pattern. The line of masters that instructs him, the new heights of cultivation he achieves, and the growing powers that he attains ultimately and necessarily lead to his supreme power and enlightenment.

After enlightenment is achieved, two more traditional elements appear in Li's biography. First, he passes his knowledge on to disciples: *Zhuan Falun*, literally "Turning the Wheel of the Law," significantly borrows its title from the standard translation of the first sermon of the Buddha. Second, he demonstrates his spiritual attainments to the world at large and is honored for them—in his case at the Oriental Health Expos of 1992 and 1993. The final chapter of a standard religious biography is, of course, missing in Li's case. Typically, the subject would ascend bodily into heaven, pass into nirvana, or enter into holy bliss. One remarkable aspect of Li's holy life as it appears in the biography is that his existence in this world has not ended.

Two other characteristics of the biography should be noted. First, traditional forms of religious biography—and indeed the secular Chinese tradition of biography as it appears in the dynastic histories—demand that their subject has demonstrated his or her powers, or at least potential to attain powers, while young. In this way the later august position that the subject reaches can be seen as having been prefigured, if not preordained. Extraordinary early attainments are prominent in this narrative of Li's life. Second, a common goal of much traditional Chinese religious biography is the establishment of genealogy. Thus, in an individual biography the subject's masters are noted. When that biography is read in conjunction with each master's own biography, where his masters are noted in turn, a set of biographies becomes a de facto lineage map. Li Hongzhi's biography is fascinating in this regard, as it grants him a kind of genealogy in the bounds of his own life. The typical sequential model outlined above is compressed by the narrative into the "more than 20 masters" that instruct him. In this way, he is represented, not just as the inheritor of the various lineages his masters belong to, but as their culmination and unifier.

The *Zhuan Falun* biography begins by stressing the originality and novelty of Falun Gong's principles, and the cultivators' amazement and fascination with the "profound power" of Li's "cultivation energy" and its "marvellous efficacy." It says, "Falun Gong is like a bright shining pearl that dispels the dirt out of the practitioner's mind with its radiance and lights the beacon on the great way of cultivation." According to this biography, Li was born on May 13, 1951, the eighth day of the fourth lunar month in that year, the day when the birth of the Śākyamuni Buddha—the historical Buddha—is traditionally celebrated. This became the first point of contention in the government's attacks on this text, to be discussed below. Li was born in the town of Gongzhuling in the province of Jilin, just south of the provincial capital of Changchun, "into an ordinary intellectual's family." He was apparently a "gifted and compassionate" child who helped his mother with her tasks and looked after his younger brothers and sisters.

Li's spiritual training began at the age of four with a master whose name translates as "Complete Enlightenment." This master, the biography claims, was the tenth-generation inheritor of the Great Method of the "Buddha School," and it was he who first introduced Li to Falun Gong's three-part morality, namely *zhen, shan,* and *ren,* or truth, compassion, and forbearance, in the standard Falun Gong translation. We will see in the next chapter how *zhen, shan,* and *ren* are understood to be the fundamental components of the universe, and in chapter 5 how practitioners are expected to embody them in their lives. Thus, this biography claims that the moral system of Falun Gong is not a recent development. Li did not invent it but received it from his first master. Complete Enlightenment introduced Li to these verities by inculcating a moral sense in the boy, regarding him disapprovingly when he did wrong, causing his hand to be cut, or sending "some big boys who would give him a good beating." Conversely, he would smile at Li when he did a good deed or confessed to having done wrong. When he was eight, "Li Hongzhi suddenly felt something in the corner of his eyes." This turned out to be the words *zhen, shan,* and *ren,* which Complete Enlightenment had imprinted there. The words were invisible to other people, but Li could always see them.

By this time, Li had also attained supernatural powers that enabled him to perform feats beyond the abilities of normal people. He could render himself invisible in games of hide-and-seek, pull old nails out of wood with little effort, and "rise high into the air" and stop boys from fighting by preventing them from moving. However, perhaps the following anecdote is the most remarkable:

Once, when he was in the fourth grade, he forgot his schoolbag when he left school. When he returned to fetch it, he found the door of the classroom locked and the windows shut. Then, an idea came to him: "It would be good if I could get in!" As soon as the thought flashed into his mind, he suddenly found himself in the classroom. And with another thought, he was out again. Even he was amazed at what had happened. Then another idea occurred to him: "What would it feel like if I stopped right in the glass?" And with that, he was in the middle of the window, his body and brain all filled with pieces of glass. He was in such pain he wanted to get straight out. And with that thought, he was.

In addition to his spiritual prowess, Li also continued to show great compassion, clearing roads of stones in case someone should fall on them, rescuing an adult from drowning without a thought to his own safety, and weeping at the sufferings of noble characters in films or novels. When he was twelve, Complete Enlightenment informed Li that another master would take his place. The second master, called "Realized Man of the Eight Extremes," taught Li "Daoist gongfu." This largely consisted of physical exercises and gymnastic forms, including those involving swords and spears. The Realized Man trained Li for two years, between 1963 and 1965.

Li started his life in employment in 1972, when he was already more than twenty years old. What happened to him as a youth is not described, but the period from 1965 to 1972 neatly encompasses the most extreme years of the Cultural Revolution when teenagers were often politically active. Similarly, no details of his job history are given; rather, it is the arrival of his third master that warrants attention, "a master of the Great Way with the Daoist name, Master of the Realised Dao," who came from the Changbai Mountains in Jilin Province on the Korean border. The Master of the Realised Dao apparently wore normal clothes and taught inner cultivation. In a rare reference to the historical circumstances of the time, the biography notes that "at that time, people did not dare to practise *qigong* openly," so Li practiced at night. "Sometimes," it says, "his master would take Li's chief consciousness out for cultivation practice. When he was asleep he could often feel his master putting things into his brain and Celestial Eye." Again, this master stressed the importance of the cultivation of his moral character. True Daoist left Li in 1974.

Li's fourth master was an unnamed woman, "a female master of the Buddha School" who taught him Buddhist cultivation and exercises. No more is revealed about her apart from the date that he first encountered her—the biography says he was twenty-three or twenty-four years old, so this occurred in 1974 or 1975, when "the power of his cultivation energy had reached a very high level." Another silence descends on Li's life story until 1982 when, the biography states, he moved to Changchun for civilian employment—presumably implying that his previous work had been for the military. This agrees with the official government version of his life, to be discussed below.

At this point in the official Falun Gong narrative, the enumeration of each of Li's masters gives way to the bald statement that "over the next ten years or so, as he reached a new level he would have a change in master, some were Buddhist and some were Daoist." After this exhaustive process, "his powers were difficult for ordinary people to imagine or understand." The anecdote that follows this claim appears to show Li in control of the weather, or perhaps simply as a perspicacious forecaster. In July 1990, when he was practicing with some disciples outdoors, the sky turned stormy and his disciples became apprehensive. Li continued "as steadily as a mountain without the slightest wavering or intention to withdraw," assuring them that it would not rain for half an hour—and the storm held off for exactly that long.

After this brief narrative of Li's life, the biography shifts its concerns to Li's development of the Falun Gong system of cultivation. Through his compassion for the plight of humanity, whose "spirits are corroded" and whose "bodies are abused," Li became determined to devise a "Great Method suitable for ordinary people to cultivate."[11] This would not be the same system of cultivation he was taught, as his practice comprised "grand cultivation teachings that could not be popularised on a large scale." The process of developing Falun Gong began, according to the biography, in 1984. Studying the methods of *qigong* available at that time, and with the assistance of his masters, who all returned to help him in this work, Li had finalized the method by 1989. Because of the input from all the masters, and thus all the different cultivation schools, Falun Gong "assembled all the mystical powers of the cosmos; it is the quintessence of the whole cosmos." This, as noted above, makes Li the unifier and culmination of the lineages of his masters. The period between 1989 and 1992 was apparently spent testing the new cultivation system on some disciples; then, conforming to the traditional model, he passed on his new teachings.

In May 1992 Falun Gong was made public. Beginning with its acceptance and support by the Chinese Association for Research into Qigong Science, the biography says that at the time of writing, Li had given dozens of lectures and classes in which he taught the exercises, and that several hundred thousand people across China had attended these sessions. At this point it summarizes Li's character and importance: he is enlightened with "a deep insight into the mysteries of the cosmos, which enables him to dispel the miasma in which the present-day world of *qigong* is shrouded"; he is "magnanimous, amiable and easy of approach"; he is solely dedicated to teaching Falun Gong; and he "works excessively and

11. This quotation and those that follow, through to the next paragraph, appear in the official English translation of the biography cited above, but not in the 1994 print edition of *Zhuan Falun*. I have not been able to locate a Chinese source for them.

knows no Sundays and holidays, often having no time to eat or rest." This paean culminates in a way that is redolent of the rhetoric of the Cultural Revolution in China rather than the early 1990s, when it was written:

Falun Dafa founded by Mr Li Hongzhi is like a red sun rising from the east, whose radiance with unlimited vitality will illuminate every corner of the earth, nourish all the living things, warm the whole world and play an unparalleled role in the realisation of an ideal and perfect human society on this planet.

The biography concludes with Li's attendance at the 1992 and 1993 Oriental Health Expos in Beijing.

The Government Attacks

Li's biography was a prime target for criticism by the Chinese government when the suppression was launched on July 22, 1999. One of the press releases issued that day through the research department of the Ministry of Public Security was called "The Life and Times of Li Hongzhi," and the biography was firmly in its sights. The government clearly wished to destroy Li's credibility because, by doing so, it would undermine the primary foundation of Falun Gong itself. Its attacks focused on three specific points. First, it provided evidence from the relevant police station in Changchun that on September 24, 1994—more than two years after Falun Gong was launched—Li formally changed his date of birth from July 7, 1952, to May 13, 1951, and acquired a new identity card. It noted that in 1951, May 13 was the eighth day of the fourth lunar month, the traditional date for the birthday of Śākyamuni. "By changing his birthday to fall on the same day of the birth of the founder of Buddhism," the press release says, "Li Hongzhi could claim that he is 'a reincarnation of Śākyamuni.'"[12]

The second point of attack related to "investigations and interviews" with "former schoolmates, teachers and neighbours." One Pan Yufang, who claimed to have been the midwife present at Li's birth, said that there were no auspicious signs when he came into the world.[13] Various

---

12. Gonganbu yanjiushe, "Li Hongzhi qiren qishi," *Renmin ribao*, July 23, 1999, p. 4, reprinted in *Jiepi falun dafa xieshuo*, ed. He Ping (Beijing: Xinhua chubanshe, 1999), p. 64. For a full translation, see *Chinese Law and Government* 32, no. 5 (September/October 1999): 56–64; quotation is on p. 57. This article also lists the other items of bureaucratic registration that have the changed birth date, and some documents issued in 1986 and 1991 on which the original birth date stands.

13. Anon., "Li Hongzhi's Mother's Midwife Says Li Is a Swindler," *People's Daily Online*, July 30, 1999, online at english.people.com.cn/special/fagong/1999073000A107.html.

witnesses to Li's past reported that far from being miraculous or possessed of supernormal powers, he was merely an ordinary child whose school results were unexceptional. They also reported that his claimed cultivation history was "nonsense" or "impossible," or remarked, "I have never seen or heard of that." His People's Liberation Army colleagues, with whom he worked as a trumpeter and then as an attendant at a guesthouse between 1970 and 1982, said that "the full schedule of rehearsals and performances and the strict military discipline and work timetable could never have left him any time to practise any *qigong*."[14] Finally, his employers at the Changchun cereals and oil company where he worked from 1982 until 1991 said that Li had no knowledge of any *qigong* before attending "the *qigong* training class in 1988."[15] Thus, it was part of the government's case that Li's acquaintance with *qigong*, far from dating back deep into his childhood, was actually very recent.

The final specific attack related to the development of the Falun Gong exercises. The Ministry of Public Security press release claims that Li made up Falun Gong based on two other *qigong* systems he had learned—Chanmi Gong, literally "The Practice of Zen and Tantric Buddhism," and Jiugong Bagua Gong, "The Practice of the Nine Palaces and Eight Trigrams"—and added "some movements from Thai dance that he picked up during a visit to relatives in Thailand." The names of these two *qigong* forms indicate their respective Buddhist and Daoist derivation. The government claims that Li did not develop Falun Gong alone but was helped by two early followers, and that far from being tested exhaustively beforehand, it was complete only one month before its official launch. Other early followers allegedly collaborated with writing teaching materials and touching up photographic images. Even Li's clothes were part of an act: "the yellow garments worn by Li Hongzhi were an opera costume purchased in a store."

In sum, the government attack was designed to prove that the biography of Li Hongzhi was simply untrue, a fabrication like the Falun Gong system itself, according to the authorities. To demonstrate its falsity was to open the eyes of the credulous to Li's deceits.

It is very difficult to find alternative sources of information for Li's life and career that are not associated with either Falun Gong or the Chinese authorities, and often the two versions of Li's life simply cannot be reconciled. Since the initial barrage of criticism in the period immediately

---

14. Gonganbu, "Li Hongzhi qiren qishi," p. 64; Research Office of the Ministry for Public Security, "Li Hongzhi: The Man and His Deeds," p. 58.

15. Gonganbu, "Li Hongzhi qiren qishi," p. 65; Research Office of the Ministry for Public Security "Li Hongzhi: the Man and His Deeds," p. 58.

following the suppression of Falun Gong, further details of Li Hongzhi's life have become available. Bearing in mind that information about Falun Gong published in the People's Republic is necessarily part of a negative publicity campaign, these details should be treated with caution. Nonetheless, some are corroborated by Falun Gong or independent sources, and some, at least, do not seem to advance the government's campaign in any specific way except insofar as to produce an image of a man with an ordinary, if fraught, family background.

We find, for instance, that Li Hongzhi married a woman some six years his junior called Li Rui, and that they have a daughter called Li Meige who was born in the early 1980s.[16] The fact that he has a wife and child is not controversial, and it does not appear to be important for practitioners. We also discover that he is the eldest in a family of four, with two younger sisters, Li Jun and Li Ping, and that the youngest sibling is a brother called Li Hui. Li Hui was clearly the source of some of the information about Li Hongzhi that appears in the book *Power of the Wheel: The Falun Gong Revolution*, published in Canada in 2000, where his name is given as Li Donghui. His sisters are also named in this book, which also claims that Li and his wife have two children.[17]

According to Chinese sources, Li's mother, Lu Shuzhen, and his father, Li Dan, both worked in the medical field. Lu was Li Dan's second wife, and apparently he went on to marry twice more before his death in 1996. Li Hongzhi's mother followed her son, his wife, and their daughter to the United States, as did his elder sister, Li Jun, and his brother, Li Hui, or Donghui. His younger sister, Li Ping, married a Thai-Chinese and lives in Thailand.[18] Li Hongzhi's wife, Li Rui, featured briefly in the Western press in 1999 when the *Wall Street Journal* published an article alleging that a Falun Gong practitioner had bought a house for Li Hongzhi and registered it in Li Rui's name.[19] Not long after, the practitioner concerned wrote to the paper, explaining he had done this without Li Hongzhi or his wife knowing, and that when they found out, they insisted he transfer his name onto the title.[20]

These accounts of Li's early life contain two more intriguing details. First, government sources claim that he was originally named Li Lai, but

---

16. Anon., "Investigation and Analysis."

17. Ian Adams, Riley Adams, and Rocco Galati, *Power of the Wheel: The Falun Gong Revolution* (Toronto: Stoddart, 2000), pp. 5, 23.

18. Anon., "Investigation and Analysis."

19. Craig S. Smith, "American Dream Finds Chinese Spiritual Leader," *Wall Street Journal*, November 1, 1999.

20. Jon Sun, "For Joy and Fulfillment, Not Money," *Wall Street Journal*, November 17, 1999.

during the Cultural Revolution, along with very many other young people, he changed his name to sound more revolutionary.[21] *Hongzhi* translates roughly as "vast will." Second, in 1988 Li went through a period during which he was seriously interested in Buddhism, studying under a master at the Huguo Bore ("Protecting the Country Prajñā") Temple in Changchun, where he lived.[22]

The government's attacks on the biography of Li Hongzhi were, of course, part of an attempt to justify the suppression. On the other hand, the biography itself, from some six years earlier, sought to construct a narrative of Li's life that proved him to be a supreme spiritual master, the rightful leader of a new movement that would bring healing and salvation.[23] The Falun Gong account of Li's early life, and the government's accumulation of data that were intended to discredit it, therefore present two entirely different versions of the life of the founder of Falun Gong. This is not surprising, as they were designed to achieve different goals. In addition to these two sources on Li's life before Falun Gong was launched, however, we may add a third that tells us not so much about the events in his life as it does the mental world he inhabited: the books that he read, including translations of Western books on the paranormal. The evidence for this comes from within Li's writings themselves and serves to place him in a specific bibliographic context in the years before the launch of Falun Gong.

Li Hongzhi's Reading

Li Hongzhi is a child of the Chinese Revolution, born in 1951 (or 1952, depending on the source). Consequently, his reading always would have been restricted to works approved by the relevant government authorities, until he ventured overseas in 1995. Of course, the rules governing what books were available in China have varied considerably over the years; but certainly from the age of thirteen or fourteen until he was in his late twenties, during the period of high Maoism, the range of books available to him would have been very limited. With the launch of the so-called reform period in the late 1970s, many more reading materials covering a much broader variety of topics became available, including books and magazines translated into Chinese from Western languages

21. Anon., "Investigation and Analysis."
22. Ibid.
23. See Penny, "The Life and Times of Li Hongzhi."

and Japanese. Nowhere does Li discuss his own library or the books he was brought up with, but an examination of his scriptures allows us to identify a few books, or a few kinds of books, that he certainly read, and that were formative in the development of Falun Gong.

Among Li's extensive writings, including those on Buddhism, he rarely mentions the titles of any books apart from his own. He does refer to the *Diamond Sutra* by name in *Zhuan Falun* and the Buddhist and Daoist Canons in general terms, but despite the fact that, according to government sources, he may have had a serious interest in Buddhism in 1988, he does not seem to be very familiar with the religion as a whole. Barend ter Haar has asked perspicaciously

whether Li Hongzhi's knowledge of Buddhist teachings and practices stems from living Buddhist tradition or from his reading in Buddhist texts. The absence, to my knowledge, of traditional Buddhist ritual practices and the recourse to essentially Daoist inspired *Qigong* practices suggest that Li Hongzhi has combined book knowledge of Buddhist doctrine with actual experience in *Qigong* practices.[24]

Indeed, we might add to ter Haar's observation the possibility that Li's book knowledge of Buddhism may have come from reading discussions and summaries of scriptures rather than the scriptures themselves. One intriguing exception to this is a short Buddhist book called *Travelogue of the Western Paradise*, as its title is translated in *Zhuan Falun* (the original title is *Xifang jile shijie youji*), that Li appears to have read more thoroughly. He says,

It's about a monk who meditated and his original spirit went to the Western Paradise and saw some scenes. He strolled around for a day there and came back to the human world, where a good six years had passed.[25]

This booklet is commonly distributed free in Buddhist temples across the Chinese world, and concerns the visions of a Buddhist monk and "living Buddha" called Kuanjing (1924–). These spiritual journeys occurred in 1967 while he was in meditation. Anecdotal evidence suggests that Chinese Buddhist monks commonly recommend the *Travelogue of the Western Paradise* to interested visitors to their temple, as it is both introductory and captivating.

24. Barend ter Haar, "Falun Gong: Evaluation and Further References," online at website .leidenuniv.nl/~haarbjter/falun.htm.

25. Li, *Zhuan Falun* 1/2, p. 6; p.11.

Apart from Buddhist texts, however, it is possible to determine the content of some of Li's reading from certain topics he examines in *Zhuan Falun* and later writings. These discussions reveal a perhaps unlikely source for some of his ideas: Western books about the paranormal from the 1970s and 1980s. An example of this comes from the following passage included in "Teaching the *Fa* on Lantau Island" from *Zhuan Falun, Volume II*:

The moon, in fact, was created by prehistoric man, and its interior is hollow. Prehistoric man was quite advanced. Today people hold that the pyramids were built by the Egyptians, and have tried to determine where the stones were transported from. But it is nothing of the sort. The pyramids in fact belong to a prehistoric culture, and were submerged at one point beneath the sea. Because of subsequent changes on Earth—namely, multiple shifts in the continental plates—the pyramids emerged anew. With time, the number of persons in that area grew, with the new residents gradually coming to realize the functions [of the pyramids]—that is, they could preserve things for great lengths of time. They thus placed human corpses inside them. But these persons were not the ones who built the pyramids; the Egyptians merely discovered them and made use of them. At a later point the Egyptians erected smaller versions of the pyramids based on the originals, and thus confused scientists.[26]

And later in the same essay:

There are people who reside in the sea. . . . There are people on the ocean floor, several kinds. Some of them resemble us, and some are rather different. Some have gills, while some are human from the waist up and fish from the waist down; others have human legs with upper bodies that are fish.

In these richly evocative passages are echoes of several topics known in Western paranormal circles; some are regarded as quite mainstream by aficionados and some as fringe, even by the standards of these circles. The first of these is a concern with the pyramids. In "Teaching the *Fa* on Lantau Island," Li refers obliquely to three perennial obsessions of writers in this field: first, that the pyramids of Egypt hold occult secrets and that "orthodox scholarship" is ignorant of their real history; second, that it would have been impossible to build them using any known ancient engineering methods; and finally, that they have a mysterious capacity for preservation. This is grist to many a speculative best seller's mill, and the relevant literature on pyramidology is too vast to assay here. Li's use

26. Li Hongzhi, "Teaching the *Fa* at Lantau Island," in *Zhuan Falun, Volume II*, pp. 5–6; "Zai Dayushan jiangfa," in *Zhuan falun juan er*, p. 6. For more on *Zhuan Falun, Volume II*, see below.

of these pyramid tropes, however, raises another common topic in the literature of the paranormal, namely Atlantis.

There are two elements in the way Li links the pyramids with Atlantis, both of which derive from Western authors.[27] First, it has long been claimed in some circles that the ancient Egyptians were not advanced enough to have constructed the pyramids themselves. One school, exemplified by Erich von Daniken, author of *Chariots of the Gods* and related books, claims that their construction is one of many proofs that aliens visited earth in ancient times and instituted human civilization. While Li appears to believe in extraterrestrial civilizations,[28] his understanding of the "history" of the pyramids does not follow this theory. Instead, he seems to be referring to a tradition that holds that the pyramids were built by the Atlantaeans. This theory goes back at least to Edgar Cayce, known as "the sleeping prophet," who was famous in the 1930s, and to Rudolph Steiner, founder of "biodynamic" agriculture and the educational system that bears his name. More recently, it has reappeared in works that claim to have discovered "irrefutable evidence" of vast and ancient human construction activity that now lies under the oceans—off Okinawa most recently, but earlier "discoveries" found such evidence near the Bahamas. Some of these remnants of ancient engineering are apparently pyramidical.[29] In Li's understanding, the pyramids sank below the waves along, presumably, with their builders when continental plates shifted, only to rise again by the same process in a later era. The idea that the civilization that "really" built the pyramids became aquatic seems to have led him to observe that "there are humanoids on the ocean floor" who are either human above the waist and fish below, or else fish above and human below. Thus, the third topic that Li refers to is the possible existence of mermaids and other semihumans who live in the sea.

Finally, going back to the beginning of these passages, Li maintains that "the moon, in fact, was created by prehistoric man, and its interior is hollow." "Hollow moon theory" is part of a larger field—fringe even in paranormal circles—that claims that all planets, including the earth, are hollow. Made famous by Jules Verne in *Journey to the Center of the Earth*, this idea dates at least to the eighteenth century. Sometimes peopled by advanced races and superb civilizations, the hole in the middle of the

27. A classic, though older, work on Atlantis lore is L. Sprague de Camp, *Lost Continents: The Atlantis Theme in History, Science and Literature* (New York: Dover, 1970; reprint of 1954 Gnome Press edition).

28. William Dowell, "Interview with Li Hongzhi," *Time Asia*, May 10, 1999, online at www.time.com/time.asia/asia/magazine/1999/990510/interview1.html.

29. See Charles Berlitz, *Atlantis: The Eighth Continent* (New York: G. P. Putnam's Sons, 1984).

planet has more recently been proposed as the home of the "extraterrestrials" who pilot the UFOs that are occasionally sighted. It is unclear how Li Hongzhi might have heard about hollow moon theory, but books on Atlantis, the pyramids, Nostradamus, the Bermuda Triangle, and other mainstream paranormal topics were certainly translated into Chinese by 1990 as part of the publishing boom in the People's Republic.[30]

The source for one element of Li's teachings that derives from the Western paranormal is very clear. In *Zhuan Falun* he writes,

There's someone in the United States who specializes in electronics research, and he teaches people how to use polygraphs. One day he was struck by a sudden inspiration and connected the two electrodes of a polygraph to a dragon plant. Then he watered its roots. After doing that he discovered that the needle of the polygraph quickly drew a type of curve, the same type of curve, it turns out, that's generated by a human brain when it experiences excitement or happiness. He was stunned, how could plants have emotions! He almost wanted to go out and shout in the streets, "Plants have emotions!" With the inspiration he got from all this, he soon opened up this field of research and did lots and lots of experiments.[31]

This passage continues for some paragraphs and is taken almost directly from the first chapter of *The Secret Life of Plants* by Peter Tompkins and Christopher Bird, first published in 1974. A Chinese translation of *The Secret Life of Plants* appeared in 1989 under the title *The Supernormal Abilities of Plants*. "Supernormal abilities" translates *teyi gongneng*, a term that by 1989 was most commonly applied to the special powers *qigong* practitioners acquired as they became more adept, such as telekinesis, superhuman strength, and so on. The use of the term *supernormal abilities* in the translated title thus entailed a recontextualization of Tompkins and Bird's book using the vocabulary of *qigong*. In some ways this can be seen as nativizing the book by integrating it into the history of Chinese cultivation. It also grants to *qigong* the cachet of foreign sophistication at a very particular time in China's recent history. The translation would

30. Among the notable works of this genre translated into Chinese and published in the People's Republic before 1990 are Erich von Daniken's *Chariots of the Gods* [*Zhongshen zhiche? lishi shangde weijie zhimi* (Shanghai: Shanghai kexue jishu chubanshe, 1981)], Charles Berlitz's *The Bermuda Triangle* [*Baimuda sanjiuo* (Beijing: Beijing chubanshe, 1981)], and Peter Tompkins and Christopher Bird's *The Secret Life of Plants* [*Zhiwude teyi gongneng* (Beijing: Xinhua chubanshe, 1989)]. There were, of course, many more books of this sort published in Hong Kong and Taiwan. In addition, knowledge on paranormal topics would have been transmitted through popular journals such as *Feidie tansuo* (the *Journal of UFO Research*) that began publication in 1981, and *Aomi* (the Chinese version of *Omni* magazine) that began in 1983.

31. Li, *Zhuan Falun* 8/3, p. 155; p. 268.

have been produced at the high-water mark of the infatuation with the West (and the disillusionment with supposedly traditional Chinese ways of thinking) among many young Chinese that coincided with the democracy movement of 1989, brutally suppressed on June 4 of that year.

Three years after the Beijing massacre and the appearance of the Chinese translation of *The Secret Life of Plants*, Li Hongzhi launched Falun Gong. Less than a year after that, his own book, originally called *China Falun Gong*, was published. This marked the beginning of a stream of writings and published speeches that formed the core of his teachings.

Li Hongzhi's Writings

The first two Falun Gong books to be published were *China Falun Gong* (in the original and revised editions) and *Zhuan Falun*, followed not long afterward by *Zhuan Falun, Volume II*. These will be discussed in turn, but we should remember that *Zhuan Falun* is the most important of Li's works: from the time it was launched in January 1995, it has been the primary scripture of the movement. Other essays and the many lectures Li has given, as well as his poetry, are of course read and respected by practitioners, deriving as they do from their Master. Nonetheless, these writings do not rival *Zhuan Falun* as expositions of the teachings. At a lower level again are the copious works found on Falun Gong websites that have been submitted by practitioners. Even though they are vetted and approved by editors, they are regarded as subsidiary.

China Falun Gong

The first book to appear under Li Hongzhi's name was *China Falun Gong*, published in April 1993 by the Military Affairs Friendship and Culture Press. The sponsor of this publishing company is the second section of the People's Liberation Army General Staff Headquarters, a military intelligence organization where one of the five Falun Gong representatives at the Zhongnanhai demonstration worked. *China Falun Gong* was intended as an introductory book, a function it still has, according to Falundafa.org, the movement's main website for the general public rather than practitioners. This website claims that it "gives an introductory level discussion of the principles of Falun Dafa and the concept of cultivation."[32]

---

32. Anon., "Falun Dafa: How to Learn," 2007, online at www.falundafa.org/eng/howtolearn
.html.

China Falun Gong is divided into three parts. The first is an introduction that treats general conceptions of *qigong*, supernormal abilities, and the Celestial Eye, as well as the relationship of Falun Gong to Buddhism. The second section deals with the practice of Falun Gong itself, while the third discusses the importance of *xinxing*, "character" (as it is often translated in Falun Gong works) or "mind-nature" (in a literal rendering), in cultivation. It also includes instructions on how to perform the five sets of exercises that have become the most common public manifestation of Falun Gong to outsiders.

A revised edition of *China Falun Gong* was released only eight months after the first edition was published, in December 1993.[33] The title was later simplified to *Falun Gong (Revised Edition)* or just *Falun Gong* (as I refer to it from now on in this book). A detailed comparison of these two editions would be both lengthy and complex, but a few points are worth making. First, both versions of the book appear to be based on Li's sets of nine lectures. *Zhuan Falun*, as we will see below, is closer to the original form of the lectures, but *Falun Gong* covers many of the same topics. The main difference between *Zhuan Falun* and *Falun Gong* is that the earlier work is arranged more cogently and logically, and is also much shorter. Despite this apparent clarity of organization, there is much that a reader now would find hard to comprehend. Certain sections of *Falun Gong* refer to particular features of the *qigong* world of the early 1990s that no longer exist, but these historical references are never explained. For instance, one section entitled "Righteous Cultivation Ways and Evil Ways" criticizes various practices that were common in the *qigong* world when Li Hongzhi launched Falun Gong, but which have since disappeared.[34] The function of these criticisms was clearly to differentiate Falun Gong from the many other forms of *qigong* being taught at the time *Falun Gong* was published. Notable among Li's targets is "cosmic language," a kind of *qigong* glossolalia. This was closely associated with Zhang Xiangyu, a self-declared *qigong* grandmaster who propounded "Nature-Centred *Qigong*" in the late 1980s and who was famously arrested in December 1990 because she had "used superstition and created false rumours to swindle others out of money and goods."[35]

A second major difference between the two editions of *Falun Gong* is that the first, from April 1993, includes the original version of Li's biographical essay, which disappeared in the revised edition of Decem-

---

33. Strangely, the first edition of *China Falun Gong* continued to be reprinted at least until May 1994, six months after the revised edition had appeared. Both versions were published by the same press.

34. Li, *Zhongguo falungong* (1993), pp. 29–33.

35. See Palmer, *Qigong Fever*, pp. 151–53; Zhu and Penny, "The Qigong Boom," 27–32.

ber 1993. Although *Falun Gong* appeared under Li Hongzhi's name, this essay, as noted above, has a different author, the *qigong* journalist Zhu Huiguang, mentioned earlier. Given that none of Li's numerous subsequent writings approach the clarity and organization of this book, we might speculate that *Falun Gong* as a whole was actually ghostwritten, in all likelihood by Zhu, based on the lectures that were later rendered more directly in *Zhuan Falun*. Also absent from the revised edition of 1994 is an extensive collection of testimonies from grateful recipients of the curative powers of Falun Gong. This change indicates that while healing was a primary attraction in Falun Gong's early phase, Li's ideas about what lay at the core of its teachings had shifted profoundly a mere two years or so after Falun Gong had been launched.

This contention is strengthened by the inclusion in the first edition of photographs showing Li healing the sick at the 1992 Oriental Health Expo. His patients included Liu Ying, the widow of Long March veteran and senior Communist revolutionary Zhang Wentian, as well as three of the people whose testimonies appeared later in the book. These pictures were not included in the revised edition. In addition, the later version concludes with a chapter of questions and answers, presumably based on actual queries practitioners had raised during the lectures Li had by then been delivering for about a year and a half. Only a handful concern Falun Gong's healing powers, and in answer to each Li downplays the importance of curing illness in favor of stressing the need for cultivation. He does, however, allow for his own healing practice in the interests of "promoting" Falun Gong: "By giving health consultations and healing people we let everybody witness Falun Gong, and in terms of publicity the results have been excellent. So we didn't do it entirely for healing people."[36]

Another difference between the first and revised editions of *Falun Gong* is that certain changes were made in important aspects of the teachings. One example concerns the nature and purpose of the *falun* itself. In the revised edition, and in Falun Gong teachings since, the *falun* appears to be of a fixed size, but in the first edition it varies depending on "the predestined fate of the practitioner and their capabilities." It also seems to be able to change once it has been inserted in the practitioner's body.

When the *falun* is big it is limitlessly big, such that common people can only glimpse a spot of it; when small it is limitlessly small, like a speck of dust or a grain of sand, so common people do not perceive its existence.[37]

36. Li, *Falun Gong* 5/2, p. 70; p. 119.
37. Li, *Zhongguo falungong* (1993), p. 38.

Similarly, in the first edition, practitioners appear to be able to have multiple *falun*s rotating at different speeds.

In the transmission classes, the *falun*s that I implant into the abdomen of each student spin at a uniform velocity and they assist in the student's cultivation. The *falun*s in other parts of the students' bodies have variable velocities.[38]

According to one passage from the first edition, these extra *falun*s can move about the body along the *qi* meridians, or they "can proceed anywhere the cultivator needs them to go. For example, they can go to where the cultivator has an infection, or help to eliminate the *qi* of illness, or open up the meridians, etc." Indeed, if the cultivator requires it of the *falun*s, they can go in "any direction or to any location inside or outside the body, to accomplish any mission." In fact, "when cultivation reaches a certain level, the cultivator is able to send out *falun*s to cure other people's diseases or use them to develop the body's latent abilities and take part in scientific research activities, etc."

Three features of this short passage conflict with later orthodoxies. First, sending *falun*s out of the body is unknown in Li's subsequent teachings and implies a kind of active use of the powers that a practitioner might acquire in the course of their cultivation that Li is explicit in opposing later. Second, after the first edition of *Falun Gong*, Li is adamant that Falun Gong practitioners never use their powers for healing others. Third, the idea that Falun Gong cultivators should use *falun*s to develop supernormal powers—powers that are latent in all people—so that they can take part in scientific research would come to be regarded as anathema.

Li implicitly addresses the changes in the teachings between the first and revised editions of *Falun Gong* in the speeches he gave to Falun Gong Assistants during 1994. For instance, in a talk to Assistants in Changchun from September of that year, Li noted,

When our first book, *China Falun Gong*, was written, its contents were in some respects similar to low-level *qigong*. The second book, *China Falun Gong* (*Revised Edition*), is much higher than *qigong*.[39]

38. Ibid., p. 39.
39. Li Hongzhi, "Explaining the *Fa* for Falun Dafa Assistants in Changchun" (September 18, 1994), in *Explaining the Content of "Falun Dafa,"* p. 8; "Wei Changchun falun dafa fudaoyuan jiangfa," in *Falun dafa yijie*, p. 8.

Finally, it is important to note the role of the military in Falun Gong's early phase. In chapter 1, links between sections of the military establishment and the national *qigong* hierarchy were noted, as was the military background of the national *qigong* association's first president, Zhang Zhenhuan, the man who smoothed the way for Falun Gong to receive official accreditation. It is not surprising in this context that the Military Affairs Friendship and Culture Press published both editions of *Falun Gong*. In addition, four of Li's Beijing lecture series took place in the auditorium of the Second Artillery, China's missile unit, while another four were in government aerospace establishments, and he gave one set in the hall of a nuclear equipment factory. In light of the present antagonism between Chinese authorities and Falun Gong, the military's apparent willingness to sponsor this new *qigong* group may seem hard to credit; but Falun Gong was, at the time, perfectly legal and in possession of all the required accreditations.

Zhuan Falun

The last of Li's series of nine lectures in China was given in Guangzhou in late December 1994. Just a few days later, on January 4, 1995, he launched what was to become the primary scripture of the movement, *Zhuan Falun*. In it, Li explains that it is an edited version of his lectures.

All of it is my words, every sentence is my words, and they were transcribed from the tape recordings word by word, and copied down word by word. It was done with the help of my disciples and students. They transcribed my words from the recordings, and then I revised the book over and over again.[40]

Zhuan Falun's origin in Li's lectures is very clear. Rather than being divided into chapters, the book is made up of nine "lectures" or "talks" (depending on the translation). Each one is subdivided into between five and ten sections. If these transcribed and edited "lectures" accurately represent the versions he delivered in person, it is clear that Li's lecturing style was not lucid. From lecture to lecture and from section to section, he raises topics only to drop them, and then repeats what he has said in a later place and in a different context. Li digresses, tells anecdotes whose relevance is often unclear, and jumps between apparently unrelated issues. Practitioners seeking understanding on specific aspects of

---

40. Li, *Zhuan Falun* 6/7, pp. 131–32; p. 228.

the teachings often have to search for guidance in many different places throughout *Zhuan Falun*. In this, the contrast with *Falun Gong* could not be starker. This aspect of Li's writings places scholars wishing to accurately represent his teachings in a difficult position. On the one hand, to explain Falun Gong doctrine in a clear, logical, and comprehensible way (as I have tried to do in this book) is arguably to misrepresent it. On the other, to render it as Li does (especially in *Zhuan Falun*) would test any reader's patience.

Although Li does not address the issue of the comprehensibility of his scriptures directly, an implicit response to it occurs in a note concerning the language of *Zhuan Falun* that he wrote on January 5, 1996, a year after the book was launched, and appended to the text. "On the surface," Li writes, "*Zhuan Falun* is not elegant in terms of language. It might even not comply with modern grammar." If he complied with grammatical rules, he says, the style of *Zhuan Falun* "might be standard and elegant," but "it would not encompass a more profound and higher content." In other words, the truths contained in *Zhuan Falun* cannot be adequately expressed in standard linguistic forms, because they are too large and all-encompassing. In his 1998 lecture in Singapore, Li went further, insisting that since his teachings are good for the whole cosmos, and all the various kinds of being that exist in it, to express them while abiding by "the grammatical standards of a human language" would be impossible.[41] With this in mind, it is easy to imagine how Li would respond to the charge that his lectures were neither laid out logically nor easy to follow: the issues he is discussing cannot be restricted by small-minded, mundane, and merely human considerations of clarity and structure.

In the speech he gave at the launch of *Zhuan Falun*, just after presenting his final lectures in China, Li explained that reading the scripture would accomplish the same goals as its being taught in person.[42] However, as we have seen, the lectures themselves were not simply a means of imparting information. Rather, they were spiritually powerful processes whereby Li intervened in the bodies of practitioners to prepare them for cultivation. *Zhuan Falun* is similarly powerful. Reading it, Li claims (in the book itself), will induce the same effects as attending one of the lec-

---

41. Li Hongzhi, "Teaching the *Fa* at the Conference in Singapore" (August 22–23, 1998), online at www.falundafa.org/book/eng/pdf/singapore1998.pdf, p. 33; "Falun dafa Xinjiapo fahui jiangfa," p. 74. On this topic, see also Li Hongzhi, "Using at Will" (June 28, 2000), in *Essentials for Further Advancement, II*, p. 15; "Suiyi suoyong," in *Falun dafa jingjin yaozhi er*, pp. 21–22.

42. Li Hongzhi, "Teaching the *Fa* in Beijing at the *Zhuan Falun* Publication Ceremony" (January 4, 1995), in *Zhuan Falun Fajie*, pp. 35–36; "Beijing zhuan falun shoufashi shang jiangfa," in *Zhuan falun fajie*, p. 47.

tures, since his power imbues it. He says specifically that it will help open a practitioner's Celestial Eye[43] and assist a practitioner in giving up smoking,[44] and can be used to consecrate a Buddha statue.[45] More than this, "Every single word in my books has my image and Law Wheel [*falun*],"[46] and if practitioners have their Celestial Eyes opened, they "can see that this book is full of dazzling colors, and sparkling with golden light."[47] As befits a holy scripture, *Zhuan Falun* must be treated with reverence, and Li is explicit that readers are not to make any marks on it.[48]

In later writings, Li's descriptions of *Zhuan Falun*'s special characteristics become even more extraordinary. Not only does every word in it contain Li's own image and a *falun*, but he claims that if practitioners look at the book with an opened Celestial Eye, as he explained in his 1996 lecture in Houston, he or she would see that each word is also

a *srivatsa* (卍), and that each character is a Buddha. . . . In addition, each character has layer upon layer of Buddhas, because this book contains principles from different levels of the cosmos.[49]

Even more wonderfully, as Li proclaimed to an American audience in 1997, if an advanced practitioner were reading *Zhuan Falun* in English translation, he or she might see "gods dressed like Saint Mary or Jesus— Gods with Caucasian images—in each and every word."[50] Li's most recent characterization of the text—from 2004—places the book in the context of his multidimensional cosmos, to be discussed in the next chapter. Apparently, "*Zhuan Falun* manifests differently in each dimension, and the *Zhuan Falun* in the heavens looks completely different from the one on earth."[51]

Clearly, *Zhuan Falun* is no ordinary book. Not only does it proclaim the teachings of Master Li, it also carries the power of those teachings in

43. Li, *Zhuan Falun* 2/1, p. 26; p. 46.

44. Ibid., 7/2, p. 140; p. 242.

45. Ibid., 5/7, p. 103; p. 178.

46. Ibid., 6/7, p. 130; p. 225.

47. Ibid., 9/5, p. 186; p. 320.

48. Ibid.

49. Li Hongzhi, "Teaching the *Fa* at the Conference in Houston" (October 12, 1996), not paginated, online at www.falundafa.org/book/eng/pdf/houston1996.pdf; "Falun dafa Xiusidun fahui jiangfa," p. 43.

50. Li Hongzhi, "Teaching the *Fa* in New York City" (March 23, 1997), in *Lectures in the United States*, p. 53, online at www.falundafa.org/book/eng/pdf/mgjf.pdf; "Niuyue fahui jiangfa," in *Falun dafa Meiguo fahui jiangfa*, p. 112.

51. Li Hongzhi, "Teaching the *Fa* at the 2004 International *Fa* Conference in New York" (November 21, 2004; no PDF); "Erlinglingsi nian Niuyue guoji fahui jiangfa," p. 25.

the ink and paper of the physical object that practitioners hold in their hands. At the same time, it has a cosmic existence, across all the different dimensions. Finally, since its publication coincided with Li's final transmission lectures in China and, as he says, reading it performs the same functions as attending those lectures, it can be said to embody Master Li himself.

Zhuan Falun, Volume II

Since *Zhuan Falun* was published, Li Hongzhi has continued to give talks and write short essays. In the mid-1990s these writings appeared in print collections, although after Falun Gong had established its websites they were generally first published online. The first collection of Li Hongzhi's short pieces was *Zhuan Falun, Volume II*, published in November 1995.[52] The title is misleading, as this volume has neither the status of *Zhuan Falun* itself, nor is it patterned on the original. It contains twenty-seven separate items, the longest being "Teaching the *Fa* on Lantau Island," a lecture Li delivered in Hong Kong in May 1995. "Teaching the *Fa*" is placed first in the collection, but that position does not necessarily indicate that it was written first, as none of the pieces in this collection are dated. *Zhuan Falun, Volume II* has been available in Chinese since it was published, both in print and on the Internet. However, although it was translated into English by 1996, this version was unavailable online for several years and reappeared only in 2008.

One possible reason why *Zhuan Falun, Volume II* was unavailable in English translation for so long may have been the perception that Westerners would find the content more challenging than other Falun Gong books. First, it focuses on specific aspects of Buddhism, or displays attitudes toward Buddhism, that may be unfamiliar to people not brought up in East Asian societies. For instance, Li argues that Buddhist monks who do not succeed in completing their cultivation before they die are often reborn as high-ranking officials as a reward for their hard work in the previous lifetime.[53] Li is also very critical of Zen Buddhism, a position that many Westerners may find strange, as Zen has generally been represented in a positive light across much of the English-speaking world.[54]

52. David Palmer notes that *Zhuan Falun, Volume II* appeared on *Beijing Daily*'s best seller list for April 1996. See Palmer, *Qigong Fever*, p. 249.

53. Li, "Teaching the *Fa* at Lantau Island," p. 3; "Zai Dayushan jiangfa," p. 1.

54. Li Hongzhi, "Zen Buddhism Is Extreme," in *Zhuan Falun, Volume II*, pp. 27–28; "Chanzong shi jiduande," in *Zhuan falun juan er*, pp. 44–46.

In addition, he indicates that some Buddhists and other religious figures are not what they seem.

Taiwan, in particular, now has many renowned monks and lay Buddhists who are actually demons. . . . Human society is terrifying. Many of the well-known, supposed "masters" in India are possessed by giant pythons. Among the *qigong* masters in China, quite a large number are possessed by foxes and weasels, though there are snakes as well. . . . The head of Aum Shinrikyo in Japan is the reincarnation of a ghost from Hell who came to the human world to foment chaos.[55]

Li also ventures to make statements about other religions in this collection. Although he had mentioned Jesus in some lectures delivered earlier than the publication of *Zhuan Falun, Volume II*, in this book he discusses the founder of Christianity in contexts that might surprise many familiar with that faith. Jesus had, he claimed, cultivated only to the same level as Laozi, author of the *Daode jing* (*The Way and Its Power*); and when he spoke of men being made from clay, "it wasn't clay as ordinary people know it. Rather, in higher dimensions all material, including clay, is high-energy matter of a more microcosmic plane."[56] Li also claims that the Crucifixion occurred because Jesus had upset certain deities in the cosmos who believed they had rights over the ultimate destiny of individual humans. When Jesus proclaimed that he had come to save all people, it provoked a conflict with these deities.

Ultimately their disagreements intensified to such an extent that they were reflected in human society. It seemed like it was a conflict in human society and in its intensity it was directed at Jesus. Jesus could not free himself of it, but with one death—being crucified—he dissolved the enmity between them. With his ordinary body of flesh gone, there was no Jesus to make enemies with, and his countless troubles were gone. That is why it's said that Jesus is a martyr for all living things.[57]

55. Li Hongzhi, "The Decline of Mankind and Dangerous Notions," in *Zhuan Falun, Volume II*, pp. 37–38; "Renlei de huapo yu weixian de guannian," in *Zhuan falun juan er*, pp. 62–63. Aum's Sarin gas attack on the Tokyo subway occurred on March 20, 1995, so it would have been fresh in Li's mind.

56. Li Hongzhi, "The Story of Creating Man out of Clay," in *Zhuan Falun, Volume II*, p. 20; "Nitu zaoren de gushi," in *Zhuan falun juan er*, p. 33. On Li's knowledge of Jesus, see Penny, "Master Li Encounters Jesus: Christianity and the Configurations of Falun Gong," in *Flows of Faith: Religious Reach and Community in Asia and the Pacific*, ed. Lenore Manderson, Wendy Smith, and Matt Tomlinson (New York: Springer, 2012).

57. Li Hongzhi, "No Demonstrations When Saving People and Teaching Fa," in *Zhuan Falun, Volume II*, p. 33, amended; "Duren jiangfa buzuo biaoyan," in *Zhuan falun juan er*, pp. 53–54.

Finally, in *Zhuan Falun, Volume II*, Li makes perhaps his most explicit remarks about the current degenerate state of society. While railing against the all-pervasive power of money and its corrupting influence on personal relationships and behavior, Li reflects on the subject of sex.

Television programs, newspapers, magazines, and literary works are full of talk about sexual liberation. People go so far as to commit incest across generational lines, and the irrationality of our times is reflected in the filthy psychological abnormality that is repulsive homosexuality.[58]

In these statements Li reveals himself to be, in Western terms, at the extreme of social conservatism; his opinions would probably be regarded as bizarre and repressive outside, and to a lesser extent inside, China. This reaction may be especially prevalent among Westerners attracted to alternative spiritual movements whose social and sexual politics have tended to allow, or even encourage, the expression of sexual variety, including those that, like Falun Gong, come from East Asia.

Other Writings

In August 1995, just a few months before *Zhuan Falun, Volume II* was published, the first set of Li's occasional lectures appeared under the title *Explaining the Content of Falun Dafa*. This volume is made up of talks Li had given in 1994 and 1995 in Changchun, Beijing, and Guangzhou to the leaders of Falun Gong's regional centers. Also deriving from this period is *Zhuan Falun Fajie*, or *The Law of Zhuan Falun Explained*, which, although published in 1997, consists of Li's answers to practitioners' questions following lectures given in 1993 and 1994 in Changchun, Zhengzhou, Jinan, Yanji, and Guangzhou, as well as a speech he gave at the launch of *Zhuan Falun* in January 1995.

Two sets of Li's shorter writings have been published as volumes 1 and 2 of *Essentials for Further Advancement*. The essays in these collections are

---

58. Li Hongzhi, "Humanity during the Final Kalpa," in *Zhuan Falun, Volume II*, p. 40, amended; "Mojie shi de renlai," in *Zhuan falun juan er*, p. 67. Li evidently has strong feelings about homosexuality. After his 1998 lecture in Switzerland, a practitioner asked, "Why is it that homosexuals are considered evildoers?" He answered, "Let me tell you, if I weren't teaching this *Fa* today, gods' first target of extermination would be homosexuals. It's not me who would exterminate them, but gods. . . . Homosexuals not only transgress the standards that gods gave to mankind, but also violate the moral norms of human society. In particular, the impression it gives children will turn future societies into something demonic" (Li Hongzhi, "Teaching the *Fa* at the Conference in Switzerland" (September 4–5, 1998), online at www.falundafa.org/book/eng/pdf/switzerland1998.pdf, pp. 25–26; "Falun dafa Ruishi fahui jiangfa," pp. 31–32).

dated and appear in chronological order, beginning in late January 1995. Similarly, more collections of lectures, such as *Guiding the Voyage*, which includes four delivered in North America in 2000 and 2001, or single lectures from across the world, complete with their question and answer sessions, continue to appear online or in print. Finally, two volumes of Li's poetry have been published. Known by their Chinese name of *Hong Yin*, translated as *The Grand Verses*, these books contain poems from as early as 1976, although most come from 1993 or later. Written in the traditional Chinese style of five or seven character lines, and therefore appearing to conform to the pattern of the sublime poetry of imperial times, Li's verse does not obey the relevant rules of rhyme or prosody. Were it not by him, it would be of little interest.

The canon of Falun Gong scriptures comprises many volumes, but as most practitioners typically now live far from Li's base in the northeastern United States and create their community online, the movement's websites now form the focus of adherents' attention. Apart from their use as a means of keeping in touch with followers from across the world and receiving direction from the coordinators of Falun Gong activism, these sites have become the library and the archive of Falun Gong. Master Li's works have a privileged position among the texts posted there, but in terms of the sheer volume of words available on them, his scriptures, lectures, and shorter writings only amount to a fraction of the material. In many ways, Falun Gong is now, more than ever, a textual phenomenon. Indeed, as we have seen, *Zhuan Falun* itself functions as a kind of master in textual form, a version of Li Hongzhi himself. In the final section of this chapter, other forms of Master Li will be examined, from his spiritual surrogates who act as if they were Li Hongzhi, to the way practitioners understand his status and being.

Master Li's Great Powers

In *Zhuan Falun*, Li Hongzhi describes the effect he has on some practitioners.

When some people see me they tug at my hand and shake it, and they won't let go. And then when other people see folks shaking hands with me, they get into the act, too. I know what they're up to. Some folks want to shake hands with their teacher, since it makes them happy, while others want to get "information," so after they grab my hand they just won't let go. We're telling you: true cultivation is something you do yourself, and we don't do healing and fitness things here or give you "information" to heal you. We don't talk about that.

The practitioners Li criticizes in this passage clearly regarded him as having potent personal charisma. The people who grasped his hand wanted something from him: "information" (*xinxi*) that was spiritually powerful and could cure diseases.[59] This is misguided, Li insists, as "true cultivation" is something they must do themselves. However, we should not assume because of this that he regards himself as a teacher like any other. This passage continues:

I'll directly remove your health problems for you. At the practice sites they're removed by my Law Bodies, and people who learn the practice on their own by reading the books have my Law Bodies to remove theirs, too. You think your *gong* energy will increase by touching my hand? Are you kidding?[60]

Zhuan Falun makes it clear, then, that Master Li is more than just a teacher. He has the power to cleanse bodies and make them healthy. He can intervene in them directly with the insertion of the *falun*, and as will be described in chapter 6, he alone can convert the white material "virtue," or *de*, into *gong*, the substance that is fundamental for progression in cultivation. In addition, this passage indicates that he has countless emanations, called "Law Bodies," that do his bidding. These emanations are, as we will see, functionally equivalent to Li himself.

According to Li, Law Bodies are spiritual beings that are created when people's cultivation takes them far beyond the normal human condition. These are born in the *dantian* or cinnabar field of such people, a numinous part of the body just below the navel, but they "manifest in other dimensions."[61] Since Law Bodies are emanations of a particular person, they act exactly as that person would, despite each of them being "a complete, independent, and real individual life in its own right." Li says, "When I want to do something, like adjust the bodies of disciples who truly cultivate, I have my Law Bodies do it."[62]

59. In *qigong*, the idea that a small package of "information" could change the nature of a person's body was not uncommon. The usual image used was that of a television with a remote control. When the viewer presses the button to change channels, a small amount of "information" is transferred to the television, but this completely changes the way it functions. I thank Utiraruto Otehode for his assistance in elucidating this point. Later in this section of *Zhuan Falun*, Li refers to other *qigong* masters sending such "information" through the mail to heal people.

60. Li, *Zhuan Falun*, 3/8, pp. 63–64, amended; p. 111.

61. Ibid., 5/6, p. 99; p. 172. Strictly speaking, Li is referring to the lower *dantian*, or cinnabar field, here. See Fabrizio Pregadio's article *"Dantian,"* in *The Encyclopedia of Taoism*, ed. Pregadio (Abingdon, UK: Routledge, 2008), pp. 302–3.

62. Li, *Zhuan Falun*, 5/6, p. 99; p. 172.

"Law Body" (or *fashen* in Chinese) is a clear case of Li's redefinition of orthodox Buddhist terminology—it is the Chinese rendering of the standard East Asian translation of *dharmakāya*, literally the body of the dharma, or Buddhist doctrine. This term is rich with meanings in orthodox Buddhist schools, but given Li's background in China perhaps the primary meaning in his context would have been the Mahayanist doctrine of the Buddha's three bodies: the *dharmakāya*, the *saṃbhogakāya*, and the *nirmāṇakāya*. Donald Lopez describes the doctrine in this way:

[In Mahayanist literature] we find references to the *dharmakāya* as almost a cosmic principle, an ultimate reality in which all buddhas partake through their omniscient minds. After the *dharmakāya* comes the enjoyment body (*saṃbhogakāya*), a fantastic form of a buddha that resides only in the highest pure lands, adorned with thirty-two major and eighty minor physical marks, eternally teaching the Mahāyāna to highly advanced bodhisattvas; the enjoyment body does not appear to ordinary beings. The third body is the emanation body (*nirmāṇakāya*). It is the body that appears in the world to teach the dharma.[63]

Clearly, Li's conception of what a Law Body is varies considerably from orthodox Buddhist tradition. Characteristically, he radically redefines a Buddhist term in a way that gives it a physical presence, in the same manner as he redefined *falun* itself, where the wheel of the Buddhist Law (understood as equivalent to the doctrine itself) became an actual, physical object, albeit one that exists in another dimension.

Li's Law Bodies are truly extraordinary. In different parts of *Zhuan Falun* he claims that they "know your every thought,"[64] "are aware of everything . . . and they can do anything."[65] They are too numerous to count,[66] and protect practitioners until they are sufficiently advanced in cultivation to protect themselves.[67] Unlike "those who transmitted the Way in the past" who apparently only had individual followers, Li has to protect disciples "on a large scale."

I'm telling you that I can do that, because I have countless Law Bodies which have my vast Spiritual Abilities [*shentong*] and Law-Power, and they can display their great

63. Donald S. Lopez Jr., *Buddhism in Practice* (Princeton, NJ: Princeton University Press, 1995), p. 22.

64. Li, *Zhuan Falun*, 2/5, p. 40; p. 71.

65. Ibid., 4/4, p. 85; p. 149.

66. Ibid., 3/1, p. 46; p. 82.

67. Ibid., 3/8, p. 68; p. 119.

Spiritual Abilities and great Law-Power. . . . When you really cultivate on the true path nobody will dare to give you any trouble, and what's more, you have my Law Bodies protecting you, so you won't run into any danger.[68]

On the other hand, practitioners must not transgress the rules of Falun Gong, as Li's Law Bodies will take action against them. This is apparently the case especially with the injunction against healing. If Li's followers try to heal people, "my Law Bodies will take back all of the cultivation things that were put in your body."[69] The same consequences would follow for adherents who charge money for passing on Falun Gong teachings.[70] Law Bodies are not, however, without compassion. If someone has erred, if he corrects his behavior, the Law Bodies will relent, as in this anecdote related by Li:

I have a student who saw my Law Body come one day. He was full of joy—"Teacher's Law Body is here. Teacher, please come in." My Law Body said, "Your room is too messy, and there are too many things here." And then he left. Generally speaking, if there are too many spirits in other dimensions, my Law Bodies will clean them out. But this student's room was full of this awful mess of *qigong* books. He realized it and cleared them out by burning them or selling them. Then my Law Body came back. This is what the student told me.[71]

Essentially, Li's Law Bodies are his surrogates, as in this incident where they defend the supremacy of Falun Gong over ordinary or low-level *qigong*. As versions of Master Li that can be multiplied many times over, the Law Bodies bear comparison with a practice of Daoist adepts that is found as early as the third century, namely "the Way of Body Division." In this practice the adept could produce many copies of himself, each of which was able to act independently. Thus, the fourth-century author Ge Hong, known as Baopuzi, or the "Master who Embraces Simplicity," wrote of his uncle Ge Xuan,

When guests were present there could be one host speaking with the guests in the house, another host greeting guests beside the stream, and still another host making casts with his fishing line, but the guests were unable to distinguish which was the true one.[72]

68. Ibid., p. 67, amended; pp. 116–17. On *shentong*, see chapters 5 and 6.
69. Ibid., 2/5, p. 44; p. 77, 7/4, p. 144; p. 249.
70. Ibid., 3/10, p. 69; p. 121.
71. Ibid., 6/5, p. 124, amended; p. 215.
72. Quoted in James Ware, trans. and ed., *Alchemy, Medicine and Religion in the China of A.D. 320: The Nei P'ien of Ko Hung* (Cambridge, MA: MIT Press, 1966), p. 306.

Li's Law Bodies also directly assist practitioners in the dissemination of Falun Gong. When instructors are "spreading the practice," they can be assured that a Law Body—"and not just one"—is behind every student. If adherents practice together, they gain the advantage of an energy field created by the Law Bodies.

My Law Bodies sit in a circle and there's a cover over the field where we cultivate *gong* energy. On the cover there's a huge *falun* and above it a great Law Body guards the field. . . . A lot of us who have abilities have seen this Falun Dafa field. It's enveloped in red light, the whole thing is red.[73]

Li does not always rely on his Law Bodies to do his work. In some Falun Gong scriptures he appears in his own right as a supremely powerful figure in the spiritual realm. He relates an incident in *Zhuan Falun* that shows him exerting these powers directly, and that also demonstrates Li's belief that the spirit world is ever present. As we will see in the next chapter, Li teaches that the cosmos is full of spiritual entities, from lowly animal spirits that can possess people to the "Buddas, Daos and Gods" of the upper dimensions. The events he narrates took place in Guizhou Province in southwest China. This was not one of the core regions of Falun Gong's early strength in the north and northeast of the country; it is also less developed economically than those regions and is home to many people of non-Chinese ethnicities. It is still considered a kind of backwater, if not a frontier, by many people from the large cities.

Li writes that when he first went to Guizhou to teach, a person arrived during one of his classes who invited him to call on the visitor's own grandmaster. Li was unimpressed and did not accept the invitation, because "this guy carried yin *qi*, it was awful, and his face looked a sickly yellow."[74] Incensed by Li's snub, the local grandmaster started causing trouble, but Li, apparently, fought him off with ease. This grandmaster, Li writes, was actually a snake spirit that had taken over a person's body at the time of his cultivation during the Ming dynasty (1368–1644). When the spirit returned to challenge Li, it changed back into its snake form, so "I caught it in my hand and used an extremely powerful *gong* called Dissolving Gong to melt its lower body into water. Its upper body slithered back to where it came from." Subsequently, another follower of this false grandmaster approached one of Li's Assistants at Falun Gong's Guizhou center, saying that his master wanted to see her.

---

73. Li, *Zhuan Falun*, 3/10, p. 70, amended; p. 124.
74. Ibid., 5/7, p. 104, amended; pp. 180–81.

She entered a pitch black cave and couldn't see anything, except for a shadow that was sitting there, with its eyes emitting green light. When the eyes opened the cave lit up, and when the eyes closed the cave went dark. He said in a local dialect, "Li Hongzhi is coming again. This time none of us will do those things. I was wrong. Li Hongzhi is here to save people." His follower asked him, "Grandmaster, please stand up. What's wrong with your legs?" He replied, "I can't stand anymore. My legs were injured." After he was asked how they got injured, he began to talk about how he made trouble.[75]

Li, it would appear, not only triumphed over an evil snake spirit but also brought the truth to his antagonist: the latter accepted Li's salvific role, confessed his transgressions, and resolved to reform his ways. We should not overlook Li's insistence that the snake spoke "in a local dialect." Stories of powerful and righteous religious masters whose message is not bound by region, who defeat local but powerful spirits that enslave and exploit their followers and demand excessive offerings or sacrifices, are found throughout the religious literature of China.[76] Li's victory over just such an entity in Guizhou, far from the capital, recalls this long tradition and would have powerful resonances for a religiously inclined Chinese audience, elevating his status to that of a supreme and national master who can subdue malevolent local spirits. Unfortunately, the fine resolve of the reformed snake spirit did not last, and he made his way to Beijing to challenge Li: "In 1993 at the Oriental Health Expo he made trouble again. That yokel was always doing terrible things and tried to ruin my transmitting of the Great Law, so I eliminated him completely."[77]

Li Hongzhi therefore presents himself as a highly cultivated person with supreme spiritual powers and with an infinitely large contingent of surrogate beings, his Law Bodies. As we saw at the beginning of this chapter, as early as the first version of his biography some followers were said to wonder whether Li was not also, in fact, a Buddha. As recently as 2005, this uncertainty about Li's real state was not resolved. In answer to a practitioner's question at a lecture in Los Angeles about how they should refer to him, Li sidestepped the question of his Buddhahood, but at the end of his answer he allowed for his followers to continue believing that he has attained that august state, at the very least.

---

75. Ibid.

76. Three classic essays on this topic can be found in Holmes Welch and Anna Seidel, eds., *Facets of Taoism* (New Haven, CT: Yale University Press, 1979): Hisayuki Miyakawa, "Local Cults around Mount Lu at the Time of Sun En's Rebellion," pp. 83–101; Rolf A. Stein, "Religious Taoism and Popular Religion from the Second to the Seventh Centuries," pp. 53–81; and Michel Strickmann, "On the Alchemy of T'ao Hung-Ching," pp. 123–92.

77. Li, *Zhuan Falun*, 5/7, p. 104, amended; pp. 180–81.

I've actually made clear since I first taught the *Fa* that people can address me in what-ever way: you can call me by my name, call me Teacher, call me Master—whatever is fine. Master isn't a stickler for these things. But if you are a true Dafa disciple, you can't address me directly by my name. It doesn't matter if ordinary people call me by my name—they can call me whatever they want. But Dafa disciples should call me "Master," or "Teacher." It's up to you, and you can address each other however you like. But be sure not to address me as "Buddha." That's because whatever the case, Master is teaching the *Fa* with a human body and saving you using a human form, he is manifesting in this world with a human body. A human body cannot be called a Buddha. Calling a human body Buddha blasphemes Buddhas. Some students might think, then: "I know in my heart who you are." Well, that's you knowing in your heart then (audience laughs, applauds), and it's fine for you to call me whatever you want to in your heart. (Teacher laughs)[78]

One set of essays that appeared on Falun Gong websites beginning in 2000 goes further than this by implying the very specific identification of Li Hongzhi with the Maitreya, or future Buddha. The Sakyamuni, or historical Buddha, lived in the first millennium BCE, and Maitreya is considered his successor.[79] In orthodox Buddhism, Maitreya is believed to be in the Tuṣita heaven, awaiting the time when he should descend to earth. For most Buddhists, Maitreya-related hopes centered on either being reborn in the Tuṣita heaven itself, or else being fortunate enough to be alive during Maitreya's time on earth and be present when he expounds the dharma. The advent of Maitreya was generally thought to be far in the future. In Chinese tradition, however, another stream of Maitreya-focused belief arose, namely that instead of Maitreya's advent being distant, it was, in fact, close at hand or had even occurred.[80] The implication that Li Hongzhi is the Maitreya Buddha thus plays directly into this tradition.

The website essays that make this identification concern various traditions of prophecy from around the world. They begin with a discussion of Nostradamus that Li Hongzhi published in June 2000—evidence, perhaps, of his continuing interest in subjects associated with the paranormal and the New Age. In this essay, he claims that one of the quatrains in *Les*

78. Li Hongzhi, "Teaching the *Fa* at the Western U.S. International *Fa* Conference" (February 26, 2005; no PDF), amended; "Meixi guoji fahui jiangfa," in *Falun dafa gedi jiangfa qi*, p. 32.

79. On the Maitreya Buddha, see the collection of essays edited by Alan Sponberg and Helen Hardacre, *Maitreya, the Future Buddha* (Cambridge: Cambridge University Press, 1988).

80. On this model where Maitreya has already arrived, see Jan Nattier's comments on what she calls the "Here/Now" version of Maitreya teachings in her essay "The Meaning of the Maitreya Myth," in Sponberg and Hardacre, *Maitreya, the Future Buddha*, 23–47.

Propheties had predicted the suppression of Falun Gong the year before (this quatrain is unusual in Nostradamus's work in that it gives a specific date, 1999, for his prediction).[81] Li's essay prompted, or more probably encouraged, practitioners worldwide to offer other readings from Nostradamus, as well as from several Chinese and Korean prophetic works, the Mayan and Hopi prophecies, and the biblical book of Revelation. One such reading concerns the alleged writings of Korean scholar and astronomer Nam Sa-go (1509–1571); the text concerned was apparently hidden from the world for 450 years and "reappeared" only in 1986. A "Korean practitioner" finds evidence for Li's true identity in Nam's text: "This sage is the king of all kings in heaven, that is, the Falun Sage King. People will refer to him as Buddha Maitreya when he descends to the world."[82]

Similarly, a practitioner called Rong Fa examines some famously gnomic verses supposedly deriving from the hand of the Ming-dynasty literatus and statesman Liu Bowen (1311–1375) to find prophecies of the appearance of Falun Gong. Like the Korean practitioner, he also identifies Li Hongzhi with the "'*Buddha of the Future*,' who is also called Maitreya."[83] More recently, in 2005 an anonymous Chinese practitioner recalled a short book of prophecies owned by his father, the title of which translates as the *Cloth Bag Sutra*. "Cloth Bag" (*budai* in Chinese) is one of the names for Maitreya. Thus, not surprisingly, this short text is concerned with the return of the future Buddha; moreover, as the author writes, "I was excited to discover that Master Li was the saviour mentioned in my father's prophecies."[84]

Thus, on Falun Gong websites, which are strictly policed by officially authorized editors, various followers of Li Hongzhi seem convinced that he is the Maitreya Buddha. Edward Irons also reports that "Falun Gong practitioners in Hong Kong have confirmed to me their belief that Li is Maitreya Buddha returned to earth." But as he notes, "the acknowledge-

81. Li Hongzhi, "In Reference to a Prophecy" (June 28, 2000), in *Essentials for Further Advancement, II*, p. 14; "Yuyan cankao," in *Falun dafa jingjin yaozhi er*, pp. 19–20.

82. A Korean Practitioner, "Letter from a Practitioner: Reflections after Reading 'A Reference for Prophecies'" (September 7, 2000), online at www.clearwisdom.net/emh/articles/2000/9/8/8293 .html, amended; "Hanguo zhuming yuyan shuji 'Ge An yilu' de qishi," www.minghui.org/mh/ articles/2000/9/7/2274.html.

83. Rong Fa, "Prophecies of Liu Chi in China's Ming Dynasty" (October 24, 2000), online at clearwisdom.net/html/articles/2000/11/3/6308.html; "Du Liu Bowen yuyan yougan," www.ming-hui.org/gb/0001/Oct/26/liubowen_yuyan_102600_shishi.html.

84. A Falun Dafa Practitioner from China, "My Father's Cloth-Bag Prophesy Book" (July 25, 2005), online at www.clearwisdom.net/emh/articles/2005/8/24/64214.html, amended; "'Budaijing' he bei zhonggong haisi de fuqin," www.minghui.org/mh/articles/2005/7/30/107213.html. On the essays about prophecy, see Penny, "Falun Gong, Prophecy and Apocalypse."

ment of Li as Maitreya is not spelled out clearly in Falun Gong textual materials."[85] However, even if this identification is not regarded as the official teaching of Falun Gong, it is clear that Master Li himself teaches that his powers in the spiritual realm are supreme, that his Law Bodies can accomplish his every wish, and that, as we will see in the next chapter, he brooks no challenges from evil beings in the cosmos.

Yet for most of Li Hongzhi's followers since 1995, in China and beyond, direct contact with their Master has been rare, and displays of his powers have not been made known to Falun Gong adherents, or society, at large. He makes few public appearances, and those are only for set-piece speeches at selected Experience Sharing Meetings, the highly choreographed conferences for practitioners, or other functions open only to a select few. Until 2009, the number of lectures he gave, all of which were delivered in North America, had diminished year by year: from a high of nine in 2003, he gave six lectures in 2004, five in 2005, three in 2006, two in 2007, and only one in 2008. In 2009, however, he gave five, with another two in 2010. Of course, since 1999 he has not been able to return to China. Thus, the most direct link practitioners inside as well as outside his homeland have with Li is through his books and lectures.

––––––––

In this chapter we have seen how Master Li is more than just a teacher; he is a supreme spiritual being with awesome powers and immense compassion. His scripture, moreover, embodies his teachings in such a way that it becomes a kind of master in textual form. For some practitioners, Li is so exalted that they consider him the Maitreya Buddha returned to earth. This identification points to a role beyond the time and place of Falun Gong's emergence in China or its current position in exile. Indeed, it locates Master Li in a position of importance in cosmic history and across the universe. Within this broadest of frameworks, the work of practitioners takes on new meanings, and the reasons why adherents to Falun Gong cultivate according to Li's teachings are revealed. Consequently, the next chapter examines Li's teachings on history, the cosmos, and the constitution of the human body.

85. Edward Irons, "Falun Gong and the Sectarian Religion Paradigm," *Nova Religio* 6, no. 2 (April 2003): 244–62; quotation is from p. 253.

FOUR

Spiritual Anatomy, Cosmos, and History

For followers of any religion, the tradition to which they belong takes two forms. In a day-to-day sense, it demands adherence to codes of law or behavior, prescribing certain actions and forbidding others. Some of these instructions might relate to how believers organize their financial affairs, what and how they eat, or how they interact with different classes of people. Some forms of religion might demand particular kinds of worship, the observance of specific holy times or seasons, or the practice of certain spiritual exercises. These considerations are often the ones that are uppermost in the minds of religiously active people, as they affect the way their lives are organized and experienced hour by hour.

However, behind these embodied forms of religion—and generally less pressing for ordinary believers throughout their waking hours—lie frameworks of understanding based on the way that their religion answers fundamental questions about how the world works and how humanity fits into it. These questions will usually include that most central issue for us across time and cultures: what happens to us when we die? This question is itself intertwined with another: what part of us, if any, survives death, and how does this entity relate to us during life? Any religion will also, typically, address questions about how the universe is arranged: Is there a heaven? Is there a hell? Are there multiple heavens and hells? Where are they in relation to this earth? How do we travel there? Depending on their view of time, believers might also posit a historical role for their faith: Does this religion bring a new revelation? Does its appearance change history? How does its founder relate to religious figures of the past? Perhaps the most fundamental answer any particular religion must provide is to the question, why should anyone believe and follow it?

Falun Gong is no different from any other religion in providing instructions for everyday life as well as assaying answers to the fundamental questions outlined above. Although the way Li Hongzhi understands the meanings of cultivation, practice, and morality is central to how Falun Gong practitioners choose to live their lives, it is necessary first to outline certain crucial conceptions that underpin those ideas. Thus, this chapter begins with a consideration of Li's basic notions concerning the human body and how it is constituted, addressing, initially, his ideas on reincarnation. It continues by outlining Falun Gong teachings on what I have called "spiritual anatomy," that is, how human existence is understood beyond the corporeal. The next part discusses Li's teachings on the nature of the cosmos, especially its multidimensional character and the various nonhuman beings that populate it. Having laid out the basic religious conceptions underlying his teachings, we are in a position to address Li's sense of the purpose of Falun Gong. Consequently, the last part of this chapter discusses his ideas of cosmic history and the role of both Falun Gong—and himself—in them.

Reincarnation

Li Hongzhi teaches that people are reborn after death, living successive lives in a cycle broken only by the ultimate achievement of Consummation, or the punishment of annihilation. In the West, rebirth is generally thought of as a Buddhist or Hindu doctrine, and indeed, Li uses specifically Buddhist vocabulary to describe it. However, as is often the case in Falun Gong, the meanings he attaches to these terms often differ significantly from standard Buddhist definitions. Perhaps surprisingly, such a fundamental feature of Falun Gong doctrine as reincarnation is rarely mentioned in Li's early books, appearing, for instance, only once in *Zhuan Falun*, where he simply remarks that if a person is not successful in his or her cultivation, "what's in store for you is continued reincarnation and destruction."[1] The likely explanation for this apparent lapse is that

1. Li, *Zhuan Falun* 3/5, p. 54; p. 96.

these texts were written with a specifically Chinese audience in mind, and for most Chinese people without a serious commitment to a religion in which a particular doctrinal position is prescribed—say, Christianity or Islam—reincarnation would be accepted as a default position. It would not, therefore, be something that Li felt he had to elaborate on, or to assert as true.

In "Practicing Cultivation after Retirement," a short essay that appeared not long after *Zhuan Falun* was published, Li urges practitioners to grasp the opportunity to maintain their cultivation even though they were busy in their work. "Once you miss the opportunity," he warns, "when will you be able to get a human body again in the sixfold path of reincarnation?"[2] Two elements of this sentence echo Buddhist doctrine. The first is the understanding that being born into human form is a rare and precious event in a being's history of births and rebirths, while the second is the use of the concept "the sixfold path of reincarnation." A widely circulated Buddhist story relates that the chances of being born human are the same as those of a lone, one-eyed turtle in the ocean coming to the surface to breathe so that its head passes exactly through the hole in the center of a single ox's yoke that happens to be floating nearby. Although Li does not refer specifically to this story, similar ideas undoubtedly lie behind his insistence that practitioners make use of the human form they possess in this lifetime; he noted in a lecture given in the United States in 1997 that "it takes several hundred or a thousand years to reincarnate into a human being once."[3]

"The sixfold path of reincarnation," in Chinese simply the "six paths" (*liudao*), refers to the six possible routes of rebirth. In Buddhism, these are understood to be heavenly beings or *deva*s, humans, demigods or *asura*s, animals, hungry ghosts, and hell beings. The category into which any sentient being is reborn is dependent on his or her karma, where rebirth as a heavenly being, human, or demigod is positive, but returning as an animal, hungry ghost, or hell being is negative. Li departs from this enumeration when he discusses the six categories of beings. When asked by a practitioner at a lecture in Singapore in 1998 what the six paths are, he first mentioned the paths of demigods, animals, humans, and heaven—the first four of the traditional enumeration of the six—and then listed "humans, animals, substances, plants, and living beings in

---

2. Li Hongzhi, "Practicing Cultivation after Retirement" (October 11, 1995), in *Essentials for Further Advancement*, p. 12; "Tuixiu zai lian," in *Falun dafa jingjin yaozhi*, p. 19.

3. Li, "Teaching the *Fa* in New York City," p. 7; "Niuyue fahui jiangfa," p. 16.

other dimensions within the Three Realms."[4] If we can assume that the beings who live in other dimensions are the heavenly beings and demigods, it would appear that the remaining four of Li's six paths must be humans, animals, plants, and substances. This also appears to be what Li meant when, in his lecture in Sydney in 1996, he said that "a human life can be reincarnated and [in addition to the possibility of rebirth as a human could] become an animal, a physical substance, a plant, a being of a high-level dimension, or a being of a low-level dimension."[5] Thus, Li's six paths appear to include two categories—plants and substances—that are not typically found in Buddhism.

The discussion in Buddhism about whether plants have sentience goes back to the early stages of its development, although it is not a generally accepted belief across the contemporary Buddhist world.[6] As we have seen, however, Li does appear to subscribe to this belief; but rather than citing the sutras, his authority is the work of the contemporary authors Peter Tompkins and Christopher Bird. Whatever may have influenced his ideas, Li is explicit in his assertion that people can be reborn as plants or may have been plants in a previous life. In his 1998 lecture in Frankfurt, he referred to the possibility of reincarnating as a tree, and to some people who "knew what kind of plant they had reincarnated from."[7] On the other hand, the sentience of substances is not, as far as I am aware, ever argued in Buddhism. Li does not often say which particular substances take part in the cycle of death and rebirth; yet in his talk to Assistants in Changchun from September 1994, he raised one possibility in a discussion about practitioners making the best use of their present life as a human.

If you reincarnate as an animal, it might take hundreds or thousands of years before you obtain a human body again. If you reincarnate as a rock, you won't get out of it until it weathers away, and that may be ten thousand years.[8]

4. Li, "Teaching the *Fa* at the Conference in Singapore," p. 12, amended; "Falun dafa Xinjiapo fahui jiangfa," p. 28.

5. Li Hongzhi, "Lecture in Sydney" (August 3, 1996), www.falundafa.org/book/eng/pdf/sydney .pdf, p. 22; "Falun dafa Xini fahui jiangfa," p. 55.

6. See, for instance, Lambert Schmithausen, *The Problem of the Sentience of Plants in Earliest Buddhism* (Tokyo: International Institute for Buddhist Studies, 1999); Ellison Banks Findly, "Borderline Beings: Plant Possibilities in Early Buddhism," *Journal of the American Oriental Society*, 122, no. 2 (April/June 2002): 252–63; T. H. Barrett, "Devil's Valley to Omega Point: Reflections on the Emergence of a Theme from the No," in *The Buddhist Forum*, vol. 2, ed. T. Skorupski (London: SOAS, 1991), pp. 1–12.

7. Li Hongzhi, "Teaching the *Fa* at the Conference in Europe" (May 30–31, 1998), online at www .falundafa.org/book/eng/pdf/europe1998a.pdf, p. 48; "Falun dafa Ouzhou fahui jiangfa," p. 115.

8. Li, "Explaining the *Fa* for Falun Dafa Assistants in Changchun," p. 18, amended; "Wei Changchun falun dafa fudaoyuan jiangfa," p. 28.

Li Hongzhi's teachings on reincarnation might give the impression that humans (and the other five categories of beings) have control over their destiny, if only by adjusting their behavior to improve their karmic situation. Clearly this must be so; otherwise there would be no point to becoming one of Li's adherents and following the path of cultivation. On the other hand, as noted earlier, Li also teaches that the adoption of Falun Gong by practitioners was predestined, and that more basic elements in human life are also determined before birth. Thus, Li maintained in 1998 that "a person's lifespan is predetermined. When he reaches a certain time he's supposed to die and then be reborn. The person over there is already pregnant, waiting for him to reincarnate, waiting for him to be born."[9] At the same time, it would appear that Li believes that between their death and rebirth, some people can influence their destination in the next life. Thus, parents who follow Falun Gong may find that their children actually chose to be born into a practitioner's family, the better to pursue cultivation in their next life.[10]

Indeed, Li's view on the immutability of human destiny is strong. In 1997, a practitioner at a lecture Li gave in New York asked whether abortion was considered killing. Li strongly agreed with the contention but expanded on the situation of the aborted fetuses in a way that, while ghoulish, also reveals his views on the predestined nature of human life span.

We've discovered that in the space surrounding maternity hospitals there are many babies with nowhere to go—they're missing body parts, or have complete bodies, but they're all lives of immature babies. Had such a life reincarnated, he might have had a future, he might have lived a number of years, and then been reincarnated again. But you kill him before he's even born. Then he has to struggle painfully for many long years—that little life all by itself, it's so sad! He has to wait until all of the years allotted to him by heaven are over, and only then can he be reborn.[11]

When Li referred to an allotted life span in this passage, he perhaps unconsciously echoed a belief that is deeply rooted in Chinese history and was certainly present centuries before Buddhism arrived there almost

9. Li, "Teaching the *Fa* at the Conference in Europe," p. 37; "Falun dafa Ouzhou fahui jiangfa," p. 89.

10. Li Hongzhi, "Teaching the *Fa* at the *Fa* Conference in Australia" (May 2–3, 1999), online at www.falundafa.org/book/eng/pdf/australia1999.pdf, p. 36; "Falun dafa Aodaliya fahui jiangfa," p. 78.

11. Li Hongzhi, "Teaching the *Fa* at a New York Meeting" (March 22, 1997), in *Lectures in the United States*, p. 48, amended; "Niuyue zuotanhui jiangfa," in *Falun dafa Meiguo fahui jiangfa*, p. 101.

two millennia ago.[12] This belief holds that at birth, each person has a fated length of life, and while a man or woman could suffer a premature death through such causes as war, violence, or execution, living beyond his or her allotted span is possible only through the rigorous application of particular forms of biospiritual cultivation. People could lose days, weeks, or years of their lives through committing a range of transgressions (and there were widely distributed books that told them which crime incurred which penalty), but in Li's view, someone clearly needed to be born before they could be reborn. If someone died before birth, that person had to live out his allotted span in a nether world before he could pass on to his next life.

Spiritual Anatomy

A perplexing question for followers of Buddhism has always been, exactly what part of them is it that gets reborn? Doctrinally, one's personality is as impermanent as any other element in the cosmos, dissolving upon death just as the body itself decays into its constituent parts; there is no conscious "I" that passes from life to life. Instead, each new birth is generated through the implacable, impersonal workings of karma, and it is the "karmic load" that is passed on. A new fire can be started from a flying spark, a Buddhist explanation runs, and a third can begin from an ember of the second. Each fire is undeniably different but is causally bound to the one before it; in the same way, each life is caused by its predecessor, but is itself distinct.

In Falun Gong, however, an unchanging and immortal element survives into the new life: the *yuanshen*, which can be rendered literally as "the original spirit." Two other main terms are related to *yuanshen* in Li's writings: *zhu yuanshen* and *fu yuanshen*. *Zhu* and *fu* form a common pair of prefixes in Chinese usage and mean, respectively, "principal" and "subordinate"—or, in the case of organizations, "the one in charge" and "the deputy." Thus, *zhu yuanshen* might be rendered "the chief original spirit," and *fu yuanshen* "the deputy original spirit." As different versions of *Zhuan Falun* and other writings by Li Hongzhi have very different translations of these terms, it is less confusing in this case to adopt these literal renderings

---

12. A useful collection of essays on the ideas of fate and life span in China is Christopher Lupke, ed., *The Magnitude of Ming: Command, Allotment, and Fate in Chinese Culture* (Honolulu: University of Hawai'i Press, 2005).

of them in the discussion that follows. Quotations from official translations have been altered accordingly to maintain consistency.[13]

The original spirit, Li repeats throughout *Zhuan Falun*, "does not perish."[14] It is that element of all sentient beings which survives death and is
reborn. In one place in that scripture, however, Li says that "the chief original spirit is in charge of the body and has the last word. . . . When his life
comes to a close his deputy original spirit leaves and they go their separate
ways."[15] From this we can deduce that a person's chief original spirit and
the deputy original spirit do not pass on to the next life together. Since, as
we will see below, Li regards Falun Gong as special because it cultivates the
chief original spirit, it would appear that the chief original spirit is that part
of us which is reborn. Thus, it follows that when Li speaks of the "original
spirit"—*yuanshen*—and of the "chief original spirit"—*zhu yuanshen*—he
means the same thing.[16] In general, when he is discussing the characteristics of the original spirit by itself he uses the term *yuanshen*; yet when he is
discussing how it differs from the deputy original spirit—*fu yuanshen*—he
uses "chief original spirit"—*zhu yuanshen*—to make the distinction clear.

In addition to surviving death, the original spirit is the fundamental
constituent of humanity. As Li says,

> If someone's body doesn't have its original spirit—if he doesn't have his temperament,
> disposition, or characteristics, if he doesn't have these kinds of things—it's just a lump
> of flesh, not a complete human being with its own personal character.[17]

13. The translations of the relevant terms in the 1998, 2000, and 2003 versions of *Zhuan Falun*
are as follows:

	Literal translation	1998	2000	2003
yuanshen	original spirit	true spirit	primordial spirit	soul
zhu yuanshen	chief original spirit	chief spirit	main spirit	master soul
fu yuanshen	deputy original spirit	assistant spirit	assistant spirit	subordinate soul
zhu yishi	chief consciousness	main consciousness	main consciousness	master consciousness
fu yishi	deputy consciousness	paraconsciousness	assistant consciousness	subordinate consciousness

14. See, for example, Li, *Zhuan Falun* 1/6, p. 15; p. 26, 2/3, p. 34; p. 60, 3/8, p. 66 ; p. 115, 4/2,
p. 73; p. 128, 6/2, p. 112; p. 195, 9/3, p. 181; p. 312.

15. Ibid., 8/4, p. 159; p. 274.

16. The position I have taken here is an attempt to clarify an ambiguity in Li's writings. The
2000 and 2003 translations of *Zhuan Falun* understand the relationship between the *yuanshen*, the
zhu yuanshen, and the *fu yuanshen* differently. In the earlier version, the *yuanshen* is considered to be
divided into two separate parts: the *zhu yuanshen* and *fu yuanshen*, and a glossary entry stating this
explicitly is provided. The 2003 version, however, implicitly accepts the position that the *yuanshen*
and the *zhu yuanshen* are different terms for the same thing.

17. Li, *Zhuan Falun* 9/2, p. 174, amended; p. 299.

The original spirit is also what makes people different from one another. Moreover, Li says that "since an individual's true life is the original spirit, only the mother who gave birth to your original spirit is your true mother."[18] Nonetheless, it need not be the same gender as the body of the person it inhabits: men can have a female original spirit and vice versa.[19]

Li explains in his teachings that the original spirit is usually located in the center of the brain in a region known in Daoism as the Upper Cinnabar Field, located near the pineal gland (to be discussed in chapter 6; it is opposed to the Lower Cinnabar Field in the abdomen, mentioned in chapter 3). Yet the original spirit has the ability to move about the body. It is also that element of each of us which thinks. These two features of the original spirit—its location and its thinking ability—are linked. Li notes that in China, the organ of thought was traditionally held to be the heart, but he also claims that people today sometimes sense that their stomach, calf, or heel is thinking. These intuitions, he says, are actually founded in reality, as in such cases the original spirit is transporting itself to different parts of its host and doing its thinking from there. The function of the brain, he maintains, is only to process the thoughts of the original spirit (which come in "a type of cosmic 'information,' representing a certain meaning") into language, gesture, or other body movements.[20]

Apart from moving around inside the body, the original spirit can also journey beyond it. In chapter 3, we saw that Li was familiar with a popular Buddhist tract called *Travelogue of the Western Paradise*. By Li's account, in the *Travelogue* it is actually the original spirit of a monk that travels to the Paradise of Ultimate Bliss while in meditation.[21] He also tells the story of a practitioner whose original spirit leaves his body during the Falun Gong sitting meditation. It sees "many levels of heaven" but can go no further, as the original spirit apparently travels by sitting on the practitioner's *gong* column, a pillar of energy produced during cultivation that grows as the practitioner progresses, as we will see in chapter 6.[22] Finally, the original spirit is the means by which the results of good and bad actions are passed from life to life. The *gong* energy created through cultivation in one life is attached to the original spirit as it finds a new body at rebirth, but equally, the virtue (*de*) and karma accrued in one life also follow it into the next.[23]

18. Ibid., 6/3, p. 118, amended; p. 205.
19. Ibid., 3/5, p. 56; p. 98.
20. Ibid., 9/2, p. 174; p. 300. On "information," see chapter 3, note 59 of the present text.
21. Ibid., 1/2, p. 6; p. 11.
22. Ibid., 2/4, p. 39; p. 70.
23. See, for instance, ibid., 4/1, p. 73; p. 127, 9/3, p. 181; p. 312, 9/5, p. 185; p. 318.

The term *yuanshen* originated in Daoism, where it has the sense of the "true self" that "resides in emptiness, free from the contents of the discursive mind."[24] Clearly, Li Hongzhi is not relying on this Daoist meaning when he deploys it in Falun Gong. Another possible source for Li's conception is indicated by the translation "soul" given in some English-language Falun Gong texts, including the 2003 translation of *Zhuan Falun*. This rendering invites comparison with its counterpart in Christianity, although it should be noted that the Chinese word for the Christian soul is *linghun* rather than *yuanshen*. They are alike in that both constitute that part of our being which survives death and suffers, or enjoys, the results of our behavior in this life. Adding to this impression is Li's repeated use of a phrase that translates as "the original spirit does not perish." The Chinese version—"yuanshen bu mie"—strongly echoes another phrase that had been in circulation in Chinese Christian circles far earlier, namely "linghun bu mie," which translates as "the (Christian) soul does not perish."

In Li's discussions of the chief original spirit, also known as the original spirit, and the deputy original spirit as a pair, he insists that they are both part of each person. The chief original spirit is that part of us which has awareness of itself, which controls what we do in a conscious state. "The chief original spirit we talk about here," Li says, "refers to one's thinking self."[25] We have seen that morally speaking, he considers human society to be on an inexorable downward spiral. It is not surprising, therefore, that he generally regards chief original spirits as rather disappointing. They are, he says, "extremely deluded."[26] Deputy original spirits, on the other hand, are often much more advanced. Indeed, Li says that the deputy original spirit "usually comes from a higher level than his chief original spirit," sometimes from a "really high" level, and typically attempts to make the chief original spirit follow the path of righteous cultivation.[27] It is vital for the chief original spirit to follow the straight and narrow, as in Falun Gong it is this spirit that is cultivated. Li insists on this point, as well as that cultivation should occur when practitioners are fully conscious of what they are doing. Distinguishing Falun Gong from other forms of *qigong* circulating in the early and mid-1990s, Li says, "Our practice isn't like the typical *qigong* practice, where people get all

24. Poul Andersen, "Taiyi," and Monica Esposito, "Gushen," in Pregadio, *The Encyclopedia of Taoism*, pp. 958 and 466.

25. Li, *Zhuan Falun* 8/4, p. 157, amended; p. 271.

26. Ibid.

27. Ibid., 3/5, p. 56; p. 99.

in a daze, they get absentminded and distracted, and they get obsessed." He continues,

In our practice you have to cultivate yourself with full awareness. . . . We have said that your chief consciousness [i.e. chief original spirit; see below] has to be aware, and that's because this practice cultivates your own self. You have to improve yourself in full awareness. We also have a meditation [that is, *jinggong*, literally a "practice of stillness"]. And how do we practice meditation? As a rule, we say that no matter how deep your concentration gets, you must know that you're practicing here. It is absolutely forbidden when you enter that state to become unaware of where you are.[28]

Li goes so far as to say that Falun Gong is the only cultivation method that cultivates the chief original spirit. All others, he claims, cultivate the deputy original spirit.[29]

This point becomes crucial when Li Hongzhi considers the position of people who are mentally ill. Several times in his writings and lectures he explicitly states that people who have a "mental disorder" are not allowed to attend his classes. This intolerance stems from his understanding that mental illness is not caused by any "injuries or pathogens"; rather, the chief original spirit of people so afflicted is weak and has no control over their bodies. In this condition, he says, the body may be possessed by external spirits or controlled by karma. Falun Gong cultivation relies on a person's consciousness having full control over his body. "If his chief original spirit isn't taking control," Li asks rhetorically, "to whom is Dafa given?"[30]

In some ways, the relationship between the chief original spirit and the deputy original spirit appears to parallel that between the human mind subject to temptation and the conscience. Li describes this relationship in *Zhuan Falun*.

When people think about some issue or do things in their daily lives, it's their chief original spirit that has the last word. What the deputy original spirit mainly does is restrain the chief original spirit so that he does as few bad things as possible. But when the chief original spirit is very attached to a course of action, the deputy original spirit

---

28. Ibid., 8/6, pp. 168–69, amended; pp. 290–92.

29. Li, "Teaching the *Fa* at the *Fa* Conference in Australia," p. 23; "Falun dafa Aodaliya fahui jiangfa," pp. 50–51.

30. Li Hongzhi, "Lecture at the First Conference in North America" (March 29–30, 1998), online at www.falundafa.org/book/eng/pdf/north_america.pdf, p. 48; "Falun dafa beimei shoujie fahui jiangfa," p. 94. See also *Zhuan Falun* 6/1, p. 106; p. 183; Li, "Lecture in Sydney," pp. 33–34; "Falun dafa Xini fahui jiangfa," pp. 79–80.

is powerless. The deputy original spirit isn't deluded by the ordinary society, while the chief original spirit succumbs easily to those delusions.[31]

Li also refers to the chief original spirit as the "chief consciousness" (*zhu yishi*) and the deputy original spirit is called the "deputy consciousness" (*fu yishi*).[32] *Yishi* in Chinese carries all the connotations of the word *consciousness* in English with the broad meaning of "mentality," but also the connections present in specific phrases such as "false consciousness" and "national consciousness." It is also possible that Li uses the word *yishi* because of its Buddhist connotations, specifically derived from the Yogācāra, or "Consciousness-Only," school.[33] Yogacara Buddhism holds that there are eight varieties of Consciousness. The first five relate to each of the five senses. The sixth, *yishi* in Chinese, is that form of consciousness which involves thought, intention, emotion, and judgment. These are clearly characteristics of the chief consciousness in Falun Gong as Li Hongzhi describes it.

Apart from its Buddhist echoes, Li's use of "consciousness" probably adds to the sense among many of his followers that his teachings are cognizant of the modern world, and modern psychology in particular. Thus, in *Zhuan Falun*, Li aligns the deputy consciousness (that is, the deputy original spirit) with the subconscious.

Now as for the subconscious that people talk about, that's pretty easy for us to explain. If you go by how a subconscious state is defined, it usually refers to a person being muddleheaded while doing something. People will often say that he did that thing unconsciously, or not intentionally. The subconscious is exactly the same as the deputy consciousness that we talk about.[34]

The deputy original spirit, in Li's view, sometimes takes control of a person in the same way that the subconscious is considered in popular psychology to rise occasionally to the surface when the conscious mind is somehow distracted or impaired. Thus, as Li says, "when one's chief consciousness relaxes and stops controlling the brain," the deputy consciousness can take over. Actions taken under these circumstances are

31. Li, *Zhuan Falun* 3/5, p. 56, amended; p. 99.

32. Ibid., p. 56; p. 98.

33. On Yogacara Buddhism, see Dan Lusthaus, "What Is and Isn't Yogācāra," online at www.acmuller.net/yogacara/articles/intro-uni.htm.

34. Li, *Zhuan Falun* 9/2, p. 176; p. 303. It should be noted that Li shows no particular knowledge of Freud's work in his writings. His use of concepts such as the subconscious derives from a more popular level of knowledge.

commonly thought of as "unconscious" behavior, and he maintains that such actions often turn out for the best, even though we are not aware of what is happening. Artistic inspiration, in his understanding, is also explained by the deputy consciousness breaking through when the chief consciousness is somehow temporarily impaired.[35] It can also take over when we are drunk. To illustrate this point, Li refers to the reputation of some famously drunken Daoist masters from Chinese history. Though often thought to be expressing their disregard for conventional society and its mores, Li reveals that each was actually putting his chief original spirit to sleep so he could concentrate on cultivating his deputy original spirit.[36] Since it is the goal of Falun Gong practitioners to cultivate the chief original spirit in a clear state, they should have no interest in putting it to sleep. Thus, drinking alcoholic beverages is banned in Li Hongzhi's teachings.

In this discussion, I have referred to a person's chief original spirit or chief consciousness and his or her deputy original spirit or deputy consciousness as if they were singular. While it is true that in Li Hongzhi's spiritual anatomy, each person has only one chief original spirit, apparently he or she can have "one, two, three, four or even five" deputy original spirits. In addition, and like the chief original spirit, the deputy original spirit need not be the same gender as the body of the person it is a part of, but it "shares the same name as you, for it is part of your body." Indeed, "he was born together with you from your mother's womb."[37] However, each Falun Gong practitioner cultivates his or her chief original spirit, not his or her deputy original spirit. The chief original spirit constitutes the real you, whereas the deputy original spirit or spirits apparently do not.

As for what your deputy original spirit does, you really have no clue. He was born at the same time as you, has the same name, controls the same body, and looks the same as you, but strictly speaking, though, he's not you.[38]

Since the deputy original spirit is generally more advanced than the chief original spirit, it is located in a different and higher dimension. Nonetheless, Li says that "what your deputy consciousness knows is still really limited"; it can only know about its own dimension and has no access

35. Ibid., p. 177; pp. 304–5.
36. Ibid., 7/2, p. 139; pp. 240–41.
37. Ibid., 3/5, p. 56; p. 99.
38. Ibid., 8/4, p. 157; p. 271.

to, or knowledge of, the totality of the cosmos.[39] It is to Li Hongzhi's teachings on the nature of the multidimensional cosmos that we will now turn.

The Nature of the Cosmos

Li Hongzhi's understanding of the cosmos is central to his teachings, as it underpins the core moral injunctions of Falun Gong. For Li, as he often repeats in *Zhuan Falun*, the special characteristic or particular nature of the cosmos is the moral triumvirate of *zhen* (truth), *shan* (compassion), and *ren* (forbearance). He does not mean this metaphorically; for him *zhen*, *shan*, and *ren* are the basic organizing principles of all things. "Air particles, stone, wood, soil, steel, the human body—all matter has this nature," he says.[40] As a result, it is embedded in the very essence of everything in the universe that they adhere to the principles of truth, compassion, and forbearance. Thus, as he says in the revised edition of *Falun Gong,*

A complete human being is composed of his flesh and his temperament. The cosmos is the same. Apart from its material nature, it also has the properties of Truth, Compassion and Forbearance. These properties exist in every particle of air.[41]

It follows, then, that the way people are organized should follow the same principles. Human society in general should adhere to them; and, Li says later in this passage, alignment with the cosmic principles he has identified will bring reward, whereas departing from them will bring punishment. Unfortunately, many people lost their moral bearings as they increasingly failed to abide by the dictates of the universe—a consequence, Li observes, of the period of reform in China during the 1980s and 1990s when people have "been forced to ride the wave of the commodity economy."[42] In addition, in Falun Gong cultivation adherence to the code of truth, compassion, and forbearance is not just regarded as the right and responsible course of action for practitioners; it is an essential part of the cultivation process. Lapsing from it will render any other efforts in cultivation worthless. These principles are not defined for Li

39. Ibid., 9/2, p. 178; p. 306.
40. Ibid., 1/3, p. 7; p. 12.
41. Li, *Falun Gong* 3/1, p. 28, amended; p. 50.
42. Li, *Zhuan Falun* 9/2, p. 175, amended; p. 301.

by culture or history: "It doesn't matter how mankind's moral standard changes," he says. "The nature of the cosmos *doesn't* change, and *it* is the only standard for determining who's good and who's bad. So to be a cultivator you have to take the nature of the cosmos as your guide for improving yourself."[43]

Li's teachings on the creation of life make the fundamental role of truth, compassion, and forbearance clear. For him, life is produced through the interaction of "many types" of matter in the universe, although he does not specify which ones. "What this means," he says, "is that a person's earliest life originates in the cosmos." Since the entirety of existence is fundamentally structured by this moral triumvirate, "when a person is born he has the same nature as the cosmos."[44] In this context we should note that Li does not follow the Buddhist understanding of the origin of human lives, in which it is fundamental that every event has a cause, and that each cause is itself an event with its own cause, in infinite regression. Any given human life is therefore considered in Buddhism as just one event in the cosmic chain of causality, with no moment of creation.

Before moving on to discuss where humans find themselves in the cosmos and what this means for the purpose of our lives, we must first investigate Li Hongzhi's teachings on the physical structure of the universe. For him, the universe is composed of many "dimensions," as all translations of *Zhuan Falun* translate the relevant Chinese word *kongjian*. This is a standard term in the People's Republic of China for "space" and occurs in phrases such as "the space age" or "the curvature of space." Exactly what Li means by a multidimensional universe is somewhat obscure, but it is possible to trace out some basic ideas from his writings. First, and most obviously, people in the dimension in which we exist are normally unable to see into other dimensions, but those people whose Celestial Eyes have been opened to a high level are able to see beyond it. Second, some dimensions "exist at the same time and in the same place."[45] Third, the rate at which time passes varies in different dimensions: in *Zhuan Falun* Li relates that in one particular dimension, two of our hours take a year to pass there.[46] In this he echoes a long-standing trope in Chinese literature wherein the speed at which time passes varies in different realms. In stories dating back to before the Tang dynasty, a

43. Ibid., 1/3, p. 8; p. 13.
44. Ibid., 1/1, p. 2; p. 4.
45. Ibid., 2/1, p. 30; p. 54.
46. Ibid., 3/7, p. 63; p. 109.

character typically ventures to another world (often in a dream) where he might spend years, only to realize upon his return that he has been away for just a few hours—or, in reverse, while he perceives that he has only been gone a short time, whole generations have passed.[47] Finally, colors manifest differently: the red and gold of the *falun* symbol itself are seen as green and purple in another dimension.[48]

Another way of trying to define what Li Hongzhi means by these "dimensions" might be to examine some specific words and phrases that he does *not* use to describe them. Clearly, Li does not mean "dimension" in the mathematical sense (for example, "the third dimension"), as in Chinese this is *weishu*. Indeed, when his translators employ the term *dimension*, they appear to be referring to its use in popular narratives in which travelers in space time move from "our dimension" into "another dimension." If this approaches Li's meaning, then ideas such as "parallel" or "alternate" universes would appear to be a more explicit way of denoting the phenomenon he describes. However, "parallel universe" is known in Chinese through science fiction, where it has the standard rendering of *pingxing yuzhou*, a direct translation. Thus, if Li had wanted to use *parallel universe* or *dimension* (in either the strict mathematical or looser literary sense), he had standard terms available for him to use. Yet lending credence to the theory that Li's idea of a multidimensional universe resembles the "parallel universe" model from science fiction is his observation in *Zhuan Falun* that "flying saucers from outer space can just go and travel in other dimensions . . . they come and go in the blink of an eye, and it's so fast nobody can explain it."[49]

Perhaps the most striking assertion Li Hongzhi makes about the multidimensional universe is that "when you were born, a 'you' was born at the same time in many dimensions of the universe, and with you they form a complete body, they're interrelated, and their thoughts are interconnected."[50] The bodies we inhabit in this dimension, therefore, have parallel versions in many other dimensions. We would apparently recognize these other bodies of ours, as "they look the same, have the same name, and do things that are more or less the same."[51] However, they are not the same in

---

47. The classic in this genre is Shen Jiji's (ca. 740–ca. 800) "The World inside a Pillow." A fine translation by William H. Nienhauser Jr. can be found in Y. W. Ma and Joseph S. M. Lau, eds., *Traditional Chinese Stories: Themes and Variations* (New York: Columbia University Press, 1978), pp. 435–38.

48. Ibid., 5/1, p. 92; pp. 159–60.

49. Ibid., 2/1, pp. 30–31, amended; p. 54.

50. Ibid., 9/2, p. 176, amended; p. 302.

51. Ibid., 7/1, 133; p. 230.

all respects: they can become big or small, according to the conditions of the relevant dimension, and they can levitate.[52] The *falun* that Li Hongzhi inserts into practitioners' bodies is understood to exist in one of these bodies in another dimension, as does the deputy original spirit (or spirits), and any Law Bodies a practitioner may produce.[53] We will see below that the dimension we inhabit is, according to Li, the lowest one of all.

Thus, when something is located in "another dimension," it must necessarily be a more elevated one. This is, perhaps, why the deputy original spirit is not as befuddled by human society as the chief original spirit is. It also accounts for why beings who live in these other dimensions have superior vision compared with ordinary uncultivated people, and are able to see the true nature of humanity that is obscure to us. These superior beings can observe, for instance, that the bones of ordinary people are actually black, and those of people who have undergone a process of consecration, or *guanding*, in their cultivation look like white jade.[54]

Li teaches that disease is caused by an accumulation of the black substance he calls karma. People who have developed their supernormal capacities can see this in the bodies of the sick. In one part of *Zhuan Falun*, however, while acknowledging the truth of this explanation, he moves beyond it to posit what he calls the "fundamental cause of an illness." Thus, he says,

when a person has a tumor, an inflammation, a bone spur, or whatever, somewhere in their body, in another dimension there's a spirit being [*lingti*] crouching at that place. . . . After you remove it you'll find that there's nothing in the body over here.[55]

The being that causes the illness apparently "produces the field" of karma. This karmic field can be seen by those with everyday special sight, but it requires someone of the supreme powers of Master Li to observe these loathsome beings as they are found in "a deeper dimension."

The multidimensional cosmos Li describes is inhabited not only by humanity; in fact, in his writings many different kinds of beings are mentioned. Within our immediate vicinity are found, for instance, the spirits of specific animals—foxes, rats, snakes, and badgers—that can possess the unwary *qigong* practitioner who lusts after fame and profit.[56] There are also the spirits of people who have died untimely deaths, including

52. Ibid., 3/5, p. 53; p. 94.
53. Ibid., 5/6, p. 99; p. 172.
54. Ibid., 2/5, p. 45; p.79, 4/4, p. 84; p. 147.
55. Ibid., 7/4, p. 145, amended; p. 251.
56. See Penny, "Animal Spirits, Karmic Retribution, Falungong, and the State."

the aborted fetuses mentioned earlier, as well as those of large animals who have been slaughtered for meat; the spirits of such unlucky creatures must drift about the universe until all their counterparts in all the other dimensions have lived out their lives.[57]

These are, however, minor and trivial beings compared with those of the higher dimensions. The superior inhabitants of the cosmos are called Great Enlightened Beings when Li refers to them collectively, and they may be subdivided into three varieties. The first are Buddhas and related beings from the Buddhist teachings. Li follows the Mahāyāna tradition in regarding the state of Buddhahood as something that has been, and will be, achieved many times in the past and potentially as many times as there are sentient beings in the future. We have already seen that the Maitreya, or Future Buddha, features in discussions of the fundamental identity of Master Li. In *Zhuan Falun* Li also mentions other Buddhas by name, and asserts several times that "Buddhas are everywhere."[58] Some of them, he says, preside over their own paradises along with other Great Enlightened Beings, including, by implication, himself.

When Great Enlightened Beings save people they have their own heavenly kingdoms. When Tathāgatas like Śākyamuni, Amitābha, and Vairocana save people they each have a paradise that they preside over. There are over 100 of these in the Milky Way system we are in, and our Falun Dafa has a Falun Paradise.[59]

Along with fully fledged Buddhas, Li also speaks of Boddhisattvas, inhabiting the dimensions above us. Moreover, and still referring to beings from the Buddhist tradition, he provides this short negative sketch of the *asuras*, one of the categories of rebirth we encountered earlier in this chapter. They are

living creatures in different dimensions but they don't have human nature. In the eyes of Great Enlightened Beings they're extremely lowly and incapable, but to ordinary people they're terrifying. They have a certain kind of energy, and they think of ordinary people as beasts, so they like to eat them. In the last few years they've jumped at the chance to teach *qigong*.[60]

---

57. Li, *Zhuan Falun* 7/1, p. 133; p. 230.
58. Ibid., 2/5, p. 43; p. 76.
59. Ibid., 3/2, p. 49, amended; p. 87.
60. Ibid., 5/3, p. 95, amended; p. 166.

In addition to beings from the Buddhist tradition, Li acknowledges the presence of Great Enlightened Beings from Daoism. Rather than using any term found in that religion for people who have attained transcendence, he simply refers to them as "Daos" (or "Taos," as it is rendered in some Falun Gong translations, based on the older English rendering "Taoism" rather than the current "Daoism"). There is little detail provided about them in Li's writings; however, in *Zhuan Falun* we learn that "One time I had my mind connected with four or five Great Enlightened Beings, Great Daos, whose levels were extremely high. . . . They wanted to know what it was I was thinking."[61] In publications that followed *Zhuan Falun*, the most common way of referring to these Daos, as well as Buddhas and the third category of these Great Enlightened Beings, Gods, is as part of a set phrase, "Buddhas, Daos, and Gods." As Li told a practitioner in a question and answer session in Sydney in 1999, the order in which he names these three categories does not indicate any relative levels of importance. It is simply a matter of locution.

I find it smooth to say "Buddhas, Daos, and Gods." I could say "Daos, Buddhas, and Gods," but it would sound awkward. Or I could say "Gods, Daos, and Buddhas," but it just doesn't feel as smooth.[62]

In general, Li Hongzhi regards all these beings as possessing perfect wisdom and supreme insight, and, of course, they do not think like ordinary people.[63] They know the real state of everything and regard it as their role to assist Master Li in his propagation of Falun Gong.[64] Indeed, he tells us, "countless Buddhas, Daos, Gods, those in charge of different levels, and heavenly deities" are studying his teachings themselves,[65] and are prepared to protect any practitioner who is being persecuted, especially since the suppression.[66] The relationship between Li's teachings and the Buddhas, Daos, and Gods is even stronger than this. "Behind every word" of *Zhuan Falun*, he says, "there are an infinite number of Buddhas, Daos,

---

61. Ibid., 3/3, p. 51; p. 90.

62. Li, "Teaching the *Fa* at the *Fa* Conference in Australia," p. 23; "Falun dafa Aodaliya fahui jiangfa," p. 52.

63. Li, "Teaching the *Fa* in New York City," p. 4; "Niuyue fahui jiangfa," p. 8.

64. Li, "Teaching the *Fa* at the Conference in Houston," not paginated; "Falun dafa Xiusidun fahui jiangfa," pp. 19–20.

65. Li, "Teaching the *Fa* in Beijing at the *Zhuan Falun* Publication Ceremony," p. 15; "Beijing zhuan falun shoufashi shang jiangfa," p. 21.

66. Li Hongzhi, "Explaining the *Fa* during the 2003 Lantern Festival at the U.S. West *Fa* Conference" (February 15, 2003; no PDF); "2003 nian yuanxiaojie jiangfa," pp. 59–60.

and Gods" who assist practitioners in understanding its wisdom, even if the version they are reading is in translation rather than the original Chinese. When practitioners suddenly understand a passage that had previously been obscure to them, this happens, says Master Li, because one of the Great Enlightened Beings has deemed their cultivation level to be sufficiently high for them to be granted this new insight.[67]

The Buddhas, Daos, and Gods have different clothes: Buddhas wear yellow, "Gods with the form of white people" white, and "Gods with the form of black people" red, while Daos are adorned in "ancient Chinese dress," except for "Great Daos at very high levels," whose clothing is "very diverse."[68] They also protect humankind from themselves. Li Hongzhi is, for specific reasons I will explore below, suspicious of modern science and technology, which, he maintains, advances faster than humanity's moral codes. He warns that if science and technology progressed too far or too quickly, "star wars would break out in the cosmos—there could really be cosmic wars. But Buddhas, Daos, and Gods won't permit it—they absolutely cannot allow humans to bring turmoil to the cosmos."[69]

In all Li Hongzhi's writings there is only one reference, as far as I have been able to ascertain, to a being beyond the multidimensional cosmos. In his lecture in Beijing in 1996, he mentioned a "Master Buddha" (zhufo) who "is beyond all times and cosmoses."[70] As there are no parallel passages that speak of this supreme being, however, it is difficult to expand on what Li might understand it to be like or how it relates to the workings of the universe in which we live.

The beings that have been discussed here, from those who are greatly enlightened to the lowest form of animal spirit, belong in the spiritual realm. There is yet another class of beings, according to Li, who inhabit the cosmos and who occasionally interact with humans: aliens. We have seen that he refers to spaceships traveling between dimensions in *Zhuan Falun*. He expanded on this theme in the speech he gave to launch that scripture in January 1995.

---

67. Li, "Teaching the *Fa* at the Conference in Europe," amended; p. 42; "Falun dafa Ouzhou fahui jiangfa," pp. 100–101.

68. Li Hongzhi, "Teaching the *Fa* at the Discussion on Creating Fine Art" (July 21, 2003; no PDF), amended; "Meishu chuangzuo yanjiuhui jiangfa," in *Falun dafa yinyue yu meishu chuangzuohui jiangfa*, pp. 60–61.

69. Li Hongzhi, "Teaching the *Fa* in San Francisco" (April 6, 1997), in *Lectures in the United States*, p. 31; "Jiujinshan fahui jiangfa," in *Falun dafa Meiguo fahui jiangfa*, p. 66.

70. Li Hongzhi, "Teaching the *Fa* at the International Experience-Sharing Conference in Beijing" (November 11, 1996), not paginated, online at www.falundafa.org/book/eng/pdf/beijing1996 .pdf, amended; "Beijing guoji jiaoliuhui jiangfa," in *Falun dafa gedi jiangfa yi*, p. 97.

You know about aliens, right—those flying saucers that fly back and forth, that come without a trace and leave without a shadow, and that travel at a high speed and are hard to fathom. A flying saucer can even change its size to be bigger or smaller. . . . It can travel in other dimensions.[71]

In later writings and speeches, Li's understanding of aliens, especially the nature of their interactions with humans, changed. In 1999, he gave one of his only interviews to a non–Falun Gong publication. In it, published in the web version of *Time Asia* on May 10, 1999, but given "a few weeks before the [April 25] demonstration," Li spoke freely about how aliens from other planets and other dimensions have infiltrated society through science and technology, as part of their plan to take over the human race.

The aliens have introduced modern machinery like computers and airplanes. They started teaching mankind about modern science, so people believe more and more science, and spiritually, they are controlled. Everyone thinks that scientists invent on their own when in fact their inspiration is manipulated by aliens. . . . The ultimate purpose is to replace humans. If cloning human beings succeeds, the aliens can officially replace humans. . . . There will no longer be humans reproduced by humans. They will act like humans, but they will introduce legislation to stop human reproduction.

To accomplish this task, the aliens

have already constructed a layer of cells in human beings. The development of computers dictates to this layer of body cells to control human culture and spirituality and in the end to replace human beings.

When the interviewer from *Time* asked what aliens looked like, Li replied that some "look similar to human beings"; one sort, however, look like humans, but have a nose that is "made of bone." Others, he said, "look like ghosts." To prove his case, he informed his interlocutor, "U.S. technology has already detected some aliens."[72]

71. Li, "Teaching the *Fa* in Beijing at the *Zhuan Falun* Publication Ceremony," p. 18; "Beijing zhuan falun shoufashi shang jiangfa," p. 25.
72. Dowell, "Interview with Li Hongzhi," *Time Asia*. In February of 1999, Li had already spoken in these terms at a Falun Gong conference in Los Angeles: "This is the ultimate means that aliens will use to replace man—that is, cloning humans. Man is being used by aliens to destroy himself, yet he is not aware of it and is still protecting the science that is destroying the human race. If humans are cloned *en masse* in the future, those beings will all be aliens that have been reborn in human bodies, and there will be no more human race" (Li Hongzhi, "Teaching the *Fa* at the Western U.S. *Fa* Conference" [February 21–22, 1999], online at www.falundafa.org/book/eng/pdf/us_west1999.pdf,

Li's beliefs about aliens clearly changed between the beginning of 1995, when he was still living in China, and early 1999, when he had been a resident in the United States for more than two years. His earlier statements reflect a view of extraterrestrials that has them piloting flying saucers around the universe and between dimensions using technology far in advance of our own. His later statements reveal a far more developed narrative that involves at least three strands of UFO mythology. The first is that scientific technology derives from extraterrestrial sources. The best-known and most widely distributed sources for this position are the works of Erich von Daniken, whose books and television programs sought to show that major developments in human history and knowledge were derived from the visits of people from other planets. The second is that aliens routinely visit the earth and are engaged in a plan to interbreed with humans to develop a new race of intergalactic hybrids. This plan is generally attributed to the "greys," that short, large-eyed variety of alien believed by some to have crash-landed their spacecraft near Roswell, New Mexico. This strand of the mythology is typically associated with so-called alien abductions, in which unsuspecting members of the public are teleported into a waiting spaceship where they are probed, sampled, and sometimes impregnated by its occupants before returning to earth. The third strand is the belief that governments, usually the US government or secretive units within them, know about alien visitations, are aware of their plans, and in some versions are actually in cahoots with them. The UFO and alien interaction literature was already vast and growing by the time Li made his statements in 1999, especially in the realm of online publication.

It is difficult, then, to be certain where Li might have learned about this mythology. One possible source, though, where he would have encountered all the strands mentioned above is the American television series *The X-Files*, which was first broadcast in the United States in 1993 and ceased production in 2002. The years 1996–99 represented the height of its popularity and influence. Among many other countries, *The X-Files* was broadcast in both Hong Kong and Taiwan in Chinese-language versions by 1995. It would have been possible, therefore, for Li Hongzhi to have both watched, and been influenced by, the series during his first

---

p. 12; "Falun dafa Meiguo xibu fahui jiangfa," p. 29). He reiterated these thoughts in Sydney four months later when he said, "Aliens wearing the skins of humans would be replicated *en masse*, occupying the bodies of humans. The future human race, originating from this type of people, would continue to replicate man more and more, and in the end replace man entirely" (Li, "Teaching the *Fa* at the *Fa* Conference in Australia," p. 6; "Falun dafa Aodaliya fahui jiangfa," pp. 14–15).

years living in America.[73] His fascination with UFOs is consistent with Li's interest in a wide range of paranormal phenomena derived, most likely, from translations of texts such as those of von Daniken that appeared in China during the publishing boom of the 1980s. It shows the importance for Falun Gong teachings of his eclecticism, and of his ability to take elements from the culture in which he lived—that of China in the early and mid-1990s, and that of the United States in the late 1990s—and put them together in unexpected ways.

The Purpose of Falun Gong

For the Falun Gong practitioner, the goal of cultivation is Consummation. As we will see in chapter 6, Li Hongzhi lays out a path for his followers to take, indicating what will happen to them as they progress up the ladder of practice. Underpinning this path, though, are basic religious understandings, some of which have been identified in this chapter, which relate to what happens to people after they die, how the cosmos is structured, what other beings exist, and how the human body is constituted biospiritually. These questions are common to most religions (although the answers they give of course vary widely), but another is crucially important for any faith: why should somebody follow it at all? In other words, what does this religion offer? In Falun Gong, the broad answer to that question is the possibility of "a return to the origin."

As indicated earlier, Li teaches that the fundamental characteristic of the universe is the moral triumvirate of *zhen, shan,* and *ren*—truth, compassion, and forbearance. Thus, at the instant of creation of any of us—that is, our first birth before the cycle of death and rebirth began—we were at one with these principles, even though we were not at this point human. We were originally, in Falun Gong terminology, Buddhas, Daos, or Gods, and this is the state in which, ideally, we should have stayed. Unfortunately, according to Li, even at this elevated level social relationships form; for him this is necessarily a bad thing. Thus, he asserts, "during social interactions among the group, some become bad and so they drop down."[74] Such a grim view of the way people relate to one

73. Zixian Deng and Shi-min Fang suggest that Li might have been influenced by the film *Progeny* (1998), which concerns the abduction and impregnation of a woman by aliens ("The Two Tales of Falungong: Radicalism in Traditional Form," online at www.xys.org/xys/netters/Fang-Zhouzi/religion/2tales.doc).

74. Li, *Zhuan Falun* 2/3, p. 34; p. 61. This corruption is glossed in *Zhuan Falun* 3/5, p. 53; p.94, as becoming "selfish or bad."

another is reflected in his categorizing of relationships based on affection as "attachments" to be eradicated, as we will see in the next chapter. This negative slant on how people interact finds its corollary in the resolutely individual nature of the cultivation process. Consequently, Falun Gong is not a religion that places importance on the idea of a community of believers. Despite Li's encouragement of practicing in groups, he teaches a private quest for transcendence.

According to Li's teachings, once some of these originally exalted beings succumb to the corruption of social interaction and fall down a step, they fall to an even lower level if they continue to misbehave. Ultimately, irredeemably, they plummet to the level of ordinary humanity. By this time they, or perhaps better "we," have reached the nadir. "When they get to this level," Li says, "people are supposed to be destroyed, eliminated."[75] By definition, therefore, the state of being human is a condition of failure and degradation. By the standards of the cosmos, we should no longer be allowed to exist. Yet in their compassion, the Great Enlightened Beings created this earth for us to live in, though it is not, according to Li, a pleasant place. In "True Cultivation," a short 1995 essay, he refers to it as "most filthy" when compared to the "holy, pure, and incomparably splendid paradise" from which we have fallen.[76] In this dimension of last resort, we have been given eyes that blind us to anything beyond this world, and bodies that suffer the pains of birth, illness, old age, and death as well as the day-to-day discomforts of hunger, cold, and heat.

When Li speaks of "returning to the origin," what he specifically means is leaving this filthy, degraded dimension and ascending back to the upper reaches of the cosmos to regain our original forms as Buddhas, Daos, or Gods. He asserts that he has brought Falun Gong to humanity precisely to accomplish this aim. It is cultivation according to his teachings that will enable practitioners to regain their former high status as perfected beings.

A person's decision to "take the path of cultivation" is a momentous one, not just for the individual involved but for the universe as a whole. As Li says,

There's another way that a person can change his life, and it's the only way. It's when he takes up the path of cultivation. . . . Once a person wants to take up cultivation, once that idea comes out it shines like gold, and it shakes the Ten-Directional World.[77]

75. Ibid., 2/3, p. 34; p. 61.
76. Li Hongzhi, "True Cultivation" (May 22, 1995), in *Essentials for Further Advancement*, p. 6; "Zhenxiu," in *Falun dafa jingjin yaozi*, p. 5.
77. Li, *Zhuan Falun* 2/3, p. 34; p. 60, amended. The "ten directions" is originally a Buddhist concept referring to the four cardinal points, the four intercardinals, and up and down.

By following the teachings of Master Li and embarking on cultivation, the Falun Gong practitioner therefore realigns him- or herself to the characteristics of the universe. In doing so, as Li stresses throughout his writings, adherents come under his protection and receive the assistance of his Law Bodies. They are on track to return to the origin. The path they have chosen, however, is strewn with difficulties—"tribulations"—or sufferings that they must undergo in their lives. Even so, as they practice forbearance in the face of tribulation, they advance on the path; enduring suffering is actually a vital element in advancement. Thus, the burden of the pain-experiencing bodies we are given in this dimension is indeed a blessing: the more hardship you encounter, and the more painful it is, the more your cultivation will advance.

Li's teachings are therefore clearly intended as a path to salvation. His diagnosis of the present condition of humanity and his conception of the cosmos are part of the same religious model, and it is from that model that his prescription for transcending our current degraded, fallen state derives. Returning to the origin, regaining our status as Buddhas, Daos, or Gods, attaining Consummation—these all amount to essentially the same thing.

The cosmic model described and analyzed in this chapter so far has been limited to our present condition, how we arrived at it, and how we can transcend it. However, Li Hongzhi is also concerned with history, and it is to his views of the history of the cosmos and the earth, and the historical role of his teachings, that we now turn. We begin specifically with Li's ideas on the history of *qigong*.

History

Chinese medical and religious texts from the premodern period, as well as notable archeological discoveries that have come to light since the 1970s, point to activities like *qigong* being performed for more than two thousand years. This extraordinary continuity of practice is mirrored in the consistency in which masters and teachers have understood these exercises to work, as preserved in the textual archive. Authors of books and articles about *qigong* during the height of its boom were often enthusiastic about this history, and sometimes became rapturous in their descriptions. Some even placed the practice of *qigong* as far back as the period of the traditional founder of Chinese culture itself: Huangdi, the Yellow Emperor.[78]

---

78. For a more complete discussion of these issues, see Penny, "Qigong, Daoism and Science."

Li Hongzhi refers to debates over the venerability of *qigong* in *Zhuan Falun*, noting that "some *qigong* masters say that *qigong* has a 2,000-year history," whereas others nominate 3,000, 5,000, or even 7,000 years ago as the period in which it originated.[79] Li's own position is different from all these. He claims that *qigong* is in fact part of "prehistoric" culture. While common usage would imply that 5,000–7,000 years before the present would certainly include human prehistory (Stonehenge, for instance, is probably no more that 4,500 years old), Li sees *qigong* as deriving from considerably more ancient times: "*qigong* is not something that today's human race came up with, it was handed down from ages ago, and it's part of prehistoric culture." Other basic elements of Chinese culture such as the *Book of Changes* (*Yijing*), the eight trigrams, and the *taiji*, or *yinyang*, symbol are also "prehistoric," according to Li.[80]

We have seen that Li believes the pyramids were built not by ancient Egyptians but rather by an earlier race that sank beneath the oceans when the tectonic plates shifted. In fact, for him, all the apparently ancient civilizations of the world were preceded by earlier cultures that met with destruction. Li's evidence for this theory of history lies in the existence of artifacts that appear to be of an anomalously great age—much older than the ten thousand years he allows since the present instance of human civilization appeared. One of these artifacts is a carving of a human figure he claims is housed in the National University of Peru; it "is wearing clothes, he has a hat on, and he's wearing shoes, in his hand he's got a telescope and he's observing celestial bodies."[81] Li also suggests that it would have been impossible, if accepted history were correct, for the murals in caves in "France, South Africa and the Alps" to have been painted "hundreds of thousands of years ago" with their level of artistry. Most surprisingly, he claims that a two-billion-year-old nuclear reactor exists in the African country of Gabon.

In 1972 a plant in France imported . . . uranium ore, and after chemical analysis they found that the uranium ore had already been refined and used. They thought it was strange, and so they sent over some scientists and technical personnel to investigate. . . . They eventually verified that the uranium ore mine was a large-scale nuclear reactor, and the layout was technically sound. There's no way people of the present

79. Li, *Zhuan Falun* 1/4, pp. 8–9; pp. 14–15.
80. Ibid., p. 11; p. 19.
81. Ibid., p. 9, amended; p. 16.

could create something like that. So when was it built? Two billion years ago, and it operated for 500,000 years.[82]

Where Li Hongzhi found these examples of anomalous archeology is unclear. The case of the Peruvian image probably refers to the so-called Ica stones, which depict scenes of dinosaurs and humans existing side by side, as well as examples of modern technology, carved into ancient rocks. Supposedly found in a cave whose location has never been disclosed, and housed in a private museum owned by their major promoter, the Ica stones are generally regarded as a hoax.[83] One widely circulated book that specifically mentions the carving of the man with the telescope is Charles Berlitz's *Atlantis* from 1984, but as I have not been able to locate a Chinese translation of it, it may be that Li learned about the Ica stones from some other source.[84] The cave art Li mentions as coming from "France, South Africa and the Alps" was not all made in the same period, of course, but is generally much more recent than his "hundreds of thousands" of years. The site Li refers to in France is probably Lascaux, which is about sixteen thousand years old. He contends that such sites show "figures [that] are dressed like modern people, and their clothes look a little like Western-style clothes—they're wearing breeches. Some of them are holding things like tobacco pipes, and some are holding canes and wearing hats." Some rock art in the places he mentions does, in fact, show images of this sort, but these sites were often active into comparatively recent historical times. In the Drakensberg Mountains in South Africa, for instance, along with genuinely ancient paintings are depictions of local people fighting Europeans that must date from the period of colonization.[85]

The Gabon nuclear power reactor seems simply to be a case of Li misunderstanding an unusual natural phenomenon. In 1972, some uranium deposits from the mines in Oklo, southeastern Gabon, that supplied fuel for France's nuclear industry were found to show chemical configurations indicating their subjection to a nuclear fission process in the far distant past. Referred to as the "Oklo fossil reactors," the long-exhausted chain reactions in these uranium deposits have been extensively studied:

---

82. Ibid., p. 10, amended; p. 17.
83. See Robert T. Carroll, "Ica Stones," in *The Skeptic's Dictionary*, online at skepdic.com/icastones.html.
84. Berlitz, *Atlantis*, pp. 179–81.
85. See D. J. Lewis-Williams, *Discovering Southern African Rock Art* (Cape Town: David Philip, 1990).

they show no signs of being "built," and their layout, far from being "technically sound," is in fact entirely natural.[86]

In one sense, however, determining whether Li's contentions about certain historical artifacts or natural phenomena are correct or not is to misinterpret the nature of his teachings. As we have seen, the Chinese authorities challenged specific items of information in Li's biography and accused him of making them up to delude his followers, going so far as to provide witnesses from his childhood who contradicted the official Falun Gong account. Similarly, many of Li's specific claims about the past in *Zhuan Falun* or *Zhuan Falun, Volume II* can be contradicted by the findings of authoritative archeology. In both these cases, however, Li's writings should be viewed as religious texts. Thus, his biography serves the same function as Buddhist and Daoist biographies have in China for more than fifteen hundred years: that is, to demonstrate the extraordinary states a person can attain with diligent adherence to a particular faith. Li's assertions about human history serve a similar purpose. They are included in *Zhuan Falun* and other scriptures to bolster his claim that human history extends back much further than orthodox scientists and historians allow. "Audacious scientists in other countries," he asserts, accept that archeology actually demonstrates that "before this civilization of ours there were other periods of civilization, and not just one." Indeed, according to Li, numerous civilizations have existed before ours. Apparently,

many times civilization suffered a devastating blow, only a small number of people survived, they lived primitively, then gradually multiplied into a new human race, and began a new civilization. Then it would head for destruction again, and again they would multiply into a new human race.[87]

Moreover,

One time I traced it back carefully and found out that there have been 81 times when mankind lay in total ruin, and only a few people survived, only a little of the prehistoric civilization was left, and then they entered the next period and lived primitively. When the people multiplied enough, civilization would finally appear again. So it's gone through 81 of these cycles, and I didn't trace it back to the end.[88]

---

86. For an introduction, see Anon., "Oklo: Natural Nuclear Reactors," online at www.ocrwm.doe.gov/factsheets/doeymp0010.shtml.

87. Li, *Zhuan Falun*, 1/4, p. 10; p. 18.

88. Ibid., p. 11; p. 18. The number 81 here is probably not accidental: it has been numerologically and religiously powerful in Chinese culture for centuries.

Li Hongzhi's model of the repeated destruction of human civilization with a small population surviving through to the next phase of history echoes ideas present in Chinese religions for centuries. One of the most developed versions of this is found in medieval Daoism, where ideas of a forthcoming apocalypse preceded by great suffering and tribulations were widespread enough in religious circles to have been noted in the official dynastic histories.[89] Scriptures from the Six Dynasties (220–589) describe a period of devastation in which natural disasters and disease run rampant. At the climax of these end times, all the evil in the world would be destroyed and a new era of peace ruled over by a messianic figure called Li Hong would be inaugurated.[90] Only a small number of people would live through this great cosmic turning point to renew humanity. They were known as the "seed people" (*zhongmin*).[91]

As in Li Hongzhi's formulation, this process of cosmic renewal is cyclical; many ages have already flourished, declined, and expired in the distant past, only for new ones to be born and die in their turn. Stephen R. Bokenkamp evocatively translates some of the names of these ages as they appear in the scriptures: Draconic Magnificence, Extended Vigor, Vermillion Brilliance, Opening Luminary, Higher Luminary.[92] The word the Daoist scriptures give to these ages is *jie*, the Chinese translation of the Sanskrit *kalpa*, an Indian word referring to the unimaginable time periods described in Buddhist scriptures (and which the Daoists adopted). Buddhism entered China in the first few centuries CE, and it was only when this Indian religion had migrated eastward that it developed its own version of the apocalypse. These visions of the end of one temporal cycle and the beginning of another were based on preexisting ideas that the religion had entered a period of decline and that the Maitreya Buddha was waiting to descend to earth.

It was in Chinese Buddhism (rather than its Indian ancestor) that the famous three-part periodization of the Buddhist teachings—the true dharma, the semblance dharma, and the decline of the dharma—was developed and came to prominence. From its inception, Buddhism has held that all things are impermanent, even the message of Buddhism itself. Thus, since the period when the Buddha himself walked the earth,

89. On Daoist apocalypses, see Christine Mollier, *Une apocalypse taoïste du début du Ve siècle: Le Livre des Incantations Divines des Grottes Abyssales* (Paris: Collège de France, 1990).

90. As Barend ter Haar has noted, the similarity between the names Li Hong and Li Hongzhi is almost certainly coincidental.

91. On the "seed people," see Christine Mollier, "Zhongmin," in Pregadio, *The Encyclopedia of Taoism*, pp. 1285–86.

92. Stephen R. Bokenkamp, "Jie, *kalpa*, aeon (eon)," in Pregadio, *The Encyclopedia of Taoism*, pp. 545–46.

when the teachings were pure, the Buddhist clerical community was disciplined, and nirvana was possible to attain, a decline has set in until ultimately the message has become diluted and distorted, monks and nuns have become corrupt, and nirvana is no longer possible. This last period is characterized as the "decline of the dharma," or *mofa* in Chinese (*mappō* in Japanese). Li Hongzhi borrows this approach to history and takes it one step further, regarding the period we are living in as "the Age of Law's End" or "the final period of the *kalpa*'s end" (or in other translations "the final period of Last Havoc" or the "Dharma Ending Period"), which appears to mean that our age is coming to a close.[93] Thus, Li writes,

> The Law that Sakyamuni taught was for low-level ordinary people 2,500 years ago, who had just emerged from a primitive society and whose minds were relatively simple. He talked about "the Age of the Law's End." *That's today*. Modern people can't cultivate with that Law anymore. In the Age of the Law's End it's hard for monks in monasteries to save even themselves, let alone save others.[94]

Indeed, he claims that books written by monks in the present day have black *qi* permeating the text, but they are unable to see it.[95] Li expounds on the disastrous situation in which we find ourselves in a passage from the essay "Humanity during the Final Kalpa" from *Zhuan Falun, Volume II*.

> Human beings no longer have the law of the heart to restrain them, nor do they have moral norms. Spurred on by hordes of demons, they stop at no evil. Morals and standards are sliding downward as fast as can be. Man's very way of thinking and concepts have changed. The beautiful is less attractive than the ugly; the orthodox is less popular than the heterodox; good is less desirable than evil; clean-cut is less valued than unkempt; what's new is less preferable than what's used; fragrant is less favored than foul. Men sport long hair while women cut theirs short—*yin* is rising and *yang* is falling, an inversion of *yin* and *yang*. Works of art are devoid of moral norms and seek to liberate human nature, making for one giant display of the demonic. Then there's impressionism and abstraction, with their wild smearings, which are accepted as art by modern people and their perverse notions. A pile of garbage dumped somewhere on purpose becomes the work of a master modernist sculptor. And as for music, you see the blaring noise of disco and rock-and-roll ascending the stage in elegant halls. With a little hype from radio and television, blind or handicapped singers with hoarse voices

---

93. For instance, Li, *Zhuan Falun* 1/7.
94. Ibid., 1/3, p. 7, amended; p. 11. Italics in the original translation.
95. Li Hongzhi, "Lessons from Buddhism," in *Zhuan Falun, Volume II*, p. 9; "Fojiao zhong de jiaoxun," in *Zhuan falun juan er*, p. 13.

and those with repulsive looks become stars. And with children's toys, the uglier and more sinister they look, the faster they sell.[96]

Moreover, it is not just our world that has suffered this fate—"a lot of dimensions from a very high level on down have gone bad."[97] Yet all this, Li claims, has been predetermined. In a talk to Falun Gong Assistants in Changchun in 1994, he explained, "During the early period, when the cosmos was formed, the final, great event was already arranged," including the "last transmission of the Orthodox Law."[98] It is in the context of this revealed history that Li Hongzhi places his own appearance. "Right now," he says, "I'm the only person in the world who is publicly transmitting the Orthodox Law," an opportunity that occurs only every "1,000 years, or even 10,000 years."[99] In this way, Li Hongzhi places himself in the position of the sole transmitter of the teaching by which "you can be saved." At the beginning of the first lecture in *Zhuan Falun*, he asks rhetorically whether Falun Gong "is about saving people? It's saving people—you are truly cultivating yourself, and not just getting healthy or fit." Placing this statement in the context of Li's understanding of cosmic history reveals that salvation, for him, means escaping the cataclysms that occur at the end of the *kalpa* and surviving into the next age. With such a grand vision, and in making claims about the nature of Falun Gong that are so extraordinary, it becomes obvious why Li is disparaging of the *qigong* masters who simply offer better health to their practitioners.

Li Hongzhi's teachings concerning the rise and fall of human civilizations and the position of present humanity in relation to the cosmic cycle, and his role in saving people through the power of his new message, echo, consciously or unconsciously, ideas of the apocalypse that have recurred in Chinese religions for centuries. In late imperial times, these strains of apocalyptic thought took on a Buddhist, or more properly a Buddhist sectarian, hue with Maitreya, the future Buddha, playing a pivotal role. We should bear in mind, however, that the tradition of Maitreya returning to earth in the here and now to deliver a salvific message before the turning of the cosmic cycle is by no means standard in Buddhism. Typically, most Buddhists have looked forward to receiving Maitreya's teachings in the far distant future, if they are fortunate enough to be "reborn

96. Li, "Humanity during the Final Kalpa," p. 40, amended; "Mojie shi de renlei," p. 66.
97. Li, *Zhuan Falun* 3/2, pp. 49–50; p. 88.
98. Li, "Explaining the *Fa* for Falun Dafa Assistants in Changchun," p. 11, amended; "Wei Changchun falun dafa fudaoyuan jiangfa," p. 13.
99. Li, *Zhuan Falun* 3/3, p. 51; p. 90.

on earth during Maitreya's time, to hear him preach the Dharma, and ultimately to attain the final goal of nirvana," in Jan Nattier's words. Moreover, in this model the golden age that Maitreya will preside over occurs only after the decline has reached its nadir and will be preceded by an "Age of Fighting."[100] Thus, the role of Li Hongzhi as the transmitter of a message that will save his followers in times of strife echoes, rather, the sectarian model (sometimes, as David Ownby notes, referred to with the epithet "White Lotus"), where Maitreya descends in our times as savior. Ownby notes, however, that Li does not accept any link with this tradition and indeed explicitly denies the existence of the primary god of the sectarian scriptures, the Unborn Venerable Mother.[101]

The fact that some of Li's more ardent followers have considered him to be the Maitreya Buddha descended to the earth, as we saw in the previous chapter, points intriguingly to a continuity between some features of Buddhist sectarianism and Falun Gong. We will see later in this chapter, though, that these continuities are far from consistent at the level of teachings, and moreover, as Edward Irons notes, "there are no clearly discernible ties of genealogy" between Falun Gong and the possible sources from which Li Hongzhi could have obtained these ideas.[102]

Fa-Rectification

The process by which the cosmos is being scourged of evil is known in Falun Gong texts by the name of "*Fa*-rectification," or *zhengfa* in Chinese. The word *fa* in this context is the same as in *Falun Dafa*, that is, the Law or dharma. The idea of "rectification," or *zheng*, has a venerable history in Chinese thought. Confucius famously proposed that the harmony of society had to be predicated on the "rectification of names," or *zhengming*, by which he meant that people should behave according to their social or familial designations. A more recent example of rectification (here using the modern term *zhengfeng*, with a slightly different *zheng* character) occurred in the Communist base area of Yan'an in the early

---

100. Nattier, "The Meaning of the Maitreya Myth," pp. 27–29.

101. See Ownby, *Falun Gong and the Future of China*, p. 104, citing Li Hongzhi, "Teaching the Fa and Answering Questions in Yanji," in *Zhuan Falun Fajie*, p. 101; "Yanji jiangfa dayi," in *Zhuan falun fajie*, p. 145. Note, however, that Falun Gong's English translation renders the Unborn Venerable Mother as the "Birthless Matron." On comparisons between Buddhist sectarian teachings and those of Falun Gong, see, apart from Ownby's book, Edward Irons, "Falun Gong and the Sectarian Religion Paradigm."

102. Irons, "Falun Gong and the Sectarian Religion Paradigm," p. 257.

1940s when the Party leadership weeded out members who did not adhere to the ideological line of Mao Zedong.[103]

The term *zhengfa*, like many others used in Falun Gong texts, is known in orthodox Chinese Buddhist texts. In this case, it simply refers to the "true or correct dharma." In literary Chinese, words can function as different parts of speech depending on context; thus, the two-character combination *zhengfa* can mean "the correct dharma" in the Buddhist sense, or "to correct the dharma" (or "*Fa*-rectification") in the Falun Gong sense. In criminal law it also has the unrelated meaning "to perform an execution."

The earliest use in Falun Gong of the term that translates as "*Fa*-rectification" occurs in the title of a talk Li gave on January 2, 1995, which was collected in *Explaining the Content of Falun Dafa*: "Comments regarding the *Fa*-Rectification Made at the Falun Dafa Assistants Meeting in Beijing." The text of the talk itself, however, does not include the term. Li's concern at this time was that the leaders of Falun Gong's branches maintain a strict approach to the teachings and the performance of the exercises. Thus, he introduced his lecture by saying, "I'm soon going to transmit the practice overseas. . . . I have to talk to you about some things. If I didn't, some problems that have already sprouted up could affect the healthy development of our Dafa."[104] In other words, what Li means by "*Fa*-rectification" in this context is simply the correction of errors in how the teachings were being passed on.

By 1996, when the next reference to *Fa*-rectification I have been able to find occurs, the situation had changed. In a lecture called "Teaching the *Fa* at the International Experience-Sharing Conference in Beijing" delivered on November 11, 1996, Li said, "If the Three Realms and humankind play their due roles in *Fa*-rectification, the humankind of the future will have immeasurable blessings." Although Li did not elaborate on the precise meaning of *Fa*-rectification here, it clearly no longer referred to making the teachings correct in branches around China. Rather, it appears to include the whole of humanity and the Three Realms, by which he meant all beings that are subject to reincarnation. In general, in this talk Li took a more cosmic view of Falun Gong, and indeed of himself, than had hitherto been the case, claiming in the same passage that

103. On *zhengming*, see John Makeham, *Name and Actuality in Early Chinese Thought* (Albany: State University of New York Press, 1994). On *zhengfeng*, see Frederick C. Teiwes, *Politics and Purges in China: Rectification and the Decline of Party Norms, 1950–1965* (Armonk, NY: M. E. Sharpe, 1993).

104. Li Hongzhi, "Comments regarding the *Fa*-Rectification Made at the Falun Dafa Assistants Meeting in Beijing" (January 2, 1995), in *Explaining the Content of Falun Dafa*, p. 68; "Beijing falun dafa fudaoyuan huiyi shang guanyu zhengfa de yijian," in *Falun dafa yijie*, p. 139.

My mighty virtue is in control from beyond all realms. . . . The most basic elements that exist in the cosmos are in me but I am not within them. I am the source that forms all wisdom in the cosmos, yet I want nothing. . . . I manifest in the human world though I am not in the realm of the human.[105]

Thus, while this reference to *Fa*-rectification does not actually explain what Li meant by it, the context in which it appears clearly shows that its meaning had developed from the simple correction of errors less than two years earlier. By 1998, however, *Fa*-rectification as Li viewed it had developed another step. By that time, it was part of the cyclical cosmic process of creation and destruction. Thus, at a lecture in Singapore in August of that year, Li indicated that "the purpose of *Fa*-rectification is to make things more wonderful," in response to a question concerning the cosmic law of "formation, stasis, degeneration."[106] The next month, speaking in Geneva, he commented that "the purpose of [transmitting my teachings] is *Fa*-rectification. All beings in the cosmos have strayed from the *Fa*, so they have to be rectified with *Fa*."[107]

By 1999, in lectures that took place before the Zhongnanhai demonstration and subsequent suppression, Li's model of *Fa*-rectification had fully taken shape. In the 1998 Geneva lecture, he had indicated that beings in other parts of the cosmos, as well as humans, had gone astray and needed to be corrected. Speaking in Los Angeles and New York in February and March 1999, he elucidated the reasons this perilous situation had come about. "Why do I transmit the Dafa of the cosmos?" Li asked rhetorically. "It is because living beings at all levels of the cosmos have deviated from the Dafa that *Fa*-rectification has to be done." He explained that "old forces in this cosmos" are at the root of the problem. These cosmic beings only came into existence after the universe had already departed from the correct path. Thus, they have only known times when the cosmic decline was in progress, and as a result, "they have no idea that the cosmos has degenerated." Deluded in this way, Li asserted, they oppose the transmission of the teachings and the process of *Fa*-rectification. These actions are "extremely evil," but while "they hypocritically pretend that they look out for people's well-being . . . their dam-

---

105. Li, "Teaching the *Fa* at the International Experience-Sharing Conference in Beijing," not paginated, amended; "Beijing guoji jiaoliuhui jiangfa," pp. 102–3.

106. Li, "Teaching the *Fa* at the Conference in Singapore," p. 23; "Falun dafa Xinjiapo fahui jiangfa," p. 51.

107. Li Hongzhi, "Teaching the *Fa* at the Conference in Switzerland," p. 41, amended; "Falun dafa Ruishi fahui jiangfa," p. 49.

age is real." In the great cleansing of the cosmos, they will be "completely annihilated" and "eradicated by the *Fa*-rectification."[108]

Thus, by 1999, Li taught not only that his teachings were the key to surviving through the turn of the cosmic cycle but that they were also fundamental to a wholesale cleansing of the universe, a process that would, understandably, be opposed by forces for whom the maintenance of the old dispensation was vital. In short: "*Fa*-rectification is taking place up there, the old cosmos is disintegrating, and the new one is being created." Yet "*Fa*-rectification hasn't yet come to the stage of humankind. Now it's just that the *Fa* is saving you."[109]

As in most other aspects of the teachings of Falun Gong, the suppression in July 1999 had a fundamental effect on ideas about *Fa*-rectification. Li did not make any public statements, publish any essays, or appear to his followers for some months after the government ban on Falun Gong. It was not until January 19, 2000, that the photo captioned "Master Li quietly watching the world from amidst the mountains after leaving New York following July 20th, 1999" was posted on Falun Gong websites. The first of his writings to be published after the suppression was the essay "The Knowing Heart," but that did not appear until May 22, 2000 (although Falun Gong sources claim it was originally written on October 12, 1999—the publication delay has not been explained). The first of Li's new essays published was "Towards Consummation" from June 16, 2000. This heralded a flurry of writings on Falun Gong websites, including "With Reference to a Prophecy," in which he discusses Nostradamus.

More than a year after the suppression, Li raised the topic of *Fa*-rectification in this new context. The essay in which this discussion occurs, from August 12, 2000, is called "Eliminate Your Last Attachment(s)." Characterized by a portentous tone, it begins by declaring that "Dafa and Dafa students have experienced the most evil, most malicious, destructive trial—something never seen before in history." In early 1999, as we saw above, Li announced that *Fa*-rectification was occurring in the upper dimensions of the cosmos, but that it had not yet descended to the realms of humanity. His new essay brought these cosmic events up to date.

Although several wretched people are still doing evil, those most evil beings who are at high levels of the cosmic body have already been completely eliminated in the process

---

108. Li, "Teaching the *Fa* at the Western U.S. Fa Conference," p. 42, amended; "Falun dafa Meiguo xibu fahui jiangfa," p. 93.

109. Li Hongzhi, "Teaching the *Fa* at the Eastern U.S. Fa Conference" (March 27–28, 1999), online at www.falundafa.org/book/eng/pdf/us_east1999.pdf, p. 31; "Falun dafa Meiguo dongbu fahui jaingfa," p. 45.

of the *Fa*'s rectification of the cosmos. The evil ones who are at the most superficial level, that of humankind, will soon have to pay for all of their sins as they are completely eliminated during the *Fa*'s rectification of the human world. . . . This is happening at a rapid speed, and is approaching the wretches in the human world and those vicious murderers who have beaten to death or injured Dafa disciples.[110]

In this passage, significantly, Li brings the process of *Fa*-rectification into the world of human society by foretelling that people who had been involved with the suppression of Falun Gong would be "completely eliminated." It is important to recall here that the doctrines surrounding *Fa*-rectification, and the future involvement of humanity in the process, were developed before the Zhongnanhai demonstration and subsequent government actions. The actions of the government in mistreating Falun Gong practitioners were therefore easily incorporated into Li's understandings of cosmic history as part of the sufferings that would precede the turn of the kalpic cycle. In addition, though, his teachings on *Fa*-rectification indicated to his followers that the ultimate victory of Falun Gong was certain; that the police officers, prison guards, and politicians who had abused Falun Gong adherents would be wiped from the earth; and that by showing forbearance in the face of persecution, practitioners would be advancing their own cultivation. This position was reiterated the next year in an essay called "A Suggestion" from April 10, 2001.

Amidst the *Fa*-rectification, those high-level beings are in the last stage of being cleaned out. Once it is broken through, all the evil beings in the world will be knocked down into hell when the *Fa* rectifies the human world, and for all eternity they will pay for the sins they committed persecuting Dafa.[111]

The increasing focus of *Fa*-rectification on the retribution that would be meted out to the persecutors of Falun Gong perhaps reached its apogee in 2001 in "What Shanshan Saw in Other Dimensions," a series of postings concerning the visions of a child practitioner that appeared on official websites.[112] Young children, Li teaches, can have their Celestial Eyes opened much more easily than adults, so their abilities to see into other

---

110. Li Hongzhi, "Eliminate Your Last Attachment(s)" (August 12, 2000), in *Essentials for Further Advancement, II*, p. 20; "Qudiao zuihou de zhizhuo," in *Falun dafa jingjin yaozhi er*, p. 29.

111. Li Hongzhi, "A Suggestion," in *Essentials for Further Advancement, II*, p. 32; "Jianyi," in *Falun dafa jingjin yaozhi er*, p. 46.

112. Attributed to Shanshan and "summarized by his mother," "What Shanshan Saw in Other Dimensions" was posted in ten installments from April through August 2001 on the Minghui and Clearwisdom websites.

dimensions are therefore more developed. While Shanshan's visions are not the only records of children's visions posted on these websites, they are by far the most elaborated.

The introduction to these postings informs us that Shanshan was nine in 2001—he was born, therefore, in 1992, the year Falun Gong was launched—and began practicing Falun Gong when he was four. While his mother watched videos and listened to tapes of Master Li's lectures, Shanshan played nearby. Before he knew any characters or could write his name, he was apparently able to read *Zhuan Falun*. Shanshan's visions broadly concern the cleansing of the cosmos of evil in the times of *Fa*-rectification. He begins his narrative by confirming the standard Falun Gong doctrine that "in other dimensions, except the earth, it is indescribably clear and extraordinarily beautiful," while the earth itself "is fearfully dirty and filled with demons, animals that possess people, strange monsters, alien life forms and ghosts."[113]

Shanshan reveals that the earth is one of the last places in the cosmos to which such anomalistic beings have fled to escape death at the hands of *Fa*-rectification, and "most of them went to China, especially Beijing." The chief agent of good in this great battle is "a flaming red sphere" on which is written *zhen*, *shan*, and *ren*. "The sphere," he tells us,

is cleaning up the entire universe from high-level dimensions to the Earth, and it deals with and destroys all evil demons. There are also many Buddhas, Taos, Gods, and heavenly beings, even the sun, the Fire God, the God of Lightning, and the Sea God; all have come out to battle the demons. In the low-level dimensions, the original spirits of trees, flowers, and houses all watch these things happening.

In this great battle, some of the divine beings who were not sufficiently committed to the cause of good were themselves "annihilated and disintegrated," but these are not the only casualties of the fight. Shanshan tells us that anyone who "swears at Dafa" out loud or in his heart will be annihilated, along with drug addicts.

Shanshan's visions are divided into ten parts and are, to a large extent, made up of the narrative of his battles with the various demons he encounters in other dimensions, sometimes in the cosmos at large and sometimes while he and his family go about their normal lives as Falun

---

113. Anon., "What Shanshan Saw in Other Dimensions (I)" (April 16, 2001), online at www .clearwisdom.net/html/articles/2001/4/28/9140.html, amended; "Shanshan kandao de lingwai kongjian (yi)," www.minghui.org/mh/articles/2001/4/16/9994.html. This installment also provides the basis for the following paragraph.

Gong cultivators: going to protest outside the Chinese embassy, going to a practice site, and so on. These battle stories are rather repetitive: a demon appears, attacks Shanshan, and is then killed. The following example from the third section of the visions is representative:

While I was learning the Law off by heart, a gigantic wild duck, with a murderous gleam in its triangular eyes, came charging towards me. I thought to myself, "Continue reading and take no notice of it" but then suddenly realized I should do something about it. Then I thought, "You shouldn't exist. You are evil. There is no place for you in this cosmos and you should be destroyed." Instantly, a black and white *taiji* disc flew out from my chest and stopped this huge bird from approaching. Almost simultaneously, another strong beam of violet light came out from my body and struck the bird like lightning. Instantly the creature exploded and disintegrated, leaving a wisp of smoke behind.[114]

Shanshan's battles with the panoply of evil demons he encounters are reminiscent of the tradition of Chinese supernatural narratives that extends from *Journey to the West* (*Xiyou ji*) through to the contemporary Hong Kong cinema of magical Daoists with special powers.[115] Shanshan actually mentions this tradition twice in his account: in one case he notes that he had always been fascinated with the "magical devices of various deities in *Journey to the West*," and in another he uses it as a point of comparison: "For more than a year, wherever the Flaming Red Sphere and *faluns* went, there has been intense heavenly fighting . . . it is countless times more splendid than any movie, or *Journey to the West*."[116] The battles also bring to mind the dynamics of some computer games, with their characteristic incessant firing of laser beams and instantaneous annihilation of aliens and their spaceships. This is ironic, as Shanshan warns the reader against just these things.

It has been a long time since I last watched a cartoon movie or played a computer game, as many of them possess very strong demon nature. . . . As soon as the person enjoys watching the movie or playing the game from the disks, he will get possessed.[117]

114. Anon., "What Shanshan Saw in Other Dimensions (III)" (April 24, 2001), online at www.clearwisdom.net/html/articles/2001/5/3/9238.html; amended, "Shanshan kandao de lingwai kongjian (san)," www.minghui.org/mh/articles/2001/4/24/10222.html.
115. See, for instance, Sammo Hung's classic *Encounters of the Spooky Kind* (*Gui da gui*, 1980) and Ricky Lau's *Mr Vampire* (*Jiangshi xiansheng*, 1985) and its sequels.
116. Anon., "What Shanshan Saw in Other Dimensions (I)"; "Shanshan kandao de lingwai kongjian (yi)."
117. Anon., "What Shanshan Saw in Other Dimensions (III)"; "Shanshan kandao de lingwai kongjian (san)."

The visions of Shanshan, of course, demonstrate the truth of Li Hong-zhi's assertions concerning cosmic history and the nature of the evil forces arraigned against Falun Gong. He reveals, for instance, that Li's skepticism about the theory of evolution is well founded. When he focused his Celestial Eye on "scenes of primitive human beings living on earth," he found that "definitely they were not monkeys."[118] He was also able to confirm that Jiang Zemin, then president of China and, as far as Falun Gong practitioners are concerned, chief architect of the suppression, is indeed not human but instead a giant, three-legged toad demon with black, yellow, and green spots.[119] The evil nature of the Communist Party as a whole is confirmed in section 7 of the visions.

Recently, all demons in the Three Realms started to re-combine their armed forces and deployed more vicious tactics. Viewed from higher dimensions, various types of demons, such as skeleton demons, iron-sheeted aliens, monsters resembling GaFa in Disney cartoon films, were led by different ringleaders. They . . . had a meeting in a hidden space station beyond the scope of the nine planets, which is the demons' headquarters. As they manifested themselves differently in different dimensions, at the lowest level of human beings they appeared as several ringleaders of the XX Party in Beijing who were insidiously concocting a new scheme to deal with Falun Gong.[120]

Shanshan's visions represent the process of *Fa*-rectification in more explicit terms than does Li himself, but the fundamental ideas that Falun Gong and Master Li are leading a purge of all the evil in the cosmos, and that the earth is on the verge of experiencing this firsthand, is certainly common to both. They also point to the cosmically evil role of the Communist (or "XX") Party and its leadership in the universal battle.

Li's teachings on *Fa*-rectification, then, place Falun Gong and Master Li himself at the center of cosmic events. His teachings appeared, as he tells us, at the precise moment required to save humanity; his presence thus marks a turning point in human and cosmic history. The urgency he stressed as early as *Zhuan Falun*, to make best use of this life in human

---

118. Anon., "What Shanshan Saw in Other Dimensions (II)" (April 18, 2001), online at www .clearwisdom.net/emh/articles/2001/5/2/9205.html; "Shanshan kandao de lingwai kongjian (er)," www.minghui.org/mh/articles/2001/4/18/9997.html.

119. Anon., "What Shanshan Saw in Other Dimensions (IV)" (May 18, 2001), online at www .clearwisdom.net/emh/articles/2001/5/25/10373.html; "Shanshan kandao de lingwai kongjian (si)," www.minghui.org/mh/articles/2001/5/19/11246.html.

120. Anon., "What Shanshan Saw in Other Dimensions (VII)" (May 29, 2001), www.clearwisdom .net/emh/articles/2001/5/30/10591.html, "Shanshan kandao de lingwai kongjian (qi)," minghui .org/mh/articles/2001/5/29/11604.html. GaFa is probably Goofy, although his official Chinese name is Gafei.

form by pursuing cultivation, takes on an added impetus when we realize what events may be unfolding in this dimension. These teachings about the purpose of Falun Gong, and their role in saving humanity, therefore rely on the basic and fundamentally religious framework of ideas Li constructed around the constitution of the human person and our spiritual anatomy, the nature of the cosmos, and the degraded state of being that is humanity. This framework provides the foundations on which his detailed instructions about cultivation and morality are built. Li's ideas on cultivation as well as the exercises and moral life he expects practitioners to follow are the topics of the next chapter.

FIVE

Cultivation

When someone becomes a Falun Gong practitioner, he or she crosses a threshold, leaving the ranks of ordinary people to attain the status of "cultivator." Cultivators in Falun Gong have accepted Li Hongzhi's teachings; they live by different rules, and their goals and expectations differ from the people around them. Their entire life's priorities are supposed to change fundamentally as a new path is laid out before them—a path that leads, in Falun Gong language, to Consummation.

"Becoming a cultivator" indicates the acquisition of a new identity, and is not so very different from conversion to any religion, new or old. Religious conversions imply a transformation of who, in essence, the person "really" is. Becoming a Falun Gong cultivator means becoming someone new, someone who is cleansed, and someone whose life has acquired a new meaning. It is a commonplace in Li's writings to draw a distinction between what cultivators do and what occurs in "ordinary human society" or among "ordinary people"; accordingly, the concerns of ordinary people must be discarded as encumbrances, "attachments" as he calls them, so that the progress of cultivation will not stall. The new identity brings with it changes in all aspects of a person's life, including not only adopting particular new activities and casting aside specific old ones but also transforming the way in which each moment of life is lived.

Li teaches Falun Gong practitioners that their acceptance of his teachings was predestined. Thus, their new status as cultivator is doctrinally the ultimate position in life that they will attain; it was always their true and inevitable destination. For neophyte practitioners with, perhaps, some residual uncertainty over their decision, the assurance that they were always predestined to enter the world of Falun Gong is a comforting and reinforcing doctrine. By making the leap and becoming a cultivator, they have come home.

This chapter explores Li Hongzhi's teachings on cultivation. It will examine the physical exercises that are most commonly associated with Falun Gong's public group practice and the traditions that underpin them. It will then analyze the moral code that cultivators are expected to uphold, without which cultivation will not work. Chapter 6 will then proceed to describe what Li teaches will happen to a cultivator's body during the cultivation process, outlining what might be meant by Consummation, the ultimate goal of the cultivator. First, however, it is important to understand the contexts from which Falun Gong cultivation arose, and the importance of the idea of cultivation in Chinese history and culture.

Cultivation and Self-Cultivation

The idea that is it possible, and desirable, for people to perform mental or physical exercises in order to transform themselves ultimately into a superior form of being has been present in Chinese religious, philosophical, and medical traditions for as long as we have records. Generally understood to be a kind of cultivation of the body or mind, often with spiritual overtones, these activities have been undertaken for the benefit of the individual cultivator, although they have often taken place in groups. Varieties of cultivation or self-cultivation (as the various terms in Chinese are usually translated) are found across the Buddhist, Daoist, and Confucian traditions, in medical teachings which were themselves often associated with religious activities in premodern China, and in the long tradition of "biospiritual" practice that includes the *qigong* of recent times, as well as much older forms of activity such as martial arts. The vocabulary each tradition uses to describe its practices, as we would expect, is often specific to that tradition, but the idea that humans are perfectible, and that there are particular activities that can induce such a transformation, is shared in all these teachings.

The word Li Hongzhi uses in his writings that is translated as "cultivate" is the standard Chinese compound *xiulian*, which is found across all these traditions of practice. The *xiu* of *xiulian*, among its other uses, refers to studying, regulating, repairing, or cultivating, both in the sense of cultivating the body or mind as well as the more obvious sense of cultivating plants, although to draw a distinct line between literal and metaphorical usages would be misleading. The *lian* in this compound means to smelt or refine some material, usually metal, as in creating an alloy or tempering a blade, for example. The compound word therefore has the connotations of transforming a base substance into a more refined one. The root meaning of smelting is preserved in the written character with the graph for fire. Another form of *lian*, pronounced in precisely the same way, is sometimes used in the compound *xiulian*. The only difference in how the two characters are written is that the graph for fire is replaced by the graph for silk. The root meaning of this alternate form of *lian* is to boil and scour raw silk, similarly referring to a process of refinement through the application of heat. A third *lian* occurs less commonly, where the graph for metal is used in place of that for fire or silk. It is again pronounced identically and is very close in meaning to the first character, though an added usage (somewhat confusingly, given it has the metal graph) is to fire pottery. Thus, *xiulian*, literally to cultivate and refine, has connotations of the material transformation of substance; and in Falun Gong, as in many of the traditions in which cultivation occurs, it is believed to physically alter the constitution of the body in some way.

In the Chinese written record, the earliest versions of individual biospiritual cultivation occur in Daoist traditions in the last few centuries before the Common Era. In particular, as Harold Roth has shown, the "Inward Training" chapters of the *Guanzi* from the mid-fourth century BCE demonstrate that practices involving control of the breath and the importance of certain body positions or postures were already developed by that time. In addition, in these chapters the concept "guarding the one" (*shouyi*) is found—"guarding the one" became important in Daoist and Buddhist meditational practices for centuries afterward.[1] Later well-known Daoist texts such as the *Zhuangzi* and the *Laozi* also include references to self-cultivation terminology and techniques, but neither could be regarded as giving instructions.

As the religion of Daoism developed in the first centuries of the Common Era, however, cultivation systems of various forms (and the adepts who practiced them) were written about explicitly. Across different periods, the common goal of Daoist cultivation was to transform the body

---

1. See Harold D. Roth, *Original Tao: Inward Training (Nei-yeh) and the Foundations of Taoist Mysticism* (New York: Columbia University Press, 1999), and Roth, "The Inner Cultivation Tradition of Early Taoism," in *Religions of China in Practice*, ed. Donald S. Lopez Jr. (Princeton: Princeton University Press, 1996), pp. 123–48. See also Kirkland, "Varieties of Taoism in Ancient China."

we are born with into an immortal body.[2] In earlier times, this transformation was understood to be attained in a clearly physical way, typically through a combination of some, but not necessarily all, of the following: breathing techniques, visualizations, special diets, sexual regimes, moral behavior, and the ingestion of drugs concocted over long periods in alchemical furnaces. Two of the ways in which the transformation took place demonstrate that the process of acquiring an immortal body was thought to lead to actual, physical changes. In a superior form, a person who had crossed the boundary between ordinary existence and immortal life simply "rose up to heaven in broad daylight" due to the lightening of his or her body to weightlessness. A lesser candidate could become an immortal by the process of "corpse-liberation," by which he or she would undergo a false death, after which the transformation would take place. The following account, which emphasizes the presence of heat in the refinement process—echoing the root meaning of the *lian* in *xiulian*—comes from a fourth-century hagiographical text. It records the transformation of one Cai Jing, and the passage begins with the words of the immortal Wang Yuan.

"At present you have too much flesh and not enough *qi*—you cannot ascend to heaven but corpse-liberation would be appropriate. Soon you will feel like you are squeezing through a dog door." He then passed on the essentials to Cai Jing and left him alone. Later Jing's body became extremely hot and he wanted cold water to pour over himself. The whole family drew water and doused him—it was as if they were pouring water on a fire. This continued for three days while he melted away to bare bones. Then he entered a chamber and covered himself with a quilt, and suddenly he was nowhere to be seen. Looking under the quilt, all that could be seen was skin, a head and feet with everything in place, just like a cicada's shedded exuviae.[3]

In later Daoist traditions the role of the alchemical laboratory is taken by the adept's body itself. In these so-called "internal alchemy (*neidan*)" or "golden elixir (*jindan*)" methods, the adept uses techniques of mental visualization and other meditations as well as special breathing practices in order to return to the Dao.[4] By refining the three basic elements of essence

---

2. See Penny, "Immortality and Transcendence," in Kohn, *Daoism Handbook*.

3. This passage comes from Ge Hong's (282–343) *Shenxian zhuan*. No extant original of *Shenxian zhuan* survives, and all modern versions are recompilations from citations in later works. The account of Wang Yuan and Cai Jing here comes from the Song dynasty *Taiping guangji* (Beijing: Zhonghua shuju, 1994), 7:46.

4. The most accessible account is by Fabrizio Pregadio and Lowell Skar, "Inner Alchemy (*Neidan*)," in Kohn, *Daoism Handbook*, pp. 464–97.

(*jing*), *qi*, and spirit (*shen*), the male adept creates what is known as the "outer medicine" in the Lower Cinnabar Field in his abdomen, mentioned previously. This outer medicine is in turn refined into the "inner medicine," and finally an "immortal embryo" is produced. The embryo is then nourished until it grows sufficiently to leave the body it was formed in, through the adept's head, as he reaches the goal of returning to the Dao.

The first stages of the process for female adepts are different, as female inner alchemy practices "acknowledge the physiological differences between women and men. While a man's energy resides in his lower Elixir [or Cinnabar] Field, many texts assert that a woman's energy resides in a point between the breasts called . . . Cavity of Energy. . . . This energy produces secretions that become menstrual blood, which is the material aspect of the essence in a woman's body," as Pregadio and Skar relate.[5] By making this distinction between the spiritual biochemistry of men and women, the intrinsically corporeal nature of Daoist inner alchemy is made explicit.

Within the Daoist tradition of cultivation, interpreted broadly, one important stream relates specifically to physical exercises. Indeed, it is practices in this tradition that contemporary works often regard as the precursors of the *qigong* of the present, and the existence of this long tradition is one element often cited to reinforce the idea that *qigong* practice is efficacious. The earliest definitive proof we have of the ancient practice of *qigong* comes from a painted silk banner that formed part of the extraordinary haul from tombs excavated from 1972 to 1974 at Mawangdui, near Changsha in Hunan Province. The tombs, dating from the first half of the second century BCE, belonged to the first Marquis of Dai, his wife, and, in all likelihood, their son. It was from this third tomb, closed in 168 BCE, that, among many religious, medical, and astronomical texts—some of which were otherwise unknown, or that preserved previously unknown versions of surviving texts—a silk banner was discovered, showing more than forty different images of men and women in poses clearly related to a physical exercise practice. This *Daoyin tu*, or *Chart of Leading and Pulling [Qi]*, is said to show people in positions resembling those of a traditional form of biospiritual exercise known as *baduan jin*, the Eight Section Brocade, popular in the martial arts practices of the Shaolin temple and often attributed to Zhongli Quan, one of the famous Eight Immortals.[6] Other

---

5. Ibid., p. 490.

6. Mawangdui Hanmu boshu zhengli xiaozubian, *Daoyin tu* (Beijing: Wenwu chubanshe, 1979). On Zhongli Quan, see Yoshikawa Tadao, "Zhongli Quan," in Pregadio, *The Encyclopedia of Taoism*, pp. 1283–84.

figures from the Daoist tradition who were responsible for famous forms of *qigong* still known today were Hua Tuo (d. 208), who is credited with inventing the Five Animals Play (*wuqin xi*), and Zhang Sanfeng (traditionally, fourteenth century), who developed *taiji quan* (or tai chi, as it is popularly known), according to some traditions.[7]

Another early stream concerned with cultivation, but of a rather different sort, begins as a concern of rulers and was located in the realm of morality. In the earliest dynasties, a ruler's virtue (*de*) was his guarantor of power—not in the sense we might think of today, where a ruler of poor virtue could lose the trust of his people, and therefore his legitimacy; rather, it meant that his virtue would necessarily elicit a favorable response from heaven. Thus, virtue was conceived, in Philip J. Ivanhoe's words, as "a kind of *power* which accrued to and resided within an individual," and, possibly from the earliest times, "was thought to be something that one must *earn* through the accumulation of good acts."[8] As the royal courts of China developed during the Zhou dynasty in the first millennium BCE, the ideal behavior of the monarch grew increasingly regulated as the protection of his virtue, and therefore his right to rule, became paramount. This regulation was understood to consist of a codified set of behaviors—toward heaven and toward people—that "included everything from high religious ceremonies to the conduct of government and . . . such things as one's personal deportment and behavior. Since everything the ruler did contributed, in some sense, to the character of his *de*, almost everything he did took on great significance."[9]

It was on the basis of this tradition that Confucius (551–479 BCE) developed the generalized principles of behavior that constitute his philosophy in its original form. In the famous formulation in the *Great Learning* (*Daxue*), which is ascribed to Confucius himself, cultivation is placed in a pivotal position in the scheme to perfect the state. In James Legge's classic translation, it reads:

The ancients . . . first ordered well their own states. Wishing to order well their states, they first regulated their families. Wishing to regulate their families, they first cultivated

---

7. For a translation of Hua Tuo's *Hou Hanshu* biography, see K. J. DeWoskin, *Doctors, Diviners and Magicians of Ancient China: Biographies of Fang-shih* (New York: Columbia University Press, 1983), p. 149. On Zhang Sanfeng, see Anna Seidel, "A Taoist Immortal of the Ming Dynasty: Chang Sanfeng," in *Self and Society in Ming Thought*, ed. Wm. Theodore de Bary (New York: Columbia University Press, 1970), pp. 483–531.

8. Philip J. Ivanhoe, *Confucian Moral Self-Cultivation* (New York: Peter Lang, 1993), p. 2; emphasis in the original.

9. Ibid., p. 4.

their persons. Wishing to cultivate their persons, they first rectified their hearts. Wishing to rectify their hearts, they first sought to be sincere in their thoughts. Wishing to be sincere in their thoughts, they first extended to the utmost their knowledge. Such extension of knowledge lay in the investigation of things.[10]

The importance of Confucius for this discussion is that while he regarded cultivation as vital for the monarch, it was also possible, indeed valuable, for lesser men. To cultivate one's person and one's virtue was to effect a transformation that would not be confined to the lives of the people performing the cultivation but would also influence those around them. This conception of cultivation for Confucius and his immediate followers was based on the conscious regulation of behavior in the social realm. By behaving in the right way and, crucially, by having the right and sincere intentions while doing so, a person would change self and society for the better.[11]

In Buddhism, cultivation is, of course, better known as meditation, and when Buddhist doctrines entered China in the first centuries of the Common Era, meditational practices came along with them. Buddhism also changed in China (even as it changed China itself), developing new concerns, new schools of thought, new disputations, and, of course, new meditational practices. Perhaps the form of East Asian Buddhist meditation best known in the West is that practiced in Chan (or in Japanese, Zen) Buddhism, where meditation takes a central role in the life of the monastery. We should be aware, though, that Chinese Buddhist meditation practices form a much larger field than those found in Chan. Chinese Buddhist meditations of various schools include visualization, active movements, and recitation, as well as mental concentration. In general the goal of any and all of these meditational techniques is to attack the ignorance and illusion to which the human mind is prone, in order to awaken the consciousness to a state of enlightenment in which reality is truly perceived. In the Buddhist understanding, wisdom is not attainable without the purification of the mind, and purification of the mind is not possible without meditation. In summary, Buddhist meditation involves two processes, both of which are necessary for insight: one

---

10. This passage comes from Confucius, the *Great Learning*; see James Legge, *The Four Books* (New York: Paragon Book Reprint, 1966), pp. 5–6.

11. Many centuries later, the course of thinking on cultivation in the Confucian tradition changed under the influence of Zhu Xi (1130–1200) and Wang Yangming (1472–1529), who advocated a form of Confucian meditation known as "quiet sitting," or *jingzuo*, which was profoundly influenced by Buddhist and Daoist practice.

of stilling the mind and focusing concentration, and one of cognition and perception.

We should be aware, however, that the understanding of meditation that has become popular in the West differs in significant ways from that practiced in traditional ways in Asia.[12] First, meditation was typically practiced in a monastic setting by clerics. The context in which it took place was characterized by strict rules relating to how the meditator prepared himself, the arrangement of the place in which the meditation was to occur, the making of offerings, and acts of worship, including invocation of deities. It was thus typically surrounded by ritual performance.[13] Second, although the goal of meditation was to attain the perfect clarity of insight that came with enlightenment, it was also the case that in the process of attaining this state, the meditator might see visions, and his body acquire supernormal powers or "superknowledges," as they are often referred to in English (in Chinese, *shentong* or in Sanskrit, *abhijñā*).[14] Some of the specific powers that can be acquired through meditation also appear in Falun Gong's teachings, but both doctrines stress that these powers are not to be taken seriously as the goal of practice; rather, they are by-products of it and may indeed be distractions from it.

Thus, physical exercises that allegedly lead to bodily transformations beyond simply gaining fitness and strength, and the idea of cultivation itself, have been ubiquitous in Chinese culture for millennia. It should come as no surprise, then, that these ideas and practices burgeoned in China during the 1980s after the severe restrictions on social and cultural life were loosened in 1979, and continued to flourish into the 1990s when Falun Gong appeared. Furthermore, that Falun Gong cultivation echoes earlier forms of cultivation and the theories that underpinned them—even if Li Hongzhi does not explicitly refer to them or was even, perhaps, unaware of them—is easy to understand, as they remain pervasive in the mental world of contemporary China.

---

12. On Western understandings of Buddhism and in particular meditation, see Donald S. Lopez Jr.'s introduction to his *Modern Buddhism: Readings for the Unenlightened* (London: Penguin, 2002), especially pp. xxxix–xl.

13. See Robert H. Sharf, "Ritual," in *Critical Terms for the Study of Buddhism*, ed. Donald S. Lopez Jr. (Chicago: University of Chicago Press, 2005), pp. 245–70, especially pp. 260ff.

14. On *shentong*, see Bernard Faure, *The Rhetoric of Immediacy: A Cultural Critique of Chan/Zen Buddhism* (Princeton, NJ: Princeton University Press, 1991), pp. 102ff.; on the Indian Buddhist precedents, see Patrick A. Pranke, "Abhijñā," in *Encyclopedia of Buddhism*, ed. Robert E. Buswell (New York: MacMillan Reference USA, 2004), pp. 8–9.

The Falun Gong Exercises

Until practitioners began systematically to protest against the Chinese government with their antitorture displays, take part in community parades or commemorations, or perform in "New Year Spectaculars" or similar song-and-dance performances, most people first encountered Falun Gong by seeing cultivators performing their exercises in parks or other public places.[15] In the China of the 1990s, adherents of various *qigong* groups were commonly to be encountered performing their routines collectively, typically before work, at their agreed practice sites in various urban locations.[16] Falun Gong was just one of many such groups when it started, although as it grew to become perhaps the largest in the country, its activities became much more noticeable. Then, as now, public practice was one of the primary ways of attracting the attention of the general public and gaining new recruits. Falun Gong's introductory websites encourage people to learn the exercises at their "local Falun Dafa practice site," and generally note that "many students of Falun Dafa enjoy doing them together as a group outdoors." They also claim that there are hundreds of the sites around the world—outside China, of course—where everyone is welcome and can learn the exercises on the spot free of charge.[17]

The exercises are, then, the most common entry point into Falun Gong for new practitioners. In various books and writings, Li Hongzhi explains the development and purpose of the exercises. In the revised edition of *Falun Gong*, he claims that they are a simplified version of an original higher form of Falun Gong that existed in the far distant past, a highly intensive cultivation system suited only for exceptional students. The exercises that he began teaching in 1992 were "suitable for the public," but they still "far exceed average cultivation systems in terms of what they offer and the levels at which they are practiced."[18] In *The Great Consummation Way of Falun Dafa*, on the other hand, it is the *function* of the exercises that is stressed. Apparently, the exercises will open "areas in the practitioner's body where energy is blocked . . . and a great amount of

15. Li explicitly requests practitioners to "do the exercises as a group in parks" ("Environment" [October 17, 1997], in *Essentials for Further Advancement*, p. 48; "Huanjing," in *Falun dafa jingjin yaozhi*, p. 105).

16. See N. Chen, *Breathing Spaces*, especially pp. 49–56.

17. See, for instance, Anon., "Falun Dafa Australia: Introduction," online at www.falunau.org/aboutdafa.htm.

18. Li, *Falun Gong*, 4/Introduction, p. 42; p. 76.

energy will be absorbed from the cosmos. In a very short period of time the exercises will expel useless substances from the practitioner's body and purify it." This purification process will, *The Great Consummation Way* tells us, help the practitioner arrive at the state of physical transformation known as the "pure-white body," a condition discussed at more length in chapter 6.[19]

It is important to distinguish between what Falun Gong practitioners believe they are doing when they exercise and what adherents of other *qigong* forms believe and do. These differences are made clear in the earliest publicity for Falun Gong from 1993, when its name first appeared in *qigong* magazines. At that time, when Falun Gong had to create a niche for itself among all the other varieties of *qigong* that were clamoring for attention in China, two major selling points were stressed in the advertisements: the ease of learning the exercises, and the ability of cultivators to practice them anywhere and at any hour of the day, even to the point of not being able to do them at all due to pressure of time. Thus, one call for enrollments in "Falun Gong transmission classes" in Guangzhou from March 1993 makes clear that Falun Gong is suitable for busy people: "Even if people have no time to practice, the *Fa* will continue to cultivate them unceasingly so that cultivators will cultivate twenty four hours a day adding to their *gong*."[20] A similar advertisement for classes in Hefei in Anhui Province from February 1994, on the other hand, emphasizes the simplicity of the exercises: "There are five sets of exercises in Falun Gong; they are easy to learn and easy to remember."[21]

The fact that Falun Gong selected these two features as prime selling points in its early advertisements is informative. Clearly, in the early 1990s, other *qigong* groups had a reputation for teaching complicated exercises that were difficult to learn, and demanded that they be performed regularly at set times or in set places.[22] This is summed up in a passage from Li's January 1995 lecture, "Teaching the *Fa* in Beijing at the *Zhuan Falun* Publication Ceremony," where he referred explicitly to other *qigong* practices—although not by name: "We don't pay attention to which direction to face while practicing, or what time to practice and which direction to face." Li continued by considering the practitioner in

---

19. Li, *The Great Consummation Way*, 1/5, p. 5; *Falun dafa da yuanman fa*, p. 5.

20. Anon., "Zhongguo Falun Gong xuexiban zhaosheng," *Qigong yu kexue* 3 (1993): 24.

21. Anon., "Zhongguo Falun Gong Hefei chuanshouban zhaosheng," *Qigong yu kexue* 2 (1994): 46.

22. It should be noted that in this early period the now standard statement that "all Falun Dafa activities are free of charge" was not true: the Guangdong classes cost 80 yuan, with an additional registration fee of three yuan; the Hefei classes cost 50 yuan. Another class in September 1993 in Guangzhou cost 100 yuan, with a registration fee of 5 yuan (*Qigong yu kexue* 7 [1993], p. 46).

the context of the universe as a whole, where the earth, all the planets, and the galaxy itself are constantly in rotation. Earthly orientation—facing north or south, for instance—thus becomes irrelevant. "Whichever direction you face when you practice," he said, "is the same as facing all directions." Similarly, while other *qigong* groups insisted that the exercises be done in specific two-hour blocks, Li claimed that while these times may be good for practice in this dimension, they may not be good in others.[23] Consequently, the ease and unrestricted nature of the physical practice is the first major difference between Falun Gong and standard *qigong* forms that the movement emphasized.

Although newcomers to Falun Gong were—and continue to be—first introduced to the five sets of exercises, it is clear that physical practice does not encompass the whole of cultivation, or indeed its core.[24] The epigraph to *The Great Consummation Way*, Li's work that most centrally addresses the exercises, states that "movements are the supplementary means for reaching Consummation"—that is, whereas they play an important role in adherents' practice at every stage, other aspects of cultivation are actually more important. Cultivation requires a change to the whole of the Falun Gong follower's life, rather than simply performing the exercises on a regular basis. Indeed, the exercises come a distant second to reading the works of Li Hongzhi. Thus, as Li suggests in his 1998 essay "Melt into the *Fa*,"

To put it more simply, as long as you read Dafa, you are changing; as long as you read Dafa, you are elevating. The boundless content of Dafa plus the supplementary means—the exercises—will enable you to reach Consummation.[25]

Another way, then, in which Falun Gong cultivation differs from other *qigong* cultivation is that it demands the practitioners' attention in all aspects of their lives and is not limited to the performance of a routine of exercises.

The third way that Li Hongzhi distinguishes Falun Gong cultivation from other forms of *qigong* is that it is not actually standard *qigong* at all. As we saw in the introduction, *qigong* is generally understood to mean

---

23. Li, "Teaching the *Fa* in Beijing at the *Zhuan Falun* Publication Ceremony," p. 28; "Beijing zhuan falun shoufashi shang jiangfa," p. 37.

24. See, for instance, the introductory web page "Falun Dafa: How to Learn," www.falundafa .org/eng/howtolearn.html, which states, "Learning Falun Dafa (also known as Falun Gong) involves both studying the principles and practicing the exercises."

25. Li Hongzhi, "Melt into the *Fa*" (August 3, 1998), in *Essentials for Further Advancement*, p. 51; "Rong yu fa zhong," in *Falun dafa jingjin yaozhi*, p. 113.

those various physical, visualization, and meditational techniques that manipulate *qi*, literally breath, which is why breathing in special ways is often a constituent part of *qigong* practice. Li maintains that this kind of practice is simply intended to heal disease, promote health, and maintain fitness. When newcomers are introduced to Falun Gong, he cleanses their bodies, thereby ridding them of disease and enabling them to embark on cultivation. Once they complete the series of nine lectures, cultivators have apparently already attained the advanced condition known as a "milk-white body." In this way, Li takes ordinary people who were predestined to become cultivators and exempts them from the stages in cultivation that standard *qigong* slowly works its way through. This bears on one of the abiding discussions in Li's writings about the exercises: what should the practitioners think about when they are doing them? And in particular, should they use "intention" (*yinian*) or "mindwill" or "mind-intent," as Falun Gong texts variously translate it?

Miura Kunio explains how "intention" has been understood in broader *qigong* circles.

In *Qigong* physical energy [i.e. *qi*] is circulated by a movement of conscious thought as much as by physical exercise. As the thinking moves around the body so does the *qi*. This concept is usually expressed in phrases like "guiding the *qi* with the thinking" or "where there is thinking there is *qi*."[26]

A more detailed account of the relationship between thought and *qi* in *qigong* comes from a work on "medical *qigong*" published in 1990 where six different mental activities are listed.

1. "localized mind concentration" where the practitioner concentrates on a particular part of the body, often one of the three cinnabar fields, an acupuncture point, or the fingers or hands.
2. "directive mind concentration" in which the practitioner mentally follows the flow of *qi* around the body through the meridians.
3. "rhythmical mind concentration" in which the awareness follows the pulse of the breath.
4. "power-strengthening mind concentration" in which the practitioner imagines him or herself to be immensely strong or powerful.
5. "suggestive mind concentration" where the practitioner silently names or describes the goals they wish to accomplish in their *qigong* practice.

26. Miura, "The Revival of *Qi*," pp. 331–62; quotation is from p. 337.

6. "representative mind concentration" where the practitioner imagines him or herself to be performing certain actions such as "stroking a ball, pressing *qi*, instilling *qi* and expelling unhealthy *qi*, and he may feel *qi* as hot as fire, as cold as ice, as sharp as a sword, or as soft as cotton.[27]

In addition to circulating *qi* through the practitioner's own body, certain *qigong* masters have been said to be able to send *qi* out from their bodies (*waiqi*), typically to cure others of disease. However, as we have seen, Falun Gong cultivators regard themselves as having passed beyond the stage of cultivating *qi*, as they have progressed at least as far as the state of a "milk-white body." Thus, as "intention" is specifically used to guide or circulate the movement of *qi*, Falun Gong cultivation has no need of it. In the analysis of the Falun Gong exercises that follows, particular attention will therefore be paid to what Li Hongzhi says the performance of the exercises accomplishes, as well as to the place of mental activity in them, as it is in these ways that he distinguishes Falun Gong cultivation from other forms of *qigong*.

There are five exercises in the Falun Gong routine, four in which the practitioner stands and one in which he or she is seated: Buddha Stretching a Thousand Arms, Falun Standing Stance, Coursing between the Two Poles, Falun Cosmic Orbit, and Reinforcing Supernatural Powers. Each of the exercises is subdivided into different stages, although these are not readily apparent to the viewer as each part flows smoothly into the next. Before performing an exercise, the practitioner is instructed to recite a four-line verse that pertains to it or listen to that verse on tape. The verses are to be recited in Chinese only, and guides for pronunciation and translations of each line are given in the footnotes to *The Great Consummation Way*. There is nothing particularly revealing about what the verses say. The first, for example, for Buddha Stretching a Thousand Arms, reads:

The body and the spirit joined together,
Move or become still according to the energy mechanisms,
As tall as heaven and incomparably noble,
The thousand-armed Buddha stands upright.[28]

Since non-Chinese-speaking practitioners must recite these lines in Chinese when, in all other aspects of Falun Gong, translations are clearly

27. Bi Yongsheng, ed., *Yixue qigong* (Beijing: Gaodeng jiaoyu chubanshe, 1990; English title, *Medical Qigong*, chief editor Yu Wenping), pp. 25–26.

28. Li, *The Great Consummation Way*, 2/1, p. 8, amended; *Falun dafa da yuanman fa*, p. 8.

regarded as equal to the original, it must be thought that these words have some power in and of themselves that would be lost if their semantic equivalents in English or some other language were used. The idea that particular words have great power is common in Chinese and many other religions. In East Asian Buddhism, the practice of chanting words or texts that are not (or cannot be) understood is widespread. Among those chanted words or phrases are the names of sutras, the first character on each page of a sutra, the name of a deity—often the Buddha of the Western Paradise—and *dhāraṇis*, which are incomprehensible collections of syllables based on Sanskrit. Whole texts can also be chanted, even if they are not understood. George J. Tanabe Jr. has indeed argued that "chanting the *Heart Sutra* without understanding its discursive meaning is not a violation of the text, but the fulfillment of it."[29]

The closest equivalent to the Falun Gong verses in Buddhist literature are the *gāthās* found in Buddhist sutras in Chinese. Similarly four lines long and found in versions of four, five, or seven characters in each line (the Falun Gong verses have four characters per line), these *gāthās* are considered to be powerful summaries of the whole of the sutra from which they come. For instance, in the *Lotus Sutra*, the Buddha says,

If there are good men or good women who, with regard to this sutra, can accept and uphold even one four-line verse, if they read and recite it, understand the principle and practice it as the sutra directs, the benefits will be very many.[30]

In the Chinese outlines of the Falun Gong exercises these verses are called "instructions" (*jue* or *koujue*), which is rendered as "oral instructions" in the revised edition of *Falun Gong* and as "verse" in *The Great Consummation Way*. In the first edition of *Falun Gong*, however, they are given the name *yijing*, which usually refers to a mood created by viewing a work of art or natural vista. No instructions are given as to whether they should be read, spoken, or heard in this text. It may be that the verses are intended to give rise to a state of mind in which the exercise is performed or else which is induced by the exercise, a question of relevance to the discussions of "intention" raised earlier.

Similarly, in the exercises themselves, each of the stages is given a four-character name that is usually descriptive of the movements concerned. In the first exercise—Buddha Stretching a Thousand Arms—these

---

29. George J. Tanabe Jr., "Chanting and Liturgy," in Buswell, *Encyclopedia of Buddhism*, pp. 137–38.
30. *The Lotus Sutra* (trans. Burton Watson), available at www.sgi-usa.org/Buddhism/library/Buddhism/LotusSutra/text/Chap26.htm.

names, as well as the name of the exercise itself, often have Buddhist connotations, but the relationship of the movement to the terminology seems arbitrary. For instance, the second stage is called "Buddha Maitreya Stretching His Back," and while the practitioner's back is stretched in this stage, what this action has to do with Maitreya, the future Buddha, is obscure. Different stages in this exercise use other Buddhist terms, such as *tathāgata, bodhisattva, arhat*, and *vajra*, while one stage is called "Golden Monkey Splitting Its Body." The "golden monkey" here is one of the names by which the Monkey King from *Journey to the West*, Sun Wukong, is known, and splitting his body into many versions of himself is one of his methods of overcoming adversaries. This Buddhist terminology would be familiar to many Chinese people, even if they might not actually know the specific meanings or connotations of the terms in doctrinal Buddhism. However, the primary connotations of phrases like "bodhisattva touching the lotus," or "*arhat* carrying a mountain on his back," or "*vajra* toppling a mountain" would not be Buddhist ones for most contemporary Chinese people. They would be more immediately reminiscent of the names of certain moves described in martial arts novels, probably the most popular form of fiction in contemporary China.[31]

According to Li, the first exercise, Buddha Stretching a Thousand Arms, is designed to open up the meridians, to allow for the free flow of energy throughout the body. He says that this exercise opens all the meridians in the body—whereas in standard *qigong* techniques meridians are typically worked on one by one—"stretching and relaxing [so that] the areas of congested energy in the body are unblocked."[32] The way the practitioner holds his or her body, including stance and position of hips, teeth, tongue, and arms, is designed to allow unencumbered flow of energy. This exercise is done first, as it enables the practitioner to "quickly enter the state of being surrounded by an energy field."[33]

The guidelines for how the practitioner should prepare for this exercise include a good example of how Li Hongzhi's writings have been revised over the years. In this case, his changes implicitly refer to the role of "intention" in Falun Gong cultivation. In the first edition of *Falun Gong*, the practitioner is instructed, "Imagine [*yixiang*] that you are very big and tall, your awareness (*yi*) is in your two hands."[34] In the revised edition, the equivalent sentence reads: "During the exercise you will have

---

31. I would like to thank Geremie R. Barmé for pointing this out to me.
32. Li, *The Great Consummation Way*, 3/1, p. 30; *Falun dafa da yuanman fa*, p. 43.
33. Ibid., 2/1, p. 8; p. 8.
34. Li, *Zhongguo falungong* (1993), p. 89.

the feeling [*gandao*] that you are very large and tall."[35] Clearly, the way that the practitioner's mind relates to the exercise changes between the first and the revised editions of the book. In the first version, intention is undeniably present, with a decisive role granted to the imagination and the use of directed awareness. In the terms of the work on medical *qigong* cited earlier, these appear to be cases of "power-strengthening mind concentration" and "localized mind concentration." In the revised version, the sense that the practitioner is "very big and tall" comes as a *result* of the exercise rather than as an act of volition—the practitioner "feels" it—and the directed awareness has disappeared. In these revisions it may be possible to observe an increasing sensitivity on the part of Li to the possible accusation that he *does* use intention in the practice. If this is a correct conclusion, then apparently he thought it wisest to remove any possible indication that the mind played any role in the exercises: in the third version of these instructions, found in *The Great Consummation Way*, this sentence disappears completely.

The second exercise, Falun Standing Stance, involves the practitioner maintaining four different poses—all of them as if he or she is holding a large wheel—for extended periods of time. This exercise will apparently "facilitate the complete opening of the entire body. It is a comprehensive means of cultivation practice that enhances wisdom, increases strength, raises a person's level, and strengthens divine powers."[36]

The third exercise, Coursing between the Two Poles, consists of three sets of movements, the first two of which have the hands moving from high above the head to the feet. The third part of this exercise has both hands placed in front of the abdomen, where they turn the *falun* that resides inside four times. The point of this exercise is to exchange bad energy from within the body—*Falun Gong* refers to pathogenic *qi* and black *qi* being expelled—for good cosmic energy that is absorbed into the body. In this way, the practitioner can be purified, ultimately reaching the state of possessing a "pure-white body," an important and lofty achievement on the path to Consummation. In doing this exercise, spaces on the top of the head and on the soles of the feet are opened to allow for the free flow of energy in both directions. Li explains that the opened space on the top of the head "doesn't refer to the cranium in this dimension—that would prove too frightening. It's the crania in other dimensions."[37] In this exercise, as in the first, there are arguably traces of "intention." All

35. Li, *Falun Gong*, 4/1, p. 43; p. 78.
36. Li, *The Great Consummation Way*, 2/2, p. 14; *Falun dafa da yuanman fa*, p. 17.
37. Ibid., 3/3, p. 35; p. 51.

three versions of the instructions ask the practitioner to "imagine [*yixiang*, or "think of," *xiang*] yourself as two large empty barrels, standing up between heaven and earth, gigantic and incomparably tall."[38]

The fourth exercise, Falun Cosmic Orbit, is intended to circulate energy throughout the body. This circulation is to take place not just along specific meridians, but from one side of the body to the other, and from front to back, unblocking all energy paths. The "cosmic orbit" or "heavenly circuit" (*zhoutian*) of the title as it is more usually translated is a common term in *qigong* writings, where there is understood to be a smaller and a larger heavenly circuit.[39] The Falun Gong version of the "heavenly circuit," of course, goes far beyond these other practices, which Li regards as inferior. In the exercise, the practitioner passes his or her hands along each limb in turn and then over the body and head, maintaining a distance of three to four centimeters between the palm of each hand and the body.

The fifth exercise, Reinforcing Supernatural Powers—"supernatural powers" is a translation of *shentong*, referred to earlier in this chapter—is performed seated in the lotus position and features three parts. The arms and hands move above the head and out to the sides, and then come to rest in a meditation posture, with the hands in the lap. This last position corresponds to a traditional Buddhist gesture known in Sanskrit as the *dhyāna mudrā*, or gesture of meditation. At several points during this exercise, the practitioner is instructed to hold a position for as long as possible. In this respect, the fifth exercise differs from the others, which are made up of continuous movements. Li maintains that Reinforcing Supernatural Powers, unlike the other four exercises, was originally a secret practice that he made public only to help more advanced practitioners gain salvation. In *The Great Consummation Way*, he explains that it is a practice that "I used to do on my own. I'm now making it public without any modifications." Apparently the reason for this is that because he can no longer teach the exercise one to one to individuals who have attained the necessary level for it, he has made it public for everyone, including beginners.[40] Furthermore, it can be performed by itself rather than as part of a program of the five.

The fifth exercise is essentially a meditation. Li stresses that the practitioner should enter into a meditative state, which in English-language

---

38. Li, *Zhongguo falungong* (1993), p. 101, Li, *Falun Gong*, 4/3, p. 52; p. 90, Li, *The Great Consummation Way*, 2/3, p. 17; *Falun dafa da yuanman fa*, p. 21.

39. These terms are also prevalent in Daoist forms of cultivation. See Martine Darga, "Zhoutian," in Pregadio, *The Encyclopedia of Taoism*, pp. 1287–89.

40. Li, *The Great Consummation Way*, 3/5, p. 39; *Falun dafa da yuanman fa*, p.57.

works on Buddhism is usually termed *samādhi*—using the Sanskrit word—in which "you will be aware of yourself doing the exercise, but you will feel that your entire body can't move."[41] Although the practitioner may find that he or she loses awareness of the limbs and body and feels that he or she is mind only, a conscious awareness of physical state and location should always be maintained.

These five exercises, then, constitute the aspect of Falun Gong that a new practitioner will first encounter, and that most resembles standard forms of *qigong*. Indeed, we can assume that some people only perform the exercises and do not go further with Falun Gong practice. This is not, however, acceptable to Li Hongzhi, as he makes clear in his April 1994 statement, "What Is Expected of Falun Dafa Assistance Centers":

Falun Dafa practitioners must cultivate their character, along with performing the movements. Those who focus solely on the exercise movements but neglect character cultivation will not be acknowledged as Falun Dafa disciples. Therefore, Dafa practitioners need to make studying the Law [*Fa*] and reading the books the essential part of their daily cultivation.[42]

This sentiment is reiterated in *Zhuan Falun*, where he underlines the importance of character (as *xinxing* is often translated in Falun Gong works) in relation to the exercises.

So if somebody just does these few sets of movements every day, you think he counts as a Falun Dafa disciple? Probably not. The reason is, when you truly cultivate you have to discipline yourself with that character standard we talk about, you have to really improve your own character, and then, and only then, is it true cultivation.[43]

Morality and Behavior

True cultivation, as Li Hongzhi explains, consists of two features—performance of the exercises and cultivation of "character," or *xinxing*. *Xinxing* is the standard Chinese word for "temperament" or "disposition," but as usual, in Falun Gong its meaning is distinctive. In *Zhuan Falun*, Li asks himself rhetorically, "So what is character?" and provides the answer.

41. Ibid., p. 40; p. 60.
42. This is point 8 of "What Is Expected of Falun Dafa Assistance Centers," referred to in chapter 2. Li, *The Great Consummation Way*, appendices, pp. 1–2; *Falun dafa da yuanman fa*, p. 63.
43. Li, *Zhuan Falun* 3/1, p. 46; p. 82.

Character includes virtue (which is a type of matter), it includes forbearance, it includes awakening to things, it includes giving up things—giving up all the desires and all the attachments that are found in an ordinary person—and you also have to endure hardship, to name just a few things. So it includes a lot of different things. You need to improve every aspect of your character, and only when you do that will you really improve.[44]

When Falun Gong texts appear in English, *xinxing* is often left untranslated. When its meaning is expounded in glossaries, each part of the compound is translated separately; thus it becomes "mind [*xin*]-nature [*xing*]." Both elements of this compound are complex. The word *xin* literally means "heart," but in traditional China, the heart—the original form of the character depicts the actual organ—was the seat of understanding and emotion. Some translators render *xin* as "heart-mind" to encompass both aspects of the word. *Xing* refers to the nature or character of a person or a thing. In particular it refers to moral character, and so, unsurprisingly, it has become a term rich in connotation in Chinese philosophy. When Falun Gong practitioners talk of cultivating *xinxing*, they are referring to refining their behavior and improving their morality. This moral improvement is not made, however, simply for its own sake or even as a prerequisite for cultivation of the body. Improving one's *xinxing* is not "just a philosophical thing," as *Zhuan Falun* says, but has a material basis.[45] Li explains this using the analogy of a sealed bottle filled with dirt. Thrown into water, it will sink, but as some of the dirt is poured out it will gradually become more buoyant. Emptied entirely, it will float to the surface. He concludes by saying, "What we're doing when we cultivate is getting rid of every kind of bad thing that's in the body, and that's the only way to rise to higher levels."[46]

The process of change that the body of the cultivator undergoes is the concern of the next chapter, so for the moment we will simply concentrate on what is meant by cultivating character, or *xinxing*. There are two aspects to this process that may be thought of as positive and negative, or as adopting certain practices and rejecting others. In Falun Gong texts, these aspects are often described as constituting "gain and loss." The revised version of *Falun Gong* states that gain "is to gain conformity to the characteristics of the cosmos," which are truth, compassion, and forbearance—we saw in the previous chapter how Li understands that the

44. Ibid., 1/6, p. 14, amended; pp. 23–24.
45. Ibid., p. 14; p. 24.
46. Ibid., p. 14; p. 25.

universe itself is, in fact, constituted by *zhen, shan,* and *ren*—while loss "is to abandon negative thoughts and behaviors, such as greed, profit, lust, desire, killing, fighting, theft, robbery, deception, jealousy, etc." But *loss* also means "to break with the pursuit of desires."[47] Thus, the positive side of the cultivation process consists of practitioners aligning their lives with the three moral verities of Falun Gong: truth, compassion, and forbearance. The negative side is the insistence that genuine cultivators abandon their desires, or as it is usually put, "give up attachments."

Correct behavior is therefore at the core of cultivation for the Falun Gong practitioner. Given this, it is striking how little attention the positive side of the topic receives in Falun Gong writings. To be sure, giving up attachments is a theme that returns with regularity in Li's books and talks, but what it means to act in accordance with truth, compassion, and forbearance is discussed much less frequently. Notably, these three aspects of right behavior are each considered as day-to-day requirements, as well as at a level beyond our normal existences. Thus, in one of the few instances in which the topic of truth is raised explicitly, Li explains that to cultivate *zhen* a person should "say true words, do true things, be a truthful person, return to your original, true self, and ultimately cultivate into a True Person."[48]

While saying true words and doing true things refer to how a practitioner might behave in the world, "returning to one's origin and true self" and "becoming a True Person" both point to metaphysical goals. We have seen how Li teaches that all humans, by their very nature, have fallen from their original selves and the dimension in which they existed, progressively tumbling down to the cesspool that is this earth. One way of expressing the goal of cultivation is to "return to one's true self," which is achieved by a step-by-step transformation into the kind of beings that we once were. Accordingly, "becoming a True Person" is a way of describing what we will become, using in this case specifically Daoist language. What is translated here as "True Person [*zhenren*]" is rendered elsewhere in studies of Daoism, where this term occurs most frequently, as "Realized Man" or "Perfected," both of which stress that this exalted state is the culmination of a course of biospiritual transformation. Such *zhenren* are often considered heavenly beings.

Likewise, compassion has both its earthly manifestations in behavior and a more cosmic form as the motivation for saving all beings. In the revised edition of *Falun Gong*, compassion—*shan*—is described as "be-

---

47. Li, *Falun Gong* 3/1, p. 28, amended; p. 50.
48. Li, *Zhuan Falun* 1/3, p. 8; p. 14.

ing about developing great compassion, doing good things, and saving people."[49] While *Zhuan Falun* sometimes raises the topic of compassion in generalized Buddhist terms, as in "once this heart of great compassion comes out you can see the suffering of all sentient beings, so you'll be filled with one wish: to save all sentient beings," the specific context in which it discusses compassion most frequently is healing the sick.[50] Disease, as we have seen, is understood by Li Hongzhi to be derived from the accumulation of karma. Simply curing an illness is therefore only getting rid of the surface effect of a root problem, since eradicating karma is necessary to eliminate the cause of all disease. Thus, Falun Gong practitioners are not generally permitted to heal the sick; in this Falun Gong sets itself apart from most *qigong* schools, where efficacy in healing sickness was, and remains, a defining feature. However, as Li observes, because practitioners have such great compassion they are allowed to use any healing abilities they have acquired in the course of their cultivation to treat patients, but not "on a large scale." Curing diseases willy-nilly would undermine ordinary human society and the laws of karma; and besides, by doing so the practitioner would only be postponing the inevitable return of illness, as the patient's karmic load would not have been relieved.[51] Cosmically, compassion appears as the defining characteristic of Great Enlightened Beings who have saved humanity from destruction, taking pity on our benighted species when we have fallen so far due to our selfishness.

Of the three moral verities that Falun Gong practitioners must comply with, perhaps the one that receives most explanation is forbearance—*ren*. At one point in *Zhuan Falun*, Li explains,

So what's great forbearance? To be a practitioner you should, for starters, be able to "not hit back when attacked, not talk back when insulted." You have to show forbearance. If you don't, what are you calling yourself a practitioner for? Some people have said, "This forbearance thing is hard to do. I've got a bad temper." If you have a bad temper then just change it. Practitioners have to show forbearance.[52]

More than just enduring abuse, successful cultivators should not even let such verbal or physical attacks prey on their mind—they should show the equanimity of an *arhat*, one of the enlightened disciples of the Buddha.

49. Li, *Falun Gong* 3/3, p. 31; p. 55.
50. Li, *Zhuan Falun* 1/3, p. 8; amended; p. 14.
51. See ibid., 1/1, p. 2; pp. 2–3, 2/3, p. 36; p. 63, and especially 7/5, passim.
52. Ibid., 9/6, p. 190, amended; p. 326.

In explaining the meaning of forbearance, Li reaches for a well-known historical anecdote. This concerns Han Xin, a high-ranking general in the army of Liu Bang, who became the first emperor of the Han dynasty in 221 BCE. When he was young, Han carried a sword, and one day encountered a local bully. The bully dared Han to strike him with the sword, or else suffer the humiliation of crawling between his legs. Han, it is said, realizing that to accept the dare would have meant that he would face either death or execution, chose the route of humiliation. In doing this he is regarded as having demonstrated great wisdom and acuity, in a sense prefiguring his later reputation for military strategy, where engaging in a battle one cannot win is considered the height of foolishness. For Li, this "showed that Han Xin had a heart of great forbearance."[53] Enduring insult and not responding in kind has, according to Li, positive material effects. If practitioners are abused in some way, showing this kind of forbearance improves their *xinxing* and, significantly, transforms their "black substance"—that is, karma—into *de*, or virtue, the "white substance."[54]

Transforming karma into virtue is fundamental in the cultivation practice of Falun Gong. We have seen how transgressions in behavior lead to the accumulation of karma in the body, and how karma is understood in Falun Gong to be a black substance. In the next chapter, we will see how virtue, the white substance in the body, must be transformed into *gong* energy for the Falun Gong cultivator to progress up the path toward Consummation. It is therefore imperative for practitioners to be able to change their karma into *de*, the raw material of *gong* energy. Thus, in many ways, forbearance—*ren*—is at the very core of Falun Gong practice: it is through forbearance that karma mysteriously transforms into *de*.

Thus, forbearance is interpreted as the endurance of suffering—tempering your *xinxing* and aiding in the transformation of your body. Encounters that challenge practitioners, whether directly in interpersonal conflict or indirectly through unfortunate events happening in everyday life, are called in Falun Gong "tribulations." These tribulations are to be endured because the very process of suffering and endurance will be positive for cultivation.

Earlier in this section, I quoted a passage from *Zhuan Falun* that defines *zhen*, and a related passage from the revised version of *Falun Gong* on *shan*. The *Zhuan Falun* passage as a whole reads:

53. Ibid., pp. 190–91, amended; p. 327.
54. Li, *Falun Gong* 3/3, p. 31, amended; p. 56.

Daoists cultivate Truth, Compassion, and Forbearance with an emphasis on Truth. That's why Daoists strive to cultivate truth and nourish their inborn nature, say true words, do true things, be a truthful person, return to the original, true self, and ultimately cultivate into a True Person. But they also have Forbearance, and they also have Compassion, it's just that the emphasis is on cultivating the Truth part. Buddhists emphasize the Compassion of Truth, Compassion, and Forbearance, in their cultivation. Cultivation of Compassion can develop a heart of great compassion, and once this heart of great compassion comes out you can see the suffering of all sentient beings, so you'll be filled with one wish: to save all sentient beings. But they also have Truth, and they also have Forbearance, it's just that the emphasis is on cultivating Compassion. Our Falun Dafa discipline goes by the highest standard of the cosmos, to have Truth, Compassion, and Forbearance and we cultivate these all together.[55]

What is striking about this passage, where Li aligns *zhen*—truth—to Daoism and *shan*—compassion—to Buddhism, is that *ren*—forbearance—is simply mentioned as the third component without being directly aligned with any particular religion. However, given the traditional formula in the Chinese tradition of the "three teachings"—Buddhism, Daoism, and Confucianism—we might expect *ren* to find its counterpart in the Confucian tradition.

Although *ren* does appear in some of the foundational texts in that tradition, Confucius and his followers are quoted in those texts as discussing *intolerable* practices.[56] For instance, in the Confucian *Analects* we find the saying, "Confucius said of the Chi Family, 'They use eight rows of eight dancers each to perform in their courtyard'"—a form of entertainment reserved for the imperial court—"If this can be tolerated [*ren*], what cannot be tolerated?"[57] Or we find Mencius saying of the renowned eremite Bo Yi, "He would not serve a prince whom he did not approve, nor command a people whom he did not esteem. In a time of good government he took office, and on the occurrence of confusion he retired. He could not bear [*ren*] to dwell either in a court from which a lawless government emanated, or among lawless people."[58] What is clear from these short citations (and others that could be adduced) is that for Confucius and Mencius, *ren* is used as a simple verb—to tolerate, to bear—rather than carrying the weight of a fundamental moral virtue—forbearance—as

55. Li, *Zhuan Falun* 1/3, p. 8, amended; p. 14.
56. It is important, however, not to confuse the *ren* used in Falun Gong, meaning "forbearance" with a different *ren* that means "human-heartedness," which *is* fundamental in Confucianism.
57. Confucius, *The Analects*, trans. D. C. Lau (Harmondsworth, UK: Penguin Books, 1979), p. 67.
58. Mencius (trans. J. Legge), in Legge, *The Four Books*, p. 812.

it does in Falun Gong. Clearly, despite the temptation to see Li's three moral verities aligning directly with China's traditional three teachings, we must look elsewhere for another religious tradition that places forbearance and the ways of acting associated with it in such an exalted position.[59]

Consider the following passage from *Zhuan Falun*:

There are people who say, "If I'm walking down the street and somebody kicks me, I can show forbearance, since nobody knows me." I'd say that's not good enough. Maybe later on you'll be slapped in the face a couple times in front of the very person you least want to lose face around, and that's to humiliate you, to see how you handle it, and to see whether you can show forbearance.[60]

The imagery Li deploys here of being repeatedly slapped in the face seems to me to have an unmistakable parallel, namely Jesus's injunction in the Gospel of Luke at 6:29: "If anyone strikes you on the cheek, offer the other also." This possible Christian parallel is strengthened upon finding that in standard translations of the Bible into Chinese, the word *ren* features significantly.[61] In such translations it appears as part of the compound *rennai*, as in Matthew 24:13, "But the one who endures [*rennai*] to the end will be saved," or in Romans 3:25, "He did this to show his righteousness, because in his divine forbearance [*rennai*] he had passed over the sins previously committed."

59. It is important in this context to note the similarity between Li Hongzhi's "*zhen, shan, ren*" formulation and another set phrase in modern Chinese, namely "*zhen, shan, mei.*" "*Zhen, shan, mei*" is the standard translation for the phrase usually rendered in English as "the true, the good, and the beautiful" and found in philosophy, particularly in the German tradition, and made famous in China through the writings of Cai Yuanpei (1868–1940). Finding its way into China largely through the writings of Hegel on dialectics, Mao Zedong famously used the phrase in two works from early 1957: the extraordinarily influential "On the Correct Handling of Contradictions among the People" (February 27) and his "Speech at the Chinese Communist Party's National Conference on Propaganda Work" (March 12). Both of these are featured in the *Selected Readings from the Works of Mao Tse-tung*, a Cultural Revolution–period, single-volume anthology of enormous "popularity" during the late 1960s and early 1970s, when Li was in his late teens and early twenties. Whether he read them or not (although he probably would have) and whether his "*zhen, shan, ren*" formulation owes anything to Mao (or some later philosophical usage) is impossible to know. What is clear, however, is that what Li *means* by "*zhen, shan, ren*" and what Mao and others *mean* by "*zhen, shan, mei*" is completely different. All we might be observing here is an intriguing stylistic echo.

60. Li, *Zhuan Falun* 9/6, p. 190; p. 326.

61. The connections between *ren* and Chinese translations of the Christian Bible were first raised, as far as I am aware, by Barend ter Haar in his report "PR China: Falun Gong: Assessing its Origins and Present Situation," from July 2002 on behalf of WriteNet and for use by the United Nations High Commissioner for Refugees; online at website.leidenuniv.nl/~haarbjter/UNHCR.htm.

Yet it is in Paul's letters that the most striking similarities appear. In Romans 5:3–5 we find, "we also boast in our sufferings, knowing that suffering produces endurance [*rennai*], and endurance produces character, and character produces hope, and hope does not disappoint us." In these verses, endurance in the face of suffering not only is seen as characteristic of the follower of Christianity but is productive of character—which in turn is productive of hope. If we were to replace *character* with *xinxing* (and they are, after all, not so very far apart in meaning), the first part of this passage would fit comfortably within Falun Gong doctrine. Similarly, in 2 Corinthians 6:3–7 Paul writes, "We are putting no obstacle in anyone's way, so that no fault may be found with our ministry, but as servants of God we have commended ourselves in every way: through great endurance [*rennai*], in afflictions, hardships, calamities, beatings, imprisonments, riots, labors, sleepless nights, hunger; by purity, knowledge, patience, kindness, holiness of spirit, genuine love, truthful speech, and the power of God." In this passage, Christians triumph through forbearance in the face of the many tribulations they might face in their ministry. These observations on the influence of Christianity on Falun Gong are, of course, speculative—nowhere does Li admit this connection, although he certainly knew about the religion at the time *Zhuan Falun* was written, and mentions Jesus with some frequency in texts from the mid-1990s onward.[62]

Since the suppression of Falun Gong in 1999, the ideals of truth, compassion, and forbearance have acquired new meanings and force beyond the ways they were understood from the time Li Hongzhi started lecturing. In this oppositional context—the era of *Fa*-rectification—different priorities have come to the fore. On January 1, 2001, eighteen months after the Chinese authorities launched the suppression of Falun Gong, Li released "Beyond the Limits of Forbearance," in which he redefined forbearance for these new times. It begins, "Forbearance is not cowardice, much less is it resigning oneself to adversity," and goes on to say, "Forbearance absolutely does not mean giving complete free rein, as this allows evil beings who no longer have any human nature or righteous thoughts to do unlimited evil."[63] At the beginning of 2001, the "evil beings" were identified as the Chinese authorities in general, and President Jiang Zemin and a few of his close colleagues in particular. "Forbearance,"

---

62. See chapter 3, note 55.

63. Li Hongzhi, "Beyond the Limits of Forbearance" (January 1, 2001), in *Essentials for Further Advancement, II*, p. 25, amended; "Ren wuke ren," in *Falun dafa jingjin yaozhi er*, p. 35.

Li reiterates, "does not mean tolerating evil beings—that no longer have human nature or righteous thoughts—defying both human and divine laws as they corrupt sentient beings and Dafa's existence at different levels, much less is it ignoring the most heinous of crimes."[64]

This short but complex essay marked a turning point in Li's pronouncements. Whereas forbearance had been discussed in terms of the individual practitioner's path of cultivation, after 1999 Li began to reinterpret how it should be manifested in the world. So while practitioners were to maintain the practice of forbearance in their cultivation, it became necessary to "go beyond the limits of forbearance" in the cosmic battle of good versus evil, since the persecution of the Great Method—the Dafa—could not be tolerated.

Not long after this essay was published, an article appeared on the main Falun Gong website entitled "Some Thoughts regarding the Scripture 'Beyond the Limits of Forbearance'" over the signature "A US Practitioner," although the original article was written in Chinese.[65] This article stresses that while the "end for the evil in the human world is approaching closer and closer. . . . *The destiny that Jiang Zemin has chosen for himself now awaits him. There is no intention or plan, on the part of Dafa practitioners, to take any action against him.*"[66] The "US Practitioner" then goes on to explain that the cosmic law of karmic retribution will ensure that Jiang receives his just deserts; by implication, it is not the duty of Falun Gong practitioners to take action against Jiang themselves. In other words, this article appears to have been circulated to counter renewed attacks by the Chinese authorities that appeared in the first few days after "Beyond the Limits of Forbearance" was published, along with reports in the Western media, implying that the original article had given Li's imprimatur to direct action against the Chinese government, something he had not previously sanctioned.[67] The anonymous author of "Some Thoughts . . ." makes the official position clear: "Dafa disciples would never dirty their

64. Ibid.

65. A US Practitioner, "Some Thoughts regarding the Scripture 'Beyond the Limits of Forbearance'" (January 9, 2001), online at www.clearwisdom.net/emh/special_column/cultivation/some-thoughts-010114.doc; "Dui jingwen 'Ren wuke ren' de yidian geren renshi," www.minghui.org/mh/articles/2001/1/10/6649.html.

66. Ibid., amended; emphasis in the original.

67. See Anon., "Xinhua Article on Uproars Produced by Falungong," *People's Daily*, January 5, 2001, online at english.peopledaily.com.cn/200101/05/eng20010105_59639.html; Craig S. Smith, "Banned Chinese Sect Is Spurred On by Exiled Leader," *New York Times*, January 5, 2001; Martin Fackler, "Beijing, Falun Gong Trade Barbs," Associated Press, January 6, 2001; Anon., "Criminal Activities of Falun Gong Condemned," *People's Daily*, January 8, 2001, online at english.peopledaily.com.cn/200101/08/eng20010108_59812.html; and Jeremy Page, "China Lambasts Falun Gong Head after New Year Note," Reuters, January 8, 2001.

hands with those evil people."[68] Li's followers therefore did not have to take engage in direct action against the rulers of China.

During *Fa*-rectification, truth has also taken on a new significance. One of the "three things" that Li has instructed his followers to do in this period is to "clarify the truth," defined in a Falun Gong glossary in the following way:

Because of the persecution in China and the unrelenting hate campaign carried out by China's state-controlled media, Falun Gong practitioners have been actively "clarifying the truth"—explaining to the public the facts about Falun Gong and exposing the persecution. Truth clarification activities include face-to-face conversations with people, posting notices and posters, handing out flyers, and hanging banners. Outside of China, where Falun Gong is freely practiced, practitioners further expose the persecution through anti-torture reenactments, art exhibits, Internet websites, books, magazines, newspapers, movies and letter writing. The goal of clarifying the truth is to help people understand Falun Gong, to dispel the lies of the communist regime in China and to raise public support to end the persecution.[69]

The goal of truth therefore has changed from being an injunction to act in a certain way in the normal course of life, to initiating specific tasks and becoming an active agent in the political struggle, in the defense of Falun Gong against the Chinese government. In an important sense, this mirrors the model of mobilization that has been a defining feature of political, social, and economic life in the People's Republic of China, where the broad masses of the people unite and work as one, applying their energies toward a particular goal. The truth in Falun Gong thus changed from being an individualized aspiration for all practitioners, to being a field for disputation with the Chinese authorities. "Clarifying the truth" is a method of challenging the basis of the suppression itself.

Finally, as the time of *Fa*-rectification draws near—when, as Li says in his 2004 essay entitled "My Version of a 'Stick Wake-up,'" "all of the cosmos's final, remaining things will be born anew as they are disintegrated and re-created, and the moment when the *Fa* rectifies the human world draws ever nearer"—the need to save sentient beings becomes ever more urgent.[70] In these times, therefore, the practitioners' compassion is

---

68. A US Practitioner, "Some Thoughts . . ."

69. Anon., "Clearwisdom Glossary" (no date), online at www.clearwisdom.net/emh/glossary .html. This glossary was written in English and is not a translation from a Chinese original.

70. Li Hongzhi, "My Version of a 'Stick Wake-up'" (October 11, 2004), online at falundafa.org/ book/eng/articles/20041011A.html; "Ye banghe," www.minghui.org/mh/articles/2004/10/11/86392 .html. The term used here that is translated as "stick wake-up" is *banghe*, a Buddhist term more usually

demonstrated by their increased assiduity in informing the world of the benefits of Falun Gong.

The practice of truth, compassion, and forbearance thus forms the "positive" aspect of the cultivation of *xinxing*. At the same time, and just as important, is the negative aspect: "abandoning" or "eliminating attachments." In the Chinese versions of Falun Gong texts, the word for such "attachments" is *zhizhuo*. In modern standard Chinese, this word has come to mean "inflexible" or "rigid," but it was originally a Buddhist term that was used to translate the Sanskrit *abhinivésa*, meaning to cling to the world of phenomena as if it were real. In the orthodox Buddhist understanding, this kind of clinging is the result of misunderstanding the essential emptiness of all phenomena, leading to a deluded refusal to renounce the world. Thus, it includes the idea of renunciation of the self, as the self is ultimately empty. Sometimes, translations of Buddhist works into English translate *zhizhuo* or *abhinivésa* as "attachment," as Falun Gong texts do, but it would be a mistake to equate this orthodox Buddhist interpretation of "attachment" with that used in Falun Gong. The primary difference between the two interpretations is that in Falun Gong cultivation the self is nurtured and preserved, the goal here being to transform the body we currently inhabit so that we may return to the origin and attain, once more, our original godlike status. In Buddhism, however, the goal is a state of nonbeing in nirvana—where "we" no longer exist.

I began this chapter by noting that becoming a cultivator in Falun Gong means to adopt a new identity and cease to behave in the way that people do in ordinary human society. Many of these characteristic behaviors, according to Li Hongzhi, derive from everyday selfish desires that generate people's thoughts and actions. These desires, in turn, originate from becoming attached to certain goals or objects. As a result, a primary part of the cultivation practice of Falun Gong practitioners is to abandon all attachments, as they necessarily hinder their progress toward Consummation. However, apart from those attachments that new practitioners will bring along into cultivation, it is possible that during the cultivation process itself, practitioners may develop new attachments that will detract from advancement in their cultivation. As Li explains,

You have to care about character cultivation, to cultivate according to Truth, Compassion and Forbearance, the characteristics of the cosmos. You have to get rid of those

---

rendered literally as "stick and shout," referring to two means by which Chan or Zen masters would jolt their students out of their normal way of seeing things.

ordinary people's desires, those character flaws, and those thoughts about doing bad things. . . . To be a cultivator, you have to cultivate yourself right there in the environment of ordinary people, you have to temper yourself there, and bit by bit get rid of your attachments and your various desires.[71]

One of the attachments that Li most commonly insists must be abandoned is self-interest. This he interprets as greed, in the sense of seeking after material profit, as well as the desire for fame and renown: the cases he most often describes in this context involve healing. As we have seen, in the discussions of compassion, healing is proscribed for Falun Gong practitioners on the grounds that it misunderstands the etiology of disease—all it does is temporarily mask the effects of karma. The other aspect of this proscription involves the motivations of practitioners. Falun Gong cultivators must practice cultivation for its own sake, not for any benefits it might bring along the way. It is entirely possible, as Li intimates, that practitioners will acquire the power to heal the sick in the course of their cultivation, but, he insists, cultivation must not be pursued in order to gain this (or any other) specific power. People who use any form of *qigong* to heal the sick do so for selfish motives and are simply seeking renown, itself an attachment in his understanding. In addition, by attempting to heal the sick they risk taking the disease on themselves, preferring to acquire a disease over losing their reputation as a healer. As soon as they request that the illness be transferred to them, it will migrate from the sufferer to the would-be healer.[72]

On similar principles, it is profoundly mistaken to practice Falun Gong cultivation in order to acquire the supernormal powers that might be developed as a result. One danger in seeking these powers is that such "pursuit" makes practitioners susceptible to evil outside influences. Among these are the spirits of foxes and other animals, around which popular religious beliefs in China have long focused, as mentioned earlier. These animals, Li says, cannot cultivate properly, because they do not possess a human body—the only way they can attain their goal is by possession (the phrase used translates as "to get on someone"). Somehow they manage to absorb some cultivation energy from the universe and acquire supernormal powers. They are then in a position to pass these powers on to the unsuspecting practitioner who has taken up *qigong* simply to show off or make money as a healer. Li tells us that the animal thinks in this way:

71. Li, *Zhuan Falun* 1/6, p. 15, amended; pp. 25–26.
72. Ibid., 2/5, p. 42; pp. 74–75.

"If he wants them, I'll give them to him. It's not wrong for me to help him, is it?" So it gives them to him. At first the animal doesn't dare get on, so it starts by giving him a little *gong* energy to try out. So he suddenly gets what he's been seeking, and he can even heal people. The animal sees that it's worked pretty well, and it's just like playing the overture before the show really starts. "He wants them, so I'll get on and once I'm there I can give him more, I'll give him all he wants!" "You want the Celestial Eye, do you? This time I'll give you anything." So it gets right on.[73]

The person who has been possessed does therefore attain the powers he has been seeking, but they come at a great cost, as the real motivation of the animal spirit is to steal the essence from a human body in order to be able to practice cultivation itself. Having had his essence stolen, the possessed person will not be able to practice cultivation and will gradually weaken and die.[74]

Desire for money, or fame, or a good reputation are not the only attachments practitioners should be wary of. In one passage in *Zhuan Falun*, for instance, Li tells practitioners who seem to be getting sick, "Don't always be afraid that it's a health problem. Fearing that it's a health problem is an attachment in itself."[75] In this same passage he tells the story of a Buddhist who realizes he is coming close to attaining enlightenment but whose great efforts in cultivation are all for nothing, as his excitement at the prospect is itself also an attachment,

an attachment of delight. An Arhat should always be in a state of nonaction, with a mind that's unshakable. But he dropped, and he cultivated in vain. Since he cultivated in vain he had to cultivate all over again, so again he cultivated himself upward. After he put in a huge amount of effort, he again moved up in cultivation. But this time he got worried and said to himself, "I'd better not get happy this time. If I get happy again I'll drop all over again." When he got afraid he dropped again. Fear is an attachment.[76]

Thus, the development of a calm and unruffled demeanor is one consequence of abandoning attachments; a cultivator should show equanimity to all things and remain as unmoved by the prospect of success as of

73. Ibid., 3/6, p. 60, amended; pp. 104–5.

74. For an extended treatment of this topic, see Penny, "Animal Spirits, Karmic Retribution, Falungong, and the State."

75. Li, *Zhuan Falun* 6/1, p. 108; p. 187.

76. Ibid. The excitement at realizing that Falun Gong provides answers to many of life's conundrums is also apparently problematic, as it can lead to practitioners behaving abnormally. Li warns against this as the "being too engrossed" (*Zhuan Falun* 8/6, amended).

failure. In this sense, the process of cultivation should not be analyzed; the cultivator should not reflect on his or her progress.

Another set of emotions that should be abandoned are those under the heading of sentimentality or emotion—the Chinese word here is *qing*, which also covers the domains of liking, love, affection, and so on. Eliminating these attachments is, perhaps, the most difficult task for practitioners, especially painful for those brought up within the Chinese cultural world, since they constitute the basic emotional ties to family. Apparently, "even praying to get rid of bad fortune and sickness for your family is an attachment of affection for your family," and therefore not allowed.[77] Cultivation is thus a uniquely individual process in which even the bonds of family are less important than progress toward Consummation. It is clear, though, that Li is also suspicious of the sexual desire and interaction that exist between couples as just one more form of emotion, only condoning it for "everyday people," insofar as it is needed to replace the population. But emotion is a much broader category than this. In a single paragraph in *Zhuan Falun*, Li includes the following under its broad reach: "being angry . . . being happy . . . love . . . hatred . . . enjoying doing something . . . not enjoying doing something . . . thinking someone is nice or someone isn't nice . . . loving to do something or not loving to do something."[78]

Thus, as simple and as fundamental an emotion as having a preference for one thing over another is viewed as a hindrance to cultivation. Ideally, the cultivator becomes completely dispassionate, almost inert. Li Hongzhi's teachings on eating meat illustrate this well. Vegetarianism, as such, is not demanded of practitioners. However, although Li observes that many practitioners choose not to eat meat, its actual consumption is not the problem for cultivation; rather, it is the *desire* to do so that causes difficulties. "To spell it out for you," he says, "if the desire to eat meat isn't removed, isn't that an attachment that hasn't been removed? . . . Not letting you eat meat isn't the point, the point is to not let you have that attachment."[79] Once the attachment has been eliminated—that is, in this case, once the practitioner no longer has any specific desire for it—eating meat is permissible. On the basis of this rationale, we might imagine that Li's views on consuming alcohol and tobacco may be similar, but they are not. Both, of course, should be given up as attachments, but unlike eating

77. Ibid., 5/7, p. 102; p. 177.
78. Ibid., 6/2, p. 114; p. 198.
79. Ibid., 7/2, p. 137; p. 236.

meat, once the desire for them has disappeared, practitioners are still not permitted to drink liquor or smoke cigarettes. Cultivation energy and supernormal powers apparently abhor the smell of alcohol, and "'whoosh' they leave your body instantly" if their host imbibes. Smoking, on the other hand, says Li at his most pragmatic, "doesn't do the body one bit of good."[80]

As in other aspects of Falun Gong teachings, the suppression led to reinterpretations of the meaning of attachments, or perhaps more accurately, the range of attachments was defined more broadly. In August 2000—a little over a year after the suppression was launched—Li wrote "Eliminate Your Last Attachments," an important essay that strikes a powerful apocalyptic tone. Its language is direct and urgent. In it, he declares, "Dafa disciples . . . are getting rid of all ordinary human attachments—*including the attachment to their human lives*—in order to reach the realms of higher beings."[81] Here, arguably, we see the appearance of the idea that being unwilling to die—presumably as a result of being an active Falun Gong practitioner after the suppression was declared—is also an attachment. It should be remembered, however, that in the period following the suppression many of Li Hongzhi's followers continued to protest against the government's actions publicly, most notably in Tiananmen Square. To do so meant certain arrest and, for Chinese citizens, imprisonment, usually in "Re-education through Labor" camps. Foreign protesters were generally detained, then promptly deported. By August 2000, allegations that Falun Gong practitioners had died in custody had been reported for several months. Thus, rather than a call to martyrdom, Li's essay was probably an attempt to create a doctrinal explanation for these deaths, to explain them not as failures in cultivation but as demonstrations of the epitome of practice. "It is in fact time," Li says, "to let go of your last attachments. As cultivators, you already know that you should, and in your actions you have, let go of all worldly attachments (including the attachment to the human body) and have made it through the process of letting go of life and death."[82]

"Is being attached to reaching Consummation an attachment?" Li goes on to ask rhetorically. His answer: "As a matter of fact, those cultivators who are truly approaching Consummation don't have this attachment."[83] We have seen that practitioners are not supposed to get

80. Ibid., pp. 139–40; pp. 240–41.
81. Li, "Eliminate Your Last Attachment(s)," p. 20; "Qudiao zuihou de zhizhuo," p. 29; emphasis added.
82. Ibid., p. 20; p. 30.
83. Ibid.

excited about the progress they have made toward Consummation. In the context of the suppression, however, the reason for Li's concerns about the attachment to Consummation seems to be that the people who possess this attachment are the ones who he feels are weakest in the face of the authorities' brutality. Those too attached to the goal of individual Consummation do not want to sacrifice themselves for the cause of Falun Gong when they are so close to the conclusion of their cultivation practice—and this, in turn, is detrimental to the struggle.

Those Dafa students who are unable to endure the suffering are especially likely to have thoughts of leaving the human world and reaching Consummation soon. This allows the evil to take advantage of their gaps.[84]

He goes on to explain:

Over the past year, students' own karma, inadequate understanding of the *Fa*, inability to let go of attachments amidst tribulations, inability to deal with things using righteous thoughts amidst painful trials, and so on, are the main reasons behind evil's escalation of the persecution, and are truly the fundamental excuses that the evil has used to damage the *Fa*. . . . So you should be able to let go of everything. If you weren't attached right now to reaching Consummation, the evil would not have been able to take advantage of this last gap.[85]

In the age of *Fa*-rectification, cultivation has therefore become unavoidably political and has had serious consequences for practitioners' lives. But even before Falun Gong was suppressed by the Chinese government, electing to begin cultivation according to the teachings of Li Hongzhi was a life-changing decision. Not only did it entail the performance of the Falun Gong exercises that are most commonly associated with the movement, but also that in every aspect of a practitioner's life, his or her behavior was to be adjusted according to the moral dictates of cultivation. These two new features of an "ideal" practitioner's life were, however, merely outward manifestations of the acceptance of Li's teachings as a whole. A new cultivator would also have begun to read, and reread, his works, in particular *Zhuan Falun*, and gradually gain insight into his view of the world and the cosmos. Accepting Li's writings as true means accepting that Master Li himself is no ordinary person, that his teachings go beyond the possibility of discussion, and thus that his

84. Ibid., pp. 20–21; p. 30.
85. Ibid., p. 21; p. 31.

instructions concerning how a practitioner's life ought to be led are more than simple suggestions.

Before the suppression of Falun Gong in July 1999, these dictates would have been challenging to fulfill; afterward, as Li's teachings were adjusted to the new realities in China and the different demands of leading a movement in exile, they have become life-consuming. Essentially apolitical before 1999, the political stance of Falun Gong in China has gradually become oppositional: first toward specific members of the leadership of the Chinese government, then toward the lower-ranking officials at the cutting edge of the suppression, such as policemen and prison officers, and finally toward the Communist Party as a whole and Communism itself as an ideology. In other words, as the suppression became more effective in China, Falun Gong practitioners inside and outside the country have been expected to add a political and activist dimension to their conception of how a proper life should be led; for those who remained in China, this has meant an immensely increased risk to their liberty and livelihood.

These demands may have proved too much for some. In China before the suppression, when there were possibly tens of millions of people who thought of themselves as Falun Gong adherents, it is likely that many of these people took little interest in what we might think of as Falun Gong cosmology or doctrine. For them, perhaps, Falun Gong represented nothing more than a convenient and efficacious *qigong* (or quasi-*qigong*) practice, one, moreover, in which the people they met at the local group exercise site were earnest, polite, cooperative, and encouraging—people, in other words, who embodied the ideals of truth, compassion, and forbearance. When the Chinese government launched the suppression with all the brutality it had at its disposal, many of these more loosely connected followers would have simply been scared away from taking part in public practice.

But, as the detention camps of China attest, there was a considerable number of practitioners for whom the teachings of Li Hongzhi were central to their lives, for whom the idea of simply giving up, or of practicing in secret, would have been anathema. For these people, Falun Gong cultivation led in one direction only, toward Consummation. Clearly, the period since the suppression has been characterized by severe tribulations for Falun Gong as a movement and for individual practitioners alike. But, as we have seen, overcoming tribulations is a necessary requirement for the transformation of the cultivator's body. Whatever the appalling consequences for practitioners, for the zealous and committed among them it may also have been seen as an opportunity for immense forbearance that would have accelerated their progress toward Consummation.

Whether cultivators are involved with current political activities or not, before the suppression and since, the goal of Consummation has always remained the end point of their path. To achieve this goal is a long journey and an arduous one, full of possible traps and pitfalls. Nonetheless, Li Hongzhi describes the stages to this goal in his writings, arguing that new practitioners ultimately can attain Consummation if they cultivate with a true heart and do not deviate from his instructions. The steps along this path to Consummation are the concern of the next chapter.

SIX

Steps to Consummation

For a Falun Gong practitioner, the path of cultivation leads step by step to the ultimate goal of Consummation. The various activities of those who cultivate according to the doctrines of Li Hongzhi—performing the prescribed exercises and cultivating *xinxing*—lead inexorably toward this final destination. As cultivation progresses, Falun Gong texts instruct readers that various changes will occur in the practitioner's body; these changes act as signposts that indicate to the cultivator that he or she is on the right track, but as we shall see, they can also act as distractions. Succumbing to these distractions can be disastrous for progressing in cultivation. Despite the fact that Falun Gong has always claimed to be a form of cultivation that is easy to learn and convenient to practice, maintaining the degree of concentration required to progress requires extraordinary discipline.

This chapter outlines the progress of Falun Gong cultivation from the point of the adoption of the teachings of Li Hongzhi by a new adherent, to the attainment of the ultimate goal of Consummation. Some of these stages are explained in detail in Falun Gong writings while some others are only hinted at, but this is, in a certain sense, to be expected. Religious writings in many traditions tend to become less specific and more metaphorical as the experience of the practitioner departs increasingly from the quotidian. In addition, according to Li, most of the changes that occur in practitioners' bodies actually take place in their counterpart bodies in other dimensions, so their outward appearance is typically unchanged, although not in every instance. Likewise, in most cases practitioners will not feel the changes taking place in their bodies, so they rely on Li's teachings during their cultivation as much as any observer of Falun Gong doctrines does in his or her analysis.

The Milk-White Body, the *Falun*, and Energy Mechanisms

In the first few years after Li Hongzhi "came down from the mountains" and presented Falun Gong to the world, his primary method of disseminating the message was through his lecturing, first in China, then overseas. As we have seen, these lectures followed a standard pattern of daily talks over a nine-day period. Although Falun Gong had no formal initiation procedure whereby new recruits were granted entry into the faith, attendance at one of the series of these nine lectures could be a kind of informal declaration of becoming a practitioner. Yet the lectures were neither simply a means of introducing the general public to Li Hongzhi's teachings (although they did function in this way) nor an experience of the powerful presence of a master's *qi*, as was quite common during the heady days of the *qigong* boom. What was apparently distinctive about Li's lectures was that over their course he supposedly engendered changes in the bodies of practitioners. These changes were threefold: first, he cleansed the bodies of those attending the lecture and transformed them into a state he calls the "milk-white body"; second, he inserted into the abdomen of each person a *falun*—a Wheel of the Law; and third, he installed "energy mechanisms (*qiji*)" around their bodies.

The Milk-White Body

Li teaches that the "milk-white body" is a state in which the body no longer contains *qi*. In general, as we have seen, all forms of *qigong* manipulate *qi* in the practitioners' bodies in a variety of ways: by exercising, by visualizing the movement of *qi* around the body, or by some other means. In Li's understanding, this cultivation of *qi* is aimed simply at gaining health and longevity; on the other hand, he asserts that the eradication of *qi* should lead to the eradication of sickness. Thus, he writes in *Zhuan Falun*,

As long as there's still *qi* in the body that person is at the level of healing and fitness, so he's not a cultivator yet. As long as somebody has *qi* it means his body hasn't been purified to a high degree, and it still has pathogenic *qi*. . . . So to put it another way, if you've got *qi*, you've got sickness.[1]

For a practitioner of a standard *qigong* form to reach the state of possessing a "milk-white body" is an arduous task that can take "more than a decade, several decades, or even longer."[2] But for practitioners of Falun Gong, Li Hongzhi performed this cleansing process during the nine lectures. Asked a question about the "milk-white body" after a lecture he gave in Zhengzhou in "the early period of disseminating the *Fa*," Li said,

> For the vast majority of you here who attended my class, you passed the stage of the Milk-White Body before you even had a chance to feel it. Actually, I pulled you up and then pushed you forward to another stage. If you were to practice and go through this process by yourself, you'd have to practice for a lifetime. I finished doing it for you in eight days.[3]

Indeed, in several places in his writings, Li emphasizes that although he has taken new practitioners directly to the state of possessing a "milk-white body," they may not have noticed any change themselves. For instance, in *Falun Gong* he writes, "this level might pass by before you even feel it. It might last only several hours. There will be one day when you feel quite sensitive, and only a little while later you won't feel as sensitive."[4] Thus, as far as Li is concerned, the "milk-white body" is the culmination of orthodox *qigong* practice. To achieve it is, however, only the beginning of the practice of Falun Gong. Moving practitioners to this level is the first part of Li's preparation of the bodies of Falun Gong cultivators in order to enable them to begin the cultivation of *gong*, a topic that will be discussed later in this chapter.

The Falun

The second task that Li Hongzhi performed for his new practitioners during the original series of nine lectures was to install a *falun*—a "Wheel of the Law"—into their bodies. In the years after he stopped lecturing, the question of how a new practitioner could acquire a *falun* was often raised.

1. Li, *Zhuan Falun* 8/2, pp. 152–53, amended; p. 264.
2. Li, *Falun Gong* 2/6, p. 25; p. 46.
3. Li Hongzhi, "Teaching the *Fa* and Answering Questions in Zhengzhou," in *Zhuan Falun Fajie*, p. 56; "Zhengzhou jiangfa dayi," in *Zhuan falun fajie*, p. 80.
4. Li, *Falun Gong* 2/6, pp. 25–26; p. 46.

In a speech and question-and-answer session he gave on September 18, 1994, published as "Explaining the *Fa* for Falun Dafa Assistants in Changchun," a practitioner asked him whether people who had not attended his lectures can "develop a *falun* through cultivation." Li Hongzhi answered that "reading the book," by which he meant *Zhuan Falun*, "is the same. As long as you truly cultivate according to Dafa, it's not a problem even if you live in the most remote place all by yourself."[5]

However, asserting that practitioners have a *falun* in their bodies and that, as we shall see below, it is in a constant state of rotation does raise questions of exactly where it resides and whether those people who have one inside them should be able to feel it move. These questions gained importance when the *falun* itself was at the core of some of the Chinese government's most virulent attacks on Falun Gong after the movement's suppression. The authorities damned as scientifically absurd Li Hongzhi's claim that he inserted one into practitioners' bodies. They also asserted that some practitioners had gone insane through practicing Falun Gong, mutilating themselves by cutting their guts open to find the *falun*, and subsequently dying. Indeed, explicit photographs purporting to show such self-mutilation were displayed in anti–Falun Gong publications and exhibitions in the years following the suppression. Yet as far as Li's teachings are concerned, there is no confusion on this point. He addresses the question of the location of the *falun* directly in several places in his writings, stating at one point, "I send forth a *falun* and plant it in your lower abdomen. It's not in our physical dimension, but a different one."[6]

Nonetheless, practitioners quizzed Li Hongzhi about whether they could, or should, feel the rotations of the *falun* in their abdomens. It might be presumed that he would simply dismiss such questions on the grounds that the *falun* exists in a counterpart body in another dimension, but this is not the case. In the questions and answers included in *Falun Gong*, he states, "Some people are sensitive and will feel the *falun*'s rotation. During the initial period after the *falun* is planted, you might not be used to it in your body, and have abdominal pain, feel like something is moving, have a sense of warmth, and so on."[7] In his speech at the launching of *Zhuan Falun* in January 1995, Li Hongzhi used his powers to demonstrate the physical reality of the rotations of the *falun*. To do this he sent *faluns* out into the audience and instructed those present:

5. Li, "Explaining the *Fa* for Falun Dafa Assistants in Changchun," p. 12; "Wei Changchun falun dafa fudaoyuan jiangfa," p. 16.

6. Li, *Falun Gong* 5/1, p. 67, amended; p. 113.

7. Ibid., p. 66, amended; p. 112.

Let's all stick out one hand and lay the hand flat. Don't use force with your hand, but keep your palm as straight as possible. Good, I will now send out a *Falun* to each of you, and have it turn in the palm of your hand so that you can tell for yourself. Is it turning? (*"It's turning!"*) For those upstairs, is it turning? (*"It's turning!"*) Okay, that was just to let everyone experience it.[8]

The word *falun*, like much of Falun Gong's specialist vocabulary, has an original meaning in Buddhism that differs from that ascribed to it in Falun Gong. In Buddhism, the *falun*, or *dharmacakra*, to give it the original Sanskrit name, is a symbol of the Buddhist Law (or dharma) itself and is often depicted in iconography. The wheel typically has eight spokes representing what is known as the Noble Eightfold Path, which defines proper Buddhist behavior and thought, and in its circularity it represents the perfection of the Buddha's teachings. The historical Buddha is said to have "turned the wheel of the dharma" when he began his teachings in Sarnath in northern India. The standard Chinese translation of "turning the wheel of the dharma" is *zhuan falun*, the title of Li Hongzhi's basic scripture.[9]

The shape of the *falun* derives from Indian religions and became central in Buddhism, appearing in iconography across the Buddhist world. Pictures of it in books, on posters, and in videos reveal it to be what Li Hongzhi calls a *śrīvatsa* (sometimes using the Latin alphabet even in Chinese-language texts),[10] better known in English as a swastika, a word that, like *śrīvatsa*, derives from Sanskrit. Li explains that this symbol is pronounced *wan* in Chinese. In the religions of Asia, it has always had entirely positive connotations, and indeed was not regarded as a negative symbol in the West until its adoption by Nazi Germany. The Falun Gong swastika, like those in contemporary Buddhism, has its arms pointing to the left, whereas the Nazi version generally had its arms pointing right—although it has been noted that if a Nazi flag was seen from the obverse side, the arms of the swastika would point in the "Buddhist" direction. Falun Gong is clearly sensitive to the possible connotations of its major symbol: the page entitled "The *Falun*" on the Falundafa.org website refers readers to a short history of the swastika that stresses its ancient, non-Nazi, roots.[11]

8. Li, "Teaching the *Fa* in Beijing at the *Zhuan Falun* Publication Ceremony," p. 27; "Beijing zhuan falun shoufashi shang jiangfa," p. 36.

9. On Falun Gong use of Buddhist terms, see Penny, "Falun Gong, Buddhism and 'Buddhist Qigong.'"

10. See, for example, Li, *Falun Gong* 2/2, p. 18; pp. 33–34.

11. See Anon., "The *Falun*" (2007), online at www.falundafa.org/eng/falun.html, linking to "The Swastika Revisited" (no date), at www.clearwisdom.net/emh/articles/2007/9/16/89609.html. On the swastika and the *falun*, see also Li, *Zhuan Falun* 5/1, pp. 91–92; pp. 158–61.

In the Falun Gong renditions of the *falun*, the large central swastika is surrounded by four small ones that differ slightly in shape, their arms being curved and pointed, "similar in shape to electric fans," as the first edition of *Falun Gong* puts it.[12] Between these four outer, small swastikas are four *taiji* symbols, usually called *yinyang* signs in English. Just as the swastika is an unmistakably Buddhist symbol in China, the *taiji* is primarily associated with Daoism. This can be understood as a kind of parallel to the truth—*zhen*—and compassion—*shan*—of Falun Gong's moral triumvirate of *zhen, shan*, and *ren*, where *zhen* is typically Daoist and *shan* is typically Buddhist, as we have seen.

The section in the revised edition of *Falun Gong* that deals explicitly with the *falun* begins with a sentence that Li Hongzhi often repeats with small variations in later writings, and is likely to be the description of the nature of the *falun* that a new cultivator seeking guidance would first encounter. It is therefore important to examine the terms it uses in detail: "The *falun* of Falun Gong is an intelligent, spinning body of high-energy matter."[13] In the English translations of his works, as here, the *falun* is consistently described as "intelligent"—the word in Chinese is *lingxing*. *Lingxing* certainly has this meaning in contemporary, somewhat colloquial, Chinese. However, there is another and, in this context, arguably more apposite meaning that the standard English translations of Falun Gong scriptures miss. Apart from "intelligent," *lingxing* also means "numinous" or "spiritual," which in China generally refers to the possession of the quality of *ling*, or spiritual potency, rather than being concerned with a "spirit" or "soul" that animates the body, as it does in the West. Whether Chinese readers of Falun Gong scriptures would opt for the "intelligent" reading of *lingxing* or its "numinous" reading is hard to determine—they may indeed read both meanings into the word— but an English-speaking reader who could not read Chinese would undoubtedly accept the reading of "intelligent" without being aware of the alternative.

This first sentence also describes the *falun* as a "body." In this case, the first and revised editions of *Falun Gong* differ in the words they use. In the first edition this is simply a *ti*, which can be a literal body (more often expressed in general language as *shenti*) or, more generally, a substance. In the revised edition a longer expression is used, namely *wuzhi ti*, presumably to clarify the meaning. *Wuzhi* means "material"; thus the simple "body" or "substance" of the first edition has become a "material body"

---

12. Li, *Zhongguo falungong* (1993), p. 37.
13. See ibid., p. 36, and Li, *Falun Gong* 2/2, p. 18; p. 33.

or "material substance" in the revised edition. Exactly how the *falun* is material will be discussed below. What should be noted here is that in this defining sentence the *falun* appears to be simultaneously spiritual and material. This may not be the paradox it appears at first, as in traditional Chinese understandings the opposition between the spiritual and the material is by no means as prevalent as in some Western traditions, where the things of this world (including our bodies) are rejected as sinful, empty, or ultimately worthless, and all value is thought to reside in things of the spirit. In Chinese religions, material objects, including man-made ones, can be imbued with spiritual potency as much as the natural world and its components are.

At the same time, however, from the latter part of the nineteenth century, as China adopted and reinterpreted Western terminology from many academic and technological fields, it also absorbed some of the basic philosophical dichotomies of Western social analysis. One crucial pair of terms that appeared in modern Chinese vocabulary at this time translate as "science" and "religion," and with these words came the understanding that they were intrinsically opposed: in this formulation science could be made to stand for a materialist view of the world in which matters of the spirit were sidelined, if not rejected, and religion was made to stand for a spiritual view which took the opposite position. Thus, the traditional Chinese understanding that the material could possess spiritual potency (and its corollary, that the spiritually potent could also be material) was overlaid from at least the beginning of the twentieth century with a notion that the two are somehow also in opposition. Li Hongzhi's formulation that the *falun* is simultaneously both spiritual and material therefore places it in a kind of paradoxical relation in which two of its major characteristics are both opposed, and not opposed, to each other.

This sentence that defines the nature of the *falun* also describes it as "spinning." Li Hongzhi goes on to explain why it should spin by arguing that the *falun* is an intrinsic part of the universe, and rotation characterizes all things in the universe, including galaxies. While the whole of the *falun* rotates on its own axis, elements within the *falun* simultaneously rotate on their axes. The eight elements of the *falun* in its outer ring—the four *taiji* and the four small swastikas described above—also spin. However, it would appear from short videos on Falun Gong websites that the four *taiji* spin in the same direction as the *falun* as a whole, while the swastikas spin the opposite way.[14]

---

14. An illustrative video can be viewed at www.falundafa.org/bul/audio-video/audiovideo_video .html.

The final part of this first sentence claims that the *falun* is made up of "high-energy matter," the Chinese phrase *gao nengliang* literally meaning "high energy." It is a distinctly scientific term, typically used to describe elements of the nuclear cycle, as for instance in "high-energy fission reactions," or in the names of commercial products, to appeal to a sense of cutting-edge science (in much the same way that American products in the 1950s included *atomic* in their names). Such scientific vocabulary pervades Li Hongzhi's writings, and in many cases, including this one, the use of such terms serves two purposes: the first is clearly to describe the actual nature of the *falun*, as he sees it, but the second is to locate Falun Gong in a modern world of science, in which his readers are educated and informed. They know, for instance, that galaxies rotate on their axes. That he regards it as important to define Falun Gong in this way is indicative of the power of the appeal to science in the People's Republic.

In addition to the features of the *falun* that are summed up in this defining sentence, another intriguing aspect is apparent from the way it is illustrated in Falun Gong books and websites, where the *falun* seems to be two-dimensional. While this may be difficult to avoid in a depiction on the printed page, Falun Gong videos show *faluns* spinning and flying about in the cosmos as flat discs. These depictions of the *falun* without thickness appear strikingly at odds with Li Hongzhi's descriptions of it as a "material body," which seem to imply that it has depth as well as shape.

Energy Mechanisms

After the purification of practitioners' bodies and the insertion of a *falun*, the third change that Li Hongzhi made to the bodies of new practitioners when they attended his initial nine lectures was to install "energy mechanisms" in them, or more precisely, on or near them. Compared with the extensive discussion the *falun* receives in Falun Gong writings, the energy mechanisms are dealt with in a very cursory way. Typically, mention of them is made simply as part of the list of three things that occur for new practitioners: their bodies will be adjusted, and a *falun* and energy mechanisms will be installed. They do, however, appear in the instructions for some of the five exercises that were discussed in the previous chapter. Thus, for the third exercise, Coursing between the Two Poles, Li Hongzhi says, "The hands should glide slowly along with the energy mechanisms outside the body. The energy inside the body moves up and down simultaneously with the hand movements."[15]

15. Li, *The Great Consummation Way* 2/3, p. 18; *Falun dafa da yuanman fa*, p. 23.

In a question and answer session following a speech Li Hongzhi gave to American practitioners in New York in 1999, a student raised an issue related to performing this exercise in cold weather. In the instructions for Coursing between the Two Poles, students are told that the hands should remain at a distance of no more than ten centimeters from the body, but that they should not touch it. Thus, the student asked, "In winter, we have to wear very heavy clothes when doing the exercises outdoors, and it's very easy for our hands to touch our clothes. Will this interfere with the energy mechanisms?" Li was pragmatic in his answer, saying that touching clothes will not affect the practice, and that practitioners should wear gloves if they need to.[16] His response confirms that he understands the energy mechanisms to be located outside the body.

At an earlier teaching meeting in New York in March 1997 a student elicited a relatively extended answer from Li on the nature of the energy mechanisms.

Energy mechanisms are dynamic mechanisms composed of *gong*'s very microscopic substances—substances that humans can't see. These mechanisms have a form, but humans can't see it. When your cultivation reaches a certain point in the future and your Celestial Eye is opened fairly well, you'll be able to see it. It's like a belt, a white belt that operates around your body. But it is connected to the *falun* inside your *dantian*. It's continually strengthened when you do the exercises. The stronger these mechanisms are, the better they drive your automatic practice. That is, they're revolving even when you aren't doing the exercises—they're helping you practice automatically. All five of the exercises we teach have these mechanisms at work. So although you see yourself standing here without movement, your body's mechanisms are moving back and forth, driving the transformation of your entire body.[17]

This passage introduces several terms that are unfamiliar, two of which—*gong* and the Celestial Eye—will be discussed below. The third, *dantian*, here simply refers to the Lower Cinnabar Field in the abdominal area. What is made clear, however, is that like the *falun*, the energy mechanisms have an actual physical existence, but one which cannot be apprehended by the uncultivated mass of humanity.

Also like the *falun*, or at least the word *falun*, Li's term that translates as "energy mechanisms" has an existing meaning in Chinese that differs from the meaning he attributes to it. In this case, the original meaning

16. Li, "Teaching the *Fa* at the Eastern U.S. Fa Conference," pp. 59–60; "Falun dafa Meiguo dongbu fahui jiangfa," pp. 83–84.
17. Li, "Teaching the *Fa* at a New York Meeting," p. 52; "Niuyue zuotanhui jiangfa," pp. 100–111.

comes not from Buddhism but from Chinese medicine. The word that is translated as "energy mechanisms" is *qiji*, which originally referred to the four ways in which *qi* can move around the body, namely rising and falling, and entering and leaving. Thus, a more accurate way of translating *qiji* in this medical context might be "the operations or functioning of *qi*." As a result, in diagnosis, a doctor of traditional Chinese medicine might employ particular terms that incorporate the word *qiji* to describe various pathogenic states such as "the operations of *qi* are not beneficial (*qiji buli*)" or "the operations of *qi* are out of adjustment (*qiji shitiao*)." However, the *ji* that appears in *qiji* generally means some kind of machine or mechanical device—for instance, an airplane is a *feiji*, literally a flying machine. So, when Li uses *qiji*, he adopts what might be the meaning a Chinese person without medical training would read into it at first viewing—that is, a device associated with *qi* or a "*qi* machine," or as it is rendered in the authorized translations of his works into English, "energy mechanism."

Li noted, in this last passage, that people with their Celestial Eyes "fairly well" opened could see the energy mechanisms around practitioners' bodies. The opening of the Celestial Eye is one of the supernormal powers acquired by practitioners in their cultivation, as we shall see later in this chapter. Before that, however, it is important to investigate the cultivation of *gong*.

Gong, Gong Cultivation, and *Gong* Columns

Li Hongzhi maintains that Falun Gong is not really *qigong* at all, as *qigong* cultivates *qi*, and the bodies of Falun Gong practitioners have been cleansed of *qi* before they set out on the road to Consummation. What, then, do Falun Gong practitioners cultivate when they perform the exercises and work on their *xinxing*? The answer is that they cultivate something called *gong*. Gong, according to Li Hongzhi, is "a high-energy substance that manifests in the form of light, and its particles are fine and its density is high. . . . More simply put, *gong* is energy."[18] In Falun Gong cultivation, the accumulation of *gong* is fundamental to progressing toward Consummation; indeed, the more *gong* that is accumulated, the closer a practitioner is to achieving his or her final goal. *Gong* cultivation requires the creation and acquisition of something new, and in this way it can be distinguished from *qigong*, which manipulates a component part

18. Li, *Falun Gong*, 1/2, p. 3; p.5.

of our bodies—*qi*—that has been present from birth, just as weightlifting, say, develops the muscles we are born with.

The creation of *gong* is a two-stage process. The first stage is the transformation of karma into *de*, or virtue, which was explained in chapter 5. That transformation provides the basic building blocks of *gong*, but the virtue that has been created requires a secondary transformation to become *gong*. While the first stage is understood to take place through the agency of practitioners, the second depends on Li Hongzhi. As he says, repeatedly, in *Zhuan Falun*, "cultivation is up to you, *gong* is up to the Master."[19] There are two kinds of explanations in Falun Gong writings for how Li performs this transformation. In the first, exactly what he does is not clearly explained, but it is clear that the ability to turn virtue into *gong* is not something that ordinary people can do. Thus, he says in *Zhuan Falun*,

"Cultivation is up to you, *gong* is up to the Master"—if you just have that wish you're all set. When it comes to who's actually doing it, it's the Master. There's no way you could do that. You've just got an ordinary human body, and you think you can evolve a higher being's body that's made of high-energy matter? Not a chance. It's a joke to even mention it.[20]

In the second explanation, as outlined in his 1995 speech at the launch of *Zhuan Falun*, Li says he provides the practitioner with a special kind of *gong*—different, presumably, from the kind that adherents strive for in their cultivation—that performs the transformation of virtue.

When the Master sees that you have cultivated quite well, that your *xinxing* has improved, and that the cosmos's special nature is not restricting you as much, then you will be able to increase your *gong*. Then, at that time the Master gives you a kind of *gong*, which we call a capability for increasing *gong*. It transforms your virtue into *gong* in a spiral fashion around the body, and it grows upwards in a spiral-like form.[21]

Whichever way the transformation happens, it is worth emphasizing that in this most fundamental aspect of an adherent's practice, advancement depends on the actions of the Master. The achievement of Consumma-

19. Li, *Zhuan Falun* 1/6, p. 15; p. 26, 1/7, p. 23; p. 40, 2/1, pp. 27–28; p. 48, 4/2, pp. 84–85; p. 148, 8/5, p. 162; p. 280.

20. Ibid., 1/6, p. 17; p. 29.

21. Li, "Teaching the *Fa* in Beijing at the *Zhuan Falun* Publication Ceremony," p. 13, amended; "Beijing zhuan falun shoufashi shang jiangfa," p. 18.

tion or indeed any of the stages leading to it cannot be attained except through his actions.

The passage cited above indicates that *gong* grows up around the body in a spiral. Once the spiral has grown as far as the head, it starts to form a pillar or column of *gong* that extends vertically above the cultivator. The *gong* column continues to grow upward as the cultivator's "*gong* power" strengthens, and is impossible for ordinary people to see. As the practitioner continues to cultivate, the column continues to grow higher and higher, sometimes reaching prodigious dimensions. At one point in *Zhuan Falun* Li refers disparagingly to a *qigong* master whose *gong* column was only "two or three stories tall,"[22] and one from the past, which went beyond the Milky Way.[23] Like the *falun*, the *gong* column exists in another dimension, but it can be sensed in this one. In a 1998 lecture, a practitioner is troubled by what appear to be headaches: "every now and then I feel as if something is pressing on my head, but I can't figure out what it's related to." Li replied that the feeling should be ignored, since the pressure on the practitioner's head was simply the *gong* column pressing down as it grew.[24]

As practitioners become more advanced and their level of *gong* rises, the body itself undergoes profound changes, as will be discussed below. During the height of the *qigong* boom, *qigong* masters became famous for sending out *qi* to perform cures, or were tested for the effects their emitted *qi* would have on various living organisms and processes. Further insight into the nature of *gong* can be gathered from a passage in which Li discusses his role in this testing regime. In it, he claims that the *gong* energy emitted by *qigong* masters actually contains elements that can be sensed by scientific instruments: these include "infrared rays, ultraviolet rays, ultrasonic waves, infrasonic sounds, electricity, magnetism, gamma rays, atoms, and neutrons."[25] However, there are some parts of *gong* that cannot be sensed, as there is no device thus far invented that can detect them. The implication here is not that a part of *gong* will be forever mysterious; rather, Li Hongzhi is insisting on *gong*'s essential materiality. Ultimately, when the proper instruments are developed, all the elements

22. Li, *Zhuan Falun* 4/4, p. 84; p. 147.

23. Ibid., 2/4, p. 39; p. 70.

24. Li Hongzhi, "Teaching the *Fa* at the Assistants' *Fa* Conference in Changchun" (July 26, 1998), online at www.falundafa.org/book/eng/lectures/19980726L.html, p. 26; "Changchun fudaoyuan fahui jiangfa," p. 59. A possible parallel to the *gong* column can be seen in an early biography of a Daoist immortal, Wu Yan, who is said to have had a column of purple *qi* rising up out of his head for "more than one *zhang*," or about three meters (*Taiping guangji* 11:73).

25. Li, *Zhuan Falun* 2/4, p. 37; p. 65.

of *gong* will be known. As far as Li's own experience of this scientific investigation was concerned, he says,

I've been tested, too, and they found that I emit gamma rays and thermal neutrons 80–170 times greater than the radiation of normal matter. At that point the needle of the testing instrument had hit the limit, and since the needle had hit the maximum point they couldn't tell exactly how strong it was.[26]

As practitioners cultivate, turning their karma into virtue that Li Hongzhi then transforms into *gong* energy, their bodies also undergo changes in their material structure. At the beginning of the cultivation practice, Li Hongzhi says that the *gong* produced by practitioners will have "large particles with gaps between them and low density, and so it has little power." However, as the level of cultivation rises, "it's possible that the density of [their] energy will be 100 times, 1,000 times, or 100 million times higher than ordinary water molecules. That's because the higher the level, the higher the density, the finer the grains, and the greater the power."[27] When practitioners are suffused with this high-grade *gong* energy, it fills each cell in their bodies in this dimension and all the infinitesimally small parts of the parallel bodies in other dimensions, "the molecules, atoms, protons, and electrons, and all the way down to the extremely microcosmic cells, they're all filled with that energy."[28] Gradually, as the density of this energy increases at a microscopic level, it starts to replace ordinary human cells, and normal metabolic processes cease. An important feature in Li's explanation of this process is that the *gong* energy does not alter the molecular structure of the body, just the matter or energy that makes it up. The physical characteristics of blood or bones do not change since "molecular cells still keep their former structure and configuration," all the while being replaced by "high-energy matter."[29]

In other words, cultivators' bodies have been transformed, but their broad features remain the same. This, however, does not mean that these bodies behave in the same way or that there are no changes in appearance: the aging process stops, as the cells that make up each practitioner's new body no longer die. As Li Hongzhi says, "Their skin becomes

26. Ibid., p. 37; p. 66.
27. Ibid., pp. 37–38; p. 66.
28. Ibid., p. 38; pp. 66–67.
29. Ibid. p. 38; p. 68.

delicate and fair, it glows with health, and older people begin to have fewer wrinkles—some will hardly have any. . . . Also, older women are likely to get their period back."[30] The idea of bodily transformation has been a consistent feature in Chinese religious and medical thought for millennia. Here we see Li Hongzhi directly tapping into that tradition, clearly echoing a refrain heard especially in descriptions of Daoist immortals. Typically, once they had attained the elixir, their teeth regrew, their white hair once again became black, and their skin looked youthful. In Li's analysis of bodily transformation, then, he refers both to the vocabulary of science—"high-energy matter," "molecular cells"—and to a trope as old as Chinese religion. This commingling or juxtaposition of the ancient to the modern not only is rhetorical but runs through all Falun Gong teachings, and is one of the most characteristic features of the doctrine.

Another aspect of Falun Gong teachings discussed earlier in relation to the terms *karma* and *virtue*, among others, is Li's tendency to use terminology from Buddhism but change its meaning, specifically to make something understood in spiritual terms into something material. *Gong* is another such case. In standard Chinese, *gong* means "skills," "results," "power," or "valuable achievement," and is, of course, the second half of the compound *qigong*. However, in Buddhist contexts, it specifically refers to the idea of meritorious actions that bring a reward—in John Kieschnick's words, "the idea that there is an invisible moral order governing the universe, and that under this system one is rewarded in this life or the next for good deeds."[31] In many parts of the Buddhist world, the making of merit is thought to correspond directly to attaining a better rebirth, and is often associated with making charitable donations to the clergy or to projects that benefit society as a whole. Yet in Li Hongzhi's teachings, as we have seen, *gong* has become a kind of energy, parts of which can be measured on present-day scientific instruments; the rest, he says, could be measured if suitable devices existed. It is thus a phenomenon of this world, something with a physical reality that acts in observable ways to those having the power to see it. That power requires the acquisition of the Celestial Eye, the major supernormal ability that Falun Gong practitioners can hope to gain through their practice.

30. Ibid., 1/7, p. 20; p. 35.
31. John Kieschnick, *The Impact of Buddhism on Chinese Material Culture* (Princeton, NJ: Princeton University Press, 2003), p. 157.

Supernormal Abilities and the Celestial Eye

During the years of the *qigong* boom, China was awash with people who claimed to have superhuman strength, walk through walls, and heal people of all maladies, as well as other kinds of special powers. Of course, when such claims were made—and even more noticeably when people purported to demonstrate these skills on television—there were experts at the ready to debunk them. Li Hongzhi seems to have watched some of these programs, as in various places in his writings, he cites American illusionist David Copperfield as an example of a person who has attained genuine supernormal powers. He especially noted Copperfield's feat of walking through the Great Wall on one of his television specials, which was broadcast in China and became famous throughout the country. In *Falun Gong*, Li claims that while *qigong* is found in countries apart from China—he cites the United States and Great Britain as examples—in these places it is called magic. According to him, though, Copperfield knew that many people in China have supernormal powers, so when he walked through the Wall, he covered the places where he entered and left with white cloth canopies to shield him from their interference.[32]

In interviews Li gave with foreign journalists in 1999, he also credited David Copperfield with the abilities of levitation and flight.[33] These beliefs about Copperfield's powers are shared by at least some of Li's followers and are endorsed by official Falun Gong websites. A "North American practitioner" wrote about Copperfield on the website PureInsight.org. Noting that Copperfield often tells his audience that "it was only a trick" after one of his feats of magic, this practitioner then summarizes an article from the *Detroit Free Press* concerning Copperfield's prediction of the winning numbers in a German lottery in 2001. When he proved successful, Copperfield in this case denied trickery, saying that he was conducting an experiment in using the untapped potential of the human brain. The practitioner concluded that Copperfield seemed to have the ability to see into the future.[34]

---

32. Li, *Falun Gong* 1/1; p. 2; pp. 3–4. David Copperfield walking through the Great Wall has been posted to Youtube (www.youtube.com/watch?v=jtG6t6LcNAU).

33. See Dowell, "Interview with Li Hongzhi"; Craig S. Smith, "Revered by Millions, a Potent Mystic Rattles China's Communist Leaders," *Wall Street Journal*, April 26, 1999. Li Hongzhi also spoke about David Copperfield in his interview in Sydney on May 2, 1999; see chapter 2, note 53.

34. A North American Practitioner, "Revelation from David Copperfield" (October 26, 2001), online at www.pureinsight.org/node/973, "Dawei de qishi," www.zhengjian.org/zj/articles/2001/10/26/12210.html.

Copperfield's feat of walking through the Great Wall is paralleled on a much smaller scale by a nine-year-old practitioner from Taiwan. A posting on the Clearwisdom website relates how, finding herself unable to sleep due to her father's snoring, she leapt down from her bunk and rushed off to find somewhere quieter. Suddenly, after a loud noise, she found herself in the next room feeling sore in the head, but with only a small red spot where she expected a huge lump. Her younger sister, apparently, saw her disappear bodily through the wall. They concluded that through cultivation, her body had been replaced by high-energy matter, the constituent parts of which were smaller than those of the wall, allowing her to pass through "like a gust of wind."[35]

Walking through walls is only one of many supernormal abilities that Falun Gong practitioners may obtain. Li Hongzhi says they can acquire clairaudience, telepathy, precognition, and the opening of the Celestial Eye. People who are not Falun Gong practitioners can also acquire these powers, but some, he says, such as "the ability to transmute objects in this physical dimension," are not for "everyday people."[36] As we have seen, it is regarded as profoundly misguided—and also potentially dangerous—for a practitioner actively to seek supernormal abilities. It is also wrong, Li Hongzhi stresses, to display them, either from humanitarian and compassionate motives or simply to show off: either way, if the practitioner demonstrated his or her abilities they would be liable to disrupt society. This is also one of the primary reasons Li gives for his followers not to use their powers to heal the sick.

Sometimes the powers can become active without the practitioner's willing them to be so. In a question and answer session in Guangzhou, a practitioner asked, "Another person's thoughts came into my mind and made me unable to become tranquil or even sleep well. I wonder if that's a good thing." Li Hongzhi replied that this is a "supernormal ability called telepathy that allows you to know others' thoughts. If you can read other people's minds, this is a good thing, but you need to handle yourself well." Clearly, in this case at least, the practitioner was not aware he had experienced telepathy.[37]

35. A Young Practitioner in Taiwan, "A Miraculous Experience: A Young Practitioner Walks through a Wall" (January 30, 2003), online at www.clearwisdom.net/emh/articles/2003/2/9/31913.html; "Xiao dizi chuan qiang er guo de shenqi jingli," www.minghui.org/mh/articles/2003/1/31/43667 .html.

36. Li, *Falun Gong* 1/3, p. 4; p. 6.

37. Li, "Teaching the *Fa* and Answering Questions in Guangzhou," in *Zhuan Falun Fajie*, p. 183; "Guangzhou jiangfa dayi," in *Zhuan falun fajie*, p. 256.

The word Li uses here to describe telepathy is *ta xintong*, the fourth of the six Buddhist *shentong*, or "superknowledges," which bear a clear resemblance to the supernormal abilities that Li Hongzhi says Falun Gong practitioners may acquire. Bernard Faure lists the *shentong* as

(1) wonder-working powers . . . which allow a Bodhisattva to pass through obstacles, be ubiquitous, fly through the air, tame wild animals, and perform all kinds of magic transformations; (2) the "heavenly eye" . . . which allows a Bodhisattva to see the death and rebirth of all things; (3) the "heavenly ear" . . . which allows a Bodhisattva to hear all the sounds in the universe; (4) the discernment of the mind of others . . . ; (5) the memory of one's own previous existences and those of others . . . ; and (6) last but not least the knowledge of the destruction of defilements . . . ; i.e., the end of ignorance . . . which takes place in the formless realm and marks the attainment of Buddhahood.[38]

In this scheme, the special powers are acquired through meditation and come as the by-product of high levels of cultivation, as is the case in Falun Gong. However, it is clear in Buddhism that these powers are available only at extremely high levels of attainment, whereas in Falun Gong it would appear that they can be gained by practitioners at a relatively low level of cultivation—though Li Hongzhi would maintain that even a low level of Falun Gong cultivation is high compared with other systems.

The supernormal ability that Li Hongzhi refers to most frequently is the possession of the Celestial Eye or "Third Eye," as some Falun Gong translations render *tianmu*, using a more familiar English term. The opening of the Celestial Eye is regarded in Falun Gong as a sign that a practitioner has made great progress in cultivation. With the Celestial Eye open, people can see into other dimensions, may observe *faluns* in operation, and also discern the height of the *gong* columns of others. In Falun Gong thinking, the world that we live in, the world we can see with our ordinary eyes, is not fundamental to the nature of the cosmos, and the ability to see with the Celestial Eye is seeing things as they really are—as little Shanshan did in his visions, described in chapter 4.

Li Hongzhi understands Celestial Eye vision as being different from ordinary sight. He points out that the images of the things we look at form not in the eyes but in the brain. More specifically, he says that "what we see" passes through the optic nerves, and images then appear in the pineal gland. This, he says, "is something modern medicine now understands." Opening the Celestial Eye means "bypassing your optic

---

38. Bernard Faure, *The Rhetoric of Immediacy: A Cultural Critique of Chan/Zen Buddhism* (Princeton: Princeton University Press, 1991), p. 102.

nerves and opening a passageway between your eyebrows, which makes it possible for your pineal gland to see outside directly."[39] Since it can see the outside world without the interference of the ordinary eyes and optic nerves, Li claims that the Celestial Eye

doesn't produce a false picture of things like our regular eyes do. It can see the essence of any thing or any kind of matter. So, people with a high-level Celestial Eye can penetrate our dimension to see other space-times, and they can see scenes that ordinary people can't.[40]

As outlined in this passage, Li Hongzhi is clearly mistaken in his explanation of ordinary human sight. The optic nerves do not send visual information from the eyes to the pineal gland, where the image "really appears"—they carry information from the eyes to a series of hierarchically arranged perceptual centers in the brain, notably the lateral geniculate nucleus in the thalamus (which, coincidentally, surrounds the pineal gland), and the visual cortex located at the rear of the brain above the cerebellum. The pineal gland plays no part in visual perception. Nonetheless, in Li Hongzhi's understanding of both ordinary sight and Celestial Eye sight, the pineal gland is fundamental, and in this he is in fact echoing unorthodox Western medical theory of considerable standing, as will be discussed below. In this passage, Li also notes that our ordinary eyes "produce a false picture of things." In other places in Falun Gong writings, he goes further than this, asserting that our ordinary eyes act as "shields" to the true nature of the cosmos beyond our restricted corner of it.

We usually see things with our two eyes, and it is exactly these two eyes that block our channel to other dimensions. Since they function as a screen, we can only see objects that exist in our physical dimension. Opening the Celestial Eye allows you to see, bypassing this pair of eyes.[41]

In orthodox medicine, the anatomy and function of the human pineal gland are now largely understood: this small gland or "body," as it is sometimes known, is about eight millimeters wide and is found in the center of the brain between the two hemispheres. Its primary function is to manufacture melatonin, which it does at different rates over the daily

39. Li, *Zhuan Falun* 2/1, p. 25; p. 44.
40. Ibid., amended.
41. Li, *Falun Gong* 1/4, p. 6, amended; p. 11.

cycle, producing more during the dark hours. Thus, it is understood as a vital organ for the regulation of sleeping and waking. The discovery of the pineal gland's functions is relatively recent, but speculation about its role in the body began in ancient times and was famously discussed by the seventeenth-century philosopher René Descartes (1596–1650), who thought it "the seat of the soul." In the mid- to late nineteenth century H. P. Blavatsky (1831–1891), founder of the Theosophical movement, took up discussion of the pineal gland, linking it with her theories of the origin and development (or regression) of humanity. For Madame Blavatsky, the pineal gland represented the vestige of the sole organ of vision we possessed at the earliest stage of humanity, when our spiritual aspect was paramount. In the later stages of this great span of human history, our physical and intellectual aspects triumphed. As we degenerated into our present form, "the Third Eye withdrew, *pari passu*, into the central cavity of the developing brain. There it has remained until the present—a symbol of that past spiritual vision which we will regain as we progress consciously along the upward arc of the evolutionary cycle," as the *Encyclopedic Theosophical Glossary* expresses it.[42]

The Third Eye has also become a popular topic in contemporary New Age circles, partly through the influence of the best seller *The Third Eye* (1956), supposedly by a Tibetan monk called T. Lobsang Rampa but actually by one Cyril Henry Hoskin, a native of Plympton in Devonshire, England.[43] Percolated with ideas related to seeing the true reality of the cosmos and altered consciousnesses—often with the assistance of psychotropic drugs—Third Eye discourse became a commonplace in Western hippie culture of the 1960s and 1970s, and its derivatives. This is, then, a largely Western tradition; but from Blavatsky and Hoskin until recent times, the influence of actual Asian thought and practice has been present, if generally filtered through several layers of "interpretation." Thus, there are actual religious and meditational traditions in Asia that make use of ideas of the Third Eye and the special vision associated with it—its traditional location between the eyebrows is a particularly powerful point on the body named, for example, as a chakra in yogic practice and as the Upper Cinnabar Field in Daoism—but none of these traditions associated the Third Eye with the pineal gland before Western contact. In

42. G. de Purucker, ed.-in-chief, *Encyclopedic Theosophical Glossary: A Resource on Theosophy*, Theosophical University Press Online Edition, www.theosociety.org/pasadena/etgloss/tem-thn.htm.

43. T. Lobsang Rampa, *The Third Eye: The Autobiography of a Tibetan Lama* (New York: Ballantine Books, 1964). See also Donald S. Lopez Jr., *Prisoners of Shangri-La: Tibetan Buddhism and the West* (Chicago: University of Press, 1998), chap. 3, "The Eye."

other words, the linking of the pineal gland with the Third Eye is a late addition derived from the West and grafted onto older Asian traditions.

Although it is typically spoken of in Falun Gong writings as a process that occurs in the same way for all people, in some places Li Hongzhi adds nuance to our understanding of the opening of the Celestial Eye, to use the term that comes closest to the Chinese version. In particular it would appear that the Celestial Eye can open, or perhaps better, be opened, at different levels. In his discussion of this question, Li adopts an orthodox Buddhist taxonomy of five levels of vision. These are the standard physical eye (translated in Falun Gong texts literally as "flesh vision"); the heavenly eye, which *deva*s, or spiritual beings, have and which humans can acquire while in a meditative state ("divine vision"); the wisdom eye, which *arhat*s have ("wisdom vision"); the dharma eye, which bodhisattvas have ("law vision"); and the Buddha eye ("Buddha vision"). When Li Hongzhi opens a practitioner's Celestial Eye, he is very specific about the level at which he opens it. He rejects the level of "divine vision," or literally "heavenly eye," one step up from normal sight, on the grounds that this gives people the kind of X-ray vision that self-declared *qigong* masters use to perform tricks. If he gave this kind of special vision to everyone, Li Hongzhi says, it would cause chaos.

State secrets couldn't be kept, it'd make no difference if people wore clothes or not, you'd be able to see people in their rooms from outside, and when you saw lottery tickets while you're out and about you'd pick the top prizes. That would be impossible! Think about it, if everybody had their Celestial Eyes opened at divine vision, would this be human society?[44]

Similarly, he says that he will not open peoples' eyes at the exalted levels of law vision or Buddha vision—these are appropriate only for bodhisattvas and Buddhas—as their "*xinxing* wouldn't be sufficient." Thus, he opens the Celestial Eye of practitioners specifically at the level of the wisdom eye or wisdom vision, where, he says, "you don't have the ability to see things through walls or to look inside a human body, but you are able to see scenes that exist in other dimensions."[45] This, he says, is useful, because it enables practitioners to see things beyond the capabilities of ordinary people and to get a sense of the true nature of the cosmos. In this way, wisdom vision gives them confidence in their

44. Li, *Zhuan Falun* 2/1, p. 26, amended; p. 45.
45. Ibid., amended.

cultivation. Put differently, the kinds of powers that this level of Celestial Eye sight grants cannot be parlayed into a stage performance or a money-making scheme.

A prerequisite for opening the Celestial Eye, says Li Hongzhi, is a sufficient level of what he calls "quintessential *qi*," or "vital essence," as it is translated in different places. The Chinese term Li uses—*jinghua zhi qi*—seems to be his own coinage: it is not found in Chinese medical vocabulary or in *qigong* writings. *Jinghua* simply means (as one of the translations implies) the quintessence, or the finest parts, of something. He explains the function of this "quintessential *qi*" in this way:

It's just like the fluorescent screen of a television: if it doesn't have fluorescent powder in it, after you turn the television on it will just be a bulb, with light but no pictures. It's the fluorescent powder that allows it to display pictures. Of course, this example isn't exact, because we see directly, while it displays pictures through the fluorescent screen.[46]

This important substance, by analogy, appears to be something like the material on which images seen by the Celestial Eye are projected. In this passage, Li goes on to explain that the "quintessential *qi*" is "extracted from virtue that's even more refined." Yet this special substance can be lost as well as gained. Indeed, Li says that the Celestial Eyes of children under the age of six are most easily opened—and sometimes just open by themselves—because their quintessential *qi* has not yet dissipated, as it does when people get older and "unhealthy education, being spoiled, and turning bad" have their deleterious effect.[47]

Like the acquisition of the *falun*, the Celestial Eye can be opened in two ways: the first is directly by Li, the second is through cultivation. Li opens the Celestial Eye at the time he talks about it in his lectures; those present will feel their "forehead become tight, with the flesh gathering and drilling inward." When practitioners' Celestial Eyes are opened through cultivation, the process is much more gradual. In meditation, they observe their forehead where the opening will occur. It begins by appearing dark, but as cultivation progresses it gradually brightens, then reddens, then blossoms, "just like a bud opening its petals instantly, like you see on TV or in the movies."[48]

46. Ibid., p. 26; p. 46.
47. Li, *Falun Gong* 1/4, p. 7, amended; p. 13.
48. Li, *Zhuan Falun* 2/1, p. 29; p. 51.

Higher Levels of Cultivation

As we have seen, Falun Gong practitioners' bodies transform themselves as they practice the exercises, refine their *xinxing*, and transform their karma into virtue in the sure knowledge that their *gong* column is growing. In this process, each practitioner begins to acquire supernormal powers, but this should not be allowed to become a distraction, as the task of cultivation has not been completed. The path upward to Consummation continues, and practitioners cannot let up in their energies; as they progress higher, new signs start to appear, and more profound and mysterious changes take place in their bodies.

Before describing and analyzing these mysteries, it is important to describe the major turning point on the path to Consummation. This occurs when the cultivator moves from the realm of what Falun Gong texts call "In-Triple-World-Law" to "Beyond-Triple-World-Law." These ungainly translations render phrases that come from Buddhism, but the English that the Falun Gong translators use in this case is strangely non-literal. The Chinese for "In-Triple-World-Law" is *shijian fa*, which means the Law, or dharma, of the world of the passing generations: this world of suffering and death, of rebirth after rebirth in the pitiable cycle of *saṃsāra*, the realm of desire and impermanence. It is the dharma of the world of the unenlightened. By contrast, "Beyond-Triple-World-Law"— *chu shijian fa*—refers to the dharma of beings who have left (*chu*) this world by gaining enlightenment. This is a realm of the spiritual, or to use Buddhist language, the enlightened. Li Hongzhi explains that cultivation in the realm of In-Triple-World-Law is concerned with constant purification, with the body continuously being replaced by high-energy matter. Beyond-Triple-World-Law cultivation, on the other hand, is the cultivation of a "Buddha-body," or in other words, a body already entirely composed of high-energy matter.[49] The details of what happens to a practitioner's body in these upper reaches of cultivation, including the acquisition of a Buddha-body, will form the basis for the remainder of this chapter.

Now, as will be obvious, the Chinese terms *shijian fa* and *chu shijian fa* do not contain any explicit reference to "three," so the question arises as to why Falun Gong texts refer to the "Triple-World." This term, a direct translation of the Buddhist term *sanjie*, is more commonly rendered "Three Realms" in English versions of Buddhist texts. These realms are

---

49. Ibid., 1/1, p. 3; p. 6.

the realm of sensual desire—our world, its hells and six heavens; the realm of form—where minor spiritual beings reside; and the world of formlessness—where higher deities exist. As wonderful as the latter two (and parts of the first) might appear, the reason why a Buddhist practitioner would ultimately want to go beyond them is that beings in these Three Realms are still subject to the cycle of death and rebirth and the possibility of retrogression.[50] Thus, in Buddhism, both leaving this world of the unenlightened—*chu shijian*—and being beyond the Three Realms amount to much the same thing, that is, gaining enlightenment and no longer being part of the world of *saṃsāra*.

However, important and extraordinary changes take place in the practitioner's body long before he or she leaves behind In-Triple-World-Law, to revert to Falun Gong language. Some of these changes relate to the generation of two new kinds of being inside the practitioner's body. These are what *Zhuan Falun* calls "cherubs (*yinghai*)" and "cultivated infants (*yuanying*)."[51]

Cherubs will not detain us long, as Li Hongzhi says very little about them. Produced during "high-level Triple-World-Law" cultivation, they are "small, lively, and mischievous," and he simply leaves the description at that.[52] In the question and answer session after his 1999 Sydney lecture, a practitioner pursued the issue, claiming that a little girl between the ages of three and five would appear, jumping on her pillow and laughing, when the practitioner was half-asleep. The practitioner wondered whether this was a cherub. Li Hongzhi replied, rather obscurely, that this might be a good thing or it might not—she could be a cherub, or possibly "someone you brought along from the past"—in any case, he said, "don't pay attention to her. Just mind your cultivation."[53]

More insight is gained into the phenomenon of cherubs through the eyes of a child, a nine-year-old called Nana, whose experiences were transcribed by her mother and published on PureInsight.org. In this narrative,

---

50. The concept "Three Realms" does appear in *Zhuan Falun*, notably in a context in which Li Hongzhi seems to be referring to the writings or speeches of some *qigong* masters his audience may be familiar with. In this passage, Li Hongzhi explains it as what "religions" refer to as "the nine levels of Heaven, or the 33 levels of Heaven, in other words, Heaven, Earth, and the Underworld," and that "all living things within the 33 levels of Heaven have to go through the sixfold path of reincarnation. What the sixfold path of reincarnation means, is that while somebody is a human being in this life, maybe he'll be an animal in the next life" (*Zhuan Falun* 2/4, p. 39; p. 69, amended).

51. These are the renderings from the 2003 translation of *Zhuan Falun*. The 2000 translation has "immortal infant" instead of the 2003 translation's "cultivated infant" and—confusingly—"cultivated infant" instead of "cherub."

52. Li, *Zhuan Falun* 4/5, p. 87, amended; p. 151.

53. Li, "Teaching the *Fa* at the Conference in Switzerland," p. 85, amended; "Falun dafa Ruishi fahui jiangfa," p. 99.

Nana woke up in the middle of the night and, going into her mother's bedroom, saw a baby asleep in the bed next to her. Nana says that since then she has often "played with the Cherub. I named her Beibei, because she's an immortal baby." Beibei would sometimes take Nana with her to heaven, where they would go to a "Japanese barbecue restaurant" and order tempura and other dishes that Beibei liked. For some reason, the owner of the teriyaki restaurant refers to Nana as "Yumi."[54] This story is accompanied by a drawing of Beibei in which she is depicted as a small baby angel drawn in the manner of a cute Japanese cartoon.

Compared with cherubs, cultivated infants are much more serious and play an important role in the cultivation process itself. The generation of the cultivated infant—which takes place in the practitioner's body, specifically in the Lower Cinnabar Field—is in fact the first stage in the development of a Buddha-body. Li explains that this is "the Indestructible Adamantine Body, which Buddhists call a Buddha-body, and Daoists call a Cultivated Infant."[55] The Lower Cinnabar Field is described in *Zhuan Falun* as being "above the *huiyin* acupuncture point, inside the body in the lower abdomen."[56] Unlike the cherubs that move about, the cultivated infant—and each practitioner generates only one of them—sits cross-legged on a lotus flower and is microscopic when it comes into being.

The cultivated infant grows slowly, and "by the time he's the size of a ping-pong ball, the shape of his whole body can be seen, and his nose and eyes are developed."[57] At this time a small round bubble appears at his side that proceeds to enlarge alongside the infant. By the time he is "seven to eight inches tall," all the petals of the lotus flower on which he sits have appeared, and "the brilliant golden Cultivated Infant sits on a golden lotus plate—it's beautiful."[58] At about the same time—Li says when it is "five to seven" inches tall—the bubble separates from where it has been connected and begins to rise through the practitioner's body, visiting important acupuncture points in its circuit. It first goes to the *danzhong* point in the middle of the chest, where it stays for a while, becoming "enriched." It then rises up through the neck to the head, where it squeezes out through the channel that runs from the pineal gland to the forehead, the channel that was cleared in the development of the

54. Yang Ning, "Nana's Fairy Family (3)" (June 5, 2006), online at www.pureinsight.org/node/4048, amended; "Nana de shenxian jiating (3): Xiao yinghai beibei," www.zhengjian.org/zj/articles/2006/6/5/37985.html.
55. Li, *Zhuan Falun* 4/5, p. 87; p. 153. The "Indestructible Adamantine Body" is regarded in Buddhism as the Buddha's incorruptible body.
56. Ibid., p. 87, amended; p. 151. The *huiyin* point is located at the perineum.
57. Ibid., p. 87; p. 152.
58. Ibid., p. 87, amended; p. 153.

Celestial Eye. Here it leaves the practitioner's body and hangs out of the forehead. After "a month or so," it returns inside the head and moves to the *yuzhen* acupuncture point at the back of the skull, where again it forces its way out of the body. As before, it returns inside and descends to the *mingmen* point between the kidneys, where it leaves the body for the third time. From here the bubble goes back to the infant, who has been sitting quietly in the elixir field all the while, enveloping him and continuing to grow with him. Ultimately, the Cultivated Infant is allowed to leave the practitioner's body a fourth and final time, continuing to grow in what Li Hongzhi calls "a very deep dimension" until he reaches the size of the practitioner's ordinary body.[59]

The passage of the bubble that is generated alongside the cultivated infant is closely associated with a traditional Chinese internal cultivation technique known as the "microcosmic orbit," or "lesser heavenly circuit" (*xiao zhoutian*). In this practice the adept visualizes *qi* moving around his or her body, beginning, as does the bubble, in the Lower Cinnabar Field and passing through the same important places on the body. However, the passage of the *qi* around the body in traditional cultivation techniques takes the opposite direction from the way Li Hongzhi describes the path of the bubble. In these standard methods, the *qi* proceeds to the base of the spine, rises to the top of the head, and then travels down the front of the body, whereas in Falun Gong the bubble rises up the front and travels down the back. Techniques such as this, known by names such as "guiding the *qi*," or *xingqi*, have been present in the Chinese world from several centuries BCE, while the specific term that translates as "microcosmic orbit" dates from the Song or Yuan periods in circles associated with the development of *neidan*, or Daoist Inner Alchemy.[60]

Similarly, the cultivated infant itself has parallels in the Daoist Immortal Embryo (*xiantai*), where the Inner Alchemy adept unites the three components of *jing*, or essence; *qi*; and *shen*, or spirit, into one. This Embryo grows as the adept practices cultivation—in this case cultivation of the *xing*, or the original nature—until it is able to leave the body and unite with the Dao. Although the precise outline of this process, and the specific terminology associated with it, only appears with the rise of Inner Alchemy, Fabrizio Pregadio has demonstrated that closely related terms and practices reach much further back in Chinese religious history. By

---

59. Ibid., pp. 88–89; pp. 153–56; Li, *Zhuan Falun* 8/5, pp. 167–68; p. 289.
60. On the *zhoutian*, see chapter 5, note 40. On *xingqi*, see Catherine Despeux, "Xingqi," in Pregadio, *The Encyclopedia of Taoism*, p. 1108.

the late second century CE, an inner embryo is mentioned in relation to cultivation practices, and, he argues, by the fifth century at latest, the idea that such an embryo is actually generated within the body is present.[61]

Three Flowers Gathering at the Head and the Pure-White Body

When Falun Gong practitioners reach the highest level of cultivation before they leave In-Triple-World-Law, they attain a state in which "three flowers appear at the head," or *sanhua juding*. Li Hongzhi says that those who can see this phenomenon with their Celestial Eyes—"even folks whose Celestial Eyes aren't that high can see it"—find it striking. As has been noted in other contexts, images like this in Falun Gong tend to be interpreted in an entirely physical way: these are three actual flowers. One is a lotus flower, but "it's not the lotus flower of our material dimension. The other two flowers are also from other dimensions, and they're extraordinarily splendid."[62] These three flowers revolve above the head on their own axes, and simultaneously rotate around it. The flowers also appear to have individual *gong* columns rising up to heaven, but "they're not *gong* columns, they just take on this form. They are extremely mysterious—if you were to see them you would be startled."[63]

"Three flowers gathering at the head," like the idea of the Cultivated Infant, has close parallels in Inner Alchemy, from which this phrase derived. However, typically for Falun Gong the meaning ascribed to the phrase is different from its original connotation. The word *hua*—"flowers" of the Falun Gong reading can be read equally as "glories," and this appears to be the meaning implied in the Inner Alchemy context, where these three *hua* are the same essence, *qi* and spirit, that we have seen in relation to the Cultivated Infant. The gathering of these "three glories" represents the same important union that gives rise to the Immortal Embryo. The close connection to Inner Alchemy can also be seen in an alternative form of the phrase—"three flowers gathering in the cauldron," where the word for "cauldron" (*ding*) is pronounced in exactly the same way as

---

61. See Fabrizio Pregadio, *Great Clarity: Daoism and Alchemy in Early Medieval China*, pp. 204–11.
62. Li, *Zhuan Falun* 8/5, p. 167; p. 288.
63. Ibid., amended.

that for "head" (*ding*)—a corporeal parallel to the alchemist's cauldron in which Daoists of earlier centuries concocted the elixir of immortality.

At the stage when "three flowers gathering at the head" has been attained, Li tells practitioners that their Cultivated Infants are by then "the size of a one or two year old child," if they have cultivated well.[64] Their bodies at this point will be "pure and white" with "smooth and delicate" skin, having been "transformed by high-energy matter." In other dimensions, meanwhile, the bodies of the cultivators have undergone other changes, and apparently develop eyes and images of bodhisattvas and Buddhas all over them.[65]

Pressing further on in cultivation and breaking through the barrier of In-Triple-World-Law, the practitioner attains a state that Li calls the "pure-white body." He explains that at this point a cultivator's entire body is made of high-energy matter. If somebody whose Third Eye is open were to look at them, they would appear transparent. The pure-white body, he says, is a transitional level between In-Triple-World-Law and "Beyond-Triple-World-Law"; once a practitioner passes beyond this point, he or she is no longer on the path of successive rebirth. Li Hongzhi summarized this process in the early period of his teaching, in answering a Guangzhou practitioner's question.

In our Falun Dafa cultivation, when someone reaches the level of Three Flowers Gathering at the Head, he has reached the highest level within the In-Triple-World-Law cultivation practice, but he hasn't gone beyond the Three Realms. So when he cultivates further, he will enter the state of Pure White Body and his body will be completely transformed into high-energy matter. Only at that point has he reached the transitional period between In-Triple-World-Law and Beyond-Triple-World-Law. A lot will be done for you during this transitional period. Of course, only when your cultivation has gone beyond In-Triple-World-Law will you have truly escaped the cycle of reincarnation and gone beyond the Three Realms.[66]

Once the practitioner has gone beyond the Three Realms, the processes he or she passes through and the changes he or she undergoes are, understandably, not easily described to those of us still mired in ordinary human circumstances. Li Hongzhi says that the pure-white body is, in fact, a Buddha Body, a kind of body that has become completely different

64. Li, "Teaching the *Fa* and Answering Questions in Guangzhou," p. 161; "Guangzhou jiangfa dayi," p. 227.

65. Li, *Zhuan Falun* 8/5, p. 167; p. 288.

66. Li, "Teaching the *Fa* and Answering Questions in Guangzhou," p. 172; "Guangzhou jiangfa dayi," p. 241.

in its constitution from normal human bodies. And although cultivation must continue even at this exalted state, albeit of a different kind from the cultivation that takes place at lower levels, the practitioner is truly on the path to Consummation.

Consummation and Righteous Attainment

As practitioners enter the realm that is beyond In-Triple-World-Law, their whole bodies, Li Hongzhi tells us, are made of high-energy matter. Here they must "start cultivation all over again," but instead of developing the supernormal abilities that were a by-product of the first cultivation process, this time they develop what he calls "Buddha Law divine powers, [which] control things in every dimension. They're unimaginably powerful." Yet Li seems unwilling to provide much information about what practitioners must do in their cultivation in these latter stages of the process, simply indicating that they will know what forms cultivation takes at those levels when they get there.[67]

The goal of cultivation is Consummation (*yuanman*), or "Spiritual Perfection," as it is rendered in the translation of some Falun Gong texts. In his early works, Li Hongzhi seems reluctant to go into very much detail about what Consummation actually is, and such statements as there are do not provide much detail. For instance, in *Falun Gong* he says, "Dedicated cultivators find a true cultivation way and achieve Righteous Attainment, which is Consummation."[68] Achieving "Righteous Attainment," then, appears to be equivalent to Consummation. "Righteous Attainment" (also translated variously in Falun Gong texts as "Right Achievement," "Right Fruit," and "True Attainment Status") is a rendering of the Chinese term *zhengguo*. Originating in Buddhism like so many Falun Gong terms, *zhengguo* refers to the reward or punishment that inevitably comes about in response to human actions or speech through the workings of karma. Answering a question from a practitioner in Jinan during Falun Gong's early years, Li explained that "True Attainment Status means successfully reaching Consummation through cultivation of an orthodox Law."[69] The word used here for orthodox—*zheng*—is the same as that translated as "righteous" above and "upright" or "true" elsewhere.

---

67. Li, *Zhuan Falun* 8/5, p. 168; p. 290.
68. Li, *Falun Gong* 2/6, p. 27, amended; p. 48.
69. Li Hongzhi, "Teaching the *Fa* and Answering Questions in Jinan," in *Zhuan Falun Fajie*, p. 91, amended; "Jinan jiangfa dayi," in *Zhuan falun fajie*, p. 128.

Within the category True Attainment Status, however, are different levels of achievement: Li lists them as "Arhat Attainment Status," "Bodhisattva Attainment Status," and "Buddha Attainment Status."[70] Thus, Consummation means cultivating by means of an "orthodox Law," which includes Falun Gong but also apparently some other cultivation methods, until one of these high states has been reached. All these states or levels of attainment are necessarily beyond the Three Realms—that is, they are beyond In-Triple-World-Law—and the practitioner has therefore gone beyond the point at which reincarnation occurs. In another place in his writings, Li says that Arhat Attainment Status is the first stage a practitioner reaches after the Three Realms, but that even within this level of attainment there are subsections, such as "First Attainment Arhat, Righteous Attainment Arhat, and Great Arhat, with a huge distance separating each level." Once a successful cultivator has passed beyond the Three Realms, incidentally, he or she "manifests with a male body and appearance, no matter what his or her sex was."[71]

To complicate matters, however, another element enters into the question of what constitutes Consummation for any individual practitioner. This element is predestination, or, to put it another way, the original state of any individual. In chapter 4, we saw how people who are living on the earth have necessarily fallen far from their original homes in a high dimension. The goal of Falun Gong cultivation is, therefore, to return us to our original places. This notion affects the idea of Consummation in the sense that "regaining our original place" will not be the same for every practitioner, because we were not the same in our original states. Specifically, we were different both in level and in kind. I will discuss how we were different in kind below, but here it is important to recognize that in our original states some of us were, say, no higher than Righteous Attainment Arhats, whereas others were fully fledged Buddhas. Thus, cultivators who were originally Buddhas but who fell from grace to this earth would be able to regain Buddha status if their cultivation was appropriate; consequently, regaining Buddha status for them would be Consummation. On the other hand, if they were unable to regain Buddha status because of shortcomings in their cultivation, they may still be able to gain a Righteous Attainment at a lower level, but still beyond the Three Realms. If, however, a cultivator were originally at a lower status—say, the level of Righteous Attainment Arhat—their Consummation would occur at that

70. Ibid.
71. Li, "Explaining the *Fa* for Falun Dafa Assistants in Changchun," p. 9; "Wei Changchun falun dafa fudaoyuan jiangfa," p. 9.

lower point, and no matter how well they cultivated would not be able to attain Buddha status. At whatever level a cultivator attained Consummation, it would necessarily be beyond the Three Realms.

Until now in this discussion of Consummation, much of the terminology has been inspired by Buddhism—Arhats, Buddhas, Righteous Attainment—but in Falun Gong cosmology, as we saw in chapter four, there are not just Buddhas but also Daos and Gods—that is, the three classes of divine beings in the cosmos that correspond to Buddhism, Daoism, and "the rest," respectively. Thus, when we speak of what we were originally, before we plummeted to this earth, we must take into account the possibility that we were not necessarily divine beings from a *Buddhist* heaven. Thus, as Li Hongzhi said in his lecture in Switzerland from 1998, "If you were a Buddha, you will be a Buddha; if you were a Dao, you will be a Dao; and if you were a God, you will be a God."[72]

Nonetheless, no matter in which direction a cultivator finds him- or herself progressing, Li assures us that "one who has reached Consummation is a Buddha, Dao, or God with boundless radiance."[73] The position a cultivator will eventually regain if he or she successfully attains Consummation will depend on which class of divine being he or she was originally. In the speech to practitioners in Switzerland, Li addressed this issue by drawing an equivalence between Consummation and the ultimate attainments in some other religions: "Consummation takes many different forms." In the Buddhism that Śākyamuni, the historical Buddha, taught, Consummation is nirvana, whereas in Tibetan Buddhism it is "rainbow transformation," Li claims. In Daoism, when practitioners go through "corpse-liberation" or "ascend in broad daylight," this is reaching Consummation.[74] Thus, these various culminations are all equally types of Consummation, but they take different forms in different practices. In an important sense, then, Consummation simply refers to the final goal of a righteous method of cultivation, irrespective of what that method is. Li Hongzhi, we should remember, does not deny the efficacy of systems of cultivation apart from Falun Gong—it is simply that they are less profound, more troublesome, and less efficient.

Just as all cultivators who attain Consummation will regain their original divine states, which may be very different from one another, so the places they came from and will return to may also be very different. These

72. Li, "Teaching the *Fa* at the Conference in Switzerland," p. 76; "Falun dafa Ruishi fahui jiangfa," p. 89.

73. Li, "Eliminate Your Last Attachment(s)," p. 21; "Qudiao zuihou de zhizhuo," p. 32.

74. Li, "Teaching the *Fa* at the Conference in Switzerland," pp. 97–100; "Falun dafa Ruishi fahui jiangfa," pp. 112–15.

places may also require the cultivator to be in a physically different condition to exist there. Thus, Li has addressed the question of whether the body, as such, is preserved in every form of Consummation. Clearly it is in Falun Gong: "Those who are going to the Falun Paradise will take their bodies with them," he says unequivocally.[75] However, in Buddhism, Śākyamuni's paradise "is composed of the elements of discipline, meditation and wisdom," so a body is not required. The Buddha body that Tibetan Buddhists have cultivated, Li claims, transforms into a red beam of light that departs upon an adherent's death to its appropriate paradise. This contrasts with Daoists, who preserve their bodies at Consummation by either liberating their corpse or ascending bodily into heaven in broad daylight. In an intriguing parallel to the Daoist case, Li Hongzhi says that "in our practice system, I use the method of Ascension in Broad Daylight for those who are to go to the Falun Paradise."[76]

Attuned primarily to the model of Semitic religions, Westerners are accustomed to thinking of a religion as having a single destination for its faithful: all good Christians will go to the Christian heaven, for example. Counterintuitively, then, the Falun Paradise is not the destination for all successful Falun Gong cultivators. In a 1994 speech to Assistants in Changchun, Li made his position clear in answering a practitioner who asked about this directly: "My Falun Paradise wouldn't be able to hold them all! . . . A large percentage of our students come from different high levels and they'll go back to their own original paradises after attaining the *Fa*."[77] And, as we saw in chapter 4, in these different paradises the deities—Buddhas, Daos, Gods in the image of white people, and Gods in the image of black people—wear different clothes. The reference in this passage to black people raises the issue of race.[78] Speaking in the United

---

75. Li, "Teaching the *Fa* at the Assistants' *Fa* Conference in Changchun," p. 11; "Changchun fudaoyuan fahui jiangfa," p. 26.

76. Li, "Teaching the *Fa* at the Conference in Switzerland," p. 100, amended; "Falun dafa Ruishi fahui jiangfa," p. 115.

77. Li, "Explaining the *Fa* for Falun Dafa Assistants in Changchun," p. 40; "Wei Changchun falun dafa fudaoyuan jiangfa," pp. 72–73.

78. In his 1999 lecture in Sydney, Li explained his theory of racial origins: "During the previous cycle of civilization the continental plates were different from those of today. But roughly speaking, people of the yellow race lived in the regions of South America and North America. The Native Americans who live there at present are classified as being of the yellow race. The people of the yellow race who live in China—at that time the heart of their territory was in Kazakhstan—migrated to the great desert region of Xinjiang after the Great Flood. At that time it was fertile. Later, they continually migrated eastward. Strictly speaking, Indians, Egyptians, Persians, the yellow race, the white race, and the black race are the six major races of the modern world. All the other ones are mixed races." Li, "Teaching the *Fa* at the *Fa* Conference in Australia," p. 39, amended; "Falun dafa Aodaliya fahui jiangfa," p. 83.

States in 1997, Li was quite clear that paradises are racially segregated.[79] But several questions from practitioners asked the difficult question of what happens to people of "mixed race." Fortunately, they too can attain Consummation, but apparently, despite the "mixed" status of their bodies, their original spirit maintains one fixed racial identity.

If they're cultivators, their outward appearances are no longer important and it all depends on the person's original spirit. If his original spirit is white, he's white; if his original spirit is yellow, he's yellow; if his original spirit is black, he's black.[80]

So far, we have seen what happens to cultivators who successfully attain Consummation. What is the fate of practitioners who for one reason or another cannot reach that state? Li addresses this specifically and holds out two possibilities for perhaps a rather large number of practitioners who recognize that either their abilities at cultivation are unlikely to bring their quest to a successful fruition, or simply that they were too old when they discovered Falun Gong to imagine realistically that they might attain Consummation in this lifetime. He comforts them by saying that

if at the end of their lives and before they approach death they vow to cultivate in their next life, then they will carry *faluns* and cultivation things with them as they reincarnate, and they will continue their cultivation from the previous life.[81]

If, however, returning to this earth is simply too painful, they can, as it were, cash in their current cultivation and be reborn in a heaven corresponding to the level they have attained, either within or beyond the Three Realms, as is appropriate. They may end up in a paradise beyond the Three Realms, but not at the status of a deity, as someone who attained Consummation would. Instead, they will exist in that paradise as a simple sentient being, a "heavenly commoner," as Li puts it.[82] A third possibility appeals to the traditional Chinese sense of filiality. If "a practitioner's son has reached Consummation," but his practitioner father has not, the son would be able to take his father along with him

---

79. Li, "Teaching the *Fa* at a New York Meeting," p. 50; "Niuyue zuotanhui jiangfa," p. 105.

80. Ibid., p. 47, amended; p. 99.

81. Li, "Teaching the *Fa* at the Conference in Houston," (not paginated), amended; "Falun dafa Xiusidun fahui jiangfa," p. 33.

82. Ibid. (not paginated); p. 34.

to the appropriate paradise. His father would, however, have the status of only a sentient being.[83]

The idea and goal of Consummation is clearly central to Falun Gong. Of all aspects of its doctrine, it would also appear to be the least mutable, as it concerns the ultimate destiny of practitioners who have managed successfully to complete their cultivation. As this is the case, we might presume that Li Hongzhi's teachings on Consummation have remained stable. Yet in the later writings, a new element has entered into his teachings. Earlier texts give the impression that individual practitioners would attain Consummation at the time they complete their course of cultivation; but more recently the idea has appeared that all people who have attained Consummation will receive their rewards simultaneously on a particular day in the future, irrespective of when they actually completed their cultivation.[84] It is tempting to see echoes of the Christian Day of Judgment in this idea, particularly the influence of American Protestant teachings that Li has lived among since the mid-1990s.

Moreover, based on one of Li's lectures from 2003, this parallel can arguably be drawn even more closely. In his speech "Teaching and Explaining the *Fa* at the Metropolitan New York *Fa* Conference" from April of that year, there are clear echoes of the evangelical Christian doctrine of the Rapture, which states that living Christians will rise up bodily to meet Jesus in the air, shielded from the subsequent seven-year period of "great tribulation," in which the unrighteous will suffer terribly. This postulation and the smug triumphalism that often accompanies it have been popularized in Left Behind, the best-selling series of apocalyptic novels by Tim LaHaye and Jerry B. Jenkins, the first of which was published in 1995.[85] The 2003 lecture refers to the Day of Consummation, linking with the Daoist idea of ascension in broad daylight:

When the day of Consummation really comes, I say to everyone, Dafa disciples really will ascend in broad daylight, and the whole world will be able to see it. (*Applause*) On that day, those who couldn't Consummate—you will sit and cry! For the ones who haven't cultivated well, I'd say it will be too late for tears.[86]

---

83. Li, "Teaching the *Fa* at the *Fa* Conference in Australia," p. 33; "Falun dafa Aodaliya fahui jiangfa," p. 72.

84. This idea is probably found first in Li Hongzhi, "The Knowing Heart" (October 12, 1999), in *Essentials for Further Advancement II*, p. 10; "Xin ziming," *Falun dafa jingjin yaozhi er*, p. 13.

85. See www.leftbehind.com for a full range of products associated with the Left Behind series.

86. Li Hongzhi, "Teaching and Explaining the *Fa* at the Metropolitan New York *Fa* Conference" (April 20, 2003; no PDF), amended; "Da Niuyue diqu fahui jiangfa," in *Falun dafa gedi jiangfa san*, p. 60.

In the final calculation, then, there will be a time of reckoning for those who attain Consummation and those who do not, according to Li Hongzhi. This may be the point at which two of his verities—truth and compassion—come into conflict. If it is true that the Day of Consummation will see the division of humanity into winners and losers, there will be no place for compassion toward those left behind. In this context it is tempting to slip into language that is redolent of Christianity—the sheep and goats of the twenty-fifth chapter of Matthew, for instance—but what this demonstrates is the profoundly religious nature of Falun Gong. We have seen earlier that the goal of Falun Gong is "saving people."[87] Here, Li is explicit about what constitutes that salvation.

Compassion also has its limits in the way practitioners cultivate. In East Asian forms of Buddhism, a bodhisattva vows to forestall his own departure from the cycle of endless birth, death, and suffering in order to shepherd all sentient beings to Buddhahood. In Falun Gong, on the other hand, the goal of cultivation is profoundly individual—all forms of emotion, including the desire that one's family not suffer illness or bad fortune, are attachments, impediments to a practitioner's progress. The sole object the Falun Gong practitioner seeks to transform is his or her own body. On the Day of Consummation, it will be these individual practitioners who ascend alone and return to their origin, regaining their godlike status in whichever paradise they had originally dwelled.

87. Li, *Zhuan Falun* 1/1, p. 1; p. 2.

Transformations

Transformation and change have been core ideas in Chinese scientific, philosophical, and religious texts for more than two and a half millennia. One of the important words in this field of meaning, *hua*, generally refers to profound change for the better. Indeed, the standard word for "culture," *wenhua*, literally means transformation through literary civilization, and those people the Chinese thought of as barbarians were *huawai*—beyond *hua*—or, in the equivalent English expression, "beyond the pale." Practitioners of different Chinese biospiritual disciplines often describe the process of developing themselves into higher, more cultivated states using the word *hua* or one of its derivatives. As we saw in chapter 5, the idea of perfectibility is common to all major traditions of Chinese philosophical and religious thought as well as to the realms of medicine and martial arts. In Falun Gong, the goal of the process of transformation is Consummation, and the object of that transformation is the practitioner's body itself. Thus, in this case, transformation is not viewed in a metaphorical way, nor is it simply thought of as becoming a more moral person. Rather, the goal is to produce a new, different, and better kind of body, and in this Falun Gong particularly echoes Daoist traditions, in which the focus of transformation is similarly corporeal, although the annals of Buddhist hagiography also feature examples of monks whose bodies behave in unexpected and marvelous ways.[1] The idea of the perfectibility of the body

1. On Daoist and Buddhist biography, see chapter 3, note 10.

has also been present in the China of modern times where it has become secularized, spreading beyond the realm of religion under the influence of discourses of physical fitness and deportment.[2]

In Falun Gong, specific transformations play a vital role in the progress of its practitioners' cultivation. At the atomic, molecular, and cellular levels, Li Hongzhi teaches that normal human tissue is gradually replaced by high-energy matter that fundamentally changes the nature of the body we are born with, even while the structure of those bodies remains intact—thus, practitioners' outward appearance will not be different in obvious ways, although they will look more youthful. We have also seen how the *de*, or virtue, that practitioners produce in their bodies through the transformation of karma must undergo a secondary transformation into *gong* energy, a transformation that the Master must perform for practitioners. Thus, the entire process of cultivation that takes place following the creation of a Cultivated Infant constitutes the transformation of a mortal body into a Buddha-body.

At the same time, of course, each practitioner's cultivation takes place at a specific point in the vast scale of cosmic time, where entire worlds are destroyed and rebuilt with the regularity of dawn and sunset, the changing seasons, the phases of the moon, the onset of the monsoon, and the rise and fall of dynasties. All these in traditional Chinese thought were equally subject to the laws of cyclical change. Transformations of this sort are also present in Li Hongzhi's ideas, especially his views of epochal change and the passing of civilizations. Li's teachings on cosmic history developed as the Falun Gong movement grew, as did his ideas on many other points of doctrine. Indeed, one of the privileges of writing about Falun Gong is the opportunity to observe the development of its teachings during a formative period.

Falun Gong's body of doctrine has not yet reached that point of fixity and stability for the interpretation of Li Hongzhi's words (either by individual practitioners or by some authorized person or group) to have become necessary or, for that matter, possible. There have been attempts, as we have seen, to forestall the unruly dissemination of unauthorized teachings, and they appear to have been successful; but while all

---

2. See Frank Dikötter, *Sex, Culture and Modernity in China: Medical Science and the Construction of Sexual Identities in the Early Republican Period* (London: Hurst, 1995), pp. 174–76. Famously, Mao Zedong was a proponent of physical fitness as a transformative process in his pre-Marxist years; see "A Study of Physical Education," in *Mao's Road to Power: Revolutionary Writings, 1912–49*; vol. 1, *Pre-Marxist Period, 1912–20*, ed. and trans. Stuart R. Schram (Armonk, NY: M. E. Sharpe, 1992), pp. 113–27.

practitioners still have the theoretical possibility of actually asking the Master himself to explain some difficult point, or seeking guidance on how his teachings apply to a situation not mentioned in *Zhuan Falun* or some other basic scripture, the motivation to develop a theology has not been present. Yet each time Li Hongzhi offers an answer to a new question, or adds to his earlier thoughts on some subject during one of his lectures, the teachings change—sometimes in subtle ways and sometimes in fundamental aspects of the doctrine.

Thus, from the earliest period in Falun Gong's existence, its teachings have been subject to reinterpretation, expansion, and arguably, in the case of Li's biography, suppression. However, the period of greatest transformation of the teachings was undoubtedly after the movement was suppressed in 1999. This great turning point in Falun Gong's history led to major shifts in fundamental tenets of the doctrine, and to profound changes in the nature of the community of practitioners. Those still in China were, and are, forced to practice in secret and receive Li's new teachings by clandestine means, if at all. Expatriate adherents are now scattered around the globe, gathering in practice groups or at experience-sharing meetings but without the sense of being part of a mass movement such as that in China in the mid-1990s. Today, Falun Gong is held together by the Internet, with far-flung practitioners regularly logging on to Minghui or Clearwisdom or one of their related sites to read about the experiences of other practitioners or to find Li Hongzhi's latest essay. They also consult the websites to seek guidance on the latest campaign against the Chinese authorities, as practitioners have added "clarifying the truth" to their assigned tasks. Put simply, the suppression turned Falun Gong into a movement with political as well as biospiritual concerns, and in subsequent years its opposition to the Chinese government and the Chinese Communist Party has broadened and hardened.

In late 2004, along with the publication of the *Nine Commentaries on the Communist Party*, the *Epoch Times*, a newspaper closely associated with Falun Gong, issued a call to members of the Chinese Communist Party and the Communist Youth League to renounce their membership. Soon afterward, according to the *Epoch Times* and Falun Gong publicity, many practitioners who were members, or whose memberships had lapsed after simply not paying their Party dues, began formally to renounce their affiliation on websites located outside China. In February 2005, Li Hongzhi published an article called "Turning the Wheel towards the Human World" in response to this new initiative, which begins by addressing concerns—held by practitioners "who haven't lived in mainland

China"—that Falun Gong adherents could *ever* have been members of the Party in the first place.[3] In this essay, pointing to the all-pervasiveness of Party culture and the way that many people joined the Party for reasons of career advancement or because they would suffer by not joining, Li admits that he, too, had once been a member of the Youth League, but claims that he was only "going through the motions."[4]

Yet the Party has changed its character since that time, Li says. In particular, its move to suppress Falun Gong and persecute practitioners demonstrated that its true nature was that of an "evil cult," an observation that turned the government's accusation back on itself. The Party's evil nature is not due, in Li's view, to the actions of the few senior officials who ordered the suppression, and those underlings who directly implemented it, as Falun Gong sources had maintained only months earlier. Rather, with this new attack on the Communist Party as such and on Communism as an ideology, the suppression took on a different meaning, with altogether more cosmic ramifications. Li Hongzhi characterizes the suppression in this article as an "enormous sin of the ages" that has "enraged all of the gods in the colossal firmament." The wrongdoings the Party has committed are, he says, unpardonable, and they have changed its nature irrevocably. Under these circumstances, in this period of *Fa*-rectification, any person, including any practitioner, who does not withdraw from the Party and any of its associated organizations "will become a target for elimination by all the gods." In his conclusion, Li returns to the primary concern for followers of Falun Gong—their cultivation practice—and declares, "No one can reach Consummation if they remain marked by, or if they acknowledge, the most evil thing in the entire cosmos."[5]

In *Zhuan Falun* and other writings from before and, indeed, for some time after the suppression, the way that practitioners of Falun Gong attained Consummation was understood in quite personal terms, even though their actions and behavior were seen to have cosmic ramifications. Increasingly for these adherents, though, the personal has become decidedly political. Their actions as participants in a political struggle, through "clarifying the truth" or through renouncing any affiliations with Party organizations, have become inextricably bound up with their

3. Li Hongzhi, "Turning the Wheel towards the Human World" (February 15, 2005), online at www.falundafa.org/book/eng/jw_122.htm; "Xiang shijian zhuanlun," minghui.org/mh/articles/2005/2/17/95688.html.

4. Ibid.

5. Ibid.

cultivation practice. To put it baldly, practitioners must cleanse themselves of any taint of Communism, or they will fail to attain Consummation, no matter what else they may do. The world of Li Hongzhi is a realm
in which politics has now taken center stage.

The suppression of Falun Gong that led to this overt politicization is
the kind of crisis that new religions in the English-speaking world rarely
face, but the movement will eventually face another that comes to all
groups in due season: the Master will pass on to another form. Whether
Falun Gong will announce that Li Hongzhi has "died," or whether he
will be reported to have undergone some other, less ordinary process
cannot be known; but whatever is the case, his final transformation will
undoubtedly lead to an equivalent one in the movement. In chapter 3,
I noted that Li's biography was unusual in the genre of religious lives,
as the typical last episode concerning the passing of the Master is missing. The eventual writing of that episode will signal the silencing of his
words—unless, of course, Falun Gong develops a practice of "spirit writing" or some other means of accessing his messages from beyond the
grave—and the pivot on which the religion revolves will disappear. As
for the future of Falun Gong, much will depend on how his passing is
interpreted. Has he really died? Does he still exist on this earth in some
form? Does his death presage other events?

It is unlikely, though, that the death of Li Hongzhi will trigger a sudden collapse of Falun Gong. We should remember, in this context, that
the movement is approaching the twentieth anniversary of its founding,
and while it does not yet have the venerable age of many religions, it has
already endured trials of great ferocity. Although we do not really know
how Falun Gong is run on a day-to-day basis, or how much influence Li
Hongzhi exerts over the strategic decisions it makes, we can be certain
that it must have some form of organizational system and a core group of
leaders that coordinate its many activities around the world. It is likely,
therefore, that the difficult question of succession has been addressed.
A new Master (or Mistress) may inherit the mantle; Falun Gong may
develop a new kind of existence in which Li's spiritual power becomes
embodied in a church structure; or the movement may construct some
other model of religious organization. Falun Gong will, however, necessarily transform into a different kind of movement. The establishment of
a new leader in a religious group whose founder has died has commonali-
ties with succession in any organization—entailing a transfer of power, a
reordering of priorities, a change in junior staff—but it also has particular
features related to religion. Falun Gong will undoubtedly face challenges
of both these types when Li Hongzhi dies, as he was both the founder

of a movement with millions of adherents and continues as its spiritual master with privileged access to the truth.

The profoundly religious nature of Falun Gong has been a major concern of this book, but the fact remains that one thing the Chinese authorities and Falun Gong itself agree on is that it is not a religion. In the first chapter, I explained that this denial is partly due to the very particular—and politicized—definitions of *religion* that hold sway under the People's Republic of China, and the immediate consequences Falun Gong would have suffered if it claimed to be one. Moreover, Falun Gong is not regarded as religion by its practitioners partly because Li Hongzhi declares it not to be, and also because their activities do not fit with their conception of what a religion looks like. Falun Gong has no buildings, no employed professional clerics, and no objects of veneration. A Falun Gong adherent does not attend a mosque to pray, or burn incense in a temple on designated days of the year, or partake of bread and wine in a regular ritual. And probably most important, unlike the five authorized religions in the People's Republic, Falun Gong is not centuries old.

On the other hand, to reiterate observations made in chapter 1, Falun Gong practitioners revere a leader whom they believe proclaims an eternal truth; who transcends all dimensions of the cosmos; who protects them in their cultivation, no matter where they are on its path; and who alone must perform spiritual transformations for them to progress toward Consummation. Li Hongzhi teaches about a cosmos no ordinary person can see, describes the existence of gods and other beings beyond our perception, offers an explanation for our existence on the earth, and brings with him a means by which we may regain our divine status. Practitioners read and reread his scripture, which is apparently of such profundity that its language cannot be restricted by standard grammar; its every printed word contains a holy image. They live by a set of moral principles that form the material basis of the cosmos and without which their attempts at bodily cultivation would fail. They have a set of spiritual exercises they are enjoined to perform at regular intervals, and—when they are allowed to do so—join with their fellows in mass gatherings to share their spiritual insights. These aspects of Falun Gong, I contend, demonstrate that it is, in all meaningful ways, a religion.

Thus, Falun Gong has represented an important focus of religious expression in China, but the fact that practitioners have not regarded themselves as "religious" points to a major and unacknowledged transformation in contemporary Chinese religiosity—that is, to the existence of mass religion that escapes the conventional, government-defined categories. Postrevolutionary China was long considered a largely non-religious country where until 1980 or so the interventions of the state systematically dismantled the structures of traditional religions. Since that time, the authorities have permitted, however begrudgingly, the rebuilding of religious structures and the revival of practice. This view of religion in the People's Republic is true enough for the recognized religions, but the phenomenon of Falun Gong forces us to see China as having developed a new way of being religious. Falun Gong is a new form of Chinese religion, even if its adherents themselves may not recognize it as being religion at all. This is the great transformation that Falun Gong has wrought: it demonstrated that at the close of the twentieth century, China was a profoundly religious country, but one that was religious in new ways. Whether Falun Gong is still widely practiced behind closed doors in the People's Republic is impossible to tell, but its spectacular growth in the 1990s demonstrated—to the Chinese government as much as to anyone else—that contemporary China still has the potential for immense religious enthusiasm and commitment.

Chinese Names and Terms

Anhui	安徽
baduan jin	八段锦
Baopuzi	抱扑子
Beibei	贝贝
Beijing	北京
Beijing Daily	北京日报
Benxi	本溪
Bo Yi	伯夷
budai	布袋
Cai Jing	蔡经
Cai Yuanpei	蔡元培
Chan	禅
Chang'an Boulevard	长安街
Changbai Mountains	长白山
Changchun	长春
Changsha	长沙
Chanmi Gong	禅密功
Chengde	承德
Chen Xingqiao	陈星桥
China Falun Gong	中国法轮功
chu shijian fa	出世间法
Cibei Gong	慈悲功
Cui Yueli	崔月犁
Dai	轪
Dalian	大连
dantian	丹田
danzhong	膻中
danwei	单位
Daode jing	道德经
Daoyin tu	导引图
Da Qigongshi	大气功师

de	德
Deng Xiaoping	邓小平
ding (cauldron)	鼎
ding (head)	顶
Dongfang qigong	东方气功
fa	法
falun	法轮
Falun Dafa	法轮大法
Falun Gong	法轮功
famen	法门
fashen	法身
feiji	飞机
fengshui	风水
fu yishi	副意识
Fuyou Street	府右街
fu yuanshen	副元神
GaFa	伽砝
Gafei	加菲
gandao	感到
gao nengliang	高能量
Ge Hong	葛洪
Ge Xuan	葛玄
gong	功
gongfu	功夫
Gongzhuling	公主岭
Guan County	冠县
guanding	灌顶
Guangdong	广东
Guangming Daily	光明日报
Guangzhou	广州
Guanzhou	冠州
guanzi	管子
gui da gui	鬼打鬼
Guiyang	贵阳
Guizhou	贵州
Guogong	国功
Guo Lin	郭林
Haikou	海口
Hainan	海南
Handan	邯郸
Hangzhou	杭州
Han Xin	韩信
Harbin	哈尔滨
Hebei	河北

He Dongchang	何东昌
Hefei	合肥
He Zuoxiu	何祚庥
Hong Yin	洪吟
hua (flowers)	花
hua (glories)	华
hua (transformation)	化
Huangdi	黄帝
Hua Tuo	华陀
huawai	化外
Hubei	湖北
Huguo Bore Temple	护国般若寺
huiyin	会阴
Hu Jintao	胡锦涛
Hunan	湖南
Jiangshi xiansheng	僵尸先生
Jiangxi	江西
Jiang Xuegui	姜学贵
Jiang Zemin	江泽民
Jianyi Yongwei Foundation	见义勇为基金会
jie	劫
Ji Liewu	纪烈武
Jilin	吉林
Jinan	济南
jindan	金丹
jing	精
jinggong	静功
jinghua zhi qi	精华之气
jingzuo	静坐
Jiugong Bagua Gong	九宫八卦功
jue	诀
kongjian	空间
koujue	口诀
Kuanjing	宽净
Laozi	老子
Liang Qichao	梁启超
Li Bo	李波
Li Chang	李昌
Li Dan	李丹
Li Donghui	李东辉
Li Hongzhi	李洪志
Li Hui	李辉
Li Jun	李君
Li Lai	李来

Li Meige	李美歌
Li Menghua	李梦华
ling	灵
linghun	灵魂
linghun bu mie	灵魂不灭
lingti	灵体
lingxing	灵性
Li Peng	李鹏
Li Ping	李平
Li Rui	李瑞
Li Rusong	李如松
Liu Bang	刘邦
Liu Bowen	刘伯温
liudao	六道
Liu Jianzhang	刘建章
Liu Ying	刘英
Luo Gan	罗干
Lu Shuzhen	芦淑珍
Mao Zedong	毛泽东
Mawangdui	马王堆
mei	美
Ming	明
mingmen	命门
mixin	迷信
mofa	末法
Nam Sa-go	南師古
Nanchang	南昌
neidan	内丹
Pan Xiao	潘晓
Pan Yufang	潘玉芳
Peng Chong	彭冲
pingxing yuzhou	平行宇宙
qi	气
Qian Xinzhong	钱信忠
Qiao Shi	乔石
qigong	气功
Qigong bao	气功报
Qigong yu kexue	气功与科学
qiji	气机
qiji buli	气机不利
qiji shitiao	气机失调
Qing	情
Qiqihar	齐齐哈尔
Qiu Yucai	邱玉才

ren	忍
rennai	忍耐
Ricky Lau	刘观伟
Rong Fa	溶法
ruanzhe	软者
Sammo Hung	洪金宝
sanhua juding	三花聚顶
sanjie	三界
sanxin weiji	三信危机
shan	善
Shandong	山东
Shanghai	上海
Shanshan	山山
Shanxi	山西
shen	神
Sheng Lijian	盛礼剑
shenti	身体
shentong	神通
Shenyang	沈阳
Shenzhen	深圳
Shifu	师父
shijian fa	世间法
Shijiazhuang	石家庄
Shijingshan	石景山
shouyi	守一
Sing Tao Jih Pao	星岛日报
Sun Wukong	孙悟空
taiji	太极
taiji quan	太极拳
taijitu	太极图
Taiyuan	太原
ta xintong	他心通
teyi gongneng	特异功能
ti	体
Tiananmen	天安门
Tianjin	天津
tianmu	天目
Tung Fang Jih Pao	东方日报
waiqi	外气
wan	卍
Wang Changsi	王长泗
Wang Yangming	王阳明
Wang Yuan	王远
Wang Zhiwen	王治文

Weifang	潍坊
weishu	维数
wenhua	文化
Wenjin Street	文津街
Wuhan	武汉
wuqin xi	五禽戏
Wu Yan	巫炎
wuzhi ti	物质体
xiang	想
xiantai	仙胎
xiao zhoutian	小周天
xie	邪
xiejiao	邪教
Xie Xiufen	谢秀芬
Xifang jile shijie youji	西方极乐世界游记
xin	心
xingqi	行气
Xinhua Newsagency	新华通讯社
Xinjiang	新疆
xinxi	信息
xinxing	心性
xiulian	修炼
Yan'an	延安
Yanji	延吉
Yan Xin	严新
Yao Jie	姚洁
Ye Hao	叶浩
yi	意
Yijing (Book of Changes)	易经
yijing (mood)	意境
yin	阴
yinghai	婴孩
yinian	意念
yinyang	阴阳
yixiang	意想
yuanman	圆满
yuanshen	元神
yuanshen bu mie	元神不灭
yuanying	元婴
Yu Changxin	于长新
Yumi	由美
yuzhen	玉枕
Zhang Hongbao	张宏堡
Zhang Jian	張建

Zhang Sanfeng	張三丰
Zhang Wentian	张闻天
Zhang Xiangyu	张香玉
Zhang Zhenhuan	张震寰
Zhao Puchu	赵朴初
zhen	真
zhengfa	正法
zhengfeng	整风
zhengguo	正果
zhengjiao	正教
zhengming	正名
Zhengzhou	郑州
zhenren	真人
zhizhuo	执著
Zhong Gong	中功
Zhongguo qigong kexue yanjiu hui	中国气功科学研究会
Zhonghua qigong	中华气功
Zhongli Quan	钟离权
zhongmin	种民
Zhongnanhai	中南海
zhoutian	周天
Zhuan Falun	转法轮
Zhuangzi	庄子
zhufo	主佛
Zhuhai	珠海
Zhu Huiguang	朱慧光
Zhu Rongji	朱镕基
zhu yishi	主意识
zhu yuanshen	主元神
Zhu Xi	朱熹
Zong Hairen	宗海仁
zongjiao	宗教

Bibliography

Primary Sources

BOOKS, LECTURES, AND ESSAYS BY LI HONGZHI 李洪志

Please note: The PDFs of Chinese versions of Li Hongzhi's books and lectures have no unique URLs, but can all be downloaded from www.falundafa.org/book/chigb.htm. The date given in many of the entries refers to the date an essay was published or a lecture was delivered.

"Bear in Mind Forever." June 18, 1997. In *Essentials for Further Advancement*, p. 40; "Yongyuan jizhu 永远记住," in *Falun dafa jingjin yaozhi*, p. 88.

"Beyond the Limits of Forbearance." January 1, 2001. In *Essentials for Further Advancement, II*, p. 25; "Ren wuke ren 忍无可忍," in *Falun dafa jingjin yaozhi er*, p. 35.

"Comments regarding the *Fa*-Rectification Made at the Falun Dafa Assistants Meeting in Beijing." January 2, 1995. In *Explaining the Content of Falun Dafa*, pp. 68–76; "Beijing falun dafa fudaoyuan huiyi shang guanyu zhengfa de yijian 北京法轮大法辅导员会议上关于正法的意见," in *Falun dafa yijie*, pp. 137–58.

"The Decline of Mankind and Dangerous Notions." In *Zhuan Falun, Volume II*, pp. 36–38; "Renlei de huapo yu weixian de guannian 人类的滑坡," in *Zhuan falun juan er*, pp. 59–63.

"Eliminate Your Last Attachment(s)." August 12, 2000. In *Essentials for Further Advancement, II*, pp. 20–22; "Qudiao zuihou de zhizhuo 去掉最后的执著," in *Falun dafa jingjin yaozhi er*, pp. 29–32.

"Environment." October 17, 1997. In *Essentials for Further Advancement*, pp. 48; "Huanjing 环境," in *Falun dafa jingjin yaozhi*, pp. 105–6.

Essentials for Further Advancement. Trans. April 2001. Online at www.falundafa
.org/book/eng/pdf/jjyz_en.pdf; *Falun dafa jingjin yaozhi* 法轮大法精进要旨, no
publication date (last essay written March 30, 1999).

Essentials for Further Advancement, II. No trans. date. Online at www.falundafa
.org/book/eng/pdf/jjyz2.pdf; *Falun dafa jingjin yaozhi er* 法轮大法精进要旨二, no
publication date (last essay written December 9, 2001).

Explaining the Content of Falun Dafa. No trans. date. Online at www.falundafa.
org/book/eng/pdf/yj_en.pdf; *Falun dafa yijie* 法轮大法义解, no publication date
(first published July 1997).

"Explaining the *Fa* during the 2003 Lantern Festival at the U.S. West *Fa* Conference." February 15, 2003. No PDF. "2003 nian yuanxiaojie jiangfa 2003 年元
宵节讲法."

"Explaining the *Fa* for Falun Dafa Assistants in Changchun." September 18, 1994.
In *Explaining the Content of Falun Dafa*, pp. 6–43; "Wei Changchun falun dafa
fudaoyuan jiangfa 为长春法轮大法辅导员讲法," in *Falun dafa yijie*, pp. 1–80.

Falun dafa gedi jiangfa yi 法轮大法各地讲法一 (Explaining the *Fa* in Various
Places, 1).

Falun dafa gedi jiangfa san 法轮大法各地讲法三 (Explaining the *Fa* in Various
Places, 3).

Falun dafa gedi jiangfa qi 法轮大法各地讲法七 (Explaining the *Fa* in Various
Places, 7).

Falun dafa yinyue yu meishu chuangzuohui jiangfa 法轮大法音乐与美术创作会讲法
(Explaining the *Fa* at the Meeting on the Creation of Music and Art).

Falun Gong. 5th trans. ed., July 2006. Online at www.falundafa.org/book/eng/pdf/
flg_2006.pdf; *Falun gong* 法轮功, no publication date (first published December
1993).

The Great Consummation Way of Falun Dafa. 3rd trans. ed., July 2006. Online at
www.falundafa.org/book/eng/pdf/dymf_2006.pdf; *Falun dafa da yuanman fa* 法
轮大法大圆满法, no publication date (first published March 1997).

"Huge Exposure." August 28, 1996. In *Essentials for Further Advancement*, pp. 31–32;
"Da Baoguang 大曝光," in *Falun dafa jingjin yaozhi*, pp. 65–66.

"Humanity during the Final Kalpa." In *Zhuan Falun, Volume II*, p. 40; "Mojie shi de
renlei 末劫时的人类," in *Zhuan falun juan er*, p. 66.

"In Reference to a Prophecy." June 28, 2000. In *Essentials for Further Advancement,
II*, p. 14; "Yuyan cankao 预言参考," in *Falun dafa jingjin yaozhi er*, pp. 19–20.

"The Knowing Heart." October 12, 1999. In *Essentials for Further Advancement, II*,
p. 10; "Xin ziming 心自明," in *Falun dafa jingjin yaozhi er*, pp. 12–13.

"Lecture at the First Conference in North America." March 29–30, 1998. Online
at www.falundafa.org/book/eng/pdf/north_america.pdf; "Falun dafa beimei
shoujie fahui jiangfa 法轮大法北美首届法会讲法."

"Lecture in Sydney." August 3, 1996. Online at www.falundafa.org/book/eng/pdf/
sydney.pdf; "Falun dafa Xini fahui jiangfa 法轮大法悉尼法会讲法."

Lectures in the United States. Online at www.falundafa.org/book/eng/pdf/mgjf.pdf;
Falun dafa Meiguo fahui jiangfa 法轮大法美国法会讲法.

"Lessons from Buddhism." In *Zhuan Falun, Volume II*, pp. 9–11; "Fojiao zhong de jiaoxun 佛教中的教训," in *Zhuan falun juan er*, pp. 13–17.

"Melt into the *Fa*." August 3, 1998. In *Essentials for Further Advancement*, pp. 50–51; "Rong yu fa zhong 溶于法中," in *Falun dafa jingjin yaozhi*, pp. 112–14.

"My Version of a 'Stick Wake-up.'" October 11, 2004. Online at falundafa.org/book/eng/articles/20041011A.html; "Ye banghe 也棒喝," online at www.minghui.org/mh/articles/2004/10/11/86392.html.

"No Demonstrations When Saving People and Teaching Fa." In *Zhuan Falun, Volume II*, pp. 32–34; "Duren jiangfa buzuo biaoyan 度人讲法不做表演," in *Zhuan falun juan er*, pp. 52–56.

"No Politics." June 4, 2001. In *Essentials for Further Advancement, II*, p. 37; "Bu zhengzhi 不政治," in *Falun dafa jingjin yaozhi er*, pp. 54–55.

"Position." June 13, 1999. In *Essentials for Further Advancement, II*, p. 5; "Weizhi 位置," in *Falun dafa jinjing yaozhi er*, p. 7.

"Practicing Cultivation after Retirement." October 13, 1995. In *Essentials for Further Advancement*, p. 12; "Tuixiu zai lian 退休再炼," in *Falun dafa jinjing yaozhi*, p. 19.

"Some Thoughts of Mine." June 2, 1999. In *Essentials for Further Advancement, II*, pp. 2–4; "Wode yidian ganxiang 我的一点感想," in *Falun dafa jingjin yaozhi er*, pp. 2–6.

"Stability." June 13, 1999. In *Essentials for Further Advancement, II*, p. 6; "Anding 安定," in *Falun dafa jingjin yaozhi er*, p. 8.

"The Story of Creating Man out of Clay." In *Zhuan Falun, Volume II*, pp. 20–21; "Nitu zaoren de gushi 泥土造人的故事," in *Zhuan falun juan er*, pp. 33–35.

"A Suggestion." April 10, 2001. In *Essentials for Further Advancement, II*, p. 32; "Jianyi 建议," in *Falun dafa jingjin yaozhi er*, p. 46.

"Talk in Guangzhou to Some Assistance Center Heads from around the Country." December 27, 1994. In *Explaining the Content of Falun Dafa*, pp. 54–67; "Guangzhou dui quanguo bufen fudaozhan zhanzhang de jiangfa 广州对全国部份辅导站站长的讲法," in *Falun dafa yijie*, pp. 105–35.

"Teaching and Explaining the *Fa* at the Metropolitan New York *Fa* Conference." April 20, 2003. No PDF. "Da Niuyue diqu fahui jiangfa 大纽约地区法会讲法," in *Falun dafa gedi jiangfa san*, pp. 1–81.

"Teaching the *Fa* and Answering Questions in Guangzhou." In *Zhuan Falun Fajie*, pp. 134–89; "Guangzhou jiangfa dayi 广州讲法答疑," in *Zhuan falun fajie*, pp. 189–261.

"Teaching the *Fa* and Answering Questions in Jinan." In *Zhuan Falun Fajie*, pp. 72–99; "Jinan jiangfa dayi 济南讲法答疑," in *Zhuan falun fajie*, pp. 101–39.

"Teaching the *Fa* and Answering Questions in Yanji." In *Zhuan Falun Fajie*, pp. 100–133; "Yanji jiangfa dayi 延吉讲法答疑," in *Zhuan falun fajie*, pp. 141–88.

"Teaching the *Fa* and Answering Questions in Zhengzhou." In *Zhuan Falun Fajie*, pp. 54–71; "Zhengzhou jiangfa dayi 郑州讲法答疑," in *Zhuan falun fajie*, pp. 77–99.

"Teaching the *Fa* at Lantau Island." In *Zhuan Falun, Volume II*, pp. 3–8; "Zai Dayushan jiangfa 在大屿山讲法," in *Zhuan falun juan er*, pp. 1–12.

"Teaching the *Fa* at a New York Meeting." March 22, 1997. In *Lectures in the United States*, pp. 37–55; "Niuyue zuotanhui jiangfa 纽约座谈会讲法," in *Falun dafa Meiguo fahui jiangfa*, pp. 77–115.

"Teaching the *Fa* at the Assistants' *Fa* Conference in Changchun." July 26, 1998. Online at www.falundafa.org/book/eng/lectures/19980726L.html; "Changchun fudaoyuan fahui jiangfa 长春辅导员法会讲法."

"Teaching the *Fa* at the Conference in Canada." May 23, 1999. Online at www .falundafa.org/book/eng/pdf/canada1999.pdf; "Falun dafa Jianada fahui jiangfa 法轮大法加拿大法会讲法."

"Teaching the *Fa* at the Conference in Europe." May 30–31, 1998. Online at www .falundafa.org/book/eng/pdf/europe1998a.pdf; "Falun dafa Ouzhou fahui jiangfa 法轮大法欧洲法会讲法."

"Teaching the *Fa* at the Conference in Houston." October 12, 1996. Online at www.falundafa.org/book/eng/pdf/houston1996.pdf; "Falun dafa Xiusidun fahui jiangfa 法轮大法休斯顿法会讲法."

"Teaching the *Fa* at the Conference in Singapore." August 22–23, 1998. Online at www.falundafa.org/book/eng/pdf/singapore1998.pdf; "Falun dafa Xinjiapo fahui jiangfa 法轮大法新加坡法会讲法."

"Teaching the *Fa* at the Conference in Switzerland." September 4–5, 1998. Online at www.falundafa.org/book/eng/pdf/switzerland1998.pdf; "Falun dafa Ruishi fahui jiangfa 法轮大法瑞士法会讲法."

"Teaching the *Fa* at the Discussion on Creating Fine Art." July 21, 2003. No PDF. "Meishu chuangzuo yanjiuhui jiangfa 美术创作研究会讲法," in *Falun dafa yinyue yu meishu chuangzuohui jiangfa*, pp. 33–86.

"Teaching the *Fa* at the Eastern U.S. *Fa* Conference." March 27–28, 1999. Online at www.falundafa.org/book/eng/pdf/us_east1999.pdf; "Falun dafa Meiguo dongbu fahui jiangfa 法轮大法美国东部法会讲法."

"Teaching the *Fa* at the *Fa* Conference in Australia." May 2–3, 1999. Online at www.falundafa.org/book/eng/pdf/australia1999.pdf; "Falun dafa Aodaliya fahui jiangfa 法轮大法澳大利亚法会讲法."

"Teaching the *Fa* at the International Experience-Sharing Conference in Beijing." November 11, 1996. Online at www.falundafa.org/book/eng/pdf/beijing1996. pdf; "Beijing guoji jiaoliuhui jiangfa 北京国际交流会讲法," in *Falun dafa gedi jiangfa yi*, pp. 79–108.

"Teaching the *Fa* at the 2004 International *Fa* Conference in New York." November 21, 2004. No PDF. "Erlinglingsi nian Niuyue guoji fahui jiangfa 二零零四年纽约国际法会讲法."

"Teaching the *Fa* at the Western U.S. *Fa* Conference." February 21–22, 1999. Online at www.falundafa.org/book/eng/pdf/us_west1999.pdf; "Falun dafa Meiguo xibu fahui jiangfa 法轮大法美国西部法会讲法."

"Teaching the *Fa* at the Western U.S. International *Fa* Conference." February 26, 2005. No PDF. "Meixi guoji fahui jiangfa 美西国际法会讲法," in *Falun dafa gedi jiangfa qi*, pp. 1–68.

"Teaching the *Fa* in Beijing at the *Zhuan Falun* Publication Ceremony." January 4, 1995. In *Zhuan Falun Fajie*, pp. 1–45; "Beijing zhuan falun shoufashi shang jiangfa 北京转法轮首发式上讲法," in *Zhuan falun fajie*, pp. 1–60.

"Teaching the *Fa* in New York City." March 23, 1997. In *Lectures in the United States*, pp. 1–22; "Niuyue fahui jiangfa 纽约法会讲法," in *Falun dafa Meiguo fahui jiangfa*, pp. 1–44.

"Teaching the *Fa* in San Francisco." April 6, 1997. In *Lectures in the United States*, pp. 23–36; "Jiujinshan fahui jiangfa 旧金山法会讲法," in *Falun dafa Meiguo fahui jiangfa*, pp. 45–76.

"True Cultivation." May 22, 1995. In *Essentials for Further Advancement*, p. 6; "Zhenxiu 真修," in *Falun dafa jingjin yaozi*, p. 5.

"True Nature Revealed." May 8, 1999. In *Essentials for Further Advancement, II*, p. 1; "Jian zhenxing 见真性," in *Falun dafa jingjin yaozhi er*, p. 1.

"Turning the Wheel towards the Human World." February 15, 2005. Online at www.falundafa.org/book/eng/jw_122.htm; "Xiang shijian zhuanlun 向世间转轮," online at minghui.org/mh/articles/2005/2/17/95688.html.

"Using at Will." June 28, 2000. In *Essentials for Further Advancement, II*, p. 15; "Suiyi suoyong 随意所用," in *Falun dafa jingjin yaozhi er*, pp. 21–22.

"Zen Buddhism Is Extreme." In *Zhuan Falun, Volume II*, pp. 27–28; "Chanzong shi jiduande 禅宗是极端的," in *Zhuan falun juan er*, pp. 44–46.

Zhongguo falungong [China Falun Gong]. Beijing: Junshi yiwen chubanshe, 1993.

Zhuan Falun. Translated by North American practitioners, February 2003. Online at www.falundafa.org/book/eng/pdf/zfl_new.pdf; translated by US practitioners, March 2000: online at www.falundafa.org/book/eng/pdf/zflus.pdf; translated by "Translation Group of Falun Xiulian Dafa," 1998: online at www.falundafa.org/book/eng/pdf/zfl_en.pdf; *Zhuan falun* 转法轮, no publication date (first published January 1995).

Zhuan falun 转法轮. Beijing: Zhongguo guangbao dianshi chubanshe, 1994.

Zhuan Falun Fajie. No translation date. Online at www.falundafa.org/book/eng/pdf/zfl_fajie.pdf; *Zhuan falun fajie* 转法轮 法解, no publication date, introductory note, July 1997.

Zhuan Falun, Volume II. Trans. June 2008. Online at www.falundafa.org/book/eng/pdf/zf12.pdf; *Zhuan falun juan er* 转法轮卷二, no publication date (first published November 1995).

INTERVIEWS AND PRESS CONFERENCES

Dowell, William. "Interview with Li Hongzhi." *Time Asia*, May 10, 1999. Online at www.time.com/time/asia/asia/magazine/1999/990510/interview1.html.

"Master Li Hongzhi Met with Chinese Media in Sydney," May 2, 1999. Online at www.zhuichaguoji.org/en/upload/docs/ThirdPartyDoc/G_3.doc; "Li Hongzhi zai Xini huijian xifang meiti jizhe huishilu 李洪志在悉尼会见西方媒体记者会实录," online at thunderer.9.forumer.com/index.php?showtopic=583.

OTHER FALUN GONG SOURCES

A Falun Dafa Practitioner from China (Dalu dafa dizi 大陆大法弟子). "My Father's Cloth-Bag Prophesy Book." July 25, 2005. Online at www.clearwisdom.net/emh/articles/2005/8/24/64214.html; "'Budaijing' he bei zhonggong haisi de fuqin '布袋经' 和被中共害死的父亲," online at www.minghui.org/mh/articles/2005/7/30/107213.html.

A Falun Dafa Practitioner from Shandong Province (Shandong dafa dizi 山东大法弟子). "My Experiences Attending Master's Fifth Lecture Series in Guangzhou." January 1, 2008. Online at www.clearwisdom.net/emh/articles/2008/2/19/94593.html; "Huiyi shifu Guangzhou diwuqi jiangfa 回忆师父广州第五期讲法," online at www.minghui.org/mh/articles/2008/1/1/169412.html.

A Korean Practitioner (Hanguo xueyuan XX 韩国学员XX). "Letter from a Practitioner: Reflections after Reading 'A Reference for Prophecies.'" September 7, 2000. Online at www.clearwisdom.net/emh/articles/2000/9/8/8293.html; "Hanguo zhuming yuyan shuji 'Ge An yilu' de qishi 韩国著名预言书籍《格庵遗录》的启示," online at www.minghui.org/mh/articles/2000/9/7/2274.html.

A North American Practitioner (Beimei dafa dizi 北美大法弟子). "Revelation from David Copperfield." October 26, 2001. Online at www.pureinsight.org/node/973; "Dawei de qishi 大卫的启示," online at www.zhengjian.org/zj/articles/2001/10/26/12210.html.

A US Practitioner (Meiguo dizi 美国弟子). "Some Thoughts regarding the Scripture 'Beyond the Limits of Forbearance.'" January 9, 2001. Online at www.clearwisdom.net/emh/special_column/cultivation/some-thoughts-010114.doc; "Dui jingwen 'Ren wuke ren' de yidian geren renshi 对经文 '忍无可忍' 的一点个人认识," online at www.minghui.org/mh/articles/2001/1/10/6649.html.

A Young Practitioner in Taiwan (Xiao dafa dizi (Taiwan) 小大法弟子 (台湾)). "A Miraculous Experience: A Young Practitioner Walks through a Wall." January 30, 2003. Online at www.clearwisdom.net/emh/articles/2003/2/9/31913.html; "Xiao dizi chuan qiang er guo de shenqi jingli 小弟子穿墙而过的神奇经历," online at www.minghui.org/mh/articles/2003/1/31/43667.html.

Anon. "Anything for Power: The Real Story of China's Jiang Zemin—Chapter 8." June 7, 2005. Online at en.epochtimes.com/news/5-7-24/30542.html; "Jiang Zemin qiren, 8: qiangtan Beijing xitong shushou《江泽民其人》八：抢滩北京希同束手," online at www.epochtimes.com/b5/5/6/7/n946915.htm.

———. "As the Tenth Anniversary of the Minghui Website Draws Near, Editors Answer Readers' Questions." April 19, 2009. Online at www.clearwisdom.net/html/articles/2009/4/22/106718.html; "Shi zhounian jianglin zhi ji, minghui bianjibu da duzhe wen 十周年将临之际明慧编辑部答读者问," online at www.minghui.org/mh/articles/2009/4/19/199284.html.

———. "A Brief History of Events Leading Up to Jiang Zemin's Irrational Persecution of Falun Gong in China." November 20, 2004. Online at www.clearharmony.net/articles/200411/23203p.html.

———. "A Chronicle of Major Events of Falun Dafa." March 2, 2004. Online at www.clearwisdom.net/emh/articles/2004/8/27/chronicle.html; "Falun dafa dashiji nianjian 法轮大法大事记年鉴（更新版三)," online at www.zhengjian .org/zj/articles/2004/3/2/26013.html.

———. "Clearwisdom Glossary." No date. Online at www.clearwisdom.net/emh/ glossary.html.

———. "Commentaries on the Communist Party—4." November 25, 2004. On-line at en.epochtimes.com/news/4-12-14/24953.html; "Jiuping zhi si 九评之四," online at www.epochtimes.com/gb/4/11/25/n727814.htm.

———. "The *Falun*." 2007. Online at www.falundafa.org/eng/falun.html.

———. "Falun Dafa: How to Learn." 2007. Online at www.falundafa.org/eng/ howtolearn.html.

———. "Falun Dafa Australia: Introduction." 2002. Online at www.falunau.org/ aboutdafa.htm.

———. "Key Statistics related to Falun Gong—2010 Annual Report." September 27, 2009. Online at www.faluninfo.net/article/909/?cid=162.

———. "Memories of Attending Master's Fourth Lecture Series in Guangzhou." May 14, 2008. Online at www.clearwisdom.net/emh/articles/2008/6/5/97893 .html; "Canjia shizun Guangzhou disi chuangong jiangfaban de rizi 参加师尊广州第四传功讲法班的日子," online at www.minghui.org/mh/articles/2008/ 5/16/178490.html.

———. "On Important Matters, Practitioners Must Pay Attention to the Atti-tude of Minghui Net." July 14, 2000. Online at www.clearwisdom.net/emh/ articles/2000/7/16/7662.html; "Zhongda wenti kan minghuiwang de taidu 重大问题看明慧网的态度," online at www.minghui.org/mh/articles/2000/7/15/ 2624.html.

———. "Positive Reports on Falun Gong by Mainland China Media before the Persecution of Falun Gong Began in 1999." August 25, 2004. Online at www .clearwisdom.net/emh/articles/2004/9/20/52631.html; "1999 nian quanmian pohaiqian dalu meiti dui falun gong de zhengmian baodao 1999 年全面迫害前大陆媒体对法轮功的正面报道," online at www.minghui.org/mh/articles/ 2004/8/25/82595.html.

———. "Reveal the Scheme of the Very Few People from Changchun." July 21, 1999. Online at web.archive.org/web/20040426043044/http://www.clear wisdom.net/emh/articles/1999/7/21/11163.html.

———. "A Second Authentic New Article of Master Li since July 22, 1999 Will Be Published in a Few Days." June 15, 2000. Online at www.clearwisdom .net/html/articles/2000/6/15/8785.html; "Jinrinei jiangyou qi yue ershier ri yilai dier pian zhenzheng de xin jingwen fabiao 近日内将有 7 月 22 日以来第二篇真正的新经文发表," online at www.minghui.org/mh/articles/2000/6/15/1461 .html.

———. "A Short Biography of Mr. Li Hongzhi, Founder of Falun Xiulian Dafa, President of the Research Society of Falun Buddha Science." Translation by "Translation Group of Falun Xiulian Dafa." Online at web.archive

.org/web/20010109225900/http://www.compapp.dcu.ie/~dongxue/biography
.html; "Brief Biography of Li Hongzhi: Founder of Falun Gong and President
of the Falun Gong Research Society," *Chinese Law and Government* 32, no. 6
(November/December 1999): 14–23; "Zhongguo falun gong chuangshiren,
falun gong yanjiuhui huizhang Li Hongzhi xiansheng xiaozhuan 中国法轮功
创始人法轮功研究会会长李洪志先生小传," in *Zhuan falun* (Beijing: Zhongguo
guangbao dianshi chubanshe, 1994); online at en.wikipedia.org/wiki/User:
Colipon/Biography_of_Li_Hongzhi.

———. "The Swastika Revisited." No date. Online at www.clearwisdom.net/emh/
articles/2007/9/16/89609.html.

———. "What Shanshan Saw in Other Dimensions (I)." April 16, 2001. Online at
www.clearwisdom.net/html/articles/2001/4/28/9140.html; "Shanshan kandao
de lingwai kongjian (yi) 山山看到的另外空间（一）," online at www.minghui
.org/mh/articles/2001/4/16/9994.html.

———. "What Shanshan Saw in Other Dimensions (II)." April 18, 2001. Online at
www.clearwisdom.net/emh/articles/2001/5/2/9205.html; "Shanshan kandao
de lingwai kongjian (er) 山山看到的另外空间（二），" online at www.minghui.org/
mh/articles/2001/4/18/9997.html.

———. "What Shanshan Saw in Other Dimensions (III)." April 24, 2001. Online at
www.clearwisdom.net/html/articles/2001/5/3/9238.html; "Shanshan kandao
de lingwai kongjian (san) 山山看到的另外空间（三），" online at www.minghui
.org/mh/articles/2001/4/24/10222.html.

———. "What Shanshan Saw in Other Dimensions (IV)." May 18, 2001. Online at
www.clearwisdom.net/emh/articles/2001/5/25/10373.html; "Shanshan kandao de lingwai kongjian (si) 山山看到的另外空间（四），" online at www.minghui
.org/mh/articles/2001/5/19/11246.html.

———. "What Shanshan Saw in Other Dimensions (VII)." May 29, 2001. Online
at www.clearwisdom.net/emh/articles/2001/5/30/10591.html; "Shanshan
kandao de lingwai kongjian (qi) 山山看到的另外空间（七），" online at minghui
.org/mh/articles/2001/5/29/11604.html.

———. "Zhengfa zhi lu 正法之路." No date. Online at photo.minghui.org/photo/
images/exhibition/newest_1.htm.

———. "Zhongguo Falun Gong Hefei chuanshouban zhaosheng 中国法轮功合肥传
授办招生." *Qigong yu kexue* 气功与科学 2 (1994): 46.

———. "Zhongguo Falun Gong xuexiban zhaosheng 中国法轮功学习班招生."
Qigong yu kexue 气功与科学 3 (1993): 24.

Falun Dafa Research Society. "Notice on Setting Up of 'Falun Dafa Bulletin Board.'"
August 8, 1998. Online at web.archive.org/web/19990429144533/falundafa
.ca/FLDFBB/index.htm.

The Foreign Liaison Group of Falun Dafa Research Society. "Falun Dafa's Transmission on Internet Notice." June 15, 1997. Online at web.archive.org/
web/19990209113803/falundafa.ca/FLDFBB/gongga0970615.htm.

Gu Anru 古安如. "On the Fifth Anniversary of the 'April 25 Appeal'—Remembering

April 25, 1999 (Part 2)." April 24, 2004. Online at www.clearharmony.net/
articles/200405/19428.html; "Zhongnanhai shijian zhenxiang (er): heping
shangfang yuanman jiejue da gongshi 中南海事件真相（二）：和平上访圆满解决
达共识," online at www.yuanming.net/articles/200404/30754.html.

Ming Xuan 明玄. "Recalling Master's Lectures in Guangzhou." February 21, 2008.
Online at www.clearwisdom.net/emh/articles/2008/3/13/95309.html; "Yi shizun Guangzhou chuangong jiangfa diandi 忆师尊广州传功讲法点滴," online at
www.minghui.org/mh/articles/2008/2/22/172909.html.

Rong Fa 溶法. "Prophecies of Liu Chi in China's Ming Dynasty." October 24,
2000. Online at clearwisdom.net/html/articles/2000/11/3/6308.html; "Du
Liu Bowen yuyan yougan 读刘伯温预言有感," online at www.minghui.org/
gb/0001/Oct/26/liubowen_yuyan_102600_shishi.html.

Yang Ning 杨宁. "Nana's Fairy Family (3)." June 5, 2006. Online at www.pure
insight.org/node/4048; "Nana de shenxian jiating (3): Xiao yinghai beibei 娜娜
的神仙家庭（3）：小婴孩贝贝," online at www.zhengjian.org/zj/articles/2006/6/
5/37985.html.

Secondary Sources

ABC Radio National. "The Religion Report." July 28, 1999. Online at www.abc
.net.au/rn/religionreport/stories/1999/39480.htm.

Adams, Ian, Riley Adams, and Rocco Galati. *Power of the Wheel: The Falun
Gong Revolution.* Toronto: Stoddart, 2000.

Alles, Gregory D. "Religion [Further Considerations]." In Jones, *Encyclopedia of
Religion,* 2nd ed., pp. 7701–706.

Amnesty International. The Crackdown on Falun Gong and Other So-Called Heretical Organizations." March 23, 2000. Online at www.amnesty.org/en/
library/info/ASA17/011/2000/en.

———. "Falun Gong Practitioners: List of Sentences, Administrative Sentences
and Those Detained." March 28, 2000. Online at www.amnesty.org/en/library/
info/ASA17/012/2000/en.

Andersen, Poul. "Taiyi." In Pregadio, *The Encyclopedia of Taoism,* p. 958.

Anon. "China Issued Anti-Cult Law." November 2, 1999. Online at www.china
embassycanada.org/eng/xw/xwgb/t38871.htm.

———. "Constitution of The People's Republic of China." Online at english
.peopledaily.com.cn/constitution/constitution.html.

———. "Criminal Activities of Falun Gong Condemned." *People's Daily Online,* January 8, 2001. Online at english.peopledaily.com.cn/200101/08/eng20010108_
59812.html.

———. "Cult Crimes Must Be Punished." *People's Daily Online,* November 16, 1999.
Online at english.peopledaily.com.cn/english/199911/06/eng199911060101
.html.

———. "Former Falun Gong Follower Leads New Life." *People's Daily Online*, November 21, 2001. Online at english.peopledaily.com.cn/200111/21/eng20011121_85012.shtml.

———. "Freedom House Honors Chinese Defenders of Religious Freedom: Annual Award Going to Five Chinese Religious Groups." Online at web.archive.org/web/20010715213704/http://www.freedomhouse.org/religion/news/bn2001/bn-2001-03–12.htm.

———. "Investigation and Analysis of Establishment and Development of Falun Gong in Jilin Province." January 11, 2008. Online at www.facts.org.cn/Data/aboutfg/200801/t76201.htm.

———. "Li Hongzhi's Mother's Midwife Says Li Is a Swindler." *People's Daily Online*, July 30, 1999. Online at english.people.com.cn/special/fagong/1999073000A107.html.

———. "Main Points of a Talk Given by Person in Charge of Bureaus of Letters and Petitions of the General Secretariat of the Chinese Communist Party (CCP) Central Committee and of the General Secretariat of the State Council When Receiving a Number of Falun Gong Appellants." *Chinese Law and Government* 32, no. 5 (September/October 1999): 19–21.

———. "Oklo: Natural Nuclear Reactors." Online at www.ocrwm.doe.gov/factsheets/doeymp0010.shtml.

———. "Recent Situation of Yao Jie: Well-Known Member of Falungong Cult (1)." Online at au.china-embassy.org/eng/zt/jpflg/t46159.htm.

———. "Xinhua Article on Uproars Produced by Falungong." *People's Daily Online*, January 5, 2001. Online at english.peopledaily.com.cn/200101/05/eng20010105_59639.html.

———. "Zhongguo qigong kexue yanjiuhui lishihui mingdan 中国气功科学研究会理事会名单." *Qigong yu kexue* 气功与科学 7 (1986): 2.

Ashiwa, Yoshiko, and David L. Wank, eds. *Making Religion, Making the State*. Stanford, CA: Stanford University Press, 2009.

Baensch, Robert E., ed. *The Publishing Industry in China*. New Brunswick, NJ: Transaction, 2004.

Barmé, Geremie R. "On New Sinology." Online at rspas.anu.edu.au/pah/china heritageproject/newsinology/.

Barmé, Geremie R., and Linda Jaivin, eds. *New Ghosts, Old Dreams: Chinese Rebel Voices*. New York: Times Books, 1992.

Barrett, T. H. "Devil's Valley to Omega Point: Reflections on the Emergence of a Theme from the No." In Skorupski, *The Buddhist Forum*, vol. 2, pp. 1–12.

Barrett, T. H., and Francesca Tarocco. "Terminology and Religious Identity: Buddhism and the Genealogy of the Term *Zongjiao*." In Krech, *Dynamics in the History of Religions*.

Bary, William Theodore de, ed. *Self and Society in Ming Thought*. New York: Columbia University Press, 1970.

Baum, Richard. *Burying Mao: Chinese Politics in the Age of Deng Xiaoping*. Princeton, NJ: Princeton University Press, 1996.

BBC Monitoring Service, April 27, 1999. "Sect Members Deliver Their Demands to Beijing in Huge Petition." *Ming Pao*, April 26, 1999.

———, April 28, 1999. "Hong Kong Paper—Mainland Schools 'Invaded' by 'Cult' of Falun Gong." *Ming Pao*, April 27, 1999.

———, April 30, 1999. "Falun Gong 'Paratroops' Reportedly Still in Beijing." *Sing Tao Jih Pao*, April 28, 1999.

———, June 7, 1999. "Report on Extradition of Falun Gong Founder Li Hongzhi 'Sheer Rumours.'" Zhongguo Tongxun She News Agency.

———, June 8, 1999. "Police Break Up Falun Gong Gathering of 70,000 in Beijing." *Sing Tao Jih Pao*, June 7, 1999.

———, July 17, 1999. "Beijing Restricting Falun Gong Sect Activities—Hong Kong Press." *Tung Fang Jih Pao*, June 28, 1999.

———, July 17, 1999. "Falun Gong Sect Members Protest against TV Programme." *Sing Tao Jih Pao*, July 15, 1999.

Benavides, Gustavo, and M. W. Daly, eds. *Religion and Political Power*. Albany: State University of New York Press, 1989.

Berlitz, Charles. *Atlantis: The Eighth Continent*. New York: G. P. Putnam's Sons, 1984.

———. *Baimuda sanjiao* 百慕大三角 [*The Bermuda Triangle*]. Translated by Tong Fu 佟富, Wang Ting 王婷, and Huang Dengpei 黃登培. Beijing: Beijing chubanshe, 1981.

Bi Yongsheng 毕永升, ed. *Yixue qigong* 医学气功 [*Medical Qigong*]. Beijing: Gaodeng jiaoyu chubanshe, 1990. Chief editor of English edition: Yu Wenping.

Bokenkamp, Stephen R. *Early Daoist Scriptures*. Berkeley: University of California Press, 1997.

———. "Jie, *kalpa*, aeon (eon)." In Pregadio, *The Encyclopedia of Taoism*, pp. 545–46.

Bumbacher, Stephan Peter. *The Fragments of "Daoxue zhuan": Critical Edition, Translation and Analysis of a Medieval Collection of Daoist Biographies*. Frankfurt am Main: Peter Lang, 2000.

Buswell, Robert E., ed. *Encyclopedia of Buddhism*. New York: MacMillan Reference USA, 2004.

Camp, L. Sprague de. *Lost Continents: The Atlantis Theme in History, Science and Literature*. New York: Gnome Press, 1954. Reprint, New York: Dover Publications, 1970.

Campany, Robert Ford. *To Live as Long as Heaven and Earth: A Translation and Study of Ge Hong's "Traditions of Divine Transcendents."* Berkeley: University of California Press, 2002.

Carroll, Robert T. "Ica Stones." In *The Skeptic's Dictionary*, online at skepdic.com/icastones.html.

Chak, Michelle. "Falun Gong Leaders Arrested." *South China Morning Post*, July 21, 1999.

Chan, Vivien Pik-kwan. "Phone Taps and Close Monitoring of Cult Members—Falun Gong Faithful Kept on Tight Leash." *South China Morning Post*, June 8, 1999.

Chang, Leslie. "China Arrests Sect's Leaders across Nation." *Asian Wall Street Journal*, July 21, 1999.

Chau, Adam Yuet. *Miraculous Response: Doing Popular Religion in Contemporary China*. Stanford, CA: Stanford University Press, 2006.

Chen, Nancy N. *Breathing Spaces: Qigong, Psychiatry and Healing in China*. New York: Columbia University Press, 2003.

Chen, Yi. "Publishing in China in the Post-Mao Era: The Case of *Lady Chatterley's Lover*." *Asian Survey* 32, no. 6 (June 1992): 568–82.

Confucius. *The Analects*. Translated by D. C. Lau. Harmondsworth: Penguin Books, 1979.

Daniken, Erich von. *Zhongshen zhiche? lishi shangde weijie zhimi* 众神之车?历史上的未解之谜 [*Chariots of the Gods*]. Translated by Wu Shengming 吴胜明, Zhou Liya 周里亚, and Lang Shengshuo 郎胜铄. Shanghai: Shanghai kexue jishu chubanshe, 1981.

Darga, Martine. "Zhoutian." In Pregadio, *The Encyclopedia of Taoism*, pp. 1287–89.

Deng, Zixian, and Shi-min Fang. "The Two Tales of Falungong: Radicalism in Traditional Form." Online at www.xys.org/xys/netters/Fang-Zhouzi/religion/2tales.doc.

Despeux, Catherine. "Le *qigong*, une expression de la modernité chinoise." In Gernet and Kalinowski, *En Suivant la Voie Royale*, pp. 267–81.

———. "Xingqi." In Pregadio, *The Encyclopedia of Taoism*, p. 1108.

De Woskin, K. J. *Doctors, Diviners and Magicians of Ancient China: Biographies of Fang-shih*. New York: Columbia University Press, 1983.

Dikötter, Frank. *Sex, Culture and Modernity in China: Medical Science and the Construction of Sexual Identities in the Early Republican Period*. London: Hurst, 1995.

Dillon, Michael. *Religious Minorities and China*. London: Minority Rights Group International, 2001.

Dow Jones International News. "Falun Gong Protests Reported in More Chinese Cities." July 21, 1999.

Duara, Prasenjit. *Rescuing History from the Nation: Questioning Narratives of Modern China*. Chicago: University of Chicago Press, 1995.

Esposito, Monica. "Gushen." In Pregadio, *The Encyclopedia of Taoism*, p. 466.

Fackler, Martin. "Beijing, Falun Gong Trade Barbs." Associated Press, January 6, 2001.

Faure, Bernard. *The Rhetoric of Immediacy: A Cultural Critique of Chan/Zen Buddhism*. Princeton, NJ: Princeton University Press, 1991.

Feldman, Gayle. "The Organization of Publishing in China." *China Quarterly* 107 (September 1986): 519–29.

Feuchtwang, Stephan. "The Problem of Superstition in the People's Republic of China." In Benavides and Daly, *Religion and Political Power*, pp. 43–68.

Findly, Ellison Banks. "Borderline Beings: Plant Possibilities in Early Buddhism." *Journal of the American Oriental Society* 122, no. 2 (April/June 2002): 252–63.

Gernet, Jacques, and Marc Kalinowski, eds. *En Suivant la Voie Royale: Mélanges en hommage à Léon Vandermeersch*. Paris: Ecole français d'Extrême-Orient, 1997.

Giles, Lionel, trans. *Sunzi: The Art of War*. North Clarendon: Tuttle, 2008.

Gonganbu yanjiushe 公安部 研究社. "Li Hongzhi qiren qishi 李洪志其人其事." *Renmin ribao*, July 23, 1999. Reprinted in *Jiepi falun dafa xieshuo* 揭批 "法轮大法" 邪说, edited by He Ping 何平, pp. 63–70. Beijijng: Xinhua chubanshe, 1999.

Goossaert, Vincent, and David A. Palmer. *The Religious Question in Modern China*. Chicago: University of Chicago Press, 2011.

He Zuoxiu. "How 'Falun Gong' Harassed Me and My Family." Online at replay.waybackmachine.org/20030121122938/http://211.99.196.218/fanduixiejiao/eng/07/001.htm.

———. "I Do Not Approve of Teenagers Practicing *Qigong*." *Chinese Law and Government* 32, no. 5 (September/October 1999): 95–98.

Hutzler, Charles. "Chinese Leaders Prepare Careful Crackdown against Secretive Group." Associated Press, May 8, 1999.

Irons, Edward. "Falun Gong and the Sectarian Religion Paradigm." *Nova Religio* 6, no. 2 (April 2003): 244–62.

Ivanhoe, Philip J. *Confucian Moral Self-Cultivation*. New York: Peter Lang, 1993.

Ji Zhe 冀喆. "'93' dongfang jiankang bolanhui teyi gongneng yanshi '93' 东方健康博览会特异功能演示." *Zhonghua qigong* 中华气功 2 (1994): 42–44.

Jian Xu. "Body, Discourse, and the Cultural Politics of Contemporary Chinese *Qigong*." *Journal of Asian Studies* 58, no. 3 (1999): 961–91.

Johnson, Ian. *Wild Grass: China's Revolution from Below*. London: Penguin, 2005.

Jones, Lindsay, ed. in chief. *Encyclopedia of Religion*. 2nd ed. Farmington Hills, MI: Macmillan Reference USA, 2005.

Kaltenmark, Maxime. *Le Lie-sien tchouan*. Beijing: Université de Paris Publications, 1953.

Kaye, Lincoln. "Traveller's Tales." *Far Eastern Economic Review*, July 23, 1992.

Kieschnick, John. *The Eminent Monk: Buddhist Ideals in Medieval Chinese Hagiography*. Honolulu: University of Hawai'i Press, 1997.

———. *The Impact of Buddhism on Chinese Material Culture*. Princeton, NJ: Princeton University Press, 2003.

King, Winston L. "Religion." In Jones, *Encyclopedia of Religion*, pp. 7692–701.

Kirkland, Russell. "Varieties of 'Taoism' in Ancient China: A Preliminary Comparison of Themes in the *Nei yeh* and Other 'Taoist Classics.'" *Taoist Resources* 7, no. 2 (1997): 73–86.

Kohn, Livia, ed. *Daoism Handbook*. Leiden: Brill, 2000.

———, ed., in cooperation with Yoshinobu Sakade. *Taoist Meditation and Longevity Techniques*. Ann Arbor: Center for Chinese Studies, University of Michigan, 1989.

Krech, Volkhard, ed. *Dynamics in the History of Religions*. Leiden: Brill, 2011.

Kyodo News International. "Chinese Spiritual Leader Cautions Beijing on Crackdown." June 16, 1999.

———. "H. K. Followers of Falun Gong Protest Arrests in China." July 20, 1999.

Landler, Mark. "Beijing Detains Leaders of Sect, Watchdog Says." *New York Times*, July 21, 1999.

———. "China Said to Prepare Ban on Sect; Protests Go On." *New York Times*, July 22, 1999.

Lawrence, Susan V. "Religion: Pilgrim's Protest." *Far Eastern Economic Review*, May 13, 1999.

Lee, Mabel, and A. D. Syrokomla-Stefanowska, eds. *Modernization of the Chinese Past*. Sydney: Wild Peony, 1993.

Legge, James. *The Four Books*. New York: Paragon Book Reprint, 1966.

Lewis-Williams, D. J. *Discovering Southern African Rock Art*. Cape Town: David Philip, 1990.

Li Jianxin 李健新. "Qigong qunxing jinghua da juhui 气功群星京华大聚会." *Zhonghua qigong* 中华气功 2 (1993): 4–6.

Lim, Benjamin Kang. "China Cracks Down on Sect, Thousands Protest." Reuters, July 21, 1999.

Lopez, Donald S., Jr. *Buddhism in Practice*. Princeton, NJ: Princeton University Press, 1995.

———, ed. *Critical Terms for the Study of Buddhism*. Chicago: University of Chicago Press, 2005.

———. *Modern Buddhism: Readings for the Unenlightened*. London: Penguin, 2002.

———. *Prisoners of Shangri-La: Tibetan Buddhism and the West*. Chicago: University of Chicago Press, 1998.

———, ed. *Religions of China in Practice*. Princeton, NJ: Princeton University Press, 1996.

The Lotus Sutra. Translated by Burton Watson. Online at www.sgi-usa.org/Buddhism/library/Buddhism/LotusSutra/text/Chap26.htm.

Lupke, Christopher, ed. *The Magnitude of Ming: Command, Allotment, and Fate in Chinese Culture*. Honolulu: University of Hawai'i Press, 2005.

Lusthaus, Dan. "What Is and Isn't Yogācāra." Online at www.acmuller.net/yogacara/articles/intro-uni.htm.

Ma, Qiusha. *Non-Governmental Organizations in Contemporary China: Paving the Way to Civil Society?* Abingdon, UK: Routledge, 2006.

Ma, Y. W., and Joseph S. M. Lau, eds. *Traditional Chinese Stories: Themes and Variations*. New York: Columbia University Press, 1978.

MacInnes, Donald E. *Religion in China Today: Policy and Practice*. Maryknoll, NY: Orbis Books, 1989.

Makeham, John. *Name and Actuality in Early Chinese Thought*. Albany: State University of New York Press, 1994.

Manderson, Lenore, Wendy Smith, and Matt Tomlinson, eds. *Flows of Faith: Religious Reach and Community in Asia and the Pacific*. New York: Springer, 2012.

Mao Zedong. "On the Correct Handling of Contradictions among the People." In *Selected Works of Mao Tse-tung*, online at www.marxists.org/reference/archive/mao/selected-works/volume-5/mswv5_58.htm.

———. "Speech at the Chinese Communist Party's National Conference on Propaganda Work." In *Selected Works of Mao Tse-tung*, online at www.marxists.org/reference/archive/mao/selected-works/volume-5/mswv5_59.htm.

———. "A Study of Physical Education." In Schram, *Mao's Road to Power*, 113–27.

Matas, David, and David Kilgour. "Report into Allegations of Organ Harvesting of Falun Gong Practitioners in China." Online at pkg.dajiyuan.com/pkg/2006-07-07/Kilgour-Matas-organ-harvesting-rpt-July6-eng.pdf.

Mawangdui Hanmu boshu zhengli xiaozubian 马王堆汉墓帛书整理小组编. *Daoyin tu* 导引图. Beijing: Wenwu chubanshe, 1979.

Mencius. *The Works of Mencius*. Translated by J. Legge. In Legge, *The Four Books*, pp. 429–1014.

Miles, James. *BBC Breakfast News*, June 11, 1998; November 6, 1998.

Minford, John. Foreword to Giles, *Sunzi: The Art of War*. Online at rspas.anu.edu.au/pah/chinaheritageproject/newsinology/.

Miura, Kunio. "The Revival of *Qi*: *Qigong* in Contemporary China." In Kohn, *Taoist Meditation and Longevity Techniques*, pp. 331–62.

Miyakawa, Hisayuki. "Local Cults around Mount Lu at the Time of Sun En's Rebellion." In Welch and Seidel, *Facets of Taoism*, pp. 83–101.

Mollier, Christine. *Une apocalypse taoïste du début du Ve siècle: Le Livre des Incantations Divines des Grottes Abyssales*. Paris: Collège de France, 1990.

———. "Zhongmin." In Pregadio, *The Encyclopedia of Taoism*, pp. 1285–86.

Moreno, Jonathan D. *Mind Wars: Brain Research and National Defense*. New York: Dana Press, 2006.

Nattier, Jan. "The Meaning of the Maitreya Myth." In Sponberg and Hardacre, *Maitreya, the Future Buddha*, pp. 23–47.

Nedostup, Rebecca. *Superstitious Regimes: Religion and the Politics of Chinese Modernity*. Cambridge, MA: Harvard University Asia Center, 2009. Distributed by Harvard University Press.

O'Neill, Mark. "Thousands Gather for Falun Gong Despite Criticism, Ban." *South China Morning Post*, May 9, 1999.

Ownby, David. *Falun Gong and the Future of China*. New York: Oxford University Press, 2008.

———. "A History for Falun Gong: Popular Religion and the Chinese State since the Ming Dynasty." *Nova Religio* 6, no. 2 (April 2003): 223–43.

Page, Jeremy. "China Lambasts Falun Gong Head after New Year Note." Reuters, January 8, 2001.

Palmer, David A. *Qigong Fever: Body, Science and Utopia in China*. London: Hurst, 2007.

Penny, Benjamin. "Animal Spirits, Karmic Retribution, Falungong, and the State." In Yang, *Chinese Religiosities*, pp. 135–54.

———. "Falun Gong, Buddhism and 'Buddhist Qigong.'" *Asian Studies Review* 29, no. 1 (March 2005): 35–46.

———. "Falun Gong, Prophecy and Apocalypse." *East Asian History* 23 (June 2002): 149–68.

———. "Immortality and Transcendence." In Kohn, *Daoism Handbook*, pp. 109–33.

———. "The Life and Times of Li Hongzhi: Falun Gong and Religious Biography." *China Quarterly* 175 (September 2003): 643–61.

———. "Master Li Encounters Jesus: Christianity and the Configurations of Falun Gong." In L. Manderson et al., *Flows of Faith*.

———. "*Qigong*, Daoism and Science: Some Contexts for the *Qigong* Boom." In Lee and Syrokomla-Stefanowska, *Modernization of the Chinese Past*, pp. 166–79.

Perry, Elizabeth J. *Challenging the Mandate of Heaven: Social Protest and State Power in China*. Armonk, NY: M. E. Sharpe, 2002.

Pollock, Simon. "Beijing Police Clamp Down on Meditation Group." Kyodo News International, July 21, 1999.

Potter, Pitman B. "Belief in Control: Regulation of Religion in China." *China Quarterly* 174 (June 2003): 317–37.

Pranke, Patrick A. "Abhijñā." In Buswell, *Encyclopedia of Buddhism*, pp. 8–9.

Pregadio, Fabrizio, ed. *The Encyclopedia of Taoism*. Abingdon, UK: Routledge, 2008.

———. *Great Clarity: Daoism and Alchemy in Early Medieval China*. Stanford, CA: Stanford University Press, 2006.

Pregadio, Fabrizio, and Lowell Skar. "Inner Alchemy (*Neidan*)." In Kohn, *Daoism Handbook*, pp. 464–97.

Purucker, G. de, ed.-in-chief. *Encyclopedic Theosophical Glossary: A Resource on Theosophy*. Theosophical University Press Online Edition, www.theosociety.org/pasadena/etgloss/tem-thn.htm.

Rampa, T. Lobsang. *The Third Eye: The Autobiography of a Tibetan Lama*. New York: Ballantine Books, 1964.

Research Office of the Ministry for Public Security. "Li Hongzhi: The Man and His Deeds." *Chinese Law and Government* 32, no. 5 (September/October 1999): 56–64.

Roth, Harold D. "The Inner Cultivation Tradition of Early Taoism." In Lopez, *Religions of China in Practice*, pp. 123–48.

———. *Original Tao: Inward Training (Nei-yeh) and the Foundations of Taoist Mysticism*. New York: Columbia University Press, 1999.

Ruwitch, John. "Luo Gan Knows Where China's Skeletons Lie." Reuters, May 11, 2002.

Saler, Benson. *Conceptualizing Religion: Immanent Anthropologists, Transcendent Natives, and Unbound Categories*. Paperback ed. New York: Berghahn Books, 2000.

Schmithausen, Lambert. *The Problem of the Sentience of Plants in Earliest Buddhism*. Tokyo: International Institute for Buddhist Studies, 1999.

Schram, Stuart R., ed. and trans. *Mao's Road to Power: Revolutionary Writings, 1912–49*. Vol. 1, *The Pre-Marxist Period, 1912–20*. Armonk, NY: M. E. Sharpe, 1992.

Seidel, Anna. "A Taoist Immortal of the Ming Dynasty: Chang San-feng." In de Bary, *Self and Society in Ming Thought*, pp. 483–531.

Seiwert, Hubert, in collaboration with Ma Xisha. *Popular Religious Movements and Heterodox Sects in Chinese History*. Leiden: Brill, 2003.

Sharf, Robert H. "Ritual." In Lopez, *Critical Terms for the Study of Buddhism*, pp. 245–70.

Shen Jiji. "The World inside a Pillow." Translated by William H. Nienhauser Jr. In Ma and Lau, *Traditional Chinese Stories*, pp. 435–38.

Skorupski, T., ed. *The Buddhist Forum*. Vol. 2. London: SOAS, 1991.

Smith, Craig S. "American Dream Finds Chinese Spiritual Leader." *Wall Street Journal*, November 1, 1999.

———. "Banned Chinese Sect Is Spurred On by Exiled Leader." *New York Times*, January 5, 2001.

———. "China's Retired Elite Aid Spiritual Group—Protest Draws Strength from Some Prominent Communist Party Members." *Asian Wall Street Journal*, April 30, 1999.

———. "Confounded China Considers Response to Challenge from Spiritual Group." *Wall Street Journal*, April 27, 1999.

———. "Revered by Millions, a Potent Mystic Rattles China's Communist Leaders." *Wall Street Journal*, April 26, 1999.

Smith, Jonathan Z. "Religion, Religions, Religious." In Taylor, *Critical Terms for Religious Studies*, pp. 269–84.

Soothill, William Edward, and Lewis Hodous. *Dictionary of Chinese Buddhist Terms*. London: Kegan Paul, Trench, Trubner, 1937.

Spiegel, Mickey. *China: State Control of Religion*. New York: Human Rights Watch, 1997.

———. "Dangerous Meditation: China's Campaign against Falun Gong." January 2002. Online at www.hrw.org/legacy/reports/2002/china.

Sponberg, Alan, and Helen Hardacre. *Maitreya, the Future Buddha*. Cambridge: Cambridge University Press, 1988.

Stein, Rolf A. "Religious Taoism and Popular Religion from the Second to the Seventh Centuries." In Welch and Seidel, *Facets of Taoism*, pp. 53–81.

Strickmann, Michel. "On the Alchemy of T'ao Hung-Ching." In Welch and Seidel, *Facets of Taoism*, pp. 123–92.

Sun, Jon. "For Joy and Fulfillment, Not Money." *Wall Street Journal*, November 17, 1999.

Taiping guangji 太平广记. 10 vols. Beijing: Zhonghua shuju, 1994.

Tan Deyin. "Ji Liewu: Falun Gong Made Me Lose My Mind." Online at www.facts.org.cn/krs/wfem/200801/t76811.htm.

———. "Li Chang: It's Tragic for Falun Gong to Go to Politics." Online at www.facts.org.cn/krs/wfem/200801/t75987.htm.

———. "Wang Zhiwen: '4·25' Affair Was Plotted in This Way." Online at www.facts.org.cn/krs/wfem/200801/t75991.htm.

Tanabe, George J., Jr. "Chanting and Liturgy." In Buswell, *Encyclopedia of Buddhism*, pp. 137–38.

Taylor, Kim. *Chinese Medicine in Early Communist China, 1945–63: A Medicine of Revolution*. London: RoutledgeCurzon, 2005.

Taylor, Mark C., ed. *Critical Terms for Religious Studies*. Chicago: University of Chicago Press, 1998.

Teiser, Stephen F. "Popular Religion." *Journal of Asian Studies* 54, no. 2 (May 1995): 378–95.

Teiwes, Frederick C. *Politics and Purges in China: Rectification and the Decline of Party Norms, 1950–1965*. Armonk, NY: M. E. Sharpe, 1993.

ter Haar, B. J. "Falun Gong: Evaluation and Further References." Online at website .leidenuniv.nl/~haarbjter/falun.htm.

———. "PR China: Falun Gong; Assessing Its Origins and Present Situation." July 2002. On behalf of WriteNet for use by the United Nations High Commissioner for Refugees. Online at website.leidenuniv.nl/~haarbjter/UNHCR .htm.

———. *The White Lotus Teachings in Chinese Religious History*. Honolulu: University of Hawai'i Press, 1999.

Tompkins, Peter, and Christopher Bird. *Zhiwude teyi gongneng* 植物的特异功能 [*The Secret Life of Plants*]. Translated by Wu Jiang 伍江, Shuang Si 霜驷, and Ouyang Zhao 欧阳朝. Beijing: Xinhua chubanshe, 1989.

Tong, James. "An Organizational Analysis of the Falun Gong: Structure, Communications, Financing." *China Quarterly* 171 (September 2002): 636–60.

Toy, Mary-Anne. "Screws Tighten on Persecuted Sect." *Sydney Morning Herald*, July 26, 2008.

Unger, Jonathan, ed. *Associations and the Chinese State: Contested Spaces*. Armonk, NY: M. E. Sharpe, 2008.

US State Department. *International Religious Freedom Report, 2010*. Online at www .state.gov/g/drl/rls/irf/2010/148863.htm.

Utiraruto Otehode. "The Creation and Reemergence of *Qigong* in China." In Ashiwa and Wank, *Making Religion, Making the State*, pp. 241–65.

Ware, James, trans. and ed. *Alchemy, Medicine and Religion in the China of A.D. 320: The Nei P'ien of Ko Hung*. Cambridge, MA: MIT Press, 1966.

Wasserstrom, Jeffrey N., ed. *Twentieth-Century China: New Approaches*. London: Routledge, 2003.

———. "The Year of Living Anxiously: China's 1999." In Wasserstrom, *Twentieth-Century China*, pp. 256–65.

Welch, Holmes, and Anna Seidel, eds. *Facets of Taoism*. New Haven, CT: Yale University Press, 1979.

Wright, Arthur F. "Biography and Hagiography: Hui-Chiao's Lives of Eminent Monks." In Wright, *Studies in Chinese Buddhism*, pp. 73–111.

———. *Studies in Chinese Buddhism*. Edited by Robert M. Somers. New Haven, CT: Yale University Press, 1990.

Xin Ping 辛平. "Fandui weikexue yao jingzhong changming 反对伪科学要警钟长鸣." *Guangming ribao* 光明日报, June 17, 1996.

Xinhua News Agency. "China Bans Falun Gong: Li Hongzhi's Role in Illegal Gathering at Zhongnanhai." August 19, 1999. Online at english.peopledaily.com .cn/english/199908/13/enc_19990813001031_TopNews.html.

———. "Official on Rumours concerning Falun Gong Practitioners." June 14, 1999.

Xu, Luo. *Searching for Life's Meaning: Changes and Tensions in the Worldviews of Chinese Youth in the 1980s*. Ann Arbor: University of Michigan Press, 2002.

Yang, Mayfair Mei-Hui, ed. *Chinese Religiosities: Afflictions of Modernity and State Formation*. Berkeley: University of California Press, 2008.

———. Introduction to Yang, *Chinese Religiosities*, pp. 1–40.

Yoshikawa Tadao. "Zhongli Quan." in Pregadio, *The Encyclopedia of Taoism*, pp. 1283–84.

Yu, Anthony C. *State and Religion in China: Historical and Textual Perspectives*. Chicago: Open Court, 2005.

Zeng, Jennifer. *Witnessing History: One Woman's Fight for Freedom and Falun Gong*. Crows Nest, NSW: Allen and Unwin, 2005.

Zhang Pengwen. "An Interview with He Zuoxiu: How He Exposes and Fights against Falun Gong." Online at www.facts.org.cn/Views/200801/t75537.htm.

Zhang Weiqing 張微晴 and Qiao Gong 喬公. *Falun gong chuangshiren Li Hongzhi pingzhuan* 法輪功創始人李洪志評傳. Taipei: Shangye zhoukan chuban gufen youxian gongsi, 1999.

Zhang Zhenhuan. "Address Given by Zhang Zhenhuan at a Meeting Held to Celebrate the Formation of the Chinese *Qigong* Scientific Research Association." In Zhu and Penny, "The Qigong Boom," pp. 13–20.

Zhao, Suisheng. "Deng Xiaoping's Southern Tour: Elite Politics in Post-Tiananmen China." *Asian Survey* 33, no. 8 (August 1993): 739–56.

Zhu Huiguang 朱慧光. "Falun changzhuan, shengming changqing 法轮常转生命长青." *Zhonghua qigong* 中华气功 3 (1993): 32–33.

———. "'Rexian' xian shengong '热线' 显神功." *Qigong yu kexue* 气功与科学 9 (1993): 15.

Zhu Xiaoyang and Benjamin Penny, eds. "The Qigong Boom." Special issue, *Chinese Sociology and Anthropology* 27, no. 1 (Fall 1994).

Zong Hairen 宗海仁. *Zhu Rongji zai 1999* 朱镕基在 1999. Carle Place, NY: Mingjing chubanshe [Mirror Books], 2001. Translated under the title *Zhu Rongji in 1999*; *Chinese Law and Government* 35, no. 1 (January/February 2002).

Index